MW01034553

ZAGAT®

Westchester Hudson Valley Restaurants 2007/08

Plus neighboring
Connecticut and
Berkshires dining

LOCAL EDITORS
John Bruno Turiano, Judith Hausman,
Lynn Hazlewood and Lorraine Gengo
STAFF EDITOR
Michelle Golden

Published and distributed by
Zagat Survey, LLC
4 Columbus Circle
New York, NY 10019
T: 212.977.6000
E: westhud@zagat.com
www.zagat.com

ACKNOWLEDGMENTS

We thank Anitra Brown, Nicholas Gengo-Lehr, Jan Greenberg, Carrie Haddad, Elizabeth Johnson, Henry Lehr, Lora Pelton, Steven Shukow, Frank Viele and Michael Zivyak, as well as the following members of our staff: Josh Rogers (assistant editor), Sean Beachell, Maryanne Bertollo, Catherine Bigwood, Sandy Cheng, Reni Chin, Larry Cohn, Carol Diuguid, Jeff Freier, Caroline Hatchett, Roy Jacob, Natalie Lebert, Mike Liao, Christina Livadiotis, Dave Makulec, Rachel McConlogue, Emily Parsons, Andre Pilette, Becky Ruthenburg, Thomas Sheehan, Kelly Stewart, Kilolo Strobert, Sharon Yates and Kyle Zolner.

Contents

About This Survey

Here are the results of our 2007/08 Westchester/Hudson Valley Restaurants Survey, covering 892 of the area's best establishments, including places in neighboring Connecticut towns. Like all our guides, it's based on the collective opinions of thousands of savvy local consumers. We've also included a guide to Berkshires dining, starting on page 217.

WHO PARTICIPATED: Input from 3,800 avid diners forms the basis for the ratings and reviews in this guide (their comments are shown in quotation marks within the reviews). Of these surveyors, 46% are women, 54% men; the breakdown by age is 6% in their 20s; 18%, 30s; 22%, 40s; 27%, 50s; and 27%, 60s or above. Collectively they bring roughly 616,000 meals worth of experience to this Survey. We sincerely thank each of these participants – this book is really "theirs."

HELPFUL LISTS: Whether you're looking for a celebratory meal, a hot scene or a bargain bite, our lists can help you find exactly the right place. See Most Popular (page 7), Key Newcomers (page 7), Top Ratings (pages 9–14), Best Buys (page 15) and Connecticut's Top Ratings (page 16). We've also provided 39 handy indexes.

OUR EDITORS: We are especially grateful to our local editors, John Bruno Turiano, managing editor of *Westchester Magazine*; Judith Hausman, an independent food critic and journalist based in South Salem, NY; Lynn Hazlewood, editor of *Hudson Valley Home & Garden* magazine; and Lorraine Gengo, senior staff writer and restaurant critic for the *Fairfield County Weekly*.

ABOUT ZAGAT: This marks our 28th year reporting on the shared experiences of consumers like you. What started in 1979 as a hobby involving 200 of our friends has come a long way. Today we have over 300,000 surveyors and now cover dining, entertaining, golf, hotels, movies, music, nightlife, resorts, shopping, spas, theater and tourist attractions worldwide.

SHARE YOUR OPINION: We invite you to join any of our upcoming surveys – just register at **zagat.com,** where you can rate and review establishments year-round. Each participant will receive a free copy of the resulting guide when published.

AVAILABILITY: Zagat guides are available in all major bookstores, by subscription at **zagat.com** and for use on mobile devices via **Zagat To Go.**

FEEDBACK: There is always room for improvement, thus we invite your comments and suggestions about any aspect of our performance. Just contact us at westhud@zagat.com.

New York, NY
May 14, 2007

Nina and Tim

Nina and Tim Zagat

What's New

WEST MEETS EAST: Though Italian holds strong as Westchester county's go-to cuisine, the area continues to diversify. Among its already-bustling new ethnic entries are Euro Asian in Port Chester and Asian Temptation in White Plains, while Zitoune is a promising Mamaroneck Moroccan transplant from Manhattan. As for stylish new Indians, check out Mamaroneck's Rani Mahal, along with Yonkers' Bukhara Grill and Pleasantville's Bollywood Bistro.

HEALTHY EATING: Sixty-seven percent of our respondents would like trans fats banned and 59% would pay more for sustainable ingredients – and restaurateurs have taken notice. Hastings' Bloom, Dobbs Ferry's Tomatillo and Mt. Kisco's new Flying Pig outpost all emphasize the use of organic and local ingredients in a nod to farm-to-table purist (and the Survey's Most Popular restaurant) Blue Hill at Stone Barns. Meanwhile, Philip McGrath (Iron Horse Grill) and Jonathan Pratt and Craig Purdy (Ümami Café) opened healthy fast-food options Pony Express and Mex-to-go near their more-established restaurants.

LOOKING AHEAD: Peter Kelly of Xaviar's acclaim has a seafooder, X20 Xaviar's on the Hudson, set to open by summer on the historic Yonkers pier. Chef Mark Filippo, who left Hartsdale's popular Cafe Mezé (which closed after a 12-year run), will head the kitchen at the forthcoming Morgans Fish House in Rye. And perhaps most exciting: Mario Batali's partner and Greenwich, CT, resident Joe Bastianich fed the rumor mill with the purchase of the fire-damaged Tarry Lodge in Port Chester. Could Babbo Due be coming?

HUDSON VALLEY HAPPENINGS: Despite bidding adieu to longtime favorite Aubergine, Columbia County residents have something to cheer as its antiques-filled river town, Hudson, celebrated the opening of Northern Italian Vico and American-Scandinavian DABA. The county got another bright trendy newcomer in nearby Philmont, the New American Local 111, all industrial chic in a onetime garage. In Dutchess County, Beacon continues to shine with New American Tonique taking over the space once occupied by Oll. Madalin's Table is a fashionable oasis in the restored Madalin Hotel in Tivoli. Downtown Poughkeepsie lost its sweet Demitasse Cafe, but gained the sleek New American Artist's Palate. On the city's riverfront, Shadows on the Hudson (with American cooking) is already hopping. And finally, the Hudson Valley itself is officially on the culinary radar with its own Restaurant Week, scheduled for this November, with over 100 eateries participating.

COST COMPARISON: With an average meal cost of $36.41, Westchester is less expensive than New York City ($39.43), but on par with Connecticut ($36.39) and New Jersey ($36.95).

Southern New York
May 14, 2007

John Bruno Turiano
Judith Hausman
Lynn Hazlewood

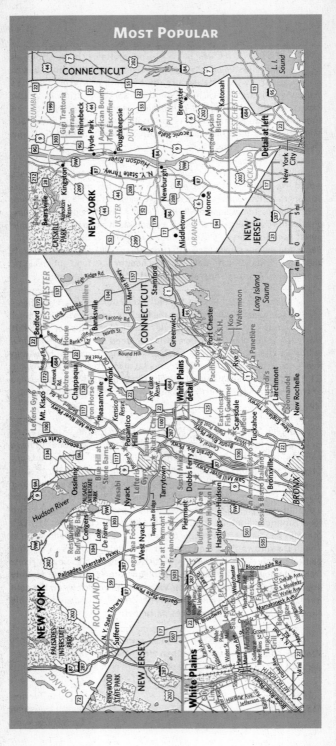

Most Popular

Each surveyor has been asked to name his or her five favorite places. This list reflects their choices.

1. Blue Hill/Stone Barns
2. Xaviar's/Piermont
3. Crabtree's Kittle House
4. Harvest on Hudson
5. Rest. X/Bully Boy Bar
6. Freelance Café
7. Iron Horse Grill
8. La Panetière
9. Coromandel
10. City Limits Diner
11. Morton's Steak
12. Mulino's
13. Equus
14. Tengda Asian Bistro
15. Sonora
16. Lusardi's
17. American Bounty
18. An American Bistro
19. Cheesecake Factory
20. Terrapin*
21. Legal Sea Foods
22. Watermoon
23. Eastchester Fish
24. Pacifico
25. Tango Grill*
26. Koo
27. Sushi Mike's
28. La Crémaillère
29. F.I.S.H.
30. Valbella
31. Wasabi*
32. Ruth's Chris Steak
33. Buffet de la Gare
34. Gigi Trattoria
35. P.F. Chang's*
36. Escoffier
37. Lefteris Gyro*
38. Bengal Tiger
39. Bear Cafe
40. Rosie's Bistro

It's obvious that many of the restaurants on the above list are among the Westchester/Hudson Valley area's most expensive, but if popularity were calibrated to price, we suspect that a number of other restaurants would join the above ranks. Given the fact that both our surveyors and readers love to discover dining bargains, we have added a list of 86 Best Buys on page 15. These are restaurants that give real quality at extremely reasonable prices.

KEY NEWCOMERS

Following is our editors' take on some of the year's most notable arrivals. (For a full list, see page 205.)

Artist's Palate	One
Belle Havana	Phoenix
Bloom	Shadows on Hudson
Bollywood Bistro	Vico
Madalin's Table	Zitoune

---

* Indicates a tie with restaurant above

Ratings & Symbols

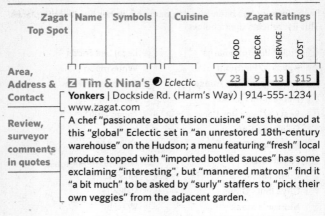

Zagat Top Spot	Name	Symbols	Cuisine	Zagat Ratings			
				FOOD	DECOR	SERVICE	COST

Area, Address & Contact

☒ **Tim & Nina's** ◖ *Eclectic* ▽ 23 | 9 | 13 | $15

Yonkers | Dockside Rd. (Harm's Way) | 914-555-1234 | www.zagat.com

Review, surveyor comments in quotes

A chef "passionate about fusion cuisine" sets the mood at this "global" Eclectic set in "an unrestored 18th-century warehouse" on the Hudson; a menu featuring "fresh" local produce topped with "imported bottled sauces" has some exclaiming "interesting", but "mannered matrons" find it "a bit much" to be asked by "surly" staffers to "pick their own veggies" from the adjacent garden.

Ratings

Food, Decor and **Service** are rated on a scale of 0 to 30.

0	–	9	poor to fair
10	–	15	fair to good
16	–	19	good to very good
20	–	25	very good to excellent
26	–	30	extraordinary to perfection
▽			low response	less reliable

Cost reflects our surveyors' average estimate of the price of a dinner with one drink and tip and is a benchmark only. Lunch is usually 25% less.

For **newcomers** or survey **write-ins** listed without ratings, the price range is indicated as follows:

I	$25 and below
M	$26 to $40
E	$41 to $65
VE	$66 or more

Symbols

☒	Zagat Top Spot (highest ratings, popularity and importance)
◖	serves after 11 PM
☒	closed on Sunday
Ⓜ	closed on Monday
⊘	no credit cards accepted

Top Food Ratings

Ratings are to the left of names. Lists exclude places with low votes, unless indicated by a ∇.

29 Xaviar's/Piermont	Zephs'
28 Freelance Café	Sapore
27 Blue Hill/Stone Barns	Buffet de la Gare
Rest. X/Bully Boy Bar	Valley/Garrison
Aroma Osteria	Le Petit Bistro
Ocean House	25 Emilio Ristorante
La Panetière	Johnny's Pizzeria*
La Crémaillère	Café Les Baux
Iron Horse Grill	Serevan
Le Pavillon	DePuy Canal House
Il Cenàcolo	Beso
Azuma Sushi	Calico
Wasabi (Nyack)	French Corner
26 Caterina de Medici	Sonora
Il Barilotto	Twist
American Bounty	Arch
Coromandel	La Fontanella
Equus	Le Château
Escoffier	Valbella
Busy Bee	Sal's Pizza

BY CUISINE

AMERICAN (NEW)

29 Xaviar's/Piermont
28 Freelance Café
27 Blue Hill/Stone Barns
Rest. X/Bully Boy Bar
Iron Horse Grill

AMERICAN (TRAD.)

24 Sweet Sue's
23 Lu Shane's
22 Catherine's
Miss Lucy's Kitchen
Traphagen

CHINESE

24 Aberdeen
23 Hunan Village
22 Pagoda
21 China Rose
20 P.F. Chang's

CONTINENTAL

24 L'Europe
21 Monteverde/Oldstone
20 Swiss Hütte
19 Off Broadway
Grande Centrale

ECLECTIC

26 Zephs'
25 Beso
Calico
Arch
Relish

FRENCH

27 La Panetière
La Crémaillère
Le Pavillon
26 Equus
Escoffier

FRENCH (BISTRO)

26 Le Petit Bistro
25 Café Les Baux
24 Le Canard Enchainé
23 Bistro 22
Le Provençal

INDIAN

26 Coromandel
24 Jaipore Indian
23 Tandoori Taste
Bengal Tiger
Mughal Palace

ITALIAN

- 27 | Aroma Osteria
  - Il Cenàcolo
- 26 | Caterina de Medici
  - Il Barilotto
- 25 | Emilio Ristorante

JAPANESE

- 27 | Azuma Sushi
  - Wasabi (Nyack)
- 25 | Sushi Mike's
- 24 | Yama Sushi
  - Hajime

MEDITERRANEAN

- 25 | Serevan
- 24 | Trotters
- 23 | Turkish Meze
  - Gigi Trattoria
  - F.I.S.H.

MEXICAN/TEX-MEX

- 23 | Cafe Maya/Maya Cafe
- 22 | Armadillo B&G

  - Sunset Grille
- 21 | Tomatillo
  - Santa Fe (Tivoli)

PIZZA

- 25 | Johnny's
  - Sal's
- 24 | Riverview
- 23 | Baba Louie's
  - Modern Rest.

SEAFOOD

- 27 | Ocean House
- 24 | La Villetta
  - Eastchester Fish
- 23 | Aquario
  - F.I.S.H.

STEAKHOUSES

- 26 | Sapore
- 24 | Tollgate
  - Morton's
- 23 | Ruth's Chris
  - Willet House

BY SPECIAL FEATURE

BREAKFAST

- 26 | Equus
- 25 | Calico
- 24 | Sweet Sue's
  - Apple Pie Bakery
- 21 | Wobble Café

BRUNCH

- 27 | Rest. X/Bully Boy Bar
- 26 | Equus
- 25 | DePuy Canal House
  - Calico
- 24 | Crabtree's Kittle House

BUSINESS DINING

- 27 | Rest. X/Bully Boy Bar
- 26 | Caterina de Medici
  - Il Barilotto
  - Equus
  - Escoffier

CHILD-FRIENDLY

- 26 | Busy Bee
- 25 | Johnny's Pizzeria
  - Twist
  - Relish
- 24 | Thai Garden

HOTEL/INN DINING

- 24 | Crabtree's Kittle House
  - Crabtree's Kittle House Inn
  - Aberdeen
  - Marriott Residence Inn
- 23 | Ruth's Chris Steak
  - Marriott Westchester
  - Would
  - Inn at Applewood
  - Old Drovers Inn
  - Old Drovers Inn

MEET FOR A DRINK

- 27 | Rest. X/Bully Boy Bar
- 25 | Sonora
- 24 | Le Canard Enchainé
  - Mulino's
  - Trotters

NEWCOMERS (RATED)

- 24 | Artist's Palate
- 23 | Haiku Asian Bistro
- 22 | Goldfish Oyster Bar
- 21 | Lanterna Tuscan
  - Mo's NY Gril

SINGLES SCENE

- 24 Trotters
- 23 Zuppa
- 22 Frankie & Johnnie's
- Armadillo B&G
- 21 121 Rest./Bar

TRENDY PLACES

- 27 Blue Hill/Stone Barns
- Rest. X/Bully Boy Bar
- 24 Koo
- 23 Gigi Trattoria
- 20 Flirt Sushi∇

BY LOCATION

WESTCHESTER

BRIARCLIFF MANOR
- 24 Yama Sushi
- 20 Terra Rustica
- Flames Steak
- Amalfi
- Guadalajara

BRONXVILLE
- 23 Haiku Asian Bistro
- Rosie's Bistro
- Il Bacio Tratt.
- 22 Japan Inn
- 21 Underhills Crossing

HARRISON
- 25 Emilio Ristorante
- 24 Hajime
- 22 Tratt. Vivolo
- Halstead Ave. Bistro
- 21 Gus's Franklin Park

HARTSDALE
- 27 Azuma Sushi
- 23 Tsuru
- 21 Lia's
- 20 K. Fung's
- Global Gatherings

KATONAH
- 23 Tengda Asian Bistro
- 22 Blue Dolphin
- 21 Le Fontane
- 19 Deer Park Tavern
- 18 Willy Nick's

LARCHMONT
- 24 La Villetta
- Plates
- 23 Lusardi's
- 22 Pascal's
- 21 Lanterna Tuscan

MAMARONECK
- 25 Sal's Pizza
- 24 Tollgate Steak

- 23 Turkish Meze
- Le Provençal
- 22 Toyo Sushi

MT. KISCO
- 22 Conte's Fishmkt.
- 21 Fish Cellar
- Temptation Tea House
- Piero's
- La Camelia

PORT CHESTER
- 25 Sonora
- 23 Willett House
- Tandoori Taste
- Alba's
- Giorgio's

RYE
- 27 La Panetière
- 24 Koo
- Watermoon
- 22 Frankie & Johnnie's
- 21 Ruby's Oyster Bar

TARRYTOWN
- 26 Equus
- 23 Ruth's Chris Steak
- Chiboust
- 21 Lago di Como
- Café Tandoor

WHITE PLAINS
- 24 Morton's Steak
- Aberdeen
- Mulino's
- Trotters
- 23 Tango Grill

YONKERS
- 23 Zuppa
- Hunan Village
- Valentino's
- 22 Kang Suh
- 20 Patang Indian

COLUMBIA COUNTY

- 24 Swoon Kitchenbar
- 23 Pillars Carriage House
- Baba Louie's Pizza
- 21 Ca'Mea
- 20 Swiss Hütte

DUTCHESS COUNTY

- 27 Aroma Osteria
- Le Pavillon
- 26 Caterina de Medici
- Il Barilotto
- American Bounty

ORANGE COUNTY

- 27 Il Cenàcolo
- 24 Nina
- Cena 2000
- 22 Catherine's
- 21 River Grill

PUTNAM COUNTY

- 26 Valley/Garrison
- 25 Arch
- 24 Riverview
- Jaipore Indian
- 22 Cathryn's Tuscan

ROCKLAND COUNTY

- 29 Xaviar's/Piermont
- 28 Freelance Café
- 27 Rest. X/Bully Boy Bar
- Wasabi
- 25 Relish

ULSTER COUNTY

- 25 DePuy Canal House
- Beso
- French Corner
- 24 Le Canard Enchainé
- Harvest Café

Top Decor Ratings

Ratings are to the left of names.

28	Equus Blue Hill/Stone Barns	24	Bird and Bottle American Bounty Wasabi (Nyack) Mount Fuji Escoffier Arch Zuppa Mulino's
27	La Panetière Le Château		
26	Harvest on Hudson La Crémaillère Rest. X/Bully Boy Bar Monteverde/Oldstone		
25	Vertigo Caterina de Medici DePuy Canal House Old Drovers Inn Aroma Osteria Valley/Garrison* Xaviar's/Piermont* Artist's Palate Cena 2000 Purdys Homestead Mohonk Mtn. House Plumbush Inn	23	Traphagen Torches on Hudson Crabtree's Kittle House Bull's Head Inn Sapore Locust Tree Valbella Il Barilotto Chart House Terrapin Le Pavillon Hudson House Inn

OUTDOORS

Blu	F.I.S.H.
Bull's Head Inn	Harvest on Hudson
Bywater Bistro	Le Jardin du Roi
Cena 2000	Northern Spy Cafe
Chart House	Stoneleigh Creek

ROMANCE

Arch	Emilio Ristorante
Bird and Bottle	Equus
Bistro 22	La Panetière
Buffet de la Gare	Le Château
DePuy Canal House	Locust Tree

ROOMS

Asian Temptation	Haiku Asian Bistro (Cross River)
Backals	La Crémaillère
Croton Creek Steak	Local 111
Egg's Nest	Phoenix
Equus	River Bank

VIEWS

Blue Hill/Stone Barns	Mohonk Mtn. House
Chart House	Monteverde/Oldstone
Equus	Shadows on Hudson
Harvest Café	Valley/Garrison
Harvest on Hudson	Vox

Top Service Ratings

Ratings are to the left of names.

27 Xaviar's/Piermont
    Blue Hill/Stone Barns

26 La Panetière
    Freelance Café
    Rest. X/Bully Boy Bar
    La Fontanella

25 Iron Horse Grill
    La Crémaillère
    Arch
    Valbella
    Valley/Garrison
    Riverview
    Equus
    Escoffier

24 Buffet de la Gare
    Caterina de Medici
    Le Petit Bistro*
    Le Pavillon
    Aroma Osteria
    La Villetta

    Mulino's
    Emilio Ristorante
    Purdys Homestead
    Le Château

23 Zephs'
    Le Fontane
    Zuppa
    American Bounty
    Calico
    Il Cenàcolo*
    Yvonne's Southern
    Il Barilotto
    Twist*
    Artist's Palate
    Ocean House
    Bistro 22
    Le Canard Enchainé
    Plumbush Inn
    Sapore
    Crabtree's Kittle House

Best Buys

In order of Bang for the Buck rating.

1. Walter's	21. Village TeaRoom
2. Red Rooster	22. Egg's Nest
3. Bagels & More	23. Grandma's
4. Apple Pie Bakery	24. Reality Bites
5. Sal's Pizza	25. Taro's
6. Irving Farm Coffee	26. Blazer Pub
7. Sweet Sue's	27. Lefteris Gyro
8. Bread Alone	28. China Rose
9. Eveready Diner	29. Lotus King
10. Lange's Deli	30. Osaka
11. Wobble Café	31. Candlelight Inn
12. Così	32. Johnny's Pizzeria
13. Temptations Cafe	33. Piper's Kilt
14. Portofino Pizza	34. Piggy Bank
15. Chefs On Fire	35. Harvest Café
16. Cafe Maya/Maya Cafe	36. Hickory BBQ
17. Tomatillo	37. Yvonne's Southern
18. Daily Planet	38. Thai Garden
19. Baba Louie's Pizza	39. Modern Rest./Pizza
20. Brooklyn's Famous	40. Bloom's Kosher Deli

OTHER GOOD VALUES

Beehive	Little Mexican Cafe
Big W's Roadside	Locanda
Bywater Bistro	Main Street Café
Cafe Mozart	Marion's Country
City Limits Diner	Max's Memphis BBQ
Comfort	Memphis Mae's
Country Inn	Miss Lucy's Kitchen
Coyote Flaco	Nestos Estiatorio
Dragonfly Caffé	Niko's Greek
Earth Foods	Oscar
Ebb Tide	Pete's Saloon
Epstein's Deli	Portobello Café
Friends & Family	Q Restaurant
Harvest Café	Roma
Hunan Village	Sam's/Gedney Way
Jackalope BBQ	Soul Dog
Jaipore Indian	Southbound BBQ
Karamba Café	Squires
Kisco Kosher	Sukhothai
Laguna	Sushi Niji
La Manda's	Tanjore
Larchmont Tavern	Totonno's
Latin American Cafe	Wunderbar

CONNECTICUT'S TOP FOOD

29	Thomas Henkelmann	24	Columbus Park
27	Jean-Louis		Thali
	Luca Ristorante		Baang Cafe
26	Bernard's		Morton's Steak
	Ondine		Elm St. Oyster
	Coromandel		Insieme
	Rebeccas		Gaia
25	Ching's		Ocean 211
	Thomas Moran's Syrah		Koo
	Valbella		Mayflower Inn & Spa

BY LOCATION

DANBURY

- 26 Ondine
- 23 Cafe on the Green
- 21 Ciao! Cafe
- 20 Hanna's
- 19 Sesame Seed

DARIEN

- 26 Coromandel
- 25 Ching's
- 22 Little Thai Kitchen
  - Aux Délices/Ponzek
- 20 Melting Pot

GREENWICH

- 29 Thomas Henkelmann
- 27 Jean-Louis
- 26 Rebeccas
- 24 Elm St. Oyster
  - Gaia

NEW CANAAN

- 25 Ching's
- 24 Thali
  - Bistro Bonne Nuit
  - Aloi
- 23 Roger Sherman Inn

RIDGEFIELD

- 26 Bernard's
- 24 Thali
  - Insieme
  - Koo
- 23 Stonehenge

STAMFORD

- 24 Columbus Park
  - Morton's Steak
  - Ocean 211
  - Mona Lisa
  - Telluride

WESTCHESTER/ HUDSON VALLEY WITH NEIGHBORING CONNECTICUT TOWNS DIRECTORY

	FOOD	DECOR	SERVICE	COST

Abatino's *Italian*   20 | 14 | 16 | $28

North White Plains | Super Stop & Shop Ctr. | 670 N. Broadway (Rte. 22) | 914-328-6579 | www.abatinosrestaurant.com

"Simple" but "solid" "comfort food" is the consensus about this "casual" North White Plains "red-sauce Italian" that specializes in "reliable" fare like "fresh salads", pastas and "outstanding" "thin-crust" "garlic pan pizzas"; while a few complain the "spotty" service "doesn't match the food" and others add the strip-mall location, "under the lights of a Super Stop & Shop", is "somewhat depressing", most agree you "can't beat the value."

Aberdeen *Chinese*   24 | 13 | 20 | $31

White Plains | Marriott Residence Inn | 3 Barker Ave. (Cottage Pl.) | 914-288-0188

"Mott Street comes to White Plains" via this "authentic", "delicious" Cantonese in the Marriott Residence Inn where "real foodies" dine on "bracingly fresh" fish and "fantastic dim sum" and other dishes "on par with the New York region's best"; disregard the "sparsely decorated space" and let the "helpful servers" guide you through a meal that will have you forgetting "the Chinese restaurants of your youth"; N.B. dim sum served at lunch only.

Abis *Japanese*   17 | 15 | 18 | $35

Mamaroneck | 406 Mamaroneck Ave. (Spencer Pl.) | 914-698-8777 | www.abisrestaurant.com
Thornwood | 14 Marble Ave. (Chestnut St.) | 914-741-5100
Greenwich | 381 Greenwich Ave. (Grigg St.), CT | 203-862-9100 | www.abis4u.com

"Decent", "family-friendly" Japanese "standbys" that get two chopsticks up for excelling at "group get-togethers", "fun" "children's parties" and "basic sushi and teriyaki dishes"; a bounty of critics suggests regardless of location, the "shop-worn" settings and "so-so food" make finding "better places" of this ilk easy to do; N.B. the Greenwich location offers hibachi tables.

Abruzzi Trattoria Ⓜ *Italian*   ▽ 20 | 18 | 19 | $30

Patterson | 3191 Rte. 22 (Rte. 311) | 845-878-6800

"From outside it appears to be an upscale pizzeria", but this Putnam County Italian offers much more than pies, with "imaginative entrees" that are a "notch above the average red-sauce" fare; the cafe-style room is "continually packed", and though one person's "lively" is another's "loud", the "staff tries hard" to please.

Ace Asian-French Cuisine *Asian Fusion*   24 | 13 | 18 | $41

Thornwood | 677 Commerce St./Rte. 141 (bet. Grant & Orchard Pls.) | 914-741-0888 | www.acecuisine.com

"Travel the Far East culinary circuit" at this Asian fusion, a "welcome addition" to Thornwood for its "sophisticated", "creative" cuisine that draws from "Japan, Vietnam, China and Indonesia"; "plain-Jane" decor makes the spacious outdoor patio especially appealing in summer, but "flaky" service is unfortunate considering "the quality of the food deserves better."

Adrienne ⓜ *American* — 23 | 20 | 23 | $51

New Milford | 218 Kent Rd./Rte. 7 (Rocky River Rd.), CT | 860-354-6001 | www.adriennerestaurant.com

Surveyors salute chef-owner Adrienne Sussman's "always excellent, flavorful and inventive" New American cuisine for providing some of the "best fine dining in New Milford"; housed in a "lovely, old" 1774 Colonial, this "charming, out-of-the-way find" boasts "intimate fireside dining" and "attentive service" – all of which add up to "a warm and delightful experience" that may be "pricey, but worth it."

Agra Tandoor *Indian* — ▽ 17 | 13 | 17 | $20

Rhinebeck | 5856 Rte. 9 (Fox Hollow Rd.) | 845-876-7510

"Flavorful", "authentic" Indian fare is hard to find in Rhinebeck's "neck of the woods", so aficionados flock to this "reliable" family-run BYO spot for a fix; decor is "hokey" but colorful (all reds and golds), and if the staff sometimes gets "overloaded", overall it's "an enjoyable atmosphere", capped by "good prices", especially if you go for the "super buffet" on Wednesday, Friday or Sunday.

Alba's Ⓧ *Italian* — 23 | 19 | 21 | $49

Port Chester | 400 N. Main St. (Rectory St.) | 914-937-2236 | www.albasrestaurant.com

"You can't go wrong" at this "wonderful" Northern Italian where "excellent pastas" and "Caesar salad prepared tableside" draw devotees into a "yellow house" with "homey" charm in Port Chester; a few complain of "a space that's too loud" and sometimes "indifferent service", but the consensus is, "it's a winner."

Aloi Restaurant ⓜ *Italian* — 24 | 18 | 22 | $51

New Canaan | 62 Main St. (Locust Ave.), CT | 203-966-4345

"Don't fly to Tuscany, come to this" New Canaan Northern Italian for "food that is consistently fresh, creative and excellent" like the signature housemade pastas from chef-owner Margherita Aloi, whose "European upbringing and work ethic" earn praise for her "presence both in the kitchen and with guests"; though the setting is a "little cramped" and the "decor could be warmer", "alfresco dining" makes for an appealing alternative in pleasant weather.

Alpine Inn *Continental/Steak* — - | - | - | M

Patterson | 2970 Rte. 22 (Rte. 311) | 845-878-3838

"Heaping plates" of signature prime rib and other hearty Continental fare await nearby Thunder Ridge skiers at this large, friendly Patterson eatery; the dining room suits families, while singles might opt to nosh in the pubby atmosphere of the bar.

Amalfi Restaurant *Italian* — 20 | 15 | 19 | $38

Briarcliff Manor | 1112 Pleasantville Rd. (N. State Rd.) | 914-762-9200

A "neighborhood" Italian where "kids are welcome", this Briarcliff Manor standby lures "locals" with "dependably" "solid" (if "not overly creative") pasta, pizza and "specials"; a "pleasant staff" gives it a "comfortable" feel in spite of "tired" digs, however, a smattering of dissenters allege it's "overpriced" given its "strip-mall" setting.

FOOD | DECOR | SERVICE | COST

A' Mangiare *Italian*

‐ | ‐ | ‐ | I

Bronxville | 26 Palmer Ave. (bet. Paxton Ave. & Pondfield Rd.) | 914-793-9224
Elmsford | 121 E. Main St. (N. French Ave.) | 914-592-8800
Pleasantville | 152 Bedford Rd. (B'way) | 914-747-2611
White Plains | 359 Mamaroneck Ave. (Livingston Ave.) | 914-683-1313
www.amangiare.com

Specialty pizzas, red-sauce favorites and homemade bread (baked twice daily) are the draws at this family-friendly Southern Italian foursome; the Elmsford location features both casual and full-service dining rooms (as well as outdoor seating), while wallet-watchers welcome the $10.95 pasta specials on Tuesday night at the Pleasantville spot; N.B. delivery is available through all branches.

Amarone's Italian Cuisine *Italian*

∇ 21 | 16 | 22 | $35

Sugar Loaf | 62 Wood Rd. (Kings Hwy.) | 845-469-4405

Eateries are scarce in Sugar Loaf, so this family-friendly Italian fills several niches with "homey" eats, signature rack of lamb for carnivores, zuppa di pesce for fish lovers, a menu for the kiddies and even special fare for the gluten intolerant; the dining room is country cozy with blue-and-yellow decor and white tablecloths, but it can get "rather noisy" when everyone troops in.

☑ American Bounty Restaurant 🕃 Ⓜ *American*

26 | 24 | 23 | $48

Hyde Park | Culinary Institute of America | 1946 Campus Dr. (Rte. 9) | 845-471-6608 | www.ciachef.edu

A "superb" menu of "delicious" New American fare featuring "high-quality local ingredients" is "tuned in" rather than "trendy" say fans of this Hyde Park cooking school restaurant, where the "blossoming chefs" earn top marks; the "elegant", "peaceful" room exudes a "lovely ambiance", and if service is "a bit bumpy", be patient, it might be "a student's first day" – "they're really out to please"; "all in all, it's a bargain" for such "outstanding" "four-star quality."

American Pie Company *American*

19 | 15 | 17 | $23

Sherman | 29 Rte. 37 Ctr. (Rte. 39), CT | 860-350-0662

This Sherman Traditional American cafe-cum-bakery "fits the bill" for lunch and Sunday brunch, but most maintain "fresh, homemade" desserts like apple pie are "the best part of the meal"; the "friendly service" runs a tad slow especially on "summer weekends" when it seems like this "family-friendly" spot "is the only game in town."

☑ An American Bistro *American*

22 | 16 | 21 | $41

Tuckahoe | 296 Columbus Ave. (bet. Fisher & Lincoln Aves.) | 914-793-0807 | www.anamericanbistro.com

"Loyal and frequent diners" applaud "excellent" "dressed-up comfort food", including "wonderful" "daily specials" and "fantastic" salads, at this "popular" Tuckahoe New American "across from the train station"; "courteous" servers also get "kudos", and though a few surveyors say the "boring" decor "detracts", "the food more than makes up for it"; P.S. they also have house wines "all under $20 a bottle."

Andrew's Restaurant *American*   ▽ 18 | 15 | 19 | $36

Elmsford | 86 E. Main St. (bet. Evarts & Goodwin Aves.) | 914-592-5446
"Andrew's a fine host" who makes dining at his Elmsford New American "a pleasure" say supporters who enjoy steaks, seafood and housemade desserts and wonder why this "local restaurant" "isn't busier"; "plain-Jane" interior and service that "could be more consistent" are two possible reasons.

Angelina's *Italian*   19 | 14 | 18 | $35

Tuckahoe | 97 Lake Ave. (Main St.) | 914-779-7944
Whether you choose the "quick and easy" "pizzeria side" or the "fancy" dining room with "angels on the walls", this Tuckahoe Italian has become a "Friday favorite" for "inexpensive" "traditional" fare; in spite of a sometimes "snooty" staff, it's still got a "homey" feel.

NEW Anna Maria's   20 | 18 | 18 | $48
Restaurant *American/Italian*

Larchmont | 18 Chatsworth Ave. (Boston Post Rd.) | 914-833-0555 | www.annamariascatering.net
"Options from fancy to familiar" abound at this "intimate" Larchmont Italian-American neophyte from "Mayor Giuliani's former chef", Anna Maria Santorelli, who makes the rounds in her "cozy" dining room "to chat" with customers; despite "expensive" tabs, locals call it "promising, so far."

Apple Pie   24 | 18 | 20 | $17
Bakery Café 🗷 *Bakery/Sandwiches*

Hyde Park | Culinary Institute of America | 1946 Campus Dr. (Rte. 9) | 845-905-4500 | www.ciachef.edu
"Sinful cakes", "fabulous croissants", "really good" sandwiches and salads, artisanal breads, plus "the best pastries this side of the Seine" keep crowds coming to this Hyde Park cooking school venue run by "amiable students"; "tasty takeout" or a "casual lunch" in the cafe overlooking a courtyard is "the perfect way" for those on a "tight budget" to "experience the Culinary Institute"; just remember, it's open until 6:30 PM, weekdays only.

Aquario *Portuguese/Seafood*   23 | 16 | 19 | $44

West Harrison | 141 E. Lake St. (Washington St.) | 914-287-0220 | www.aquariony.com
"Fish lovers" favor this "pleasant" Portuguese seafooder in West Harrison purveying "authentic", "well-executed" fare including "fabulous lobster" and "wonderful seafood stew"; if the room is "somewhat sedate", and the service "slow", both seem suited for the "older crowd" that enjoys a "leisurely" meal.

Arch 🅼 *Eclectic*   25 | 24 | 25 | $69

Brewster | 1296 Rte. 22 (end of I-684) | 845-279-5011 | www.archrestaurant.com
"Top-notch" Eclectic fare and "sublime desserts" served by a "caring" staff in "romantic", "gorgeous surroundings" add up to "elegant country hospitality" at this venerable, tucked-away Brewster "trea-

sure"; yes, it's "expensive" (though "not too pricey for brunch") but it's a "wonderful special-occasion" spot "worth traveling for"; N.B. jackets required at dinner.

Armadillo Bar & Grill Ⓜ Tex-Mex | 22 | 16 | 20 | $29 |

Kingston | 97 Abeel St. (bet. Hone & Wurts Sts.) | 845-339-1550 | www.armadillos.net

"*Olé* for the tamales!" cheer fans of the "spicy" "high-end" Tex-Mex eats at this "popular" Kingston cantina, where "friendly" owner Merle will make you "feel at home"; the "Southwestern motif" includes Mexican movie posters and a few stuffed armadillos presiding over the "lively scene"; be sure to "get there early in summer" for patio dining.

Ⓩ Aroma Osteria Ⓜ Italian | 27 | 25 | 24 | $46 |

Wappingers Falls | 114 Old Post Rd. (Rte. 9) | 845-298-6790 | www.aromaosteriarestaurant.com

"Fantastic" Italian food and a "top-notch" wine list featuring "some small vineyards" add up to "fine dining at its best" proclaim patrons of chef-owner Eduardo Lauria's Wappingers Falls "gem"; spacious Tuscan-style digs featuring textured walls, wrought-iron accents and a waterfall are deemed "classy yet warm" and service "attentive", so "the only drawback" "could be the noise level" when things get "hectic" – just "bring earplugs" along with "a hearty appetite."

Aroma Thyme Bistro American | 20 | 18 | 19 | $41 |

Ellenville | 165 Canal St. (bet. Hermance St. & Maiden Ln.) | 845-647-3000 | www.aromathymebistro.com

Carnivores, the "bean-sprout-and-organics Birkenstock crowd" – even vegans and celiacs – chow down side-by-side at self-declared health nut Marcus Guiliano's Ellenville New American, as a "very nice" staff serves "something for everyone, all done well"; the not-yet-gentrified "neighborhood provides no inkling of the fantabulous" bistro-style interior, with wainscoting topped by hand-painted green-and-gold harlequin walls lending a "civilized atmosphere."

NEW Artist's Palate Ⓢ American | 24 | 25 | 23 | $42 |

Poughkeepsie | 307 Main St. (bet. Market & Garden Sts.) | 845-483-8074 | www.theartistspalate.biz

"Rookie of the year award" is what admirers would bestow on this "trendy" New American newcomer that's considered a "bright spot" in "reviving" Downtown Poughkeepsie; toque team Charlie and Meghan Fells turn out "imaginative" "delectables" like "killer rock shrimp beignets" and lobster mac 'n' cheese in a "SoHo-like" "conversion of a 19th-century storefront" with local artists' works displayed on the brick walls; a "helpful staff" and "excellent value" are also palatable.

Asiana Cafe Pan-Asian | 23 | 19 | 19 | $33 |

Greenwich | 130 E. Putnam Ave. (Milbank Ave.), CT | 203-622-6833

"Be prepared to wait for a table on the weekend" at this "delicious", "always reliable" Greenwich Pan-Asian and "sister to Penang Grill", which seems to have "something for everyone" on the menu; still, surveyors are split over its recent expansion, with pros proclaiming "the redo brings the cafe to new heights" and critics contending "it's gotten too big for its britches and lost its charm."

NEW Asian Temptation *Pan-Asian* | – | – | – | M |

White Plains | 23 Mamaroneck Ave. (bet. Main St. & Martine Ave.) | 914-328-5151

This posh Pan-Asian newcomer in the White Plains City Center is positioned for people-watching with throbbing music and balcony seating overlooking the low-lit dining room and sushi bar; a "special snacks" menu, as well as the usual rolls, noodles and stir-fries go well with bubble teas and fruity cocktails.

Aspen Garden *Mediterranean* | 13 | 10 | 15 | $23 |

Litchfield | 51 West St. (Rte. 63), CT | 860-567-9477

At this "fixture on the Litchfield green", "lunch in the sun in the summertime" on the "nice patio" with a "pleasant" view and "reasonable prices" help offset only "decent, basic" Mediterranean eats; harsher critics contend it's this tony town's "version of a diner" that's "a ministep away from fast food", so only "go if every place else is packed."

NEW A'Tavola Bistro 385 *French/Italian* | – | – | – | M |

Harrison | Harrison Shopping Ctr. | 385 Halstead Ave. (bet. Haviland St. & Oakland Ave.) | 914-381-6050

Bistro fare goes global at this Harrison newcomer where French and Italian dishes share menu space with ceviche, satays and chicken wings; the strip-mall location is warmed up with mustard-yellow walls, while the upbeat atmosphere is made even livelier by jazz bands on weekends.

Aurora *Italian* | 19 | 19 | 16 | $44 |

Rye | 60 Purchase St. (Purdy Ave.) | 914-921-2333 | www.auroraofrye.com

"Pleasant all around", this Rye Northern Italian attracts "a nice crowd" to its warmly appointed dining room for "upscale pizzas", "Tuscan dishes" and "prix fixe lunches that are an excellent bargain"; "hit-or-miss service" and a tendency to be "earplug" "noisy during peak hours" are grievances, though it remains a "popular choice" and an "'in' spot."

Aux Délices Foods
by Debra Ponzek *American/French* | 22 | 13 | 15 | $26 |

Darien | Goodwives Shopping Ctr. | 25 Old Kings Hwy. N. (Rte. 1), CT | 203-662-1136
Greenwich | 3 W. Elm St. (Greenwich Ave.), CT | 203-622-6644
Riverside | 1075 E. Putnam Ave. (Riverside Ave.), CT | 203-698-1066
www.auxdelicesfoods.com

"Gourmets on the run" in Riverside, Greenwich and Darien rely on these "upscale delis" for their "beautifully prepared" French–New American entrees and "decadent desserts" "that you can take home and pretend (although no one will believe you) to have made yourself"; the "ridiculous" "prices may scare some away" ("$6 for 10 snow peas!" huff hyperbolists), but that doesn't keep these celebrated chef-owner shops with just a handful of seats from being "cramped" and "crowded" with tony townies.

	FOOD	DECOR	SERVICE	COST

◩ Azuma Sushi Ⓜ *Japanese*   27 | 14 | 21 | $44

Hartsdale | 219 E. Hartsdale Ave. (bet. Bronx River Pkwy. &
Central Park Ave.) | 914-725-0660

"Impeccable" "Tokyo-style sushi" for the "serious" "purist" is what
you'll find at this "costly" Hartsdale Japanese where "nothing is
cooked" and "they do one thing, and they do it great"; "don't bring the
kids" as there are "no crazy rolls or funny chefs", and while a few carp
about the "boring" "all-white" decor, "cramped tables" and occasional
"attitude" from the staff, it's a spot that "separates itself from the
pack" and is a "legit" contender for the "best" raw fish in Westchester.

Azzurri Ⓜ *Mediterranean*   ▽ 17 | 21 | 18 | $42

Thornwood | 665 Commerce St./Rte. 141 (bet. Lincoln &
Orchard Pls.) | 914-747-6656 | www.azzurrirestaurant.com

A "fine"-looking room with warm browns, golds and yellows reminiscent of a Tuscan villa sets the stage for this Thornwood restaurant,
a relative "newcomer" that offers Mediterranean cuisine with Italian
accents, including "wood-fired calamari" and "huge soft scallops";
surveyors report it's still "working out" some kinks with "slow" service and food that "needs to improve", however, with a little work,
this spot "could be a real gem."

◩ Baang Cafe & Bar *Pan-Asian*   24 | 20 | 18 | $44

Riverside | 1191 E. Putnam Ave. (Neil St.), CT | 203-637-2114 |
www.decarorestaurantgroup.com

"Sell the first-born", "wear black", then "order a fancy drink" at this
venerable Pan-Asian in Riverside, where the Greenwich crowd congregates to "people-watch, be seen" and share "excellent" "family-
style" fare like "crackling calamari salad"; even advocates find the
"raucous" "party atmosphere" "way too loud", but say all is forgiven
"once the food arrives."

Baba Louie's Sourdough Pizza *Pizza*   23 | 11 | 18 | $21

Hudson | 517 Warren St. (bet. 5th & 6th Sts.) | 518-751-2155 |
www.babalouiessourdoughpizzacompany.com
See review in The Berkshires Directory.

Babbone Fine Italian Cuisine Ⓜ *Italian*   ▽ 22 | 13 | 19 | $42

Bronxville | 502 New Rochelle Rd. (bet. Cross County Pkwy. &
Pelhamdale Ave.) | 914-665-4722

Patrons of this "local family place" in Bronxville appreciate
"delicious", "well-prepared" "old-school" Italian dishes served in
"hearty portions" accompanied by "big drinks"; adding to the appeal
are "friendly" service and "homey" ambiance – now if only they
could do something about the "parking" situation.

Bacio Trattoria Ⓜ *Italian/Mediterranean*   19 | 11 | 20 | $36

Cross River | 12 N. Salem Rd./Rte. 121 (Rte. 35) | 914-763-2233 |
www.baciotrattoria.com

"The neighborhood secret is out" say supporters of this "popular"
Cross River "roadhouse" with a "satisfying" Italian-Med menu that's
"big on flavor" and an "exceptional value" to boot; the somewhat

"plain" interior is brightened by "charming" servers who have "crayons ready for the little ones", and if "cramped" quarters have a few diners grumbling, most think it's "worth it for the food"; P.S. the "outdoor terrace" is "lovely" in warm weather.

NEW Backals *American*   16 | 22 | 16 | $56

Scarsdale | Five Corners | 2 Weaver St. (Heathcote Rd.) | 914-722-4508 | www.backals.com

A "sophisticated crowd" is impressed with the way new owners have "beautifully redecorated" this Scarsdale New American (formerly home to Heathcote Tavern) in a "smart" "modern" style, "trying to replicate" "Big Apple ambiance"; while a significant number of surveyors complain about "only ok" fare that "doesn't warrant the cost", "spotty" service and "uncomfortable" Philippe Starck-designed "plastic chairs", they also confide: if they "fix these things" it "has potential."

NEW Backyard Bistro 🅂 🅼 *American*   - | - | - | M

Montgomery | 1118 Rte. 17K (bet. Bailey Rd. & Walnut St.) | 845-457-9901
Aptly named, this New American newcomer from veteran catering couple Jerry and Susan Crocker (who once owned Yankee Kitchen) is set behind their Montgomery home; the tiny, 16-seat space with trees stenciled on creamy walls sets a snug mood for housemade breads and pastas, as well as dishes like their signature scallops in a potato basket; in summer, patrons waiting for a table can sip a cocktail in the landscaped courtyard.

Bagels & More *Deli*   18 | 7 | 14 | $10

Hartsdale | 224 E. Hartsdale Ave. (bet. Rockledge Rd. & Station Dr.) | 914-722-4444
Yorktown Heights | Triangle Shopping Ctr. | 36 Triangle Ctr. (Rte. 35) | 914-962-3040

"Authentic" New York–style bagels and "strong hot coffee" keep commuters queuing up at these Hartsdale-Yorktown delis, perfect for a "quick" breakfast, while "sandwiches and salads" make them solid "lunch spots" as well; with only a "few tables inside and on the sidewalk", "takeout" is the way to go.

Bailey's Backyard *American*   20 | 16 | 20 | $38

Brookfield | 640 Federal Rd. (Rte. 7), CT | 203-775-3392 🅼
Ridgefield | 23 Bailey Ave. (Main St.), CT | 203-431-0796
www.baileysbackyard.com

"It's like eating in your backyard" say surveyors about this small, "cozy" New American whose "consistently good food" and "summer meals on the patio" are "Ridgefield's little secret"; the notion of alfresco dining is still up in the air at the newer, slightly larger Brookfield branch, which may add outdoor seating next year.

Bangkok Thai *Thai*   21 | 7 | 17 | $24

Mamaroneck | 1208 W. Boston Post Rd. (Richbell Rd.) | 914-833-1200

There's "no" atmosphere but you'll say "yes" to the "authentic", "delicious" dishes at this "affordable" Thai "tucked away" in a

FOOD DECOR SERVICE COST

Mamaroneck strip mall; some reviewers maintain that despite a "friendly" staff, until they "upgrade the tabletops" and "fluorescent lighting" in this "humbly decorated joint", it's best "for takeout" only.

Barcelona Restaurant & Wine Bar *Spanish*

22 | 20 | 20 | $40

Greenwich | 18 W. Putnam Ave. (Greenwich Ave.), CT | 203-983-6400 | www.barcelonawinebar.com

This Greenwich "tapas temple delivers big flavors on small plates" that are "pure heaven for those who like to taste a little of everything" while sipping something from an "amazing" Spanish wine list; an "eternally hip" hacienda with "flirty waitresses" and "scantily clad ladies and slick-haired men crowding the bar", it makes for "one of the best going out experiences around", but cynics shout the decibel level will have you "screaming at your date" while you're dining on "el blando" dishes.

Basement Bistro, The Ⓜ *American*

▽ 29 | 22 | 28 | $70

Earlton | 776 Rte. 45 (Rte. 81) | 518-634-2338 | www.sagecrestcatering.com

"Surprise, surprise!" cry "foodies" who've found this "unique" "undiscovered" New American hidden in the Catskills; "engaging", "enthusiastic" chef Damon Baehrel first "meets and greets" at his "intimate" boîte in the madeover basement of his home, then "cooks and serves" his "fabulous" 10-course tasting menu "showcasing" "quintessentially perfect ingredients" (many from his own garden); it's "a labor of love", so reservations are a must.

Bastones Italian Grill *Italian*

18 | 12 | 19 | $31

New Rochelle | 1 North Ave. (Pelham Rd.) | 914-636-6611

"Bring the children" to this "friendly", "family-style" Italian eatery in New Rochelle, where you can doodle on paper tablecloths while noshing on "ridiculously large portions" of "down-home" standards; with "sports decor" and "arenalike noise levels", it's "hardly fine dining" – even so, moderate prices make it a "decent" place.

Bayou *Cajun/Creole*

21 | 17 | 17 | $28

Mt. Vernon | 580 Gramatan Ave. (Broad St.) | 914-668-2634 | www.bayourestaurantny.com

"Bayou"-buffs get their "eat and drink on" at this "kickin'" "frat house/blues joint" in Mt. Vernon with "authentic" Cajun-Creole fare like "addictive" "jambalaya" served in "huge portions"; "live bands" ("it gets very loud") and a "funky" "party" atmosphere with "voodoo knickknacks and hot sauces" shelved along the walls make the experience best-suited for less "fussy" types.

☒ Bear Cafe *American*

23 | 22 | 21 | $40

Bearsville | 295 Tinker St./Rte. 212 (Stilbel Rd.) | 845-679-5555 | www.bearcafe.com

"Models, actors", "a rock 'n' roll crowd" and other "glitterati" gather for a "well-thought-out" seasonal menu of "really delicious" New American cooking at this "relaxed" "classic hot spot" on the outskirts of Woodstock; mere mortals also find "prompt, pleasant service" and a "convivial", "unpretentious" vibe, whether they "unwind" at the busy bar, or nab "a streamside window seat" in the rustic room or the even woodsier new pavilion outside.

Beebs *American* ▽ 22 | 19 | 20 | $39

Newburgh | 30 Plank Rd. (Rte. 9W) | 845-568-6102

In olden times, this "historic roadhouse" in Newburgh welcomed weary stagecoach travelers; nowadays, the "cute" Victorian-style tavern (complete with lace curtains) makes for a "great stop after shopping or work" – or anytime there's a call for a "variety" of New American fare that's "never disappointing"; service is "good", and "the tiny bar" alone is "worth a visit."

Beech Tree Grill *American* 20 | 16 | 20 | $27

Poughkeepsie | 1 Collegeview Ave. (Raymond Ave.) | 845-471-7279 | www.beechtreegrill.com

"You may run into a professor", "students on a date" or even "the mayor's husband" at this Poughkeepsie neighborhood New American that serves as a "comfy hangout" for the Vassar set and other locals; all nosh on "solid, simple" eats that include a few "upscale" dishes, or quaff something from the "excellent beer selection", the better to enjoy the "dark, pub atmosphere" in the narrow, brick-walled space.

Beehive Restaurant *American/Eclectic* 17 | 13 | 18 | $29

Armonk | 30 Old Rte. 22 (Kaysal Ct.) | 914-765-0688

"There's a solid buzz" at this Armonk Eclectic–New American that caters to locals that laud the "terrific variety", "polite" servers and "legendary" Sunday brunch; sure, at its heart, it's "basically a dressed-up diner", but one with a "feel good" vibe and "fair" prices.

Bella Vita *Italian* ▽ 20 | 15 | 18 | $39

Mohegan Lake | 1744 E. Main St. (bet. Lexington Ave. & Strawberry Rd.) | 914-528-8233

"Come hungry" and "leave pleasantly stuffed" at this Mohegan Lake Italian "right on Route 6" where the servers make "you feel like you belong"; despite "tight" seating, it's a "solid choice", given the "rural location", but beware the prices run "high"; P.S. come summer, you can "dine under the stars" on the patio.

NEW Belle Havana 🅼 *Cuban/French* – | – | – | M
(fka Bistro Chartreuse)

Yonkers | 35 Main St. (Warburton Ave.) | 914-969-1006

Bistro Chartreuse owners Alexandre Cheblal and Stella Rodriguez-Cheblal have jettisoned their menu of modern Gallic comfort food, and remade their Yonkers Waterfront District space over into a Cuban-French hybrid with an old-world Colonial motif featuring palm leaf ceiling fans, a bamboo bar and tea-stained walls; entrees include banana leaf–wrapped snapper with sweet yam purée and Catalan rotisserie chicken with garbanzo bean and chorizo dip in addition to a tapas menu that will be offered until 2 AM.

	FOOD	DECOR	SERVICE	COST

Bellizzi *Italian* | 14 | 11 | 13 | $22 |

Larchmont | 1272 Boston Post Rd. (Weaver St.) | 914-833-5800
Mt. Kisco | 153 Main St. (Green St.) | 914-241-1200

The playroom is the main attraction at these "quick"-bite Larchmont and Mt. Kisco Italian sibs where video games, "fanciful decor" and pizzas make it a "hot spot" for the "under-12" set; be forewarned, it's "noisy beyond belief", so while "Advil", "earplugs" and "beer and wine" may help, you'll likely "pay for it later" with a "headache."

Bel Paese *Italian* | 17 | 13 | 16 | $34 |

Hawthorne | 408 Elwood Ave. (Rte. 141) | 914-741-6520

This Hawthorne Italian "right by the train station" "draws a crowd of repeat customers" who appreciate the "accommodating" kitchen staff that whips up "credible" and affordable renditions of "red-sauce" classics; doubters, however, dismiss "uneven" fare and "cramped" decor, suggesting it's best only "in a pinch."

Belvedere Mansion Ⓜ *American* | ▽ 17 | 26 | 17 | $62 |

Staatsburg | 10 Old Rte. 9 (4 mi. south of Rte. 308W) | 845-889-8000 | www.belvederemansion.com

You can count on this "wonderful" Dutchess County "hideaway" overlooking the Catskills and the Hudson River for a truly luxe setting: the mansion's "intimate dining spaces" are "beautifully appointed" with 18th-century French antiques, silk and damask; "too bad" New American cuisine is "unpredictable" claim critics – "you can't eat the decor"; N.B. rooms are available for overnight stays.

Ⓩ Bengal Tiger *Indian* | 23 | 18 | 19 | $34 |

White Plains | 144 E. Post Rd. (bet. Court St. & Mamaroneck Ave.) | 914-948-5191 | www.bengaltiger1.com

Masala mavens hail this "consistently wonderful" "upscale" Indian "jewel" in White Plains (some say the county "gold standard" for the cuisine), where "authentic" dishes are "elegantly served" by a "gracious and respectful" staff in a "dark" dining room "draped" with fabric; if some whisper it's "declined", you wouldn't know it judging from the "wait" on weekends; P.S. the "bargain" lunch buffet "can't be beat."

Bennett's Steak & Fish *Seafood/Steak* | 20 | 14 | 20 | $50 |

Stamford | 24-26 Spring St. (bet. Bedford & Summer Sts.), CT | 203-978-7995 | www.bennettssteakandfish.com

This "solid", "nothing fancy" steakhouse "on a side street" of Downtown Stamford is not only "where the beef is", it's also home to "good" "fresh fish" and one of "the best wine lists in town" (no wonder "all the important locals hang out there"); while macho types maintain it's a "great place for a guy's night out", detractors declare the "basketball-theme" decor "a decade or two past its prime."

Ⓩ Bernard's Ⓜ *French* | 26 | 25 | 26 | $65 |

Ridgefield | 20 West Ln./Rte. 35 (Rte. 33), CT | 203-438-8282 | www.bernardsridgefield.com

Fans feel like "royalty in Ridgefield" at this "friendly yet formal family-run" French, a favorite for "special occasions" that's "awesome in every way"; Bernard Bouissou's "food is perfection, the decor romance at its finest", service "cosseting" and the "wine list impressive"; just "be ready to leave your wallet with the waiter", and beware: "tables by the piano are a bit loud"; N.B. jacket suggested.

Bertucci's *Italian* | 15 | 13 | 15 | $22 |

Danbury | 98 Newtown Rd. (I-84, exit 8), CT | 203-739-0500
Darien | 54 Boston Post Rd. (I-95, exit 13), CT | 203-655-4299
www.bertuccis.com

This "family-friendly" Italian chain duo in Danbury and Darien is all about the "dough" – as in "bubbling-hot", "thin-crust pizzas" and "dumpling-shaped rolls" – as well as in the "best bang-for-the-buck" prices; but protestors pan an "unbearably loud" "place where children run wild", "tables are never cleared" and "the most depressing decor east of the Mississippi" will leave you "needing Prozac."

Beso *Eclectic* | 25 | 20 | 21 | $46 |

New Paltz | 46 Main St. (Chestnut St.) | 845-255-1426 |
www.beso-restaurant.com

At this "terrific" two-year-old New Paltz Eclectic, chef Chad Greer's "excellent", "sophisticated" dishes, prepared with an emphasis on "local ingredients", are bested only by wife Tammy Ogletree's "decadent desserts"; seating in the "pleasant" two-story skylit space may be a little "cramped" but the "atmosphere's relaxing", and if tabs are a touch "expensive for the area", that (and "professional service") just adds to the "Manhattan feel."

B4 Bistro *American/Mediterranean* | 18 | 14 | 18 | $37 |

Valhalla | 4 Broadway (N. Kensico Ave.) | 914-328-4199 |
www.b4bistro.com

They "try hard" to be "welcoming" at this "friendly" Traditional American–Mediterranean bistro near Kensico Dam Plaza in Valhalla where residents in-the-know stick to burgers, appetizers and drinks served by "knowledgeable barkeeps"; the "noise level" is "loud" and the "price way too high" for the "quality of food" but it's "nice to have in the neighborhood" – after all it's the "only place in town that's open Mondays."

NEW Big B's Reef & Beef Restaurant *Seafood/Steak* | - | - | - | E |

Stamford | 489 Glenbrook Rd. (Crescent St.), CT | 203-355-1032
Few surveyors have found this new Stamford surf 'n' turfer that's located in a blue-collar neighborhood; aptly named, it serves up "huge portions" of signature porterhouse steaks and Chilean sea bass in a "casual atmosphere."

Big Easy Bistro, The *Cajun* | ▽ 17 | 17 | 18 | $37 |

Newburgh | 40 Front St. (2nd St.) | 845-565-3939 |
www.bigeasybistro.net

Good times roll at this "energetic" Cajun on Newburgh's waterfront, where a "variety of fare" with "nice Creole highlights" comes via a "friendly staff" that also dispenses specialty drinks from the long copper-topped bar; brick walls, a stuffed alligator and a "loud" crowd add to the "Mardi Gras" mood, though the outdoor patio is a "relaxing" respite.

NEW Big W's Roadside Bar-B-Que *BBQ* | - | - | - | I |

Wingdale | 1475 Rte. 22 (Rock Hill Dr.) | 845-832-6200 |
www.bigwbbq.com

"Big W" stands for "big wow" at this Wingdale newcomer dispensing "delicious" BBQ, with "standout ribs" and "succulent" "smokin' chicken"; owner Warren Norstein first set up shop in a van parked roadside (hence the name), but moved into this former convenience store where customers can now perch at a table or picnic outside under a willow in summer; N.B. opens at 4 PM and for now, it's BYO.

Bird and Bottle Inn Ⓜ *American* | 21 | 24 | 22 | $52 |

Garrison | The Bird and Bottle Inn | 1123 Old Albany Post Rd.
(Indian Brook Rd.) | 845-424-2333 | www.thebirdandbottleinn.com

"What a makeover!" exclaim enthusiasts at Putnam County's recently restored, "utterly delightful" 18th-century country inn; "quaint" "Colonial decor" and "roaring fireplaces" conjure "George Washington's presence" as an "attentive staff" serves up "consistently" "good" New American dishes; even those finding it "a bit pricey" agree it's "the perfect place to celebrate" or indulge in a "spectacular" Sunday brunch.

Bistro Bonne Nuit *French* | 24 | 21 | 21 | $54 |

New Canaan | 12 Forest St. (bet. East & Locust Aves.), CT |
203-966-5303

"Step into this New Canaan bistro and you are transported to the warmth of Provence", from the "wonderful cassoulet" and "delicious frites" to the "rich mousse au chocolat"; some say the "welcoming" setting is "as comfortable as an old shoe", while others allege "the space is sooooo tight" you need to "overlook the tush in your salad when the waiter takes your neighbor's order (and these are very skinny waiters)."

Bistro Twenty-Two Ⓢ Ⓜ *American/French* | 23 | 23 | 23 | $62 |

Bedford | 391 Old Post Rd. (bet. Lake Ave. & The Farms Rd.) |
914-234-7333

"A class act" enthuse admirers of this "warm, romantic" "country house" in Bedford, where "sophisticated" French Bistro–New American fare is served by "pleasant", "tuxedo-clad" waiters in a "lovely", "understated" room; if a few fear it's been "inconsistent" of late, it's still "popular" with fans who consider it a "satisfying" choice for a "romantic evening" or "special occasion."

Black Goose Grille *American* | 17 | 19 | 17 | $35 |

Darien | 972 Post Rd. (Center St.), CT | 203-655-7107

"The warm bar is one of the best features (especially in the winter when the fireplace is going)" of this "old-school *Cheers* for yuppies" "in the heart of Darien"; for loyalists, it's a "steady" "neighborhood place for comfort food when you don't want to cook", but detractors dub the New American fare "boring" and "waaay overpriced."

Blazer Pub, The ⏚ *Pub Food*   21 | 9 | 16 | $20
Purdys | Rte. 22 (I-684, exit 7) | 914-277-4424

"It ain't fancy", but that doesn't stop a "funny mix" of "families", "Harley riders", "yuppies" and "IBMers" from converging on this "down-home" "roadside" Purdys pub where the "outstanding" hamburgers ("do they get juicer than this?"), "killer" steak fries and brews on tap more than "make up for the dive atmosphere"; so "take a Sunday drive" to this "staple", but keep in mind, you'll want to "avoid peak times" because "*the* place" for patties in Northern Westchester is almost "always busy"; P.S. "bring cash."

NEW Bloom *American*   ▽ 21 | 21 | 20 | $51
Hastings-on-Hudson | 19 Main St. (Warburton Ave.) | 914-478-3250 | www.bloom-restaurant.com

Eco-happy eaters flock to this "promising" Hastings newcomer where the "creative" New American menu is prepared with organic ingredients and complemented by a selection of biodynamic wines; "quiet" and "comfortable" earth-toned digs and a staff that "tries hard" smooth the sting of "high" prices; P.S. their "wonderful brunch" is a less-expensive option.

Bloom's Kosher Deli *Deli*   19 | 10 | 15 | $21
Yorktown Heights | Yorktown Green Shopping Ctr. | 339 Downing Dr. (Rte. 118) | 914-245-3900 | www.bloomskosherdeli.com

"An oasis in the deli desert" that is Northern Westchester, this Yorktown Heights eatery offers "authentic" kosher goodies from "fantastic" "overstuffed" pastrami sandwiches "on fresh rye" to "stuffed cabbage" and "homemade knishes"; if a few kvetch about "depressing" decor and "surly" service, they might want to "opt for takeout."

Blu *American*   18 | 19 | 18 | $45
Hastings-on-Hudson | 100 River St. (Southside Ave.) | 914-478-4481 | www.bluonhudson.com

"The enchanting view" of the Hudson River and the Palisades ropes in romantics to this "waterside" Hastings restaurant where the New American food is "good", but "not always on par" with the "lovely" setting (or "high" prices); if the "odd location", "wedged" next to a tennis court, confuses some critics, even they admit that "outdoor tables" make it a "nice place" to meet for "a drink" in the summertime.

Blue ⌧ *American*   19 | 19 | 17 | $49
White Plains | 99 Church St. (Hamilton Ave.) | 914-220-0000 | www.bluewhiteplains.com

A "yuppie" crowd fills this "upbeat" "Manhattan-style" New American in White Plains with a "funky" high-ceilinged setting and an "interesting" (some say "weird") Asian-inflected menu; unfortunately, a "trendy NYC scene" also means "city prices" and "noise" as well as sometimes "inattentive" servers, although in spite of that, most maintain the "nice bar" and "martini menu" still make it a "great date place" in the area.

Blue Dolphin ⑧ *Italian* — 22 | 11 | 19 | $33

Katonah | 175 Katonah Ave. (Jay St.) | 914-232-4791 | www.lefontane.net

"Squeeze" into this "tiny" "converted" "old diner" in the heart of Katonah village and you'll find "honest", "delicious" Southern Italian cooking that's well worth the "maddening" lines; "a friendly crew" and a "homey", "knickknacky" atmosphere make it a "place to feel like regulars" ("if it's not on the menu just ask"), and if the "cramped" quarters start to get to you, just remember, it's "crowded for a reason."

Blue Fountain *Italian* — ▽ 20 | 19 | 21 | $35

Hopewell Junction | 826 Rte. 376 (Hillside Lake Rd.) | 845-226-3570 | www.thebluefountain.com

"Large portions" from an "eclectic" Italian menu "always please" at this "reliable" family-run Dutchess County spot done up Tuscan-style with sunny colors and crisp white linens; rates are "reasonable" and the ambiance warmed by "kind", "courteous" servers, which explain why it's a popular venue for "large parties" and other catered events.

🄩 Blue Hill at Stone Barns 🅼 *American* — 27 | 28 | 27 | $84

Pocantico Hills | Stone Barns Center for Food & Agriculture | 630 Bedford Rd. (Lake Rd.) | 914-366-9600 | www.bluehillfarm.com

A "stunning" "conduit from earth to table", Dan Barber's Pocantico Hills New American (ranked No. 1 for Popularity in Westchester/HV) showcases "ultrafresh" ingredients grown "on a former Rockefeller estate" in "heavenly" prix fixe meals "creatively" served in a converted barn that's the picture of "unstuffy elegance"; though the less starry-eyed say the "overhyped" experience may leave you "blue" due to "timidly seasoned" fare and "absurd" prices, most urge you to snag a "hard-to-get" reservation, and "go at least once" to experience "what food is meant to be."

Blue Moon Mexican Café *Mexican* — 17 | 17 | 16 | $27

Bronxville | 7-27 Pondfield Rd. (Sagamore Rd.) | 914-337-4000 | www.bluemoonmexicancafe.com

"Tequila and tots" get equal play at this "casual" Bronxville Mexican "cantina" that caters to "singles and families alike", offering "acceptable", if "Americanized", "south-of-the-border" specialties in a "festive" setting; if the food's only "decent", the "lively" atmosphere and "reasonable prices" still make it a "pleasant experience."

Blue Plate 🅼 *American* — 18 | 15 | 18 | $37

Chatham | 1 Kinderhook St. (Central Sq.) | 518-392-7711 | www.chathamblueplate.net

"Hearty" fare "served with flair" is just part of the draw at this "homey" Columbia County "hangout" whose "wood floors, brick walls and tin ceilings" keep things "comfortably casual"; it's a "pleasant" place where locals and "ex–New Yorkers" "meet and greet" and indulge in the "special meatloaf" or other entries on the "solid" New American menu.

WESTCHESTER/HUDSON/CT

	FOOD	DECOR	SERVICE	COST

Boathouse *American* — 16 | 19 | 17 | $39
Lakeville | 349 Main St./Rte. 44 (Walton St.), CT | 860-435-2111
This "charming Lakeville spot has acquired a dedicated clientele" of "locals and rich weekenders" – particularly "prep school kids and their parents" – who come for "casual Traditional American fare", "with a curious slate of Japanese choices" thrown in; "the nearby lake" gives credence to the "picturesque" "nautical decor", but "uneven service" and "menu selections" give some surveyors a sinking feeling.

Bobby Valentine's Sports Gallery Café ● *Pub Food* — 14 | 15 | 15 | $22
Stamford | 225 Main St. (Washington Blvd.), CT | 203-348-0010 | www.bobbyv.com
"Don't bring a date or it will be your last", but if "you want to watch a game or two with the kids or the boys" and chow down on chicken wings this Stamford American "institution" owned by the namesake former Mets manager and filled with "baseball memorabilia" may fill the bill; "loudness" and "big-screen TVs" are the name of the game, but cynics say "the only homer you'll hit here is when you leave."

NEW Bollywood Bistro Ⓜ *Indian* — ▽ 24 | 21 | 22 | $29
Pleasantville | 68 Wheeler Ave. (bet. Bedford & Manville Rds.) | 914-747-4599
"Flavorful and light" options abound at this Pleasantville Indian newcomer where "fresh ingredients" play into many dishes and you "don't have to be a Bollywood actor" to receive "star treatment"; "affordable" tabs and a "warm" setting decorated with vintage movie posters have supporters saying it's "just what the neighborhood needed."

Boulders Inn Ⓜ *American* — 21 | 25 | 20 | $57
New Preston | E. Shore Rd./Rte. 45 (Rte. 202), CT | 860-868-0541 | www.bouldersinn.com
"Romantic doesn't begin to describe this" New Preston Contemporary American set in a "beautiful inn overlooking Lake Waramaug"; the "luxury log cabin" interior is "cozy", but in warmer weather the outdoor terrace and it's "unparalleled" view is "best at sunset" as "an ideal spot for drinks or dinner"; while most agree the food is "very good", the cost-conscious call it "an expensive experience."

Boxcar Cantina *Southwestern* — 19 | 16 | 17 | $31
Greenwich | 44 Old Field Point Rd. (Prospect St.), CT | 203-661-4774 | www.boxcarcantina.com
"Bring earplugs" if you venture into this upscale Greenwich Southwestern "before 7 PM when it's kiddy-central", or "sit in the bar" where it's "quieter"; amigos agree "the margaritas will kick your butt", but are in a standoff over the food ("solid" vs "standard") and the tab ("reasonable" vs "expensive").

Brasserie Swiss Ⓜ *Swiss* — 19 | 13 | 19 | $40
Ossining | 118 Croton Ave./Rte. 133 (bet. Rtes. 9 & 9A) | 914-941-0319
"Authentic and plentiful" Swiss "mainstays" like fondue and "solid" sauerbraten are dished out at this "homey", if "high"-priced,

FOOD DECOR SERVICE COST

Ossining longtimer run by "knowledgeable" "proprietors" adept at "attentive service"; yes, the "quirky" "1970s" chalet-styled interior is a "little too dark and worn" for most diners' tastes, but a few admirers admit they think the "old-school" decor is part of its "charm."

Bread Alone *Bakery/Coffeeshop*   20 | 11 | 15 | $13

Boiceville | Rte. 28 (Rte. 42) | 845-657-3328
Kingston | 34 N. Front St. (Wall St.) | 845-339-1295 🛇
Rhinebeck | 43 E. Market St. (Rte. 9) | 845-876-3108
Woodstock | 22 Mill Hill Rd. (Maple Ln.) | 845-679-2108
www.breadalone.com

Although the "famous" artisanal "bread alone is worth the visit", these mid–Hudson Valley bakeries/coffee shops are a "perfect lunch or snack spot" serving "tasty soups", "wholesome" "fresh sandwiches", salads, "scrumptious panini" and "treats" like "fudgy brownies"; "counter service" and "modest decor" don't deter those who want to "linger over a newspaper", but remember, they close early evening.

Briar's, The *American*   15 | 11 | 18 | $27

Briarcliff Manor | 512 N. State Rd. (Rte. 9A) | 914-941-9870 |
www.briarsrestaurant.com

A steady stream of "faithful customers" frequent this "friendly" Traditional American in Briarcliff Manor for "ample portions" of "comfort" fare like prime rib, onion soup and "excellent coleslaw"; though the "outdated" decor is a "step back into the 1950s", it's an "inviting" place nonetheless.

NEW Brick House Bar & Grill *American*   ▽ 15 | 13 | 16 | $22

Stamford | 244 Bedford St. (Broad St.), CT | 203-353-8892

This Traditional American newcomer to Downtown Stamford has yet to find a following, but the few respondents who've ventured in say the "pub grub is good", especially the Buffalo wings and burgers, and "the bartenders are nice."

Brooklyn's Famous Subs & Pasta *Diner*   16 | 16 | 18 | $20

White Plains | 51 Court St. (bet. Main St. & Martine Ave.) |
914-422-0115 | www.brooklynsfamous.com

You half-expect "Richie, Potsie and Fonzie" to make an appearance at this "retro diner" in White Plains, where "doo-wop" junkies lunch on "huge submarine sandwiches", burgers and egg creams amid "1950s decor"; it's a "cute distraction" if you grew up with sock hops, but despite "delightful owners" and "quick" service, the fare is "mediocre"; N.B. beer and wine now available.

Brothers Trattoria *Italian*   ▽ 23 | 18 | 21 | $22

Beacon | 465 Main St. (bet. Schenck & Tioronda Aves.) | 845-838-3300

If you're looking for a family "neighborhood Italian joint", this spot in Beacon comes "highly recommended" because service in the upscale but casual, brick-walled space "couldn't be friendlier"; "kids love the pizza", while grown-ups cite the "fine" traditional trattoria fare, the "excellent wines by the glass" and the "good food"/ "good value" ratio.

	FOOD	DECOR	SERVICE	COST

⚡ Buffet de la Gare Ⓜ *French*   26 | 21 | 24 | $61

Hastings-on-Hudson | 155 Southside Ave. (Spring St.) | 914-478-1671 | www.buffetdelagare.us

"Homesick French gourmets" head to this Hastings "jewel" where "charming" new owners Luc and Nicole Dimnet "are upholding the tradition" of "consistently sublime" "classic bistro fare" including "magnificent cassoulet" and escargots; decor is "quaint" and "warm" as ever with a pressed tin ceiling and 100-year-old oak bar, and if prices are a bit "haute" for some, it's "worth every penny, particularly for special occasions."

NEW Bukhara Grill *Indian*   ▽ 25 | 16 | 21 | $33

Yonkers | 27 Meyer Ave. (Vredenburgh Ave.) | 914-476-1910

"Finally!" masala mavens have something to cheer about at this Yonkers Indian newcomer (an offshoot of the NYC original) where a "talented team" pumps out "pungent", "carefully prepared" cuisine that goes far beyond "run-of-the-mill" "suburban" fare; "unbeatable prices" (especially for the "lunch buffet") and "consistent" service garner nods as well – just ignore the "banquet hall" feel of the room.

Bull's Bridge Inn *American*   16 | 16 | 20 | $38

Kent | 333 Kent Rd./Rte. 7 (Bull's Bridge Rd.), CT | 860-927-1000 | www.bullsbridge.com

With a view of a covered bridge, this Kent Traditional American housed in a 1762 inn is a "local hangout" that serves "reliable" prime rib and a bargain early-bird dinner in a "relaxed atmosphere"; but detractors deduce it "must be an inner craving for the boring salad bars of the patrons' youth" that "keeps this place trucking."

Bull's Head Inn Ⓜ *American*   19 | 23 | 18 | $45

Campbell Hall | 120 Sarah Wells Trail (Arbor Rd.) | 845-496-6758 | www.bullsheadinn.com

"Marvelous" murmur Orange County lovebirds looking for "romantic" ambiance, who suggest dining "in the gazebo" overlooking the pond at this "large", "very pretty" 18th-century "country home"; chef-owner Thomas Luedke's American cooking is "good", and if the less starry-eyed "expect more", it's still "a fun spot" for brunch or a "weekday gathering at the bar."

Buon Amici Ⓜ *Italian*   20 | 14 | 21 | $37

White Plains | 238 Central Ave. (Tarrytown Rd.) | 914-997-1399 | www.buonamicirestaurant.com

"Red-sauce" fare at moderate prices attracts "lots of families" to this White Plains Italian "neighborhood spot" "convenient to the County Center" with cuisine that garners reviews from "decent" to "delicious"; "waiters who know everyone" and "greet you like an old friend" make it a "pleasant" place in spite of "old decor" that "needs a redo."

⚡ Busy Bee Cafe Ⓢ *American*   26 | 17 | 23 | $36

Poughkeepsie | 138 South Ave. (Reade Pl.) | 845-452-6800

Buzz has it that "wonderful", "always delicious" New American food has patrons "licking the plate clean" at this Poughkeepsie cafe set in a modest residential area; it's sometimes "tough to get a table" in the "tiny" "cute" room that, despite a remodel, doesn't quite disguise "the deli it used to be", although "welcoming service" more than makes up for that, as do monthly "supper club"-style jazz nights.

NEW Bywater Bistro 🅂🅼 *American*　　▽ 18 | 20 | 16 | $32

Rosendale | 419 Main St. (bet. Central & Keator Aves.) | 845-658-9902

Set in the former Rosendale Cement Company space, this new Ulster County eatery's more "warm and inviting" than its predecessor; chef Sam Ullman's "diverse" New American menu ranges from burgers to "creative" dishes, with half portions of many entrees "a nice touch", while "sincere if inexperienced" service is one kink they're "making the effort" to iron out; meanwhile, dining in the garden out back remains "magical."

🆉 Café Les Baux *French*　　25 | 17 | 21 | $40

Millbrook | 152 Church St. (bet. Franklin & Merrill Aves.) | 845-677-8166 | www.cafelesbaux.com

It's "a delight!" declare Gallic groupies of this petite Millbrook "paradigm of a small French country restaurant", where "friendly patron" Herve Bochard "is at the stove" preparing "excellent", "robust, classical bistro" eats "to be savored"; *les négatives* include somewhat "cramped" seating, and "uneven service", but "no matter", "you'll smile on the way home."

Cafe Livorno 🆉 *Italian*　　▽ 19 | 17 | 20 | $45

Rye | 92 Purchase St. (Purdy Ave.) | 914-967-1909

Diners can count on "attentive service" by the "wonderful family" behind this "dependable", "romantic" Northern Italian in a "small" but "cozy" former residence along Rye's central business district; the straightforward cuisine, though, strikes a minorty of thrillseekers as lacking in "imagination" and say a "change in menu" is in order; N.B. a wine bar is reportedly in the works for the upper level.

Cafe Maya *Mexican*　　23 | 18 | 20 | $24

NEW Beacon | 294 Main St. (bet. Brett & Cedar Sts.) | 845-838-4901

Maya Cafe *Mexican*

Fishkill | 448 Rte. 9 (Van Wyck Lake Rd.) | 845-896-4042

Chef-owner Luis Pinto closed his popular Cold Spring cantina and now dispenses "excellent", "genuine" "Mexican with a twist" in this "bustling" Dutchess County duo instead; though the names flip-flop, both venues offer the same "fresh guacamole made tableside", "delicious margaritas", "low costs" and "helpful staff" in "kitschy" digs with walls painted bright yellow, green, pink and blue; N.B. it's BYO at the newer Beacon branch for now.

Cafe Mirage ◑🆉 *Eclectic*　　20 | 12 | 19 | $37

Port Chester | 531 N. Main St. (Terrace Ave.) | 914-937-3497 | www.cafemirageny.com

This "lively", "quirky" Eclectic Port Chester "late"-night spot (kitchen's open until midnight) situated in a "converted garage" has "something to appeal to everyone" on its "well-executed" menu of

| | FOOD | DECOR | SERVICE | COST |

"bistro food" that offers "often surprising" choices like rabbit and ostrich; "it still looks like a gas station, but no matter", "they pay serious attention" to the food here and "it works."

Cafe Mozart *Coffeehouse*

| 15 | 15 | 15 | $22 |

Mamaroneck | 308 Mamaroneck Ave. (Palmer Ave.) | 914-698-4166 | www.cafemozart.com

"Catch up with friends" over "good music" (there's live piano, guitar or jazz Thursday–Saturday evenings) at this "convenient" Mamaroneck coffeehouse and European style "gathering place"; the less-enthused admit it's a "nice place to hang" but assert the "inconsistent service" and "so-so main dishes" make it "best to stick to cake and coffee" "after a movie or a show at the Emelin Theatre."

Cafe on the Green *Italian*

| 23 | 22 | 24 | $42 |

Danbury | Richter Park Golf Course | 100 Aunt Hack Rd. (Mill Plain Rd.), CT | 203-791-0369 | www.cafeonthegreenrestaurant.com

"You don't need to be a golfer to enjoy" this "excellent" Northern Italian "tucked inside the clubhouse of Danbury's Richter Park Golf Course" with a "great view of the 18th hole"; surveyors cite "first-class service" and "sinfully blissful bananas Foster" as additional reasons they'd return; "the downside is that it's not convenient to find" this "hidden gem."

Cafe Portofino *Italian*

| 20 | 15 | 20 | $38 |

Piermont | 587 Piermont Ave. (Kinney St.) | 845-359-7300 | www.portofinoinpiermont.com

Rockland County residents wanting "simple", "honest" Italian chow choose this "neighborhood" "watering hole", where a "friendly bar" and a "welcoming atmosphere" attract "lots of regulars"; "supercasual" digs are politely deemed "cozy" and service "attentive"; "now, if only they had more windows" to take advantage of their Hudson River waterfront locale.

Cafe Tamayo Ⓜ *American*

| 24 | 22 | 23 | $43 |

Saugerties | 89 Partition St. (Main St.) | 845-246-9371 | www.cafetamayo.com

"Simply put, the food is superb" (and "the duck deserves its legendary reputation") swoon admirers of James Tamayo's "refined" New American prix fixe menu; the "laid-back", "charming old-style space" on Saugerties' Restaurant Row includes a sunroom and courtyard, so factor in "warm, elegant service", and this is "the place to impress a new sweetie."

Café Tandoor *Indian*

| 21 | 17 | 19 | $30 |

Tarrytown | 19 N. Broadway/Rte. 9 (bet. Central Ave. & Main St.) | 914-332-5544

This "unassuming" yet "cozy" mango-hued Indian eatery in Tarrytown convenient to the Music Hall offers "wonderfully simple" and "tasty" fare, "smooth and informed" service, and is "BYO" – "always a plus"; picky sorts point out that "parking is tough" and claim it's "not terribly authentic" but even they admit that sitting at a table "next to the large streetside windows" does make for a "lovely evening."

	FOOD	DECOR	SERVICE	COST

Café with Love ⊄ *European* ▽ | 19 | 14 | 17 | $19 |

Saugerties | 85 Partition St. (Main St.) | 845-246-1795 |
www.cafewithlove.com

Saugerties denizens squish into this "teeny, tiny" relative newcomer
for the "yummiest lunch" around; "always fresh", "tasty" soups and
salads as well as "simple" European eats are served up in the deep-red
room, which may not be "the best place for an intimate conversation" but you can "people-watch", at least until 5 PM, when they close.

Caffe Regatta *Seafood* | 19 | 20 | 20 | $43 |

Pelham | 133 Wolfs Ln. (Sparks Ave.) | 914-738-8686

Whether it's "date night" or an early dinner "with the kids", this versatile and "accommodating" seafooder "in the heart of Pelham" lures
them in with "well-prepared" fin fare in a "delightful" "nautical"-
themed room; a posse of landlubbers bemoan that, yes, they "try very
hard to please" but the quality of meals "varies" "one time to the next."

Calico Restaurant & | 25 | 16 | 23 | $37 |
Patisserie Ⓜ *American/Eclectic*

Rhinebeck | 6384 Mill St. (Market St.) | 845-876-2749 |
www.calicorhinebeck.com

Leave room when trying chef Anthony Balassone's "amazing",
"thoughtful" Eclectic–New American savories at this Rhinebeck
"treasure", because "you must have dessert" – wife Leslie makes
"to-die-for" pastries; service is "personal" but the "no-frills" bakery-
style storefront is super "petite", so some say it can be "better to
take out", but "take lots."

California Pizza Kitchen *Pizza* | 16 | 12 | 14 | $23 |

Scarsdale | 365 Central Park Ave. (S. Healy Ave.) | 914-722-0600 |
www.cpk.com

"Unusual" pizzas and a "terrific" "salad selection" have "families"
frequenting this "busy" Scarsdale sauce-and-cheese-link-in-a-
"chain" where you'll be "bombarded by kids" ("some screaming")
and "service" "can be a bit lacking"; sure, it's a "good value", but
"classic" pieheads wonder "when better places are nearby", why
"would anyone eat" this "marginal" "Californian" fare?

Ca'Mea Ⓜ *Italian* | 21 | 20 | 19 | $40 |

Hudson | The Inn at Ca'Mea | 333-335 Warren St. (City Hall Pl.) |
518-822-0005 | www.camearestaurant.com

Looks like this "trendy" four-year-old Hudson Northern Italian has
"settled in for a long stay"; chef Antonio Carchi's Ligurian specialties range from "traditional to sublimely extravagant", all served by
an "accommodating" staff in "modern" rooms done up with "works
of local artists" or, "when weather permits", on the "delightful" patio;
a new addition: guestrooms upstairs for those who want to stay over.

Candlelight Inn ◑⊄ *Pub Food* | 21 | 6 | 14 | $19 |

Scarsdale | 519 Central Park Ave. (Old Army Rd.) | 914-472-9706

Where else can you find a mix of "Hell's Angels", "college kids" and
"Edgemont parents" and their "children drawing with provided cray-

ons" but this "neon"-lit "late-night" "joint" in Scarsdale (serving till 3 AM) where "wings" "rival those in Buffalo" and the "pub" grub is deemed especially "hangover"-worthy; ignore the "sticky floors", remember it's "cash"-only and for those who find it "unbearably crowded", good news: they now deliver.

Canterbury Brook ⑤ Ⓜ Swiss
▽ 23 | 20 | 24 | $39

Cornwall-on-Hudson | 331 Main St. (off Rte. 9W) | 845-534-9658 | www.neateateries.com

If only "all neighborhood spots" were as "hospitable" as this "small" Cornwall Continental sigh patrons citing "personal attention" from a "caring" staff, "excellent" Swiss-inspired cuisine and "wonderful specials" courtesy of chef Hans Baumann; add "attractive" candlelit country-comfy rooms made "cozy" by "toasty fireplaces" in winter and a "pleasant" brookside terrace for when it's warm, and all said, it's surprising the place is "not well-known."

Capriccio Restaurant French/Italian
21 | 22 | 21 | $53

Brewster | 1250 Rte. 22 N. (I-684) | 845-279-2873 | www.capricciorestaurantny.com

"Spectacular reservoir views" outshine even the "beautiful dining room" at this popular Brewster venue where "charming" chef-owner Bruno Crosnier has added tapas to the "surprisingly good" French–Northern Italian menu; "polished service" comes via "tuxedoed waiters", and a fireplace makes winter dining snug, while the terrace is a "mid-summer night's dream"; occasional live music and valet parking are other pluses.

Caravela Brazilian/Portuguese
20 | 15 | 19 | $43

Tarrytown | 53 N. Broadway (bet. Central Ave. & Dixon St.) | 914-631-1863 | www.caravelarestaurant.com

"On a street full of restaurants", this bit of "Lisbon" in Tarrytown with a "formal", "quiet ambiance" "stands out" for "satisfying" Portuguese-Brazilian cuisine, including a variety of "fish dishes" and 1,000 bottles of wine to choose from; on the negative side are "high" prices and nautical decor that's "so old it will soon spring a leak" unless "refurbished."

Casa Maya Mexican
14 | 14 | 15 | $26

Scarsdale | 706 Central Park Ave. (bet. Mt. Joy Ave. & Old Army Rd.) | 914-713-0771 | www.racanellirestaurants.com

"Basic" Mexican fare "about as authentic as a square peso" feeds "families" at this "informal" Scarsdale restaurant with a "roaming mariachi" (Thursday–Saturday); with only "passable" fare, "rushed" service and "weatherbeaten" decor, your best bet is to "come for the margaritas and chips – and go elsewhere for dinner."

Casa Miguel BBQ/Tex-Mex
14 | 12 | 16 | $29

Mt. Kisco | 222 E. Main St./Rte. 117 (W. Hyatt Ave.) | 914-666-7588

"Employees from Northern Westchester Hospital" frequent this "old-school" Mt. Kisco Tex-Mex–BBQ "standby" for "after-hours" "margaritas" and "ordinary", "inexpensive" fare; muchos ex-amigos purport the "assembly-line food and service" is "not up to their previous standards" and the "only thing cheesier" than the "enchiladas" is the adobe and bric-a-brac decor.

Casa Rina of Thornwood *Italian*

17	12	19	$36

Thornwood | 886 Commerce St. (Marble Ave.) | 914-769-4515 | www.casarinarestaurant.com

"Familiar and filling" "red-sauce Italian" served by a "pleasant" staff in a "dated" burgundy-and-gold dining room makes this "tried-and-true" Thornwood throwback reminiscent of where "your parents would bring you in the '70s; although the $17.95 "early-bird dinners" "are hard to beat", the blasé blast you get "quantity rather than quality."

Cascade Mountain
Winery & Restaurant ▣ *American*

▽ 22	18	19	$39

Amenia | 835 Cascade Mountain Rd. (Flint Hill Rd.) | 845-373-9021 | www.cascademt.com

The "upscale menu" of Traditional American fare plus a chance to "enjoy a tasting" of the vineyard's 12 wines are the draws at this "charming" Dutchess County venue in a "gorgeous countryside" setting ("a great detour if you're on the Taconic"); some diners choose the rustic, beamed bistro-style room, though most say "it's best eating on the deck" on a "sunny afternoon"; either way, say fans, "go!"

▣ Caterina de Medici ▣ *Italian*

26	25	24	$49

Hyde Park | Colavita Center for Italian Food and Wine, Culinary Institute of America | 1946 Campus Dr. (Rte. 9) | 845-471-6608 | www.ciachef.edu

Budding chefs and "adorable" "student personnel" deliver a "phenomenal experience" at this "preeminent" Hyde Park cooking school restaurant, turning out "fabulous" "Italian classics that acknowledge the change of seasons", "elegantly presented" in a "very pretty" chandeliered "Tuscanesque" space where "no decorative cliché is left out"; as for service, you'll get the "royal treatment" (with a few "rookie mistakes") even if you opt for more casual dining in the Al Forno room overlooking the kitchen.

Catherine's ▣▣ *American*

22	14	21	$37

Goshen | 153 W. Main St. (New St.) | 845-294-8707 | www.catherinesrestaurant.net

Those in-the-know "bring a suitcase for the leftovers" at this "casual" Goshen eatery, because chef-owner Stephen Serkes' "solid" Traditional American eats come in "huge portions"; the staff is "super-friendly", and if the main dining room gets "cramped" with local politicos doing a "meet and greet", there's always the "pub downstairs", where it's less noticeable that a "decor redo" is "overdue."

Cathryn's Tuscan Grill *Italian*

22	20	21	$41

Cold Spring | 91 Main St. (Fair St.) | 845-265-5582 | www.tuscangrill.com

"Delicious" "aromas drift out to the street" from this "lovely" Tuscan set back off Cold Spring's main drag; inside, a "helpful staff" delivers "always good", "down-to-earth twists on old favorites" like the signature pappardelle with rabbit, grapes and grappa; add "nice wines at reasonable prices", "arty" digs done in earthy colors and an "attractive garden", and you've got a "perfect little charmer."

Catskill Rose ☑ *American*   ─ │ ─ │ ─ │ M

Mt. Tremper | 5355 Rte. 212 (Wittenberg Rd.) | 845-688-7100 | www.catskillrose.com

Still "waiting to be discovered", this off-the-beaten-path Mt. Tremper New American run by toque team Peter DiSclafani and Rose-Marie Dorn offers those who find it a "limited menu" of "well-prepared" seasonal dishes, including their signature house-smoked duckling, all "tastefully presented" in "unpretentious" circa-1940s digs decorated (of course) in rose tones; N.B. open Thursday–Sunday only.

Cava Wine Bar & Restaurant *Italian*   22 │ 20 │ 21 │ $45

New Canaan | 2 Forest St. (East Ave.), CT | 203-966-6946 | www.cavawinebar.com

Surveyors enjoy spelunking for "excellent grilled fish" and "homemade pastas" at this "cozy, cavelike" Northern Italian in "Downtown New Canaan", where the "wine selection is superb" (20 by the glass) and the "staff provides exceptional, friendly service"; however, some say this "lovely little basement gem" has "too many hard surfaces" so the "noise level can be deafening."

Cena 2000 *Italian*   24 │ 25 │ 20 │ $47

Newburgh | 50 Front St. (bet. 2nd & 3rd Sts.) | 845-561-7676

"A chip off" "the famous Il Cenàcolo", this "less expensive" Northern Italian on Newburgh's "bustling riverfront" is "also a winner" declare devotees, with "pleasant decor" upstaged by "breathtaking views of the Hudson" and a "knowledgeable staff" dispensing "excellent", "interesting" fare; the patio's a "must on summer evenings" as "long lines" attest, when the raw bar alone "is worth the wait."

Centro Ristorante &   19 │ 17 │ 18 │ $32
Bar *Italian/Mediterranean*

Darien | 319 Post Rd./Rte. 1 (Birch Rd.), CT | 203-655-4772
Greenwich | The Mill | 328 Pemberwick Rd. (Glenville Rd.), CT | 203-531-5514
www.centroristorante.com

"You can be a kid again and draw on the tablecloth" and "maybe it will wind up on the wall" at this "always busy" Med–Northern Italian duo; "families" and "the ladies who lunch" favor the "consistently good" "fresh" food, but others opine it's only "the same old menu" of "standard" fare that draws a clientele of *Stepford Wives* and "noisy" kids; P.S. outdoor dining is the way to go at the Greenwich branch, which "overlooks a waterfall" "down by the old mill stream."

NEW **Charlotte's** *European*   ─ │ ─ │ ─ │ M

Millbrook | 4258 Rte. 44 (bet. Deep Hollow & Kennels Rds.) | 845-677-5888 | www.charlottesny.com

Ensconced in the space once occupied by longtime Millbrook standby Allyn's, this hunt country newcomer offers a "limited" European menu that changes daily, but unchanged is decor made cozy by fireplaces in each room, and the garden in its "beautiful setting" overlooking a horse farm; it's still "too soon to comment" on much else as culinary couple Mikael and Alicia Möller deal with "start-up jitters."

Chart House *Seafood/Steak* | 16 | 23 | 16 | $45 |
Dobbs Ferry | 1 High St. (Station Pl.) | 914-693-4130 | www.chart-house.com

"Drop-dead views of the Hudson" take center stage at this riverside Dobbs Ferry surf 'n' turf chain outpost that's a "favorite" for "family celebrations" and "romantic dinners" in spite of fare that's only "average" and sometimes "amateurish" service; still, lots of windows, a fireplace and "seasonal outdoor seating" mean "if nothing else", "have a drink on the patio and enjoy the fantastic setting."

Chateau Hathorn Ⓜ *Continental* | ∇ 22 | 28 | 27 | $52 |
Warwick | 33 Hathorn Rd. (County Rte. 1A & Rte. 94) | 845-986-6099 | www.chateauhathorn.com

It's all "classy old-world elegance" at Helene and Dolph Zueger's "castlelike" "estate" in Orange County, where "beautiful dining rooms" set a "festive", "special-occasion" mood whether in the "grand" paneled ballroom with soaring ceilings or the more casual bar; "good" Continental cuisine comes via a "friendly" staff that rates high marks, oenophiles "dig" the "outstanding wine cellar" and all said, it's a "tried-and-true favorite."

Chat 19 *American* | 17 | 17 | 16 | $35 |
Larchmont | 19 Chatsworth Ave. (Boston Post Rd.) | 914-833-8871 | www.chat19.net

There's "fun people-watching" at this "busy", "casual" Traditional American in Larchmont with a "meat-market-esque" bar and "outdoor seating" where you can "meet your neighbors"; "stick to basics" like the burgers and "funky cocktails" and "enjoy the scene", but take heed: the "noise" level will have you asking how much you "value your eardrums."

☑ Cheesecake Factory, The *American* | 18 | 17 | 16 | $29 |
White Plains | The Source | 1 Maple Ave. (Bloomingdale Rd.) | 914-683-5253 | www.thecheesecakefactory.com

The "winning formula" of "to-drool-over cheesecakes" and "endless menu choices" served in "laughably copious" portions attracts "lots of families" to this Traditional American chain link in White Plains in spite of "interminable waits" and "clueless servers"; the "mass-produced" food is "surprisingly well prepared", though the unconverted claim it's "overpriced", "overbusy" and "overrated"; in short: "it does the job", but "with so many other restaurants in town", "why bother?"

Chef Antonio Restaurant *Italian* | 14 | 11 | 16 | $32 |
Mamaroneck | 551 Halstead Ave. (Beach Ave.) | 914-698-8610

This well-priced Mamaroneck Southern Italian satisfies the "neighborhood" as an "unpretentious" "place to bring the kids" for "old-fashioned" "red-sauce" "favorites"; the "tired decor" and "ordinary" fare have some suggesting it's best for "when you don't want to cook."

Chefs On Fire ☒ *American*

22 | 20 | 16 | $23

High Falls | DePuy Canal Hse. | 1315 Rte. 213 (Lucas Tpke.) | 845-687-7778 | www.depuycanalhouse.net

Set in the flagstoned wine cellar of the 18th-century DePuy Canal House, this "eccentric" High Falls New American serves "casual comfort" fare and the "yummiest" thin-crust, wood-fired pizzas, with chef-owner John Novi offering "original" creations like calamari or "taco pies" for those who "like to experiment"; the "cavelike" room is "cool" and the prices "nice", so the only drawback is "spaced-out" service; N.B. a sushi bar was added post-Survey.

NEW Chelsea's on Fifth
Bistro & Grill *American/Irish*

- | - | - | I

Pelham | 156 Fifth Ave. (bet. 2nd & 3rd Sts.) | 914-738-2193 | www.chelseasonfifth.com

This shiny new neighborhood pub in Pelham is done up in dark wood and exposed brick while lots of light from floor-to-ceiling windows give it a modern look; go for a wide selection of Traditional American dishes, a full Irish breakfast all day or hunker in at the bar with a creamy draft beer until 1 AM and catch rugby on the telly.

Cherry Blossom *Japanese*

▽ 22 | 18 | 20 | $26

Fishkill | Main Street Mall | 1004 Main St. (Cary Ave.) | 845-897-9691

Sushi's scarce in Fishkill, but this "been-there-forever" Japanese "can be counted on" to fill the void with "good, fresh" fish and "well-prepared cooked dishes" too; service is usually "enthusiastic" but if "dreary decor" gets you down, just "get takeout."

Chez Jean-Pierre *French*

22 | 20 | 20 | $45

Stamford | 188 Bedford St. (Broad St.), CT | 203-357-9526 | www.chezjeanpierre.com

The "charming owner makes sure all is *très bien*" at this "civilized" "slice of Paris transported" to "Stamford on the Seine"; the "cozy" interior is "inviting" or "sit outside on the sidewalk" when the weather's fine and enjoy "great" bistro fare like coq au vin and "a good bottle of wine"; oenophiles applaud the 50 percent discount on all bottles every Sunday evening – it takes the bite out of the otherwise "pricey" tab.

Chiboust *French/Mediterranean*

23 | 19 | 20 | $46

Tarrytown | 14 Main St. (B'way) | 914-703-6550 | www.chiboust.com

"A warm smile" greets diners at this "pricey" French-Med "bistro" and pastry shop in "quaint Downtown Tarrytown" where "creative" main dishes are done one better by "divine" "breads and desserts"; add in a "small but well-rounded wine list", "knowledgable" servers and a "modern" look with high ceilings and exposed-brick walls, and you've got a "chic" "little" "hideaway" that pleases "in all ways."

China Rose *Chinese*

21 | 17 | 19 | $26

Kingston | 600 Ulster Ave. (Rte. 32) | 845-338-7443
Rhinecliff | 1 Shatzell Ave. (2 mi. west of Rte. 9) | 845-876-7442

Locals lusting after "gourmet" Chinese are "bloody grateful" for the "terrific", "modern interpretations" of classic dishes offered by this

	FOOD	DECOR	SERVICE	COST

Mid–Hudson Valley duo now under separate ownership; "amazing" "sake margaritas" boost the "fun atmosphere" in the "quirky little" Rhinecliff setting, especially in the "boisterous bar", and if the no-rez policy makes it "hard to get in the door", in summer, you can "eat outside and enjoy the river view"; the "unpretentious-to-the-max" Kingston outpost offers mostly takeout.

⚡ Ching's Kitchen *Pan-Asian*   25 | 17 | 18 | $38
NEW Darien | 971 Post Rd. (Center St.), CT | 203-656-2225
⚡ Ching's Table *Pan-Asian*
New Canaan | 64 Main St. (Locust Ave.), CT | 203-972-8550 |
www.chingsrestaurant.com

Since there's "not a clunker on the menu", "it's hard to pass up old favorites in order to try new dishes" that spring from the chef-owner's "great imagination" at this New Canaan Pan-Asian that's "still the gold standard" for fusion cuisine in the area; it can be "noisy and crowded" and expect to hear a big "ka-ching" when it comes to the check, but the main reason it's "not a place to linger" is "a staff that rushes you out" – leaving snarky surveyors to suggest: "park out front and leave the car running"; N.B. the new Darien outpost opened post-Survey.

Chola *Indian*   22 | 12 | 19 | $31
Greenwich | 107-109 Greenwich Ave. (Lewis St.), CT |
203-869-0700

This "small", "under-recognized Indian" located on the "back side of Greenwich Avenue" may be "hard to find", but "it's also not your run-of-the-mill pakora palace"; while the food is "excellent", the staff "attentive" and the prices are "decent", the Decor score may explain why "takeout seems to generate the most business"; N.B. there's also a Manhattan sibling with the same name.

Chuck's Steak House *Steak*   17 | 14 | 18 | $33
Danbury | 20 Segar St. (bet. Lake & Park Aves.), CT |
203-792-5555
Darien | 1340 Boston Post Rd. (I-95, exit 11), CT | 203-655-2254
www.chuckssteakhouse.com

They've "been serving steaks the same way for over 35 years" and advocates allow this chain duo in Danbury and Darien "must be doing something right", like offering "consistent quality", an "extensive salad bar" and "reasonable prices" (especially the "unbeatable early-bird special"); but opponents assert "just say no" because they're "dark, old and in need of dusting."

Ciao! *Italian*   18 | 14 | 17 | $31
Eastchester | 5-7 John Albanese Pl. (Main St.) | 914-779-4646 |
www.ciaoeastchester.com

"An open kitchen" turning out "fresh pasta" and "thin-crust pizzas" is the main "attraction" at this "reasonably priced" "neighborhood" Northern Italian "joint" in Eastchester; given "uninterested" service and the fact its "overrun by screaming kids on weekends" it's really best "for families."

	FOOD	DECOR	SERVICE	COST

Ciao! Cafe & Wine Bar *Italian*

21 | 16 | 21 | $30

Danbury | 2B Ives St. (White St.), CT | 203-791-0404

"Good values" on vino (and with 25 wines available by the glass, the selection's good too) and "high-quality cuisine at a reasonable price" are reasons respondents rely on this "established" Danbury Italian as a "nice dining spot"; those who feel the "funky" decor "could use an upgrade" might consider eating out on the sidewalk patio.

Citrus Grille Ⓜ *American*

24 | 21 | 21 | $53

Airmont | 430 E. Saddle River Rd. (bet. Lake St. & Rte. 59) | 845-352-5533 | www.thecitrusgrille.com

"Wonderful, fresh, imaginative" New American fare emerges from chef-owner Steven Christianson's kitchen at this "really out-of-the-way" Rockland County spot; "pleasant service", plus a "lovely atmosphere" in a space tricked out in tropical hues hit a "home run", especially with those on "a date", so perhaps it's the "secluded" location that keeps it an "underappreciated gem."

ⓩ City Limits Diner *Diner*

19 | 15 | 17 | $26

White Plains | Westchester Mall | 125 Westchester Ave. (Bloomingdale Rd.) | 914-761-1111

White Plains | 200 Central Ave. (bet. Harding Ave. & Tarrytown Rd.) | 914-686-9000

Stamford | 135 Harvard Ave. (I-95, exit 6), CT | 203-348-7000

www.citylimitsdiner.com

"Always crowded", these "kitschily appointed", "1950s-style" "upscale diners" have "something for everyone", including "fabulous breakfasts", "innovative salads" and "terribly tempting" pastries and home-baked breads; they're "frantic" and "loud" and "you'll pay a king's ransom for an egg cream", but over the years, these "reliable" "go-to" spots for "family dining" have become area "institutions."

Cobble Stone ❶ *American*

16 | 14 | 16 | $27

Purchase | 620 Anderson Hill Rd. (bet. Lincoln Ave. & Purchase St.) | 914-253-9678 | www.cobblestone-thecreek.com

"Chow down" on "simple", "inexpensive" Traditional American fare (like burgers) at this former speakeasy in Purchase "full of corporate types and college kids" lounging in hunter-green booths; antagonists allege the "rather ordinary" menu and digs that "could use updating" make it a "lunch spot", nothing more.

NEW Coco Rumba's *Cuban/Pan-Latin*

17 | 20 | 15 | $39

Mt. Kisco | 443 Lexington Ave. (Radio Circle Dr.) | 914-241-2433 | www.cocorumbas.net

A "much needed" "alternative" to the usual dining choices in Mt. Kisco, this Cuban–Pan-Latin newcomer is "always jammed" in spite of "amateurish" service that's "still working out the kinks"; "mother country" natives say this is only a "decent" "attempt at the actual cuisine", but with "hot bartenders", "sexy waitresses", "cool Mojitos" and "throngs of women" at the "lively" bar, it looks like they're onto a successful "formula."

☑ Columbus Park Trattoria *Ⓢ Italian* — 24 | 19 | 21 | $43

Stamford | 205 Main St. (Washington Blvd.), CT | 203-967-9191 |
www.columbusparktrattoria.com

The "delicious" Italian food at this "family-run" Downtown "Stamford
stalwart" is "just like *nonna* made", from "osso buco to die for" to
"mouthwateringly good" pasta, all served by "waiters who know
their business"; it's a "local favorite" so the "cramped" quarters are
often filled with business lunchers who are "on expense account."

Comfort *Ⓢ Ⓜ American* — ▽ 20 | 10 | 12 | $18

Hastings-on-Hudson | 598 Warburton Ave. (Villard Ave.) | 914-478-4677

An "inventive" menu of "well-prepared" "organic comfort food"
makes it worth "sitting elbow-to-elbow" at this "phone boothsized"
Hastings New American newcomer where the seating is "extremely
limited" (there's no restroom or alcohol served either); considering
"the reputation it is garnering", it "needs more space", but until
then, there's always "takeout"; N.B. a second, larger location is reportedly in the works.

Conte's Fishmarket *Ⓢ Ⓜ ⊘ Seafood* — 22 | 7 | 16 | $44

Mt. Kisco | 448 Main St. (St. Mark's Pl.) | 914-666-6929

Fish "doesn't come any fresher" than at this "popular" Mt. Kisco
seafooder that's a market by day and a "BYO" restaurant come
evening serving "wonderful", "well-prepared" cuisine; despite
"spotty" service, "uncomfortable" seating and "expensive" tabs, it's
"crowded on most nights"; N.B. no credit cards.

Cookhouse, The *BBQ* — 19 | 14 | 17 | $28

Darien | 154 Boston Post Rd. (Norwalk Rd.), CT | 203-655-6663
New Milford | 31 Danbury Rd./Rte. 7 (Sunny Valley Rd.), CT |
860-355-4111
www.thecookhouse.com

"You would think the cooks all grew up down South" at this duo of
"can't-beat-it-for-'cue" Americans that serve "humongous portions"
of "excellent smoked ribs" and "the best pulled pork"; it's "noisy"
and the "service leaves a little to be desired", but most still call it
"comfort-food central."

Copper Bottom *Ⓜ American* — ▽ 19 | 17 | 19 | $37

Florida | 162 N. Main St. (Randall St.) | 845-651-5700 |
www.thecopperbottom.com

Lanterns, pots and pans, and a copper-topped bar gleam in this
Orange County American-Continental offering such "good food" as
sesame wasabi–encrusted shrimp and tuna; an "enjoyable experience" may be had in three dining rooms with wainscoted walls, high
ceilings and large latticed windows, and if that doesn't suit, there's
a bar offering burgers and such.

NEW Copper Restaurant *American* — - | - | - | M

Fishkill | 1111 Main St. (North St.) | 845-896-1000

With its brick walls and banquettes, this casual Fishkill tavern looks
the same as in its previous incarnation, but new owners and a new

chef have gussied up the New American menu, adding more upscale fare such as nut-crusted salmon, lobster ravioli and vanilla-peppercorn glazed pork chops at dinner, with chicken panini and flatbread pizza pleasing the lunch crowd.

Coppola's ⓜ *Italian* ▽ 18 | 14 | 20 | $34

Poughkeepsie | 825 Main St. (Raymond Ave.) | 845-452-3040

Pros praise "cheap" "comfort" chow at this "big, loud" Poughkeepsie red-sauce Italian institution, saying the food is "run-of-the-mill in a good way" even if digs aren't "overly fancy"; cons counter it "needs an injection of nouveau" and don't soft pedal about "dated decor", but most agree the owners "make everyone feel like they belong."

Corner Bakery *Bakery* ▽ 25 | 17 | 24 | $23

Pawling | 10 Charles Colman Blvd. (Main St.) | 845-855-3707 | www.mckinneyanddoyle.com

An offshoot of McKinney & Doyle next door, this "wonderful" wee bakery in Pawling delivers the "best cakes and pies in the area", salads, sandwiches with "unusual twists" and English muffins so good devotees declare they'd "request them for a last meal"; digs are "all country" style, but space is limited – as are certain goodies, so get there early because they tend to "run out on weekends."

Cornetta's Seafood *Seafood* ▽ 13 | 8 | 14 | $38

Piermont | 641 Piermont Ave. (bet. Bay & Kinney Sts.) | 845-359-0410 | www.cornettas.com

In summer, it's "nice" to eat in the tent overlooking the marina at this "basic" Piermont seafooder where lobsters get "good" ratings but other fare is judged just "so-so"; nautical detailing doesn't help digs that "need a face-lift", so it's best to focus on "spectacular views of the Hudson river."

ⓩ Coromandel *Indian* 26 | 17 | 21 | $33

New Rochelle | 30 Division St. (bet. Huguenot & Main Sts.) | 914-235-8390
Darien | Goodwives Shopping Ctr. | 25-11 Old Kings Hwy. N. (Sedgewick Ave.), CT | 203-662-1213
www.coromandelcuisine.com

"Bring on the heat!" boast boosters of these "top-rated" subcontinentals offering "wonderful regional selections" that appeal to "both Indian émigrés and the hair-band set"; the "outstanding cuisine and impeccable service are marred only by decor that seems not to have changed since the Moghuls ruled Delhi"; N.B. proponents particularly praise the all-you-can-eat lunch buffets.

Cosi *Sandwiches* 16 | 12 | 12 | $15

Larchmont | Ferndale Shopping Ctr. | 1298 Boston Post Rd. (Weaver St.) | 914-834-9797
Mt. Kisco | 15 S. Moger Ave. (Main St.) | 914-242-5408
New Rochelle | North Ridge Shopping Ctr. | 77 Quaker Ridge Rd. (North Ave.) | 914-637-8300
Rye | 50 Purchase St. (Elm Pl.) | 914-921-3322
Darien | 980 Post Rd. (Center St.), CT | 203-655-0335

(continued)

(continued)

Così

Greenwich | 129 W. Putnam Ave. (Dayton Ave.), CT | 203-861-2373
www.getcosi.com
Part "coffeehouse", part "sandwich and salad joints", these "step-above-a-chain" "quick-bite" "local hangouts" lure "students on a budget" and "moms and their kids" for the "addictive", "fresh-out-of-the-oven bread" and "make-your-own" s'mores dessert; detractors declare the decor "drab" and admonish an "immature staff" that "needs to get their act together servicewise."

Cosimo's Brick Oven *Italian*   20 | 19 | 19 | $29

Kingston | 14 Thomas St. (B'way) | 845-340-0550 |
www.cosimosrestaurantgroup.com
Middletown | 620 Rte. 211 E. (Rte. 17) | 845-692-3242 |
www.cosimosbrickoven.com

Cosimo's on Union *Italian*

Newburgh | 1217 Union Ave./Rte. 300 (bet. 2nd & 3rd Sts.) |
845-567-1556 | www.cosimosunion.com
Piezanos "love" the "special" brick-oven pizzas at this "lively" mid-Hudson trio, but don't overlook the "consistently-above-par" pastas or other "straightforward" Italian eats either; "warm, comfortable" surroundings, a staff that "treats you well" and "reasonable" tabs add up to "good times", especially at the tonier Newburgh branch, where you can even dine in the wine cellar.

Cosimo's Trattoria *Italian*   19 | 20 | 18 | $29

Poughkeepsie | 120 Delafield St. (bet. Rte. 9 & Spruce St.) |
845-485-7172 | www.cosimosrestaurantgroup.com
A large open space with high-ceilings, colorful tiles, tall windows and stone floors make the mood "Tuscan-type" at Cosimo's Brick Oven's "busy" Poughkeepsie sibling, where some go for "surprisingly good", "reliable" Italian entrees and others pick the thin-crust pizza; as long as you don't mind somewhat "slow" service, it's "good for gatherings."

Country Inn Ⓜ⇗ *American*   - | - | - | M

Krumville | 1380 County Rd. 2 (bet. Acorn Hill & Grassy Ridge Rds.) |
845-657-8956 | www.krumville.com
"One of the Hudson Valley's best-kept secrets", this "quirky" Ulster County "roadhouse" is "worth finding" declare locals, weekenders and "foodies" who mingle for "scrumptious" New American food "prepared by someone who cares a lot"; but nobody cares about "paper napkins, thin silverware", a pool table or a rustic space decorated with stuffed birds because the staff is "charming" and the "fabulous selection" of 500-plus beers alone make it "worth the trip."

Coyote Flaco *Mexican*   20 | 10 | 16 | $24

New Rochelle | 273 North Ave. (Huguenot St.) | 914-636-7222 Ⓜ
Port Chester | 115 Midland Ave. (bet. Armett St. & Weber Dr.) |
914-937-6969
Sure, this "no pretenses" Port Chester Mexican with an outpost in New Rochelle "could use some sprucing up" ("decor? we don't need

no stinkin' decor!"), but tortilla-groupies happily howl about the "truly authentic", "tasty" fare made from "fresh ingredients"; service "can take a while", so sip a cocktail from the "extensive" "margarita menu" on the "outdoor patio", "ignore the industrial neighborhood" and you may be on your way to becoming a "regular."

⊿ Crabtree's Kittle House *American* 24 | 23 | 23 | $60
Chappaqua | Crabtree's Kittle House Inn | 11 Kittle Rd. (Rte. 117) | 914-666-8044 | www.kittlehouse.com
For "special occasions" or a "secret rendezvous", you can't go wrong at this "sophisticated" Chappaqua country inn where "delectable", if not "overly exciting", New American cuisine is served by a "gracious" staff and "knowledgeable sommeliers" guide you through a "world-class" wine list the size of "a phone book"; "bucolic views" of "beautiful trees" and an English garden enhance the experience, and while a few detractors say service is "sometimes off" and find the 19th-century-style decor "dowdy", most agree it's a "longtime favorite" that's worth the "splurge."

Creek, The *American* ▽ 15 | 15 | 14 | $38
Purchase | 578 Anderson Hill Rd. (bet. Lincoln Ave. & Purchase St.) | 914-761-0050 | www.cobblestone-thecreek.com
This "hidden away" New American eatery in Purchase – convenient to the Performing Arts Center – caters to the pre-theater crowd with a three-course prix fixe dinner as well as with burgers and more "traditional" à la carte fare; space sticklers deride "tight quarters" and call the "limited" selection "pricey for the offering."

Crew *American* ▽ 20 | 18 | 18 | $28
Poughkeepsie | 2290 South Rd./Rte. 9 (Neptune Rd.) | 845-462-5900 | www.crewrestaurant.com
"Awesome soups" lead the popularity parade at this Poughkeepsie New American, though other "tasty", "hearty" grub at "fair prices" gets good marks too; given its mini-mall location, it's "a nice surprise" with a "modern" colorful interior, open kitchen and a "happening" "bar scene" to boot; all said, it's "easy to become a regular."

NEW Croton Creek - | - | - | E
Steakhouse & Winebar ⊠ *Steak*
Croton Falls | 4 W. Cross St. (Rte. 22) | 914-276-0437 | www.crotoncreek.com
Chic is scarce in the Northern Westchester dining scene, so this Croton Falls steakhouse with French accents and an inviting wine bar is a welcome addition; the quartet of owners (including *American Idol* finalist Kimberley Locke) has refurbished the 1875 tavern space, imparting an upscale rustic vibe.

Cutillo's *European* - | - | - | M
Carmel | 1196 Farmers Mills Rd. (bet. Meadow Ln. & N. Horsepound Rd.) | 845-225-8903 | www.cutillosrestaurant.com
Ensconced in a stucco house in Carmel, this family-run European-American offers a menu that ranges all over, from steaks and pastas to Wiener schnitzel and duck breast with brandied apricot sauce; in

winter, patrons prefer one of the pastel dining rooms made cozy with carpets, antiques and fireplaces; come summer, they choose the large enclosed porch with a bar and picture windows overlooking the lawn.

NEW DABA ⊠ American/Scandinavian ▽ 19 | 17 | 21 | $32

Hudson | 225 Warren St. (bet. 2nd & 3rd Sts.) | 518-249-4631 | www.dabahudson.com

There's "something for everyone" at this new Hudson American-Scandinavian "hot spot", where a slightly "confusing" menu ranges from hummus to "fancier fare" like signature slow-baked salmon; the "relaxing", "fun" vibe comes via walls painted warm tones, a double bar and cushy leather couches plus "attentive service"; it's "still finding its legs", but chef Ola Svedman and owner Daniel Nilsson "are trying really hard."

Daily Planet ❶ Diner 18 | 16 | 19 | $20

LaGrangeville | 1202 Rte. 55 (Taconic Pkwy., exit 55W) | 845-452-0110 | www.dailyplanetdiner.com

"You don't have to be Superman to love" this "classic" Dutchess County diner with its "predictable but always dependable" "non-stop menu" and "blue-plate specials"; a "courteous staff" "handles crowds of children well", and if a few grown-ups gripe about "tired" "throwback" TV-themed decor, at least they like the "cheap" tabs.

Dakshin Indian 23 | 18 | 19 | $29

Stamford | 68 Broad St. (Summer St.), CT | 203-964-1010 | www.dakshinrestaurant.com

"Go for the lamb" and "excellent vegetarian dishes" at this Downtown Stamford Indian where "spicy means spicy" and the $10.95 all-you-can-eat weekday "lunch buffet is a fantastic deal"; "service can be uneven", but the setting, which includes palm trees, Asian antiques and statuary, is "pleasant."

David Chen Chinese 19 | 15 | 18 | $27

Armonk | 85 Old Mt. Kisco Rd. (Rte. 128) | 914-273-6767

"It isn't Chinatown" but this Armonk "gourmet" Sino specialist attracts "big groups" and "families" (a "TV screen downstairs" "keeps the children busy") with its "extensive menu" of "above-average" selections and "friendly service"; though it's "always crowded", skeptics suspect David is "living off his previously established reputation"

NEW DaVinci's Cafe Italian - | - | - | M

New Rochelle | 22 Division St. (bet. Main St. & Westchester Pl.) | 914-235-2464 | www.davincis-cafe.com

Downtown New Rochelle condo-dwellers pining for an honest plate of pasta or a crisp pizza make their way to this Italian newcomer; weekend valet parking is a plus, as is patio dining in summer.

Deer Park Tavern American 19 | 18 | 18 | $41

Katonah | 40 Deer Park Rd. (bet. Rtes. 22 & 35) | 914-232-9104 | www.deerparktavern.net

"A little off the beaten track", this "simple", "consistent" Katonah New American lures locals "for an easy dinner with friends" or a

FOOD | DECOR | SERVICE | COST

"lovely" lunch on the "front porch"; although the "fun" bar "gets crowded and noisy" and "service can be slow" "when they're busy", the "warm atmosphere" – with hardwood floors and dark paneling – makes it a "pleasure in the country."

NEW De La Vergne M *American* ▽ 21 | 17 | 19 | $40
Amenia | 4905 Rte. 44 (Smithfield Valley Rd.) | 845-373-9972
Amenia's "new guy in town", this "friendly" American offers a "wide-ranging menu" of "delicious" fare aimed to please both locals and weekenders, who keep it simple with burgers and mac 'n' cheese, or "splurge" on upscale fare like prosciutto-wrapped veal tournedos; the "decor is cozy" both in the mustard-and-blue barroom and in the red dining room with its fireplace and weathered wood booths.

Z DePuy Canal House M *American* 25 | 25 | 22 | $62
High Falls | 1315 Rte. 213 (Lucas Tpke.) | 845-687-7700 | www.depuycanalhouse.net
"Still the grand old lady of Hudson Valley dining", this High Falls New American set in a "charming" stone Colonial house "retains the cuisine of high camp it grew famous for", with chef-owner John Novi's "original, creative" (and sometimes "weird") dishes declared "delectable" as ever; yes, it's "extravagant", but "unobtrusive service" and "ridiculously romantic" rooms furnished in period style make it perfect "to celebrate a red-letter occasion."

Diasporas M *Greek/Mediterranean* ▽ 20 | 15 | 21 | $37
Rhinebeck | 1094 Rte. 308 (Old Rock City Rd.) | 845-758-9601 | www.diasporacuisine.com
"Imaginative", "untraditional" Greek and Mediterranean fare featuring "extremely well-prepared fish dishes" are "worth the drive" to this "out-of-the-way" Rhinebeck spot devotees declare; yellow walls, faux-classical pillars and a "quiet atmosphere" in the 1920s building strike some as a bit "boring", though others say it's "very pleasant", and everybody likes the "caring" staff.

DiNardo's M *Italian* 17 | 13 | 17 | $40
Pound Ridge | Scott's Corners | 76 Westchester Ave. (Trinity Pass Rd.) | 914-764-4024
A "dependable" menu of "traditional favorites" complemented by a 300-bottle wine list is offered at this Pound Ridge Italian, with a red-and-white pizza parlor "for families" up front and more "formal" dining in back (look out for the "occasional celeb sighting"); it may be "overpriced" "for what it is", but in the end "it's the only show in town."

Division Street Grill *American/Eclectic* 19 | 17 | 18 | $41
Peekskill | 26 N. Division St. (bet. Main & Park Sts.) | 914-739-6380 | www.divisionstreetgrill.com
"City-worthy fare" is presented "in a comfortable, classy setting" at this New American–Eclectic "in the heart of Peekskill's artist district" where abstract paintings on the walls and "jazz on weekends" add to the "sophisticated" vibe; "service can be slow" and "waits are an issue" so "patience is a virtue" when dining here.

FOOD | DECOR | SERVICE | COST

Docas Ⓜ *Portuguese*

- | - | - | M

Ossining | 125 Main St. (bet. Spring & State Sts.) | 914-944-9205
"Even if you don't know" the cuisine, you'll find something "wonderful" at this "friendly" "family-owned" Portuguese in Ossining where owner Carla Pinto keeps the sangria flowing and "big portions" of "authentic" roast pork, rabbit stew and grilled seafood come courtesy of chef-husband Abel; high blue ceilings give it a seafaring feel, while much of the hand-painted pottery comes from the antiques and ceramic shop next door.

Doc's 🚫 *Italian*

22 | 11 | 20 | $34

New Preston | 62 Flirtation Ave. (Rte. 45), CT | 860-868-9415 | www.docstrattoria.com
"Bring a sweater and your own wine" to this "tiny", "charming" and "reasonably priced" New Preston Northern Italian whose "luscious pasta dishes" are "just what the doctor ordered" "after a bike ride or kayak around Lake Waramaug"; others "just don't get the point" of dining in a "cramped room" with "threadbare decor" and say it's "better for takeout."

Don bo *Japanese/Thai*

▽ 17 | 20 | 20 | $31

New Windsor | 335 Windsor Hwy./Rte. 32 (Old Forge Hill Rd.) | 845-562-0697 | www.donbothai.com
At this "very friendly" New Windsor spot, chef-owner Ko Brower mixes up a menu of Southeast Asian dishes, with Japanese sushi and tempura, Thai satay and curries, and a few Korean touches reflecting his own heritage – all spiced to suit individual patron's palates; it's a "good idea" declare locals, chowing down amid modern SoHo-style surroundings gussied up in gray and burgundy.

Doubleday's *American*

13 | 12 | 17 | $21

Dobbs Ferry | 83 Main St. (bet. Chestnut & Elm Sts.) | 914-693-9793
"See the whole town" eating burgers, fries and the like at this "reasonably priced" Dobbs Ferry Traditional American "tavern" that's "everything you'd want in a sports bar"; it's rather "typical", but "for drink" or a "quick dinner" while watching the Yankees on one of the "many screens", it works just fine.

Down by the Bay *Eclectic*

16 | 15 | 17 | $45

Mamaroneck | James Fenimore Cooper Hse. | 410 W. Boston Post Rd. (Fenimore Rd.) | 914-381-6939
"Seafood is the way to go" at this "cozy" Eclectic facing the harbor in Mamaroneck, where you "can feel the history" of the "quaint" building (aka the James Fenimore Cooper House); a "decent local choice" according to some, although adversaries consider the food "bland" and say the "run-down" decor lacks "joi de vivre."

Downtown Cafe ● *Italian*

▽ 21 | 18 | 19 | $28

Kingston | 1 W. Strand St. (B'way) | 845-331-5904 | www.downtowncafekingston.com
A "very large menu" of "solid, flavorful" Italian fare with "lots of fish choices" ("where else will you find fresh whole sardines?") satisfies

FOOD DECOR SERVICE COST

some at this spot in Kingston's Rondout district, though detractors decree eats are "overrated"; "simple" digs get a boost from live music on weekends while another plus is a patio that people "love."

Dragonfly Caffé *Coffeehouse* ▽ 15 | 19 | 18 | $9

Pleasantville | 7 Wheeler Ave. (Manville Rd.) | 914-747-7477

"You're sure to find a tasty morsel" – in the form of wraps, salads and desserts – at this "well-run" Pleasantville "coffeehouse" that's the "antidote" to generic coffee chains with a "funky" interior decked out with antiques and lanterns from Turkey; "strategically located" near the Jacob Burns Film Center, it's best for "a quick bite" "before or after a film", and though it tends to get "crowded" (especially on Fridays when there's live music), the staff "makes you truly feel at home."

NEW Dragonfly Grille Ⓜ *Eclectic* – | – | – | M

Woodstock | Woodstock Golf Club | 114 Mill Hill Rd./Rte. 212 (W. Hurley Rd./Rte. 375) | 845-679-2470

Set in an 18th-century gristmill on the Woodstock golf course, this "simple" Eclectic newcomer offers a changing menu of traditional fare such as chef-owner Johnathan Sheridan's signature meatloaf; wife Maryellen works the front of the house, and those who note decor "badly needs updating" suggest just "look out the windows" at the "lovely view of the stream", or dine by it on the terrace in summer.

NEW Dragonfly Lounge, The *Eclectic* ▽ 18 | 19 | 15 | $37

Stamford | 488 Summer St. (Spring St.), CT | 203-357-9800

Surveyors are split over this "interesting" Downtown Stamford newcomer, which has a "great" Gothic atmosphere due to its recent transformation from an Irish pub filled with antiquities; some praise the "inventive" small plates of Eclectic cuisine like General Tso's calamari, but protesters proclaim the "gimmicky" fare "pricey."

NEW Duo *European/Japanese* – | – | – | M

Stamford | 25 Bank St. (Main St.), CT | 203-252-2233

The name reflects the cooking approach at this European-Japanese hybrid in Downtown Stamford, where the key ingredients of menu items are prepared and served two different ways – for example, tempura shrimp with prawns Provençal; an offshoot of Plateau, its next-door-neighbor and Pan-Asian parent, this newcomer sports modern decor and an extensive listing of sakes to complement the East vs. West showdown displayed on every plate.

Earth Foods ⊄ *Eclectic/Vegetarian* – | – | – | I

Hudson | 523 Warren St. (bet. S. 5th & S. 6th Sts.) | 518-822-1396

Weary antiquers cruising Hudson's main drag drop into this casual Eclectic breakfast and lunch spot for soups, salads, wraps and heartier fare like shepherd's pie and such, while vegans and vegetarians are well-served too; the small space in the 19th-century building has white wainscot topped with red walls displaying the works of local artists for a casual, colorful feel.

	FOOD	DECOR	SERVICE	COST

Z Eastchester Fish Gourmet *Seafood* — 24 | 17 | 19 | $46

Scarsdale | 837 White Plains Rd. (Brook St.) | 914-725-3450 |
www.eastchesterfish.com

"Fish lovers" declare this "bustling" Scarsdale seafooder with "up-scale" nautical decor "lives up to its reputation" with "deliciously prepared" dishes "straight from the ocean", a "terrific" wine list and "fabulous desserts"; a handful of scallywags whine about "tables being too close together" and fare that's "pricey" "considering the simple preparations", but if you're watching your wallet, the $24.95 prix fixe menu is a "great value" (call for details); P.S. reservations for five or more only, so brace yourself for "waits."

East Harbor *Chinese/Japanese* — ▽ 16 | 12 | 16 | $22

Yonkers | 1560 Central Park Ave. (Tuckahoe Rd.) | 914-961-0100 |
www.eastharborrestaurant.com

"Sushi is the best choice" at this neighborhood Japanese-Chinese in Yonkers, especially considering the half-price specials that are "hard to beat" (before 3 PM and on Monday and Wednesday nights); other menu items are just "passable", as is the decor of light peach-colored walls livened up with fish and lobster tanks.

Ebb Tide Seafood & — 20 | 8 | 9 | $27
Lobster Shack M *Seafood*

Port Chester | 1 Willett Ave. (Abendroth Ave.) | 914-939-4810

They "know their fish and how to cook it" at this "no-frills" Port Chester seafood "shack" where "fresh" "lobster rolls", "steamed clams" and chowder are best devoured "sitting on the deck" in summer "with a view of the river (and Costco)"; waits are "tough", but prices "inexpensive", and though it's "not *quite* New England", "it could pass."

Eclisse *Italian* — 19 | 16 | 17 | $33

Stamford | Harbor Sq. | 700 Canal St. (bet. Henry & Market Sts.), CT | 203-325-3773

"Bring your appetite" and "a gang of friends" to this sprawling, "family-style" Stamford Northern Italian where "the garlic wafts its welcome" from "coma-inducing" portions of "penne alla vodka" at "cannot-be-beat prices"; but the less-enthused assert "everything tastes the same" and it's served amid "noisy crowds" and "tired" decor.

Edo Japanese — 21 | 18 | 20 | $33
Steak House *Japanese/Steak*

Pelham | 4787 Boston Post Rd. (bet. Fowler & Pelhamdale Aves.) |
914-738-1413
Port Chester | Pathmark Shopping Ctr. | 140 Midland Ave. (Weber Dr.) |
914-937-3333
www.edohibachi.com

The "chef's floorshow" takes center stage at this "kitschy, but so much fun" Japanese hibachi in Pelham with a newer outpost in Port Chester; both are "lively" (read: "extremely busy") and good "for groups" and "kids' birthdays"; "exotic drinks" and "fresh" fare served in "huge portions" win raves from fans who assure "you won't leave hungry."

	FOOD	DECOR	SERVICE	COST

Egane *Korean* — 20 | 15 | 17 | $30

Stamford | 135 Bedford St. (Broad St.), CT | 203-975-0209

"Kim Jong-il and George Bush would be friends" if they dined together at this "good", "reasonably priced" Downtown Stamford Korean; "the staff expertly guides first-timers through an authentic experience" of "cook-your-own barbecue" done at tables outfitted with special grills; there's also sushi for non-interactive eaters.

Egg's Nest, The ⊭ *American* — 18 | 20 | 19 | $24

High Falls | 1300 Rte. 213 (Bruceville Rd.) | 845-687-7255 | www.theeggsnest.com

"It's like being in a hippie's dream" at this "whimsical" High Falls eatery, where "over-the-top", "wild", "highly entertaining" decor covering "every square inch" takes "center stage"; "satisfying", "homestyle" Traditional American food with a few flourishes comes dished up by a "friendly" staff, so sit back, "relax and enjoy the acid flashback."

El Coqui *Puerto Rican* — ▽ 15 | 15 | 16 | $25

Kingston | 21 Broadway (bet. Abeel & W. Strand Sts.) | 845-340-1106

Kingston's Rondout district has a patch of "pure Puerto Rico" in this "festive" spot where live music on weekends has diners "dancing" in the aisles "in no time"; chef-owner Robert Bruno's paella, arroz con pollo and such are "only fair" but authentic, and even if "gringos can't tell the difference", they do notice Caribbean-style "slow service."

El Danzante *Mexican* — ▽ 19 | 12 | 14 | $16

Kingston | 720 Broadway (Liberty St.) | 845-331-7070

"There's nothing fancy" at this "very informal" Kingston cantina, just "better than ordinary", "straightforward Mexican food", which is "toned down" some "for American tastebuds", courtesy of Oaxacan chef-owner Miguel Hernandez; even those who "are not cheering *olé*" over the eats admit it's all "affordable", and the "jukebox is great."

Elms Restaurant & Tavern Ⓜ *American* — 21 | 20 | 21 | $47

Ridgefield | 500 Main St./Rte. 35 (Gilbert St.), CT | 203-438-9206 | www.elmsinn.com

Chef-owner Brendan Walsh's "always good" Traditional American is housed in an "atmospheric" 1799 Ridgefield Colonial filled with "Revolutionary War decor"; you can dine in the elegant main rooms "with roaring fires", in the more "casual" tavern or out on the covered porch "where you can watch the comings and goings on Main Street."

Z Elm Street Oyster House *Seafood* — 24 | 16 | 20 | $46

Greenwich | 11 W. Elm St. (Greenwich Ave.), CT | 203-629-5795 | www.elmstoysterhouse.com

This "congenial" chef-owned seafooder is where Greenwichers go for "impeccably fresh oysters" (six different types offered daily) and "perfectly prepared fish"; with seating for only 38, you can feel as "crammed in" as a bed of bivalves, plus the audio-impaired add the "roar of the ocean would be preferable to the noise level", but that doesn't keep most customers from being happy as clams here; N.B. reservations for lunch only.

	FOOD	DECOR	SERVICE	COST

El Tio *Mexican*

	-	-	-	I

Port Chester | 143 Westchester Ave. (bet. Broad & S. Pearl Sts.) | 914-939-1494

"Tasty", "authentic", "homestyle" Mexican fare at "reasonable prices" leaves diners "well-fed" at this bare-bones Port Chester eatery; the "friendly staff speaks limited English" so it's a "good place to practice your Spanish" while waiting for tacos *al pastor* and shrimp *mojo de ajo.*

Emerson at Woodstock 🅼 *American*

	18	22	18	$46

Woodstock | 109 Mill Hill Rd. (Rte. 375) | 845-679-7500 | www.emersonresort.com

A "nicely appointed dining room" with French doors and stained-glass light shades welcomes "locals and weekenders" alike at this "bustling" Woodstock bistro, where all "sup on" New American fare that's usually "good" but "inconsistent" (with service to match) or sip something from a "huge wine list"; techies head for the adjoining Internet cafe.

🅉 Emilio Ristorante 🅼 *Italian*

	25	18	24	$54

Harrison | 1 Colonial Pl. (bet. Harrison Ave. & Purdy St.) | 914-835-3100 | www.emilioristorante.com

"Consistently excellent" rave reviewers of this Harrison Italian located in an old Colonial house where an "amazing" "appetizer cart", "great homemade pastas", "seasonal specials that make the mouth water" and a "professional staff" make it a "pleasure to dine"; a minority maintains the "interior needs updating", although admirers insist it's an "elegant" "choice" "worthy of the high prices."

Empire Hunan *Chinese/Japanese*

	16	14	16	$23

Yorktown Heights | 1975 Commerce St. (Hanover St.) | 914-962-5500

"A favorite for office parties and birthdays", this Yorktown Heights restaurant serves "generous portions" of "decent" Chinese-Japanese specialties, including Hunan chicken and moo shu pork as well as "typical" "sushi bar" offerings; despite "lackluster" digs, "sometimes poorly executed service" and "run-of-the-mill" cuisine, it's still considered "good", "for the suburbs."

Encore Bistro Français *French*

	21	17	20	$42

Larchmont | 22 Chatsworth Ave. (Boston Post Rd.) | 914-833-1661

"*Délicieux!*" declare diners about the "classic" "bistro fare" at this "charming", if "noisy", Gallic "gem" situated in a Larchmont storefront with red leather booths and hardwood floors; a "friendly" "French-speaking staff", "great steak frites" and mussels keep this "neighborhood" "treat" "packed for a reason."

Enzo's *Italian*

	18	15	19	$42

Mamaroneck | 451 Mamaroneck Ave. (Halstead Ave.) | 914-698-2911

"Regulars" love feeling "like a special guest" at this "old-world" Mamaroneck Italian "familiar" "favorite" that's been dishing out "reliable" "red-sauce" fare for over 20 years; despite the "wonderful" staff, the disenchanted deem it "overrated", especially the "dreary" decor, and besides, "it ain't cheap."

	FOOD	DECOR	SERVICE	COST

Epstein's Kosher Deli *Deli* | 16 | 7 | 13 | $20 |

Hartsdale | Dalewood Shopping Ctr. | 387 N. Central Ave. (Rte. 119) | 914-428-5320

Yonkers | 2574 Central Park Ave. (Foothill Rd.) | 914-793-3131
www.epsteinsdeli.com

"A taste of the old country" – "as long as your old country is the Bronx" or "Brooklyn" – can be had at this "been-around-forever" Hartsdale-Yonkers deli duo where "Jewish soul food" like "thick" "pastrami" "sandwiches" and a side of "coleslaw" are washed down with "Dr. Brown's Soda"; "grumpy" waitresses are "perfect entertainment", and while the atmosphere is more "cafeteria" than "fine dining", the overall experience "satisfies the longing for the old days."

☑ Equus *American/French* | 26 | 28 | 25 | $78 |

Tarrytown | Castle on the Hudson | 400 Benedict Ave. (bet. Maple St. & Martling Ave.) | 914-631-3646 | www.castleonthehudson.com

It's no surprise surveyors vote this "posh" New American–French restaurant in Tarrytown No. 1 for Decor this year considering the "otherworldly" setting within a "beautiful" 1897 stone castle on a hill with "gorgeous sweeping views" of the Hudson River and three dining rooms (Garden Room, Oak Room, Tapestry Room), each "elegant" in its own way; the cuisine is "divine" as well, so "don a jacket", "bring a fat wallet" and prepare to be "meticulously doted upon" and made to feel "like a baron" in some "fairy tale."

Ernesto Restaurant ☒ *Italian* | ▽ 20 | 12 | 20 | $31 |

White Plains | 130 W. Post Rd. (Maple Ave.) | 914-421-1414

"Off the beaten track" from the city's core, this "cozy" White Plains Italian is the "place to go" for "classic cooking with the touch that mom used to have", including "wonderful pizza" and veal chops; although the white linens barely elevate it a step above "hole-in-the-wall" status, you'll still enjoy a "satisfying", albeit "familiar", meal.

☑ Escoffier, The ☒☒ *French* | 26 | 24 | 25 | $56 |

Hyde Park | Culinary Institute of America | 1946 Campus Dr. (Rte. 9) | 845-471-6608 | www.ciachef.edu

"Escoffier must be proud" of the chefs-to-be "trying hard to live up to the name" at this Hyde Park culinary school's "bastion of French haute cuisine"; "delicious" fare, a "beautiful", "sedate" setting and "classical service" delivered with an "abundance of grace and enthusiasm" all elicit "one word: superb", and though "booking ahead is a pain" and "prices high", "a table near the kitchen" is as good as "dinner theater"; "the Washington CIA should do as well."

NEW Euro Asian *Asian Fusion* | – | – | – | M |

Port Chester | The Waterfront at Port Chester | 30 Westchester Ave. (bet. Townsend St. & Traverse Ave.) | 914-937-3680 | www.euroasianrestaurant.com

Bright colors and loud music animate the bar at this bustling Asian fusion newcomer on Port Chester's waterfront; a selection of sushi, signature rolls, Thai-style crab cakes and Mandarin duck are paired with an extensive and well-priced wine list.

	FOOD	DECOR	SERVICE	COST

Eveready Diner ◐ *Diner* — 17 | 18 | 18 | $18

Hyde Park | 4189 Albany Post Rd./Rte. 9 (bet. Calmer Pl. & South Dr.) | 845-229-8100

"If you're into diners" there's "nothing finer" than this "fancy" "'50s-style" Hyde Park spot dispensing "plentiful" portions of "all the favorites", "from mac 'n' cheese to panini"; other "real thing" touches include "glitzy" digs, kids' meals that come in a "take-home cardboard Cadillac", "waitresses who call you 'honey'" and round-the-clock service on weekends.

⬛NEW Fifty Coins Restaurant *American* — 14 | 15 | 14 | $23

Ridgefield | 426 Main St. (Big Shop Ln.), CT | 203-438-1456 | www.fiftycoinsrestaurant.com

Named after the owner's racehorse (which also explains the equestrian-themed decor), this "new kid on the block" is "trying to carve out a niche" for itself as Ridgefield's "family-friendly" Traditional American; items like burgers and barbecue are "reasonably priced", but critics carp that it "still needs to work out service kinks" and a setting that "can get a little *Romper Roomy*."

59 Bank *American* — 18 | 15 | 18 | $33

New Milford | 59 Bank St. (bet. Main & Railroad Sts.), CT | 860-350-5995
Ridgefield | 37 Ethan Allen Hwy./Rte. 7 (Rte. 102), CT | 203-544-0059
www.59bank.com

"Once you've tasted the food, the decor doesn't matter" at these Traditional Americans in New Milford and Ridgefield, where fans favor "crispy" pizzas and "great salads" from a "wide-ranging menu" that offers "grazing options" as well as "family-friendly" meals; while foes assert the fare is only "average", penny-pinchers praise the prices.

Figaro Bistro *French* — 19 | 20 | 19 | $47

Greenwich | 372 Greenwich Ave. (Grigg St.), CT | 203-622-0018 | www.figarobistro.com

"Crowds of Greenwich locals" come to this "charming" but "noisy" bistro for "always-enjoyable" fare like "great" grilled hanger steak and pommes frites; "the staff is very French", which some say translates as "you are treated like family", while others interpret as "prima donna service"; one thing's certain: you'll pay "Parisian prices."

Finn McCool's *Pub Food* — 16 | 10 | 16 | $20

White Plains | 106 Westchester Ave. (Bloomingdale Rd.) | 914-428-0109

"Sure it's not the best food in town", "but there's a neighborhood vibe" at this White Plains Irish pub with a horseshoe bar and well-worn wood booths; though it's "showing its age", "decent" burgers, snacks, Guinness and a game of pool or darts create a "comfortable" atmosphere despite "the smell of stale beer."

☑ F.I.S.H. *Mediterranean/Seafood* — 23 | 17 | 19 | $46

Port Chester | 102 Fox Island Rd. (Grace Church St.) | 914-939-4227 | www.fishfoxisland.com

"SoHo meets Cape Cod" at this "funky" "out-of-the-way" Port Chester Mediterranean where "inventive cooking" (particularly "fabulous" "fresh fish" and "offbeat appetizers") reels in the Rye and "Greenwich crowds", and early birds who order their dinner before 6:30 PM are rewarded with a "free bottle of wine!"; the "colorful" dining room can be a "frenetic" "scene", but come summer, you can "sit outside" and watch the boats come in and out of the Long Island Sound."

Fish Cellar Ⓜ *Seafood* | 21 | 17 | 20 | $45 |

Mt. Kisco | 213 Main St. (bet. Hyatt & Lenox Sts.) | 914-666-4448 | www.fishcellar.com

Though "miles from the ocean", this dinner-only Mt. Kisco fish house with an aquatic color scheme serves up "reliably" "fresh" seafood (the "warm owners" run "a nearby market") in "straightforward" preparations and "excellent oysters" and shrimp cocktail from a "superb" "raw bar"; though at times "noisy and crowded", there's a patio that's a "delightful" "oasis" in summer; add in "efficient" servers, and it's an "enjoyable venue" that most consider a "definite repeat place."

Flames Steakhouse Ⓜ *Steak* | 20 | 18 | 20 | $58 |

Briarcliff Manor | 533 N. State Rd. (Ryder Ave.) | 914-923-3100 | www.flamessteakhouse.com

It's "not like going to the city", but fans of this Briarcliff Manor steakhouse declare it's "underrated", serving "killer", "dry-aged beauties", and insist you "take advantage of the "exceptional" 500-label wine cellar; the less-enthused complain about "stuffy" service and "overpriced" fare, but even so, it's always "busy."

NEW Flirt Sushi Lounge *Japanese* | ▽ 20 | 20 | 16 | $45 |

Irvington | 4 W. Main St. (S. Astor St.) | 914-437-5186 | www.flirtsushi.com

A self-consciously "sexy" newcomer, this Irvington Japanese features "creative", "flirtatiously" and unsubtly named sushi and maki (like their lobster-and-caviar Climax Roll) and a "cool" bar with seating for six; the dim lighting and selection of sake and cocktails make it a "girls' night out" spot and a "hip" "date place", though "service" is one area in which it's "lacking."

Flying Pig Ⓢ *American* | 21 | 15 | 17 | $39 |

Mt. Kisco | Mt. Kisco Train Station | 2 Depot Plaza (Kirby Pl.) | 914-666-4255

Flying Pig on Lexington Ⓜ *American*

NEW Mt. Kisco | 251 Lexington Ave. (bet. Moore & Smith Aves.) | 914-666-7445
www.pigcafe.com

An "innovative, market-fresh menu" with "an emphasis on local Hudson valley produce" and organic ingredients makes this "unique" and "tasty" Mt. Kisco New American "popular" with "ladies who lunch" as well as "commuters" who favor the grab-and-go offshoot at the Metro-North Station; a few frugal types find the "high" prices "piggish" while some are "disappointed" with the new "larger" digs (which lack the "charm" of the original location) and the staff that could use more "training."

Fortuna Ristorante ☒ *Italian* ▽ 22 | 18 | 22 | $49
Croton-on-Hudson | 1 Baltic Pl. (Rte. 9A) | 914-271-2600 |
www.fortunaristorante.com

"Terrific service" and a "fine" menu of Northern Italian dishes like veal chop Bolognese and eggplant rollatini bring diners "back again and again" to this 120-seat ristorante in Croton; though it's "out of the way", "tucked in among professional offices", inside is a "nice-looking" room accented with maroon velvet drapes; most consider it "a find" "in an area" where not many places "strive to be high-end."

Foundry Cafe *American* ▽ 18 | 14 | 14 | $20
Cold Spring | 55 Main St. (Fair St.) | 845-265-4504

Cold Spring's "breakfast HQ", this "cute little" spot also serves lunch and a "lazy Sunday brunch" from a "reliable" New American menu with "lots of vegetarian offerings"; despite a "staff mildly annoyed by having to serve you" and "homey" digs, it's a "popular" "hangout."

Four Doors Down Ⓜ *American* – | – | – | M
Buchanan | 265 Tate Ave. (bet. Albany Post Rd. & White St.) |
914-737-0606 | www.fourdoorsdown.com

A "solid" "little gem" say supporters of this Buchanan New American with a stainless-steel-topped bar and local art on the walls; while fans are "keeping [their] fingers crossed" that it "stays" in an area "overrun with pizzerias and diners", an equal number of disparagers decree that despite "attempts to be trendy", the "down-to-earth menu" and "limited wine list" make the experience "just ok."

Frankie & Johnnie's Steakhouse Ⓜ *Steak* 22 | 22 | 21 | $63
Rye | 77 Purchase St. (bet. Purdy & W. Purdy Aves.) | 914-925-3900 |
www.frankieandjohnnies.com

Why "drive to NYC for dinner" when Rye has this "excellent alternative" located in a "hip", high-ceilinged "old bank building" with "wonderful service", "quality" steaks and a big-time wine list; "pricey" fare and a "see-or-be-seen" "upscale crowd" ("lots of diamonds and Botox") make it "hoity-toity to the max", but despite the "high noise level", the overall experience is a "cool" "delight."

Fratelli *Italian* 21 | 14 | 20 | $34
New Rochelle | East End Shopping Ctr. | 237 E. Main St. (Stephenson Blvd.) |
914-633-1990 | www.fratellinewrochelle.com

"Gutsy cooking", including "wonderful specials", attract a steady stream of "locals" to this "unpretentious" New Rochelle Italian where a "friendly" chef greets his customers and "accommodates special requests"; there's "no atmosphere", but it's the type of restaurant "recommended by barbers" as "a nice place to bring family."

☒ Freelance Café & Wine Bar Ⓜ *American* 28 | 21 | 26 | $50
Piermont | 506 Piermont Ave. (Gerhardt Strasse St.) | 845-365-3250 |
www.xaviars.com

"Heavenly" New American dishes "graciously served despite all the hustle and bustle" make this Piermont "lower-cost sister" to "tonier

Xavier's next door" "simply outstanding" sigh the smitten; thanks to "extraordinarily pleasant" "host Ned Kelly", it "feels like family, only cooler" in the "upscale yet casual" "closet of a bistro", but no reservations means the "challenge is getting in", so "go early" or "during the week"; "you won't be disappointed" – "hip food, hip wine, hip people, hip-hip hooray!"

French Corner Ⓜ *French*   25 | 21 | 22 | $46
Stone Ridge | 3407 Cooper St./Rte. 213 W. (Rte. 209) | 845-687-0810

"Adventurous" chef Jacques Qualin and front-of-house spouse Leslie Flam "run a smooth operation" at this Stone Ridge boîte, delivering "wonderful", "genuine" French dishes you can "select with a blindfold and not go wrong"; all come "served politely" in a "delightful" room with "lovely lighting", so even though it's "upscale for the nabe", it's "worth the money", especially if you go for the $28 prix fixe.

Friends & Family II Hillside *Continental*   ▽ 21 | 15 | 19 | $28
Accord | 4802 Rte. 209 (Airport Rd.) | 845-626-7777 | www.friendsandfamily2.com

"On first sight" this "friendly" Ulster County roadhouse looks "like a very ordinary place", so newcomers are surprised to discover a "pleasant" staff serving Salah Alygad's "good, seasonal" Continental cooking; country-style dining rooms – one in coral colors, the other with a stone wall and fireplace – set the the mood for a "relaxed dinner", and flank a bar that has a "devoted fan base" of its own.

Frodo's Ⓜ *American*   23 | 15 | 23 | $44
Pleasantville | 472 Bedford Rd. (Pleasantville Rd.) | 914-747-4646 | www.tastethemagic.com

"Forget the ring", "the magic" is in chef Daniel Petrilli's New American cooking at his Pleasantville "winner" where "perfectly executed entrees" (including a few "out there" dishes like lentil-apple gnocchi) rely on "fresh local ingredients"; if the "functional" room painted with a mountainous mural doesn't have "much ambiance", that's offset by "friendly" service and an atmosphere so "noisy" and "chaotic" on weekends, that no one seems to mind.

Fuffi 2000 Ⓜ *Italian*   ▽ 17 | 10 | 20 | $36
New Rochelle | Wykagyl Shopping Ctr. | 1288 North Ave. (bet. Disbrow Ln. & Northfield Rd.) | 914-738-6200

"If no one in your group is interested in haute cuisine" then this "simple" New Rochelle Northern Italian will meet your dining needs with "traditional" cooking and a "staff and owner that always greet you" as if you were "eating in their home"; the wood-paneled decor, however, "lacks ambiance" (being in "a strip mall" doesn't help either), and most dub it a rather "ordinary" "neighborhood" place.

Fuji Mountain *Japanese*   15 | 15 | 19 | $38
Larchmont | 2375 Boston Post Rd. (Deane Pl.) | 914-833-3838

The "basic formula" of "samurai showmanship" and "flash at the big grill" is "well executed" at this "hibachi-style" Japanese in

Larchmont that's "fun with the kids" (they "love the onion volcano"); between the "noise", "limited menu" and abundance of "birthday parties", however, those without tots may want to "stay far away."

Gadaleto's Seafood Market & Restaurant *Seafood*

19 | 9 | 16 | $31

New Paltz | 1 Cherry Hill Ctr. (Main St.) | 845-255-1717

The hook is a "wide selection" of "seafood as fresh as can be" at this "minimal" New Paltz spot, a spawn of the adjacent fish market that's been supplying the Hudson Valley for 35 years; the catch is "take-a-number"-style service and digs that certainly "ain't the greatest" despite live jazz on weekends, but you can always "try takeout."

Gaia *American/French*

24 | 26 | 22 | $59

Greenwich | 253 Greenwich Ave. (E. Elm St.), CT | 203-661-3443 | www.gaiarestaurant.com

Respondents rave about the "gorgeous interior" of this soaring Greenwich French–New American housed in "a former bank", but there's a schism when it comes to some of the *sous vide* dishes, which are "cooked in mason jars": converts call the method a "wonderful culinary triumph" (especially "the mac 'n' cheese with truffles"), while those "not entirely convinced wonder 'is this stylish baby food?'"; at any rate, the $22 "prix fixe lunch is a great value", but the dinner prices will leave you "feeling that your pocket was picked after the bill comes."

NEW Gail's on the Common ⊄ *American* (fka Gail's Station House)

– | – | – | ∣

Ridgefield | 103 Danbury Rd. (Farmingville Rd.), CT | 203-438-9775 | www.gailsstationhouse.com

This BYO newcomer is a much smaller, less flamboyant incarnation of the former beloved Main Street Traditional American where all of Ridgefield went for weekend brunch until it burned down about two years ago; like the original, it's known for its homemade scones, muffins and cookies and now offers light lunch options like goat cheese salads and panini.

Garth Road Inn *Pub Food*

16 | 13 | 16 | $25

Scarsdale | 96 Garth Rd. (Grayrock Rd.) | 914-722-9472

"Pub-o-files", "locals" and a steady stream of "singles" looking for a "good" selection of pints pulled from a state-of-the-art draught system flock to this "convenient" Scarsdale spot with "Irish roots", dishing out "decent" "fish 'n' chips", "burgers" and other "basic" grub in a "dark" "tavern"-like atmosphere; a few forgo the fare for "a drink at the bar" or to chat up the "genuine" staff "imported" from Ireland.

Gasho of Japan *Japanese*

17 | 18 | 19 | $36

Hawthorne | 2 Saw Mill River Rd. (Skyline Dr.) | 914-592-5900
Central Valley | 365 Rte. 32 (I-87, exit 16) | 845-928-2277
www.gasho.com

"Ginsu-wielding chefs" "dazzle" the "crowds" at these Hawthorne–Central Valley Japanese old-timers where the "floorshow" "shtick" at "communal cooking tables" is more "enjoyable" than the "predictable" fare; as for the "staid" "1970s" decor – it could "use an upgrade."

Gates *Californian/Mediterranean* 18 | 18 | 17 | $30

New Canaan | 10 Forest St. (bet. East & Locust Aves.), CT | 203-966-8666

"Yellowstone has Old Faithful, New Canaan has this old reliable", favored for its "uncomplicated", "reasonably priced" Cal-Mediterranean fare and "family-friendly" atmosphere; local preppies proclaim it's "best for burgers, salads" and "a good Sunday brunch" all served in a "cheery" albeit "noisy" space.

Gaudio's *Italian* 17 | 17 | 17 | $31

Yorktown Heights | 2026 Saw Mill River Rd. (Rte. 35) | 914-245-0920 | www.gaudiosrestaurant.com

Yorktown Heights denizens hail this "decent" Italian for "large portions" of "traditional standards" like "veal and pasta" as well as "delicious" "brick-oven" pies "from the pizzeria next door"; muted yellow walls help offset the "storefront ambiance" but "dinerlike service" could use some work.

Gavi *Italian* 18 | 17 | 18 | $48

Armonk | 15 Old Rte. 22 (Rte. 22) | 914-273-6900 | www.gavirestaurant.com

Loyalists contend this "convenient", "unpretentious" Italian in Armonk with an "attentive professional staff" is a "solid" choice for a "weekday" dinner; the unconvinced, however, dub the "monotonous" "fare" "unspectacular" and the "specials overpriced", and conclude it's "overrated" "for what it is."

Gentleman Jim's Ⓜ *American* ▽ 17 | 16 | 19 | $26

Poughkeepsie | 1112 Dutchess Tpke. (Rochdale Rd.) | 845-485-5467

"Ladies and gentlemen" vie for "a seat near the fireplace" at this "old-school" Poughkeepsie purveyor of prime rib, steaks and other "nice Traditional American fare" that comes "well priced" and in "generous portions", while the 19th-century farmhouse setting and "friendly" service keep the welcome warm anyway.

Gianna's *American/Italian* ▽ 21 | 17 | 24 | $29

Yonkers | 1034 N. Broadway (Odell Terr.) | 914-375-0106

"Yonkers needs more places" like this "lively" candlelit Italian-American where a rising number of "regulars" appreciate the "outstanding" service and "excellent" thin-crust pizzas and homestyle entrees; "fair prices" and well-sized portions make you forget all about the "strip-mall" location of this "casual, yet sophisticated" spot.

Gigi's Folderol II *Eclectic* ▽ 24 | 23 | 23 | $47

Westtown | 795 Rte. 284 (Rte. 1) | 845-726-3822

A "local favorite", this "off-the-beaten-path" Orange County Eclectic "gem" combines "casual fine dining" and "seemingly effortless service" in an old farmhouse setting with two "comfortable" dining rooms: one a brick-floored, airy atrium, the other prettied up with flowers and paintings; factor in "enjoyable piano music" on weekends, and you've got "a winner."

	FOOD	DECOR	SERVICE	COST

☑ Gigi Trattoria 🅼 *Italian/Mediterranean* | 23 | 19 | 18 | $40 |

Rhinebeck | 6422 Montgomery St./Rte. 9 (Livingston St.) |
845-876-1007 | www.gigitrattoria.com

"Weekenders, artists, actors and filmmakers" contribute to the "hopping scene" at this "packed" Rhinebeck Italian-Med turning out "wonderful meat and fish dishes" in addition to "upscale" pastas, "wafer-thin" pizzas and "killer" "Tuscan fries"; the "attractive" if "odd-shaped space" exudes a "nice" "citylike" ambiance, so "sketchy service" is the only downside; no matter, this "hot spot" is "a keeper."

Gina Marie's Trattoria *Italian* | 19 | 13 | 16 | $39 |

Eastchester | 214 Main St. (John R. Albanese Pl.) | 914-793-6155

"Be sure to arrive hungry" to this Eastchester Italian that gives "new meaning to the word family-style" with "ridiculously" "big plates" where one "manhole-cover-sized entree" "can feed three people" (though a few complain about the $7.50 sharing charge); in all, it's "a safe bet" for "red-sauce" fare although the yellow-and-burgundy digs don't inspire any accolades and "slow servers" also detract.

Ginger Man *American* | 17 | 18 | 16 | $34 |

Greenwich | 64 Greenwich Ave. (Putnam Ave.), CT | 203-861-6400

"Cozy up by the fire in the back room or hang out at the bar", with its "vast" selection of "beers from around the world", at this "reasonably priced" Greenwich Traditional American that's an "after-dark haven for the popped-collar crowd"; though the burgers and brews are reasons to go, expect the "waiters to take forever to deliver" them.

Giorgio's *Italian* | 23 | 15 | 20 | $57 |

Port Chester | 64 Merritt St. (Ellendale Ave.) | 914-937-4906

There's "never a bad night" at this "old-time" Port Chester Northern Italian "hideaway" where "Giorgio runs the place with pride" and "warm" servers make everyone "feel welcome and well-fed"; the "menu's unchanging" but that's a plus in view of "consistently good" fare – it's no wonder "lots of regulars" consider it "the best-kept secret in Westchester."

Giovanni's *Steak* | 19 | 16 | 20 | $43 |

Darien | 2748 Post Rd. (I-95, exit 9), CT | 203-325-9979 |
www.giovannis.com

The owner is "always on hand to greet you" at this "longtime" Italian-accented steakhouse in Darien; "try the juicy and sizzling porterhouse", which, if you order as part of "the prix fixe dinner, is actually a bargain"; the only detraction is the "lackluster setting."

Giulio's of Tappan *Italian* | 18 | 20 | 20 | $46 |

Tappan | 154 Washington St. (Conklin Ave.) | 845-359-3657 |
www.giuliosoftappan.com

You take a "step back in time" at this "comfy", family-friendly Tappan Italian stalwart set in a "beautiful Victorian" house with period decor; an "attentive staff" serves the "usual fare, done well", and "what they lack in culinary perfection they make up for in effort and charm" so overall, it "makes you smile."

	FOOD	DECOR	SERVICE	COST

Global Gatherings ☑ *Eclectic* — 20 | 21 | 18 | $40

Hartsdale | 156 S. Central Ave. (bet. N. Healy & S. Washington Aves.) | 914-683-1833 | www.globalgatheringsrestaurant.net

"Price tags dangle from the chandeliers above you" at this "offbeat" Hartsdale "restaurant within a home furnishing store" where the "funky" "flea market" decor is matched by "innovative" Eclectic fare; "wonderful" desserts by chef Desiree Kelly earn high marks, as do "knowledgeable" servers, but "if you don't like clutter", stay away.

Globe Bar & Grill *American/Mediterranean* — 16 | 18 | 16 | $40

Larchmont | 1879 Palmer Ave. (Chatsworth Ave.) | 914-833-8600 | www.globegrill.com

This "lively" Larchmont New American–Med draws a "yuppie" crowd that fill up its "pretty cool" "open" dining room, "rowdy" back lounge and "outside patio" despite "inconsistent" service and "inventive" food that "looks better than it tastes"; it's got a "nice feel", but many agree: it's a "better bar hangout than restaurant."

Golden House *Chinese* — ▽ 20 | 13 | 20 | $22

Jefferson Valley | Lourdes Shopping Ctr. | 3639 Hill Blvd. (Rte. 6) | 914-962-8088 | www.goldenhousemenu.com

Northern Westchester nostalgics make this "old-school" Jefferson Valley Chinese with a "friendly staff" "a destination" for "consistently" "better than average" meals of Cantonese cuisine; despite the "strip-mall location" that "needs a face-lift", it's still "a step or so up from the rest of the crowd."

Golden Rod *Pan-Asian* — 20 | 12 | 16 | $26

New Rochelle | 55 E. Main St. (Premium Point Rd.) | 914-235-6688

The "always-fresh" dishes have a "nice light touch, whether Japanese, Thai, Chinese or Malaysian", at this New Rochelle Pan-Asian with "fair prices" and a bamboo-heavy decor; "portions tend to be small" and service "rushed"; if you don't like "all your food brought out at once", try "takeout."

NEW Goldfish Oyster Bar & Restaurant ☑ *Seafood* — 22 | 21 | 19 | $45

Ossining | 6 Rockledge Ave. (bet. Liberty St. & Revolutionary Rd.) | 914-762-0051 | www.goldfishdining.com

This "attractive", brightly colored new seafooder in Ossining with two levels of dining has become a "neighborhood splurge" for those who enjoy "watching the speed and detail in the open kitchen" as they pump out "grilled fish" and more "inventive" choices from an "ambitious menu"; though a few grumble about occasionally "absent-minded service" and "uneven" meals, most are happy that the "new kid in town" "shows promise."

Grand ☑ *American* — 21 | 23 | 19 | $41

Stamford | 15 Bank St. (Summer St.), CT | 203-323-3232 | www.stamfordgrand.com

"Chic" "singles" go to this "smart, sophisticated" Stamford New American for "after-work drinks" and an "eye-candy" clientele – not to mention an "excellent and innovative selection of small plates" like "tuna sashimi pizza" and a "truffled mac 'n' cheese", for which surveyors say they'd "sell their soul"; if food is your focus, "go early" "before the club crowd hits."

Grande Centrale *Continental/Italian*   19 | 18 | 20 | $41
Congers | 17 N. Rockland Ave. (Lake Rd.) | 845-267-3442 | www.grandecentrale.com
"A nice little surprise nestled next to the train tracks", this Congers Continental-Italian located in the "quaint" "converted station" serves as a "warm" spot for an "adult family dinner"; "good food you can count on", service likewise and a "real-deal" $19.95 early-bird menu are just the ticket, with "valet parking a big boost" too.

Grandma's of Yorktown *American*   16 | 13 | 17 | $19
Yorktown | 3525 Crompond Rd./Rte. 202 (Bear Mountain State Pkwy.) | 914-739-7770
"You only order a meal", say supporters, so you can have a "fantastic" slice of pie for dessert at this "comfortable like old slippers" Yorktown Traditional American with "nice young ladies that serve" and "kitschy" "seasonal displays" of animatronic figurines that "attract children"; negative Nellies admit it's "ok for breakfast", but the "ordinary" menu and pies that "are overrated" mean "it's time for a home, Grandma."

Granite Springs Inn *American*   20 | 19 | 21 | $37
Granite Springs | 2 Old Tomahawk St. (Rte. 202) | 914-248-8100 | www.granitespringsinn.com
This "unpretentious" Granite Springs Traditional–New American "has something for everyone", from "personal pizzas" and "seared tuna" to a "large list of nightly specials" "worth a try"; an "excellent" "wine and microbrew list" as well as a room made cozy with a "roaring fireplace" and "welcoming" staff keep customers coming back "again and again."

Grappolo Locanda 🆂 *Italian*   19 | 18 | 18 | $48
Chappaqua | 76 King St. (N. Greeley Ave.) | 914-238-5950 | www.grappololocanda.com
"Pleasant" "twists-and-turns" keep the menu "interesting" at this "neighborhood" "hangout" in the "heart of Chappaqua" where "well-heeled yuppies" sup on "enjoyable" Italian fare; mahogany floors do nothing to help a "room that is way too loud", and a vociferous minority of diners bemoans the "inattentive" servers, saying you'd expect more "at these prices."

Graziellas *Italian*   19 | 16 | 20 | $36
White Plains | Esplanade White Plains Hotel | 95 S. Broadway (E. Post Rd.) | 914-761-5721 | www.graziellasny.com
"It's the food you grew up with in Bensonhurst" at this "moderately priced", "hearty" Italian "in the heart of White Plains" that's "a good option for parties" or "special occasions" (there are private rooms with space for 200 total); "difficult" parking makes it "most convenient for [nearby] Crowne Plaza stayovers."

	FOOD	DECOR	SERVICE	COST

Greenbaum & Gilhooley's *American*   ▽ 16 | 12 | 17 | $33

Wappingers Falls | 1379 Rte. 9 (bet. Myers Corners & Old Hopewell Rds.) | 845-297-9700 | www.greenbaumgilhooley.com

It "looks like a sports bar, feels like a family restaurant" at this Wappingers Falls "staple" serving "huge portions" of Traditional American grub such as "good, solid" steaks and such; critics claim the staff could use an "attitude adjustment", but say it's ok if you just "pop in for a drink."

Guadalajara *Mexican*   20 | 16 | 16 | $33

Briarcliff Manor | 2 Union St. (Rte. 9) | 914-944-4380

"Guacamole mashed tableside" and "killer" "margaritas" are hallmarks of this "tasty", but "noisy", Briarcliff Manor Mexican with "traditional" south-of-the-border decor and mariachi on weekends; most consider it a "good choice" "in the area" despite "not terribly original" fare and "long waits for seats and service."

Gusano Loco *Mexican*   18 | 12 | 17 | $27

Mamaroneck | 1137 W. Boston Post Rd. (Richbell Rd.) | 914-777-1512

Proponents proclaim this "fun little" "dive" in Mamaroneck "the real deal" for Mexican food; yet despite reasonable prices, antagonists attest this "ordinary" spot is "slipping", though "the guacamole remains excellent."

Gus's Franklin Park *Seafood*   21 | 11 | 19 | $36

Harrison | 126 Halstead Ave. (1st St.) | 914-835-9804

"Tons of regulars" tout this Harrison seafood "time warp" (it opened in 1931) where "everyone knows everyone" and "fresh" fish from the adjacent market is cooked "deliciously" "any which way you want" and served to diners on "wooden tables and in booths"; though it "doesn't take reservations" and there's "often a long wait", it's still "worth the trip" because you don't find "places in Westchester like this anymore."

G.W. Tavern *American*   18 | 20 | 17 | $36

Washington Depot | 20 Bee Brook Rd./Rte. 47 (bet. Blackville Rd. & Calhoun St.), CT | 860-868-6633 | www.gwtavern.com

"You can feel the spirit of George" at this "charming" "circa-1850 tavern" "overlooking the Shepaug River" in Washington Depot, where patrons "people-watch" "out on the patio" "when the river is running" or inside "with the fireplace going"; Traditional American cooking like chicken pot pie makes for "reliable fare when you don't want to get dressed up for the big guns."

Gypsy Wolf Cantina Ⓜ *Mexican*   16 | 18 | 18 | $25

Woodstock | 261 Tinker St. (Dixon Ave.) | 845-679-9563

"Loud, crowded", "fun" and "very Woodstock" sums up this Mexican delivering "decent" eats all "served fast"; "have a few" "cheap" margaritas, and you can better appreciate the "funky" "colorful decor", with animal masks, "interesting artwork" and a "million little Christmas lights" festooning the place.

	FOOD	DECOR	SERVICE	COST

NEW Haiku Asian Bistro & Sushi Bar *Pan-Asian*

| 23 | 20 | 20 | $33 |

Bronxville | 56 Pondfield Rd. (Garden Ave.) | 914-337-5601
Cross River | Cross River Shopping Ctr. | Rte. 121 (Rte. 35) | 914-763-9120

"Mouthwatering sushi" plus "fabulous" Pan-Asian dishes "pack them in" to these "always crowded" moderately priced eateries in Bronxville (decorated with Japanese lanterns) and Cross River ("more spacious" and featuring "a gorgeous waterfall"); both locations have an "efficient" and "courteous staff" and are "hip" additions to the "sleepy suburbs" they're based in – and they "deliver."

Hajime M *Japanese*

| 24 | 14 | 17 | $39 |

Harrison | 267 Halstead Ave. (Harrison Ave.) | 914-777-1543

Those "discerning about their fish" "sit at the bar" at this sparsely decorated Harrison Japanese and devour the "freshest sushi north of NYC"; "cramped" conditions and "snippy" service are small prices to pay for the "top-rate" "distinctive creations" that are "worth the trip."

Halstead Avenue Bistro *American*

| 22 | 17 | 21 | $40 |

Harrison | 123 Halstead Ave. (1st St.) | 914-777-1181

"Fresh ingredients", "lovely presentation" and a "warm and inviting atmosphere" (the "fine host" "knows many of the patrons") bring in a steady clientele to this Harrison New American with a hand-carved mahogany bar and prix fixe deals (Sunday–Thursday) "that are a terrific value"; though most "would enjoy it better if it were a little quieter", the experience is "almost always a bull's-eye."

Hamilton Inn *Eclectic*

| ▽ 19 | 19 | 20 | $44 |

Millerton | 67 Main St. (Park St.) | 518-789-9399 | www.thehamiltoninn.com

Diners in search of a "gracious, old New England feeling" find it at this Millerton Eclectic set in a "stately" Victorian house complete with fireplaces and a "romantic" wraparound porch to boot; "well-executed" seasonal fare is served at a "leisurely" pace "by candlelight" so the one "tiny annoyance", some mutter, is "the muzak – it has to go."

Hanada Sushi *Japanese*

| 20 | 13 | 17 | $32 |

Pleasantville | 8 Pleasantville Rd./Rte. 117 (bet. Cooley St. & Manville Rd.) | 914-769-0638

"Solid Japanese, raw or cooked", appeases aficionados at this "authentic" Pleasantville eatery set in "unassuming" surroundings; most concur it's a "reasonable destination" considering choices "in neighboring towns", but since the "small" space is "often crowded", "takeout" is a good option.

Hanna's Z *Lebanese*

| 20 | 8 | 18 | $24 |

Danbury | 72 Lake Ave. (bet. Abbott Ave. & Lawncrest Rd.), CT | 203-748-5713

This chef-owned, moderately priced "hole-in-the-wall" may be in a "mundane Danbury strip mall", but the "always fresh, well-prepared "authentic Lebanese cuisine" "will take you to faraway places", which the lackluster decor won't; cooks cheer about the "terrific grocery right next door" for Middle Eastern ingredients.

Harney & Sons *Tearoom*
(fka W.D. McCarthur)

▬ | ▬ | ▬ | I

Millerton | 13 Main St. (bet. N. Center St. & N. Elm Ave.) | 518-789-2121 | www.harney.com

Best known as a purveyor of top-notch teas, this Millerton lunch spot also has a lounge where sippers can savor the brews along with scones, sandwiches, fresh soups and salads; pastel walls in the casual, diminutive space are hung with old engravings of kettles in keeping with the theme, while in warm weather, you can take your cup on the terrace.

Harry's of Hartsdale *Seafood/Steak*

19 | 19 | 18 | $49

Hartsdale | 230 E. Hartsdale Ave. (bet. Bronx River Pkwy. & Central Park Ave.) | 914-472-8777 | www.harrysofhartsdale.com

"Commuters" hit this Hartsdale spot – "convenient" to the train station – to slurp down oysters and "people-watch" at the "lively bar" or dine on "chophouse" fare that's "solid", if somewhat "underwhelming", given the "high" prices; service can be "slow", but still, the stainless-steel bar and open kitchen lend an "urban vibe" that definitely "works" for "cocktails" or "brunch."

Harvest *American*

21 | 21 | 20 | $43

Brookfield | 834 Federal Rd. (Station Rd.), CT | 203-740-7601 | www.harvestct.com

Supporters say "you will never regret going" to this "civilized" Brookfield New American for dishes like "delicious crab cakes" and "outstanding foie gras"; the "lovely" New England country decor "features cozy, fire-lit dining rooms", and "attentive service" adds to the "warm and friendly ambiance."

Harvest Café Restaurant & Wine Bar *American*

24 | 19 | 23 | $32

New Paltz | Water St. Market | 10 Main St. (bet. Water St. & Wurts Ave.) | 845-255-4205 | www.harvestcafenp.com

"Hidden atop" a "mini-village of shops" on the outskirts of New Paltz, this "relaxing" second-floor New American satifies with "delicious" "imaginative" dishes such as chef-owner Mark Suszczynski's signature sage-infused duck breast; a "pleasant, competent" staff works the "small", "minimally decorated" room that in warm weather plays second fiddle to the deck, where diners "watch the sunset over Mohonk mountain"; "ah, that view!"

☒ Harvest on Hudson *Mediterranean*

22 | 26 | 21 | $52

Hastings-on-Hudson | 1 River St. (W. Main St. off Southside Ave.) | 914-478-2800 | www.harvest2000.com

A "rare combination" of "spectacular" setting and "culinary excellence", this "enchanting" Hastings Med overlooking the Hudson turns out a "consistently delicious" "harvest of flavors" thanks to

	FOOD	DECOR	SERVICE	COST

"fresh-picked" herbs and vegetables "grown on the property"; a few insist the fare and service can be "inconsistent", but most devotees declare the "transporting" Tuscan feel in the high-ceilinged interior works for "group" dinners or "romantic" escapades alike.

Haymaker American   23 | 21 | 21 | $41
Poughkeepsie | 718 Dutchess Tpke./Rte. 44 (Cherry Hill Dr.) | 845-486-9454 | www.thehaymaker.com
"One of Poughkeepsie's rising stars", chef-owner Bennett Chinn's New American dispenses an "excellent variety" of "first-class", "well-prepared" (if "sometimes overly complex") fare; "attentive service" is only "uneven when it gets busy", while the strip-mall locale offers no clue of "surprisingly" "modern decor" with its light walls and dark furniture; in all, it's "well worth a stop."

Heather's Open Cucina Ⓜ Italian   21 | 17 | 18 | $46
Nyack | 12 N. Broadway (bet. Main & New Sts.) | 845-358-8686 | www.heathersopencucina.com
Nyack's "deservedly popular" Italian, this "busy" "little" bistro dishes up "consistently" "good", "inventive" "comfort food" that's "worth" the wait it sometimes takes "to get to table"; brick-walled surroundings could use "a bit of sprucing up", and it can get "noisy" and "frantic at times", but that's often the way in places this "hip", so just "relax and enjoy."

Heights Bistro & Bar, The Ⓜ American   24 | 18 | 20 | $36
Yorktown Heights | 334 Underhill Ave. (Rte. 118) | 914-962-3777 | www.theheightsbistro.com
"Excellent" New American fare (with a "great veal meatloaf") served by a staff that "tries hard" charms a loyal following at this "first-rate" Yorktown Heights "gem" where the $19.95 "early-bird" special is an "outstanding" deal; sage-green wainscoting creates a "warm atmosphere", but if some find the quarters "cramped", the "courtyard seating" in summer "can't be beat."

Hickory BBQ BBQ   18 | 12 | 20 | $24
Kingston | 743 Rte. 28 (Waughkonk Rd.) | 845-338-2424 | www.hickoryrestaurant.com
You're treated "like their favorite customer" at this "homey" Kingston BBQ joint that's "gaining a reputation" for "gargantuan portions" of "smoking good meats" and "unusual sides" courtesy of "two Jewish boys from New York" (aka owners Mark and Steven Slutzky); "yeah, the room is plain", though live music on weekends jazzes things up, and it's all "good value" too.

High Street Roadhouse Cajun/Creole   18 | 9 | 14 | $27
Rye | 12 High St. (Maple Ave.) | 914-967-4855 | www.highstreetroadhouse.com
The "lower-Westchester gentry" may not appreciate the "funky" "dive bar" setting of this "hard-to-find" Cajun-Creole restaurant in Rye, but "decent" fare (including alligator) and a "wild" "roadhouse atmosphere" make it a "good place to go with the kids" or "the boys"; occasional live blues and rock bands add to the "fun."

Hillsdale House *American*   13 | 12 | 13 | $30
Hillsdale | 1 Anthony St. (Rte. 23) | 518-325-7111
A "quintessential neighborhood hangout", this circa-1811 "country-style inn" in Columbia County is "easygoing" all around, so many don't mind the "distracted staff" or a "not very exciting" New American menu, suggesting "stick with simple choices"; it's a "pleasant standby" for pizza or a "hamburger on a cold night."

Hoffman House 🖾 *Continental*   ▽ 19 | 23 | 20 | $32
Kingston | 94 N. Front St. (bet. Crown & Green Sts.) | 845-338-2626 | www.hoffmanhousetavern.com
"Talk about atmosphere", this 1687 National Historic Landmark "gorgeous stone house" in Kingston's historic Uptown district is dripping with it, from the beamed ceilings to the wideboard floors; soak up the "serene setting" near one of the fireplaces, bask in "careful, professional service" and chow down on "well-prepared", "good" Continental fare; it all adds up to "good value."

Hokkaido *Japanese*   ▽ 24 | 20 | 24 | $32
New Paltz | 18 Church St. (Main St.) | 845-256-0621
It's as "if you died and went to Japan" exclaim enthusiasts at this "inviting" New Paltz Japanese known for "exceptional" dishes, "world-class sushi" and "wonderful service", all found in a simple room with bamboo touches that exudes a "quiet, calm atmosphere"; in warm weather, you can pretend you're in heaven on the "delightful patio."

Holy Smoke Ⓜ *BBQ*   18 | 10 | 17 | $26
Mahopac | 241 Rte. 6N (bet. Cheryl Ct. & Stillwater Rd.) | 845-628-9795 | www.holysmokebbq.net
"Sharing" is almost "a must" at this Mahopac BBQer serving "stick-to-the-ribs" ribs, "spicy chicken wings", pulled pork and such in "portions for the very hungry"; though "pine paneling and simple furniture" are about as "plain" as can be, a "well-intentioned" staff helps make up for it.

Hopkins Inn Ⓜ *Austrian*   18 | 22 | 20 | $42
New Preston | 22 Hopkins Rd. (½ mi. west of Rte. 45 N.), CT | 860-868-7295 | www.thehopkinsinn.com
Aesthetes agree that the "flagstone terrace" of this chef-owned, family-run New Preston stalwart affords "a drop-dead view" of Lake Waramaug; but customers quibble over the quality of the food: fans compliment the "consistently good" "traditional Austrian cuisine" like braised veal shank and "great schnitzel", while foes fret that the "never-varying menu" "needs to be brought out of the 19th century"; N.B. Closed January–late-March.

Horse & Hound Inn, The *American*   ▽ 16 | 14 | 16 | $41
South Salem | 94 Spring St. (Main St.) | 914-763-3108 | www.thehorseandhoundinn.com
"Comfortable and convenient", this South Salem "neighborhood restaurant" – a converted stagecoach stop with a fireplace and "old tavern"-like decor – serves somewhat "uneven" Traditional American

fare to a crowd of regulars, including "a crew at the bar"; it's an "easy night out", for sure, but locals lament it "could be so much better."

Horsefeathers *American*

17 | 15 | 16 | $25

Tarrytown | 94 N. Broadway (Wildey St.) | 914-631-6606

"Crave-able" burgers, "sweet potato fries" and a "large selection" of "seasonal brews" off a "slightly pricey", "varied menu" make this Tarrytown Traditional American "haunt" the "type of place" you'd "want in your neighborhood"; the staff is "friendly", "but slow", and while the wood interior with lots of "bric-a-brac" feels a bit "dark" and "run-down", there's always the "pleasant" patio seating that just about makes up for it.

Horseman
Restaurant & Pizza *American/Pizza*

▽ 13 | 9 | 16 | $21

Sleepy Hollow | 276 N. Broadway (Beekman Ave.) | 914-631-2984 | www.thehorsemanrestaurant.com

"Trans-fats" be damned say "families" and "college kids" crowding into the booths at this "homey" Traditional American "dive" in Sleepy Hollow for modestly priced burgers, pizza, cheese fries and beer; cynics save it for "breakfast" or a quick "lunch" and suggest that if you desire "fine dining", "go elsewhere."

Hostaria Mazzei *Italian*

21 | 19 | 20 | $50

Port Chester | 25 S. Regent St. (Westchester Ave.) | 914-939-2727 | www.hostariamazzei.com

Both "Connecticut and New York residents agree" a "festive, flavorful feast" from an "imaginative" chef awaits at this Port Chester Italian where a "competent" staff takes orders for "outstandingly prepared" "fish and meat specialties", pastas and pizza right out of their wood-burning oven; it's "pricey" "for the neighborhood", yet it remains a "solid" "local spot", hence the crowds "on weekends."

Hudson House of Nyack **M** *American*

20 | 19 | 21 | $43

Nyack | 134 Main St. (Franklin St.) | 845-353-1355 | www.hudsonhousenyack.com

"Charismatic host" and co-owner/pastry chef Matt Hudson "is a doll" coo admirers at his "lively" Nyack New American, where "clever twists on bistro standards" are followed by "desserts that can't be beat"; the onetime village hall with its pressed tin ceiling and walls is now a "cozy, modern dining room" ("check out the jail-cell wine cellar"), while the bar scene adds to the "enjoyable" vibe.

Hudson House River Inn *American*

21 | 23 | 21 | $43

Cold Spring | 2 Main St. (West St.) | 845-265-9355 | www.hudsonhouseinn.com

"On a lazy summer afternoon" you can dine on the porch and "gaze at" "sensational" views of the Hudson at this "classy" Cold Spring riverfront spot dispensing "good" "traditional as well as updated" New American fare; inside, the "beautiful, old" 19th-century inn has a "bright and airy" dining room tended by a "capable" staff, so no wonder it's a "hometown favorite."

	FOOD	DECOR	SERVICE	COST

Hudson's Ribs & Fish *Seafood/Steak*
18 | 16 | 19 | $34

Fishkill | 1099 Rte. 9 (bet. Old Rte. 9 & Smithtown Rd.) | 845-297-5002 | www.hudsonsribsandfish.com

Some "pop over" to this Fishkill surf 'n' turfer just for the famous "fresh hot popovers" – "delicious morsels" with "fabulous strawberry butter" declared "the highlight" among eats that are otherwise "good for basics"; though "no-frills" decor gets rated "subpar", there are still "waits on weekends" to get into this "popular watering hole."

Hunan Larchmont *Chinese*
17 | 11 | 17 | $25

Larchmont | 1961 Palmer Ave. (West Ave.) | 914-833-0400

This Larchmont "standby" has become a "reliable" spot for "better-than-typical Chinese food" "before the movies" thanks to an "ample selection" of specialties and a staff "that does its best to please"; some say it's "unexciting" and "old-fashioned", with decor that's "straight out of the 1970s" (green tablecloths and pink napkins) and only "gets crowded" due to its "good location."

Hunan Ritz *Chinese/Japanese*
19 | 12 | 15 | $25

Thornwood | Rose Hill Shopping Ctr. | 636 Columbus Ave. (Nannyhagen Rd.) | 914-747-0701

"Reliable" renditions of "Chinese and Japanese" "favorites" rein regulars into this "reasonably priced" "staple" "tucked away" in a Thornwood strip mall; "delivery" is a "good" bet considering the "abrupt" service and black lacquer decor could both "use some help."

Hunan Village *Chinese*
23 | 17 | 20 | $35

Yonkers | 1828 Central Park Ave. (Slater Ave.) | 914-779-2272 | www.hunanvillage.com

"Wonderfully" "creative" dishes "you won't find" elsewhere make this Yonkers Chinese, staffed with "attentive" waiters who make "excellent" "recommendations", "among the best" of Westchester Sino specialists; though it's a "big loss" to many regulars who don't see "owner Paul" around anymore and suggest the "new management" "isn't the same", almost all agree it's still "worth a detour."

Ichi Riki Ⓜ *Japanese*
21 | 16 | 20 | $33

Elmsford | Elmsford Plaza | 1 E. Main St. (Rtes. 9A & 119) | 914-592-2220

"Capable chefs" and "courteous" servers make this "authentic" Elmsford Japanese "a pleasure" for "fresh" sushi and "interesting" cooked entrees; lunch is most popular, with a $12.50 special, and though three tatami rooms counterbalance "the small tables", dining is still "a little tight" in this "tiny, neighborhood place."

Il Bacio Trattoria *Italian*
23 | 17 | 18 | $31

Bronxville | 1 Park Pl. (Pond Field Rd.) | 914-337-4100 | www.ilbaciotrattoriany.com

Admirers adore this "homey" Bronxville Italian that's an "excellent value" with "trattoria-style dishes", "fabulous pizza combinations" and a "scrumptious" "gelato bar"; "long waits" and "loud acoustics" are downsides, and if you don't like dining "surrounded by children of all ages", there's an "outdoor garden" to escape to in summer.

	FOOD	DECOR	SERVICE	COST

☑ Il Barilotto ☒ *Italian* — 26 | 23 | 23 | $43

Fishkill | 1113 Main St. (North St.) | 845-897-4300 |
www.ilbarilottorestaurant.com

"Don't go expecting" "typical" Italian food at Fishkill's "outstanding" sister to Aroma Osteria, because "innovative" is the word, with a "top-quality" "rustic" menu "surpassed" only by "fantastic" specials – and there's an "extensive list" of vinos "to boot"; "large, well-spaced tables" help create a "contemporary wine bar look" in the "intimate" space, and "professional" "service is always there when needed", so apart from "deafening acoustics", it's "a hit" all around.

☑ Il Cenàcolo *Italian* — 27 | 22 | 23 | $56

Newburgh | 228 S. Plank Rd./Rte. 52 (bet. I-87 & Rte. 300) |
845-564-4494 | www.Ilcenacolorestaurant.com

"Sublime" swoon fans at this "middle-of-nowhere" Newburgh Northern Italian that "lives up to its reputation" with "unbelievable" dishes, a "zillion specials, each better than the next", and an "amazing wine list"; it "looks like an abandoned bowling alley", but inside, "softly lit", Tuscan-style decor (complete with hanging copper pots and temptingly laid-out antipasti) is enhanced by "gracious" service, so though tabs may trigger "sticker shock", it's "fabulous", and "well worth it."

Il Continori Ⓜ *Italian* — - | - | - | M

Wappingers Falls | 2648 E. Main St. (Rte. 9D) | 845-297-9222
Cousin to Beacon's Brothers Trattoria, this "wonderful" Wappingers Falls Italian serves slightly more upscale Northern Italian fare (like signature scallops with wild mushrooms and truffle cream oil) but at the same "reasonable" rates; a few paintings and photographs brighten up "minimal decor" with pressed tin ceilings and exposed brick, while an "accommodating staff" ensures patrons "go back again and again."

Il Falco ☒ *Italian* — 22 | 18 | 21 | $44

Stamford | 59 Broad St. (bet. Summer St. & Washington Blvd.), CT |
203-327-0002 | www.ilfalco.com
This "old-school" Stamford Italian "mainstay" is "a special place for osso buco" complemented by "an extensive wine list" and "top-notch service"; loyalists "love that the owner is always coming around to see how your food is", but trendy types taunt "you'll be making your own atmosphere" due to the "tired decor."

Il Forno Ⓜ *Italian* — 20 | 15 | 19 | $29

Somers | 343 Rte. 202 (Rte. 100) | 914-277-7575 |
www.ilfornosomers.com
There's "always a wait" at this Somers Italian where "they know their stuff" and the "brick-oven pizza" and "hearty" "red-sauce" entrees are enjoyed by "families young and old"; "friendly, though harried" servers work the recently renovated dining room with wrought-iron detailing, which some call "cozy" and others dub "crowded."

Il Portico *Italian*

22 | 20 | 22 | $47

Tappan | 89 Main St. (Oak Tree Rd.) | 845-365-2100 |
www.ilportico.com

Rockland County residents who "love" the "tasty" eats at this "consistently good" yet "relatively undiscovered" Italian "hope it'll stay that way" (although the less gung-ho wish portions weren't so "sparse"); most agree that "attentive" staff and the "wonderful setting in an old house" filled with flowers and paintings make it just the thing for "a small party", or a "romantic" tête-à-tête.

Il Sorriso *Italian*

20 | 19 | 21 | $44

Irvington | 5 N. Buckhout St. (Main St.) | 914-591-2525 |
www.ilsorriso.com

The "owners care" and are "delighted to serve you" at this "upscale" Irvington restaurant serving "simple" Italian fare paired with wines from a 300-label list; if a few find the food "indifferently prepared", the ambiance alone is "appetizing", especially in "summer" on the "pretty sun-drenched patio" overlooking the Hudson – it's reminiscent of "a hillside in San Francisco."

NEW Il Teatro *Italian*

▽ 21 | 19 | 22 | $56

Mamaroneck | 576 Mamaroneck Ave. (bet. Station Pl. & Waverly Ave.) |
914-777-2200

This "enjoyable" Mamaroneck newcomer (and sister to Pelham's La Fontanella) is "already very popular" for its "creative" Northern Italian cuisine, "customer-oriented" service and theatrical setting with velvet curtains and vintage posters; "high noise levels" and "hard-to-get" reservations ("small space" alert!) are downsides, but it's still "worth the effort."

Il Tesoro 🗷 *Italian*

▽ 26 | 22 | 24 | $48

Goshen | 6 N. Church St. (Main St.) | 845-294-8373

Yes, it's "cozy, as in small", and maybe "a bit cramped", but this Goshen Northern Italian turns out such "surprisingly good", "inspired" fare and "fabulous homemade desserts" that it's becoming "a destination" "for a special night out"; an "accommodating staff" serves in a space that's mellow with yellow stucco and brick walls, so even if it's "on the expensive side", most declare "these people are really getting it right."

Imperial Wok *Chinese/Japanese*

18 | 16 | 17 | $26

Somers | Heritage Hills Ctr. | 13 Heritage Hills 202 Ctr. (Rte. 202) |
914-277-8900

North White Plains | 736 N. Broadway (bet. McDougal Dr. &
Palmer Ave.) | 914-686-2700

A "tremendous selection" of "always satisfying" "flavorful dishes" that are a "cut above standard" "suburban" Chinese and Japanese fare distinguishes this White Plains and Somers duo (the latter's got a "gorgeous lake view") where "busloads of retirees" appreciate the "huge portions" and "reasonable prices"; the decor is "somewhat dated", though that somehow seems "appropriate" given they're rather "traditional" spots.

India Cafe & Grill *Indian*   20 | 14 | 17 | $32

Armonk | 61 Old Rte. 22 (Rte. 128) | 914-273-5931 |
www.indiacafeandgrill.com

"IBMers" and other "corporate" types take a "break from the office"
and "frequent" this "tasty" Indian "on a side street away from the
main part of town" for the "lunch buffet that's a real steal (for
Armonk anyway)"; "dingy" digs "are nothing to write home about",
but "welcoming" owners make it "pleasant" nonetheless.

India House Restaurant *Indian*   23 | 17 | 19 | $30

Montrose | 2089 Albany Post Rd. (Trinity Ave.) | 914-736-0005 |
www.indiahouseny.com

"English expats" craving "authentic" "Brick Lane" curries and other
"spicy" subcontinent fare find this Montrose eatery delivers with a
"reliably good" menu that includes a variety of "vegetarian options"
and a "lunch buffet" that's "a bargain"; decor is "traditional" too
with multicolored canopies lining the ceiling.

Insieme Ristorante ⓈItalian   24 | 16 | 23 | $44

Ridgefield | 103 Danbury Rd. (bet. Copps Hill Rd. & South St.), CT |
203-894-8141

"You need a GPS" to locate this "tiny Italian gem" "hidden behind a
Ridgefield shopping center"; still, surveyors say its "delightful food"
and "friendly" service make it "worth the hunt."

Iron Forge Inn Ⓜ *American*   ▽ 21 | 20 | 20 | $44

Warwick | 38 Iron Forge Rd. (Mt. Peter Rd.) | 845-986-3411 |
www.ironforgeinn.com

Orange County fans of this "out-of-the-way" "charmer" are "trying to
keep it a secret", but word's out that the New American menu is "always different and always good", and the "welcome" is warm too,
whether in the 1760 farmhouse's four "intimate" dining rooms, the
hilltop gazebo or the taproom with its own menu of pub fare.

ⓏIron Horse Grill ⓈⓂ *American*   27 | 22 | 25 | $56

Pleasantville | 20 Wheeler Ave. (Manville Rd.) | 914-741-0717 |
www.ironhorsegrill.com

"Gracious" as both a host and a chef, Philip McGrath "pampers" his
customers with "memorable", "beautifully presented" New
American cuisine at his "elegant" Pleasantville "destination" set in a
converted 1904 railway station where "attentive service" "makes
everyone feel special"; the "small", high-ceilinged room is "convivial", though "noisy", and even if prices run "high", the "incredible"
flavor "combinations" have most everyone exclaiming that "more
restaurants should be like this."

Irving Farm
Coffeehouse *Sandwiches/Soup*   18 | 15 | 15 | $14

Millerton | 44 Main St. (Dutchess Ave.) | 518-789-6540 |
www.irvingfarm.com

"A favorite hangout" for Millerton locals to "sit, read and chat", this
"quirky", "relaxed" eatery offers "a big selection" of sandwiches,

soups, salads and baked goods as well as a "really good" "cup of joe" from 39 house-roasted varieties that can rival you-know-who's; most days they close at 6 PM, but new owners have introduced an expanded dinner menu for Fridays and Saturdays.

NEW Jackalope BBQ *BBQ*

‒ ‒ ‒ I

(fka Ümami Café)

Fishkill | 717 Rte. 9 (Main St.) | 845-896-1979

Ümami Café owner Craig Purdy has done a switcheroo with his Fishkill spot that's now on the BBQ bandwagon, bringing down-home Texas-style ribs, pulled pork and beer-can chicken to a space done up to match; old license plates, neon beer signs, cooking pans, washboards, a picket fence, moose antlers, a stuffed jackalope (natch) and a help-yourself hot-sauce trough in the middle of the room set a merry mood that's attracting kids of all ages.

Jack & Dyls Ⓜ *American*

18 15 19 $40

Tarrytown | 49 Main St. (Washington St.) | 914-631-2228 | www.jackanddyls.net

A "nice vibe" prevails at this "friendly" Tarrytown New American turning out "interesting" renditions of "comfort food" and offering well-priced sips from a USA-centric wine list; though the "tiny" space has a tendency to get "noisy", the "warm" atmosphere and "affordable" tabs make it a "decent" "neighborhood" spot.

Jackie's Bistro Ⓢ *French*

20 15 19 $45

Eastchester | 434 White Plains Rd. (Mill Rd.) | 914-337-8447 | www.jackiesbistro.com

A "touch of Paris" awaits at this "small" but "charming" "family-run" French restaurant in Eastchester where a "warm welcome" and "classic" bistro fare keeps "longtime" fans "feeling good" despite a handful of critics who fear recent "disappointing" experiences mean it's "gone downhill"; digs could use "updating", but "in an area known for Italian", this "warm" spot still makes for a "pleasant evening."

Jackson & Wheeler *American*

17 15 15 $44

Pleasantville | 25 Wheeler Ave. (Jackson St.) | 914-741-2000 | www.jacksonandwheeler.com

"Something for everyone" is the mantra at this Pleasantville New American that's "convenient to the Jacob Burns center" for a "decent" meal "after the movies" and has a Sunday jazz brunch and an in-house bakery; complaints abound, however, regarding "roulette wheel service" ("sometimes knowledgeable", "sometimes igno-rant") and an overabundance of "nightly events" that "cheapen the surroundings" – critics sum up by saying it "doesn't come together" because they "can't seem to figure out what they want to be."

Jaipore Royal Indian *Indian*

24 21 20 $33

Brewster | 280 Rte. 22 N. (3 mi. off I-684, exit 8) | 845-277-3549 | www.fineindiandining.com

"Amazing, authentic" Indian dishes served up in a "beautiful old" Victorian mansion "make for a fun contrast" at this Brewster oasis in a "sparse ethnic food area"; acolytes "drawn from miles around" adore the "gracious" service and the "Sunday buffet" – it's "a gourmand's heaven" and a "deal", as well.

Japan Inn Ⓜ *Japanese* | 22 | 13 | 20 | $34 |

Bronxville | 28 Palmer Ave. (bet. Parkway Rd. & Paxton Ave.) | 914-337-1296

A "favorite" for "locals", this "small" Bronxville "sushi joint" traffics in "wonderfully" prepared Japanese standards served by a "friendly crew" who "recognize return customers with enthusiasm"; "never mind the decor" that might be "lacking", this "dependable" "old-timer" is still a "welcoming retreat."

Jean Claude's Ⓜ✑ *Dessert* ▽ 26 | 14 | 16 | $19 |

Warwick | 25 Elm St. (Oakland Ave.) | 845-986-8900

"Fantastic pastries" and other "delicious" "dessert fare" are the raison d'étre at this petite patisserie/cafe in the "cute" town of Warwick; those stopping in at the saucer-sized spot for coffee or a quiche should heed their limited hours (Wednesday–Sunday).

☑ Jean-Louis ⒵ *French* | 27 | 22 | 26 | $75 |

Greenwich | 61 Lewis St. (bet. Greenwich Ave. & Mason St.), CT | 203-622-8450 | www.restaurantjeanlouis.com

At this "grown-up" Greenwich "foodie nirvana" "for people who appreciate the best cooking with the best ingredients", chef-owner Jean-Louis Gerin "continues to strive for and attain new heights" while staying "true to his French roots"; "gorgeous decor and superb service" lead surveyors to surmise it's a "special-occasion place" that's "worth taking someone whom you want to impress", "but it's a good thing the tab is not in euros."

Jennifer's Ⓜ *German* | 19 | 14 | 20 | $38 |

Yorktown Heights | 715 Saw Mill River Rd. (1 mi. west of Rte. 100) | 914-962-4298 | www.jennifersmenu.com

"Warm hosts" greet you at this "pleasant" German-Continental in Yorktown Heights that offers "a world beyond knockwurst" with "well-prepared" fare served in a "simply decorated" Tudor-style dining room; if a few find the "old-world" cuisine a bit "boring", it's still "a nice change" from "the abundance of Italian restaurants in the area."

J.J. Mannion's *American* ▽ 15 | 13 | 19 | $23 |

Yonkers | 640 McLean Ave. (Central Park Ave.) | 914-476-2786

They "pour a good pint of Guinness" at this "homey" "old Irish bar" in Yonkers with a "great selection" of 37 beers and "dependable" Traditional American "grub"; despite decor that's "seen better days", pub-crawlers pronounce it a "comfortable" place that's "nice for a drink" and has two private rooms that are "good for parties."

☑ Johnny's Pizzeria ⒵Ⓜ✑ *Pizza* | 25 | 7 | 11 | $20 |

Mt. Vernon | Lincoln Plaza | 30 W. Lincoln Ave. (bet. N. 7th Ave. & Rochelle Terrace) | 914-668-1957

"What a pie!" cry legions of Neapolitan disciples who liken the "thin-and-crunchy-crust", "light-on-the-cheese", "brick-oven pizzas" at

	FOOD	DECOR	SERVICE	COST

this Mt. Vernon cash-only shop to a "near religious experience"; "Italian comfort food" is also on order at this spot with "great prices" that "can stand up to the best" in "New York City."

John's Harvest Inn 🅜 *Continental* ▽ 19 | 19 | 18 | $39

Middletown | 633 Rte. 17M (Rte. 17, exit 119) | 845-343-6630 | www.johnsharvestinn.com

Customers concur, you "have to love the clocks" decorating this "old-time" Middletown Continental; where they differ is on chef-owner John Botti's "classic" cooking, with some saying it's "good" and the harder-to-please opining it's "ordinary", but either way, a "pleasant staff" keeps things ticking over in the cozy wainscoted dining room.

Julianna's *American* - | - | - | M

Cortlandt Manor | 276 Watchhill Rd. (Sniffen Mountain Rd.) | 914-788-0505

Chef Michael Carrozza "isn't afraid to experiment" claim Cortlandt Manor mavens who are "left smiling" by "large portions" of the "wholesome" New American fare he serves at this relative new-comer set in a converted schoolhouse; service is "inconsistent", but regulars recognize "owners who are trying hard" and hope they "get their timing down" at this blossoming "local place."

Justin Thyme 🅜 *Pub Food* 16 | 11 | 17 | $27

Croton-on-Hudson | 171 Grand St. (Mt. Airy Rd.) | 914-271-0022 | www.justinthymecafe.com

It's "nothing fancy", but this "pubby" Croton "haunt" "is the place to go" for an "early dinner with the kids" or "Sunday brunch", where the "basic" fare is deemed "solid", but "more ambitious dishes" on the Traditional American menu "fall short"; it "gets noisy" later on as the "lively" bar gets "crowded" with "locals" sampling "tasty martinis" from a lengthy cocktail list at the restored copped-topped bar.

Kang Suh *Korean* 22 | 14 | 20 | $34

Yonkers | 2375 Central Park Ave. (Jackson Ave.) | 914-771-4066

"Delectable" "grill-it-yourself" Korean BBQ and "generous *banchan*" (those "little appetizer plates") are augmented by a selection of Japanese standards at this Yonkers branch of the New York City original that's "fun for a date or family dining out"; an "attentive" staff that is happy to "help" makes it "pleasant", despite its bare-bones strip-mall setting.

Karamba Café *Cuban/Pan-Latin* ▽ 22 | 8 | 15 | $19

White Plains | 185 Main St. (Court St.) | 914-946-5550

"Get your arroz con pollo fix" at this "bargain" Cuban "comfort-food" haven where everyone from construction workers to office temps load up on "tons" of "freshly prepared" Latin fare; sure, the basic brown color scheme adds "little ambiance", but loyalists don't mind if the digs keep potential patrons away, whispering it's a "good thing more people don't know about this place" because they "don't want to share it!"

	FOOD	DECOR	SERVICE	COST

Karuta *Japanese*
▽ 19 | 12 | 21 | $31

New Rochelle | North Ridge Shopping Ctr. | 77 Quaker Ridge Rd. (North Ave.) | 914-636-6688

"Mrs. Karuta makes sure that everything runs perfectly" at her "small" but "solid" New Rochelle Japanese where "fresh sushi" and 20 varieties of sake are "served by a lovely staff"; the "quiet family" atmosphere, unfortunately, "was spoiled by the introduction of a TV in the main dining area" and some add an entire "face-lift is in order."

Kazu Japanese Restaurant *Japanese*
▽ 21 | 11 | 19 | $30

Hartsdale | 17 E. Hartsdale Ave. (Central Park Ave.) | 914-682-6688 | www.kazurestaurant.com

"Wonderfully fresh fish" at "moderate prices" draws devotees to this "tiny" Hartsdale "storefront" Japanese for "pristine" sushi served in "interesting combinations" and blackboard specials that change weekly; new owners "work hard to please patrons" via "unbelievable lunch deals"; in all, it proves "good things come in small packages."

K. Fung's *Chinese*
20 | 13 | 18 | $28

Hartsdale | 222 E. Hartsdale Ave. (Fenimore Rd.) | 914-472-3838

You'll "feel a little less guilty" after indulging at this "health-conscious" Hartsdale Chinese where the kitchen dishes out "fresh"-tasting Mandarin creations with an emphasis on "less-oily" preparations and "vegetarian options"; "diverse daily specials" and "helpful" service make it a "continuing family favorite" in spite of "boring" beige "suburban" digs.

Kicho *Japanese*
▽ 19 | 15 | 18 | $37

Bedford Hills | 352 N. Bedford Rd. (Cherry St.) | 914-666-3332

"Thumbs-up" for this Japanese newcomer that "injects some life into sleepy Bedford Hills" where fin fans recommend ordering "ambitious sushi combinations" especially on the "outdoor terrace" "in the summertime"; while some say it's "not as bracingly fresh" as some "competitors" and there's little "atmosphere" in the lime-green dining room, it's still a "welcome addition" to an area that needs restaurants that "try hard."

King & I, The *Thai*
19 | 15 | 18 | $32

Nyack | 93 Main St. (bet. B'way & Cedar St.) | 845-358-8588 | www.kingandinyack.com

Expect "no wows", just "well-prepared", "nicely flavored" Thai food at this "relaxed", "been-there-forever" Nyack outpost that's "a boon to the neighborhood"; new owners gave the interior a makeover that may not be reflected in the ratings, but in any case, it's "sitting by the window" to "people-watch" that's the "treat."

Kirari *Japanese*
20 | 9 | 16 | $31

Scarsdale | 30 Garth Rd. (Freightway) | 914-725-3730

"Regulars" revisit this "reliable", "local" sushi spot in Scarsdale for "fresh" fish, "creative" rolls and a standard selection of "cooked" Japanese specialties; though service is "friendly", "sparse" surroundings mean it's "worth getting takeout"; N.B. they also deliver.

	FOOD	DECOR	SERVICE	COST

Kira Steak *Japanese*   ▽ 17 | 12 | 18 | $34

Armonk | Armonk Town Ctr. | 575 Main St. (School St.) | 914-765-0707
"Kids love" this "small" but "fun" Armonk Japanese where "hibachi fare" reigns and there "always seem to be plenty of servers" on hand, including the chefs who put on a "show"; if meat and veggies aren't your thing, "order sushi" from their "connected" sister restaurant.

Kira Sushi *Japanese*   23 | 11 | 17 | $34

Armonk | Armonk Town Ctr. | 575 Main St. (School St.) | 914-765-0800
"Lazy Armonkians" don't "have to travel" far for "excellent" sushi and instead rely on this neighborhood Japanese where "chefs are masters" of both "classic and innovative rolls"; the "fresh and delicious" fish helps offset "rushed service" and a "fast-food atmosphere" that "leaves a lot to be desired."

Kisco Kosher *Deli*   18 | 10 | 14 | $21

White Plains | 230 E. Post Rd. (bet. Mamaroneck Ave. & S. Broadway) | 914-948-6600 | www.kiscokosher.com
It's "about time" a "Jewish deli" came to White Plains kvetch admirers of this kosher restaurant (recently transplanted from its original Mt. Kisco location) "that satisfies" with "large", "first-rate" pastrami and corned beef sandwiches, chopped liver and other "standard" fare; if some declare it "doesn't measure up" to "NYC quality", even they admit it's a "welcome addition" to the neighborhood.

Kit's Thai Kitchen *Thai*   23 | 12 | 18 | $22

Stamford | Turn of the River Shopping Ctr. | 927 High Ridge Rd. (Cedar Heights Rd.), CT | 203-329-7800 | www.kitsthaikitchen.com
This Stamford Asian may be "tiny", "but it delivers big flavors" and "large portions" of "reasonably priced", "wonderful authentic Thai cuisine" ("those afraid of spicy food, beware"); most don't mind the "strip-mall location" or "the downscale decor", but even those who do attest that "takeout is a great option"; P.S. a recent expansion added more seating inside, and there are "a few cute tables outdoors" for dining when the weather's nice.

☒ Koo *Japanese*   24 | 20 | 19 | $49

Rye | 17 Purdy Ave. (2nd St.) | 914-921-9888
Ridgefield | 470 Main St. (Prospect St.), CT | 203-431-8838
www.koorestaurant.com
The "closest thing" to "Nobu in the 'burbs", this "chic", "ultramodern" Japanese in Rye (with a newer Ridgefield, CT, outpost) delivers a "Zen experience" via "beautifully presented" sushi and sashimi as well as "tantalizing" "fusion" dishes; "big tables" and "amazing martinis" make it suited for a "wonderful night out with friends", and though tabs are "high" it's so much "fun", it's "worth the price."

Kotobuki Ⓜ *Japanese*   23 | 11 | 19 | $33

Stamford | 457 Summer St. (bet. Broad & North Sts.), CT | 203-359-4747 | www.kotobukijapaneserestaurant.com
"Eat at the bar" at this "hole-in-the-wall" Stamford Japanese because chef-owner Masanori Sato "knows his customers and takes care of

| | FOOD | DECOR | SERVICE | COST |

them" with "excellent" raw-fish dishes; the "plain" decor is "not impressive", but that doesn't keep the place from being "a local favorite."

Kraft Bistro *American/Mediterranean* 19 | 20 | 18 | $44

Bronxville | 104 Kraft Ave. (bet. Park Pl. & Valley Rd.) | 914-337-4545 | www.kraftbistro.com

Thrill-seekers "looking for something different" head to this "inviting" Bronxville Mediterranean–New American for "sophisticated" and "exotic" dishes like mustard-crusted salmon and skewered lamb; "candles in the window" "set the stage" for an "intimate" evening, though a minority murmurs the "high prices" aren't justified, given sometimes "spotty" service.

Kujaku *Japanese* 20 | 13 | 16 | $31

Stamford | 84 W. Park Pl. (Summer St.), CT | 203-357-0281 | www.kujakustamford.com

"Sake loosens the inhibitions" at this "festive and fraternal" Stamford Japanese "mainstay", where people who believe that "flying knives are fun" "wait in lines for the hibachi"; there's also "good sushi", but that doesn't distract detractors from noticing that the "ugly decor" "is a bit like an unfinished basement" and service is "lacking."

Kyoto Sushi *Japanese* ▽ 24 | 18 | 21 | $28

Kingston | 337 Washington Ave. (Lucas Ave.) | 845-339-1128

"See? you can get good sushi upstate" if you head for this Kingston Japanese fixing "innovative combinations" and "well-prepared" cooked dishes too; red walls and a carpeted floor add warmth to the otherwise simple, traditional setting in the small, brick building.

La Bretagne Ⓢ *French* 23 | 16 | 23 | $51

Stamford | 2010 W. Main St. (bet. Harvard Ave. & Havemeyer Ln.), CT | 203-324-9539 | www.labretagnerestaurant.com

For 30 years, "this time warp" in Stamford has been indulging diners with "delicious dishes" of rich "classical French food" like roast duckling bigarade and "wonderful desserts"; but waiters in "tuxedo"-like uniforms, "faded decor" and "an aging clientele" give thirty-somethings the feeling that they are "dining in a retirement home."

La Camelia Ⓜ *Spanish* 21 | 19 | 21 | $48

Mt. Kisco | 234 N. Bedford Rd./Rte. 117 (Knowlton Ave.) | 914-666-2466 | www.lacameliarestaurant.com

"Feast" on "wonderful" tapas and paella served by a staff that's "attentive, without being obtrusive" at this "quiet" Mt. Kisco Spanish "standby" set in a "charming" 18th-century Colonial house with Picasso and Dali reproductions hanging in the four "cozy" rooms; diners divide on decor, with a few finding it "stodgy" and "worn" while pros profess it exudes an "old-world" feel.

⛝ La Crémaillère Ⓜ *French* 27 | 26 | 25 | $75

Bedford | 46 Bedford-Banksville Rd. (Round House Rd.) | 914-234-9647 | www.cremaillere.com

Feel like a "European noble" and experience "old-world elegance" at this "romantic" Bedford French located in an "undeniably beautiful"

1750 converted farmhouse where "scrumptious" meals are served by a "knowledgeable", "gracious" staff; a few detractors declare it "overwrought" and "stuffy" (jackets are required), but they're drowned out by the majority that maintains it's "earned its reputation" as one of "the best" "splurges" "every season" of "every year."

La Duchesse Anne *French*

∇ – | 15 | 17 | $52

Mt. Tremper | La Duchesse Anne | 1564 Wittenberg Rd. (Rte. 212) | 845-688-5260 | www.laduchesseanne.com

"The jury's still out" on this veteran French spot "now under new management" declare Mt. Tremper residents, noting that chef-owner Fabrice Vittoz turns out "passable" bistro classics, but "suffers the perennial Catskills problem – no help"; still, it's in its early days, and the "romantic" Victorian inn remains the same, so it "could be very charming" with a little "care."

La Fontanella *Italian*

25 | 18 | 26 | $51

Pelham | 115 Wolfs Ln. (bet. 1st & 2nd Sts.) | 914-738-3008

"Everything is done right" at this "rare" Pelham "gem" where "fabulous" Northern Italian fare (including "melt-in-your-mouth" pasta) rivals that of "Florence" and "outstanding" "old-world service" shows they really "care"; "upscale" ambiance comes via white tablecloths and plenty of fresh flowers, and though it gets a bit "cramped" when "crowded", the "close" conditions don't detract from an otherwise "swoonable experience."

Lago di Como Ⓜ *Italian*

21 | 17 | 20 | $43

Tarrytown | 27 Main St. (bet. John & Washington Sts.) | 914-631-7227 | www.lagodicomorestaurant.com

Loyalists love this "low-key", "family-run" eatery in Tarrytown – one block from the Music Hall – where "authentic" Northern Italian specialties are "proudly served" in a "relaxing" atmosphere; design mavens dub the decor "dull", though even they admit the "charming owner makes up for" the dining room's "shortcomings."

Laguna *Italian*

20 | 19 | 18 | $32

White Plains | 189 E. Post Rd. (Waller Ave.) | 914-428-3377

"Big groups" that "love garlic" and "large portions" file into this "family-style" Northern Italian in Downtown White Plains, with "nice round tables" that make it "good" "for parties"; sure there's "lotsa noise" and service can be "kind of slow on busy nights" but all-in-all it's a "solid", "affordable" experience.

La Hacienda *Mexican*

13 | 16 | 16 | $30

Stamford | 222 Summer St. (Broad St.), CT | 203-324-0577 | www.lahaciendastamfordrestaurant.com

Surveyors are split over this Downtown Stamford Mexican: supporters say the "seriously strong margaritas", "serenading" mariachis and "garden seating out back" make them "feel like every day is Cinco de Mayo"; but detractors dismissing the "poor quality of the food" and "fake ambiance" warn "don't take a date here unless you're hoping to give her or him a hint."

	FOOD	DECOR	SERVICE	COST

La Lanterna ⓜ *Italian* `19` `15` `19` `$41`

Yonkers | 23 Grey Oaks Ave. (bet. Barney & Hearst Sts.) | 914-476-3060 | www.lalanterna.com

Diners divide on this "out-of-the-way" Yonkers Italian with a lengthy from-The-Boot wine list, patio dining and live music in summer; proponents proclaim it's "worth the trip" for "well-prepared" and "tasty" fare, however, a chorus of critics claims the food is "run-of-the-mill" and the atmosphere is marred by the "noisy" scene at the bar.

La Manda's 🕾 *Italian* `18` `6` `16` `$27`

White Plains | 251 Tarrytown Rd. (Dobbs Ferry Rd.) | 914-684-9228

"Crowds" of "regulars" "eat, eat, eat" "red-sauce basics" and "thin-crust pizza" at this "homey" "mom-and-pop" (actually father-and-son) Italian in White Plains that's been open since 1947 and is considered "one of the last of the great old-timers"; service is "hectic" and the decor "hasn't changed in decades", but with "embarrassingly low" tabs like these, "who cares?"

La Mexicana *Mexican* ▽ `17` `7` `16` `$14`

Red Hook | 19 W. Market St. (bet. Rte. 9 & St. John St.) | 845-758-6356

It's "about as close to Mexico as you can get" at this Red Hook grocery-cantina dishing up "homestyle" eats for "cheap"; it's a "student hangout", though graduates who find the digs "unappealing" just get takeout – either way, "you can't help loving the place."

Landau Grill *Pub Food* ▽ `12` `9` `13` `$27`

Woodstock | 17 Mill Hill Rd./Rte. 212 (Maple Ln.) | 845-679-8937

"Food is not the attraction" at this "funky" Woodstock New American "pub" – it's the "streetside patio" where, "if weather permits", locals linger to watch "hippies and tourists" "coming and going"; service is just "ok" and eats simply "serviceable", so most choose to chow down on burgers and quaff "an icy draft" while they view "village life."

Landmark Inn ⓜ *American* ▽ `17` `15` `18` `$40`

Warwick | 526 Rte. 94 N. (8½ mi. south of Rte. 17) | 845-986-5444

Warwick locals "feel at home" in this "old-reliable" Traditional American set in a Colonial farmhouse whose rustic decor includes a wood-burning stove and topsy-turvy touches like doors on the ceiling; critics decree the "creative cuisine attempts don't quite make it", although simpler fare in the separate pub is "good."

Lange's Deli *Deli* `18` `5` `13` `$13`

Scarsdale | 57 Spencer Pl. (Popham Rd.) | 914-472-0330 | www.langesdeli.com

"Everything you could want" in a "corner deli", this recently renovated Scarsdale "institution" satisfies supporters with "quality" overstuffed "sandwiches" and prepared foods that are "a cut above" the rest; "lines" are a regular occurrence during the "crazy lunchtime" rush, so "unless you like other people's elbows", you'll want to avoid eating in the "normally crowded" space, and opt either for "carry-out" or the "sidewalk seating area."

	FOOD	DECOR	SERVICE	COST

Lanterna Tuscan Bistro *Italian*   21 | 18 | 21 | $45

NEW **Larchmont** | 147 Larchmont Ave. (Boston Post Rd.) | 914-834-8700
Nyack | 3 S. Broadway (Main St.) | 845-353-8361
www.lanternausa.com

"Talented chef" Rossano Giannini's "popular" Nyack spot is known for "hearty" dishes, "personal", "unrushed" service and digs so "tight" the seating's strictly "for skinny people"; now he's "moved over the bridge" to add a roomier Larchmont sibling; both venues have a Tuscany-via-SoHo bistro vibe, with monthly cooking demos and "occasional celebrity sightings" as added inducements.

☑ La Panetière *French*   27 | 27 | 26 | $78

Rye | 530 Milton Rd. (Oakland Beach Ave.) | 914-967-8140 | www.lapanetiere.com

"When you can't get to Paris", a "remarkable meal" awaits at this Rye "grandmother of elegant French restaurants" that's "beautifully furnished" to resemble a Provençal country inn; owner Jacques Loupiac "oversees every detail", from the staff that "caters to every whim" to the "superb" fare and "voluminous" wine list; N.B. jacket required.

La Piccola Casa *Italian*   ▽ 21 | 11 | 21 | $42

Mamaroneck | 1422 E. Boston Post Rd. (Greenhaven Rd.) | 914-777-3766

"Personal service" and "consistently" "fine meals" await at this "underrated", "informal" Mamaroneck Northern Italian "joint"; still, comfort-hounds claim the "tight" "quarters dampen the experience", which is "a pity because it's very good on other counts."

NEW La Puerta Azul ⓜ *Mexican*   ▽ 16 | 25 | 16 | $35

Salt Point | Sicamore Sq. | 2510 Rte. 44 (Rte. 82 & Taconic State Pkwy.) | 845-677-2985 | www.lapuertaazul.com

Beyond the blue door lies "amazing decor" at this colorful Dutchess County Mexican newcomer all tricked out with mosaics, wrought-iron accents, a waterfall in the entrance and a "Spanish tiled bathroom to gawk at"; less successful are the "complicated", "overly ambitious" menu ("could you please make a normal taco?") and service that needs to get "on the ball", but locals say "give it a chance to work out the kinks" "and see what happens."

Larchmont Tavern *American*   15 | 13 | 17 | $24

Larchmont | 104 Chatsworth Ave. (bet. Boston Post Rd. & Palmer Ave.) | 914-834-9821 | www.larchmonttavern.com

This "convivial" American "tavern" open since 1933 (the original bar is still there) was "recently updated" for Larchmont "yuppies", adding flat-screen TVs, but keeping the menu "mostly intact" with "basic" grub like sandwiches, burgers and salads that are "decent enough"; "local color" and a "where-everybody-knows-your-name" "vibe" prevail, though a disappointed few lament it's "not what it used to be."

La Riserva Trattoria *Italian*   21 | 17 | 22 | $41

Larchmont | 2382 Boston Post Rd. (Deane Pl.) | 914-834-5584

"Well-prepared" "traditional Italian food" keeps a steady stream of "regulars" returning to this Larchmont "favorite" that fans are happy to report "has gotten better"; if the menu "could use some jazzing up", "spacious" surroundings and "accommodating" servers still make it a "nice quiet evening."

La Salière *French*   21 | 16 | 17 | $44

Ridgefield | 3 Big Shop Ln. (Main St.), CT | 203-438-1976
"The fish tank should be a hint that the best bets are seafood" at this "pleasant" Ridgefield French whose chef-owner was the cook for the royal family of Monaco; patrons praise the "very good food", but are less content with the "erratic service" and note that while "it's not as pricey as when it first opened", tabs are still "steep."

La Scala 🅼 *Italian*   20 | 13 | 20 | $44

Armonk | Olive Branch Shopping Ctr. | 386 Main St. (Bedford Rd.) | 914-273-3508
"Simple" and "solid", if "predictable", dishes like chicken scarpariello are offered at this "homey" Armonk Italian that's both "friendly" and "comfortable"; though the decor could use "sprucing up", "gracious" servers who "try hard" "almost make up for" the "tired-out" digs.

La Stazione *Italian*   19 | 19 | 17 | $33

New Paltz | 5 Main St. (Huguenot St.) | 845-256-9447
"When it's good, it's very good" at this "jolly" New Paltz Italian set in a "beautifully renovated" 1870 railroad station decorated with timetables and photographs from its heydey; although it is "inexperienced", service is "prompt and energetic", while carpets in the newly enlarged dining room help reduce "loud" decibels; for real peace, patrons head outside to the "well-done" patio.

Last Chance Antiques &   ▽ 21 | 18 | 23 | $23
Cheese Café *American*
(fka Last Chance Cheese Shop)

Tannersville | 602 Main St. (Railroad Ave.) | 518-589-6424 | www.lastchanceonline.com
You can "shop for gourmet gifts" and antiques too, at this "fun" Traditional American eatery-cum-store tucked in the Catskill mountain town of Tannersville; it's a "pleasant surprise", offering "a great beer selection", "onion soup to die for", "pot pies" and "macaroni and cheese made with aged cheddar" – "talk about comfort food!"

Latin American Cafe *Cuban*   20 | 9 | 18 | $23

White Plains | 134 E. Post Rd. (Mamaroneck Ave.) | 914-948-6606
This "welcoming" White Plains "mainstay" for "tasty" and "filling" Cuban fare is a "nice choice" for transplants who "miss Miami" and "generous portions" of beef, roast pork and coconut flan; the less-than-striking digs have some relegating this to a "lunch" place (with "reasonably priced" specials), while others go for "takeout."

La Trattoria 🅂 *Italian*   23 | 14 | 22 | $37

New Rochelle | North Ridge Shopping Ctr. | 77 Quaker Ridge Rd. (North Ave.) | 914-235-2727
"Kudos" for "amazingly prepared" Italian fare including "interesting specials" at this New Rochelle "neighborhood treasure" with service

FOOD DECOR SERVICE COST

that's "all in the family" – the chef-owner's "wife is the hostess" and "a daughter or two" occasionally wait tables; "quality" cuisine trumps decor, but despite the strip-mall setting, "it's always crowded."

La Villetta ⓈＩ *Italian/Seafood*   24 | 16 | 24 | $50

Larchmont | 7 Madison Ave. (N. Chatsworth Ave.) | 914-833-9416
"You can count on" "superb" cuisine at this Larchmont "gem" where "excellent service" (many dishes are finished tableside) and "fine" seafood "set it apart from other local Italian restaurants"; though candlelight and fresh flowers ratchet up the romance factor, "incredibly noisy" conditions have fans "wishing fewer people knew about it."

Lazy Boy Saloon ◑ *Pub Food*   17 | 14 | 17 | $23

White Plains | 154 Mamaroneck Ave. (bet. E. Post Rd. & Maple Ave.) | 914-761-0272 | www.lazyboysaloon.com
"Fun crowds" of boozehounds congregate at this White Plains "sports bar" for an "astounding" selection of brews from around the globe and "good" "pub grub", including nine varieties of Buffalo wings; it's "loud when busy", especially during *"Monday Night Football."*

Le Bouchon *French*   22 | 19 | 20 | $40

Cold Spring | 76 Main St. (Rock St.) | 845-265-7676
"Lusty" brasserie cuisine (with the "best pommes frites this side of Paris") keeps francophiles filing into "local Frenchman" Pascal Graff's Cold Spring "favorite"; "lots of mirrors" make the "small, welcoming" bright-red space seem "roomier", while those who "like to dine alfresco" declare the terrace in "the lovely garden" has "a certain charm", and "lunch on the porch, watching the shoppers, is fun" too.

Le Canard Enchainé *French*   24 | 22 | 23 | $42

Kingston | 276 Fair St. (bet. John & Main Sts.) | 845-339-2003 | www.lecanard-enchaine.net
Everything's *"très français"* at Jean-Jacques Carquillat's "delightful" Uptown Kingston bistro, from "excellent" "real" "country French cuisine" (and a "fabulous prix fixe lunch") to the "fine service" delivered by an authentic Gallic staff "passionate about food"; the "sharp setting" blends an "edgy" "slice of Paris" with "upstate serenity", while the "cozy little" piano bar is abuzz with *musique* on weekends.

Le Chambord *French*   22 | 22 | 20 | $61

Hopewell Junction | Le Chambord | 2737 Rte. 52 (Carpenter Rd.) | 845-221-1941 | www.lechambord.com
A Georgian manor house full of chandeliers, paintings and antiques provides a "lovely setting" for "classical French" fare, at this Dutchess County hideaway beloved of "couples on their anniversary"; detractors declare it "a bit froufrou", "not for gastronauts" and "expensive" to boot, but pros protest "it's always a pleasure."

Ⓩ Le Château Ⓜ *French*   25 | 27 | 24 | $68

South Salem | 1410 Rte. 35 (Rte. 123) | 914-533-6631 | www.lechateauny.com
A "magnificent" "pastoral setting" in an old Tudor "mansion on a hill" makes this "fantastic" South Salem French with "wonderfully

attentive service", a "fine wine cellar" and private rooms accentuated by votive candles the "place to impress someone"; it's a "special" experience from the trip "up the long driveway" to the last spoonful of "to-die-for" soufflé, so "save your money", "get gussied up" and expect "a 'memorable'" "top-of-the-line" "formal" evening.

Le Fontane Ristorante 🅼 *Italian*   21 | 18 | 23 | $40

Katonah | 137 Rte. 100 (Rte. 139) | 914-232-9619 | www.lefontane.net

"The welcome is always warm" from "caring owners" showing lots of "family pride" in their "consistent" Southern Italian in Katonah, where the chef knows "the secrets" of "preparing fine", "fresh" food; pros promise even "hard-to-please" patrons will "enjoy" the experience, enhanced by live guitar midweek and "summer dining" on the terrace.

☑ Lefteris Gyro *Greek*   21 | 9 | 17 | $21

Mt. Kisco | 190 E. Main St. (bet. Dakin Ave. & Lundy Ln.) | 914-242-8965
Tarrytown | 1 N. Main St. (B'way) | 914-524-9687
www.lefterisgyro.com

"You can't beat the price" at these "homestyle" Hellenics in Tarrytown and Mt. Kisco where *"Flintstones*-sized" portions of "warm pitas", "fat gyros" and "fresh" salads with "yummy" "home-made dressing" keep both spots "crowded" "for a reason"; the "friendly" if "frenzied" staff turns "tables quickly", so the only "major downside" is "spartan" decor.

☑ Legal Sea Foods *Seafood*   19 | 17 | 16 | $40

White Plains | City Center Mall | 5 Mamaroneck Ave. (Main St.) | 914-390-9600
West Nyack | Palisades Ctr. | 4304 Palisades Center Dr. (NY Thrwy., exit 12) | 845-353-5757
www.legalseafoods.com

For a "real New England fix", "seafood groupies" and "mall rats" doggy-paddle to these "dependable" White Plains and West Nyack chain outposts with "consistently" "decent" fish and a "chowda" that wins raves; "college kid" servers are "sometimes inattentive" and a few mutineers grumble the "quality doesn't measure up to the price", yet most feel "lucky to have them" along their stretch of the beach.

Le Jardin du Roi ❶ *French*   20 | 18 | 21 | $42

Chappaqua | 95 King St. (bet. N. Greeley Ave. & Prospect Dr.) | 914-238-1368 | www.lejardinchappaqua.com

"Solid bistro fare" – in the form of a "classy breakfast", "leisurely lunch" or "an intimate dinner" – makes this Chappaqua French "a place to return to", especially if you can "snag" a "coveted" "garden table"; "rustic" decor and "closely spaced tables" lend a "Parisian feel" while a "warm reception" from the staff ensures a "delightful" time for all; a bonus – it's "a kick" to see the Clintons "drop by every now and then."

NEW Lejends *Caribbean/Southern*   – | – | – | E

Yonkers | 22 Warburton Ave. (bet. Dock & Main Sts.) | 914-709-9840 | www.lejendsrestaurant.com

This upscale Caribbean-Southern newcomer to Yonkers' revitalized waterfront features sophisticated takes on down-home classics in-

| | FOOD | DECOR | SERVICE | COST |

cluding guava BBQ babyback ribs, three-cheese macaroni and jerk chicken; black-and-white photographs honoring music greats Ray Charles, Billie Holiday, Ella Fitzgerald and Bob Marley line the walls while exposed brick, high ceilings and two waterfalls intensify the cool factor.

Lena's *European*   21 | 22 | 21 | $50

Nyack | Nyack Seaport | 2 Spear St. (Piermont Ave.) | 845-353-7733 | www.lenasrestaurant.com

With its "romantic setting on the river", airy dining room with "lots of flowers" and French doors overlooking "nice views" of the Tappan Zee bridge, this Nyack European is just the spot for a "leisurely" meal respondents agree; otherwise opinions differ – though the staff is "well-informed", "a change of chef" has some saying the fare is "disappointing", others that it's still "terrific."

⚡ Le Pavillon 🅂🄼 *French*   27 | 23 | 24 | $45

Poughkeepsie | 230 Salt Point Tpke./Rte. 115 (bet. Bedell Rd. & N. Grand Ave.) | 845-473-2525 | www.lepavillonrestaurant.com

For the "best coq au vin", the "crispest, most succulent duck this side of Normandy" and other "perfect" "classic French fare of the *grandmère* variety", Poughkeepsie denizens head out to chef-owner Claude Guermont's tucked away "longtime favorite"; the "romantic" "country house" setting is "still elegant after all these years" and the staff "lovely", making this "genuine" experience "worth a drive", no matter how "long."

⚡ Le Petit Bistro *French*   26 | 19 | 24 | $43

Rhinebeck | 8 E. Market St./Rte. 308 (Rte. 9) | 845-876-7400 | www.lepetitbistro.com

Francophiles squash into Joseph Dalu's "absolutely charming" Rhinebeck French bistro, knowing that "anything from a snack at the bar to a romantic dinner" will be "impeccably prepared"; "brilliant specials" and "superior", "not fawning service" help cancel out the "only negative: the proximity of adjoining tables", because "petit is the word" for the super-"cozy" room; even so, "it feels great to be" at this "winner."

Le Provençal Bistro *French*   23 | 19 | 21 | $48

Mamaroneck | 436 Mamaroneck Ave. (bet. Mt. Pleasant & Palmer Aves.) | 914-777-2324 | www.provencalbistro.com

"Terrific" fare "in the true spirit" of bistro cooking can be had at this "charming", "down-to-earth" Mamaroneck French adorned with posters of Provence, where the "all-you-can-eat mussels" special (Sunday–Thursday) gets raves and you're "never rushed" by the "courteous" servers; in all, it's a "perfectly charming experience every single time", even on "noisy" "weekends."

L'Escale *French*   21 | 24 | 20 | $63

Greenwich | Delamar Hotel | 500 Steamboat Rd. (I-95, exit 3), CT | 203-661-4600 | www.lescalerestaurant.com

Sit under the chandeliers or out on the terrace and enjoy the "beautiful view" of the Long Island Sound at this Greenwich "power-dining

FOOD DECOR SERVICE COST

scene" and "fabulous summer spot" ensconced in "a wonderful boutique hotel"; "hedge-fund honchos and their diamond-clad trophy wives" favor the "excellent" French Provençal cuisine, but others find it "overpriced" and "overhyped" and observe that the bar is often "filled with throngs of fortysomething cougars looking to secure their futures by picking up a banker."

L'Europe Restaurant Ⓜ *Continental*   24 | 20 | 23 | $68

South Salem | 407 Smith Ridge Rd./Rte. 123 (Tommys Ln.) | 914-533-2570 | www.leuroperestaurant.com

A "very mature" crowd "dresses up and eats well" at this "pretty" South Salem Continental, set on four acres on the Connecticut border, that's a "lovely throwback" to "civilized grown-up dining"; a "superior Sunday brunch" and "old-world courtliness" make it a "choice for special occasions", though the drapes that look straight out of "your grandmother's house" have a handful of reviewers grading the atmosphere as "stuffy."

Lexington Square Café *American*   18 | 19 | 18 | $40

Mt. Kisco | 510 Lexington Ave. (Rte. 117) | 914-244-3663 | www.lexingtonsquarecafe.com

There's "something for everyone" cheer champions of this "lively", "local" spot in Mt. Kisco that's "a cut above the typical bistro" with "wide-ranging", "tasty" New American cuisine and "helpful" servers; "soaring ceilings" and a "hopping bar scene" give the space a "NYC" feel, though the "overbearing noise level" can be an "intrusion" into an otherwise "enjoyable" experience.

Lia's Ⓜ *Italian*   21 | 18 | 18 | $43

Hartsdale | 202 E. Hartsdale Ave. (Rockledge Rd.) | 914-725-8400

"Original" "top-notch" fare that's "not your usual Italian" garners raves from reviewers who are "greeted warmly every time" at this "intimate" Hartsdale "neighborhood" spot; though a few grumble about "spotty" service and tabs "too costly" for the "understated" environment, they're outnumbered by supporters who swear it's a "great" "find."

Lia's Mountain View Ⓜ *Italian*   ▽ 16 | 9 | 18 | $27

Pine Plains | 7685 Rte. 82 S. (Rte. 83) | 518-398-7311 | www.liasmountainview.com

Pine Plains denizens in pursuit of "basic", "home-cooked", "red-sauce Italian" eats find it at this "neighborhood" spot, where the "value's good" and the welcome "friendly"; two fireplaces help make up for "sparse" decor in the rustic room, as does a view of Stissing mountain from the deck.

Lighthouse on the Hudson *American*   16 | 20 | 15 | $38

Piermont | 701 Piermont Ave. (bet. Bay & Ritie Sts.) | 845-365-1986 | www.lighthousehudson.com

"It's a lot of fun in summer" at this riverfront Piermont American, where the "Hudson is practically lapping at your toes", so most sit at an "umbrella table on the large deck", overlook the "mundane menu" and "clueless service" and just drink in "gorgeous views" of the Tappan Zee bridge while sipping something "stiff" from the tiki bar.

Lipperas' at the Chatham House *Continental*

| 19 | 21 | 19 | $40 |

Chatham | The Chatham Hse. | 29 Hudson Ave. (bet. Maiden Ln. & School St.) | 518-392-6600 | www.thechathamhouse.com

"What a find!" exclaim enthusiasts of this "upscale-for-Columbia-County" Continental two-year-old housed in a "magnificently restored" 19th-century hotel; a "terrific staff" serves diners as they tuck into "high-quality" – if sometimes "uneven" – fare in the "spacious" main room with its brick arches, by the fireplace in the "casual taproom" or "on the porch in summer."

Little Mexican Cafe ● *Mexican*

▽ 23 | 14 | 20 | $23 |

New Rochelle | 581 Main St. (Centre Ave.) | 914-636-3926

"Authentic flavors of Mexico" including "guacamole, margaritas" and tacos *al pastor* (with chile-rubbed, spit roasted pork) have made this "cheap" New Rochelle cafe "with a big heart" a favorite; "kind service" awaits in either of the two seating sections – one for full-service dining and the other for watching satellite TV and eating at the bar.

Little Sorrento *Italian*

| 18 | 11 | 17 | $25 |

Cortlandt | Parkside Corner Shopping Ctr. | 3565 Crompond Rd. (bet. Bear Mountain State Pkwy. & Lexington Ave.) | 914-736-6767 | www.littlesorrento.com

Carboholics count on pizza, pasta and "fantastic homemade bread" ("crusty and fresh from the brick oven") at this "old-style" Italian tucked into a Cortlandt strip mall where a "friendly" staff and "fair" prices ensure it's a "pleasant" "neighborhood" spot; the "casual" "storefront" setting is stocked with foodstuffs and pottery for sale (and is browsing-friendly) making "waits" just a little more bearable.

NEW Little Thai Kitchen *Thai*

| 22 | 11 | 17 | $26 |

Darien | 4 West Ave. (Boston Post Rd./Rte. 1), CT | 203-662-0038
Greenwich | 21 St. Roch Ave. (Gerry St.), CT | 203-622-2972
www.littlethaikitchen.com

"Don't spread the word about the favorable reviews too far" order admirers of this "delicious, genuine" "hole-in-the-wall" Thai duo; with "food as good as you'd get in Bangkok", these "great finds" "get very busy", leaving some to grouse that "they can't handle their take-out business"; N.B. the new Darien outpost serves beer and wine, but it's still BYO at the Greenwich original.

NEW Local 111 Ⓜ *American*

| – | – | – | M |

Philmont | 111 Main St. (Summit St.) | 518-672-7801 | www.local111.com

"Relying on regional farms" for produce makes this "friendly" New American newcomer in Columbia County "something special" advise advocates, who enjoy "stellar" meals at "very good prices" in the "really cool" space – a converted garage now all industrial chic with a golden-brown concrete floor, walnut tables edged in steel and an L-shaped bar to match; even though it's "still finding its way, it's very promising."

NEW Locust Restaurant & | - | - | - | M |
Pizzeria *Italian*
Fishkill | 1105 Main St. (Hopewell Ave.) | 845-896-4100
Another entry from Sali Hadzi, who owns the highly rated Il Cenàcolo and Cena 2000, this family-oriented Fishkill yearling is more down-home than its tony siblings, offering simpler Southern Italian red-sauce classics like veal francese, zuppa di pesce and lasagna; the building welcomes patrons with a gingerbread Victorian porch, while the small, casual dining room is warmed by brick walls and earthy colors.

Locust Tree *European* | 21 | 23 | 21 | $45 |
New Paltz | 215 Huguenot St. (Mulberry St.) | 845-255-7888 | www.locusttree.com
"Screamingly romantic, especially when the fire's going" or "the candles are lit", this Northern European set in a "lovely" 18th-century stone house hidden outside New Paltz is "worth the trouble to find"; inside, "talented chef" Barbara Bogart prepares "very good", "imaginative" meals (like signature suckling pig), while hubby Robert Khimeche heads up "sincere" service, so why not just "kick back and let the staff spoil you rotten."

Long Ridge Tavern *American* | 15 | 19 | 17 | $35 |
Stamford | 2635 Long Ridge Rd. (Rte. 104), CT | 203-329-7818 | www.longridgetavern.com
An inviting "fieldstone fireplace", a "cozy *Cheers*-esque bar" and "jazz bands on Saturdays" are reasons this "lively" North Stamford tavern attracts "locals"; but even some of them say "if only" the "average and unremarkable" American food "matched the surroundings."

Lotus King *Chinese* | 18 | 15 | 20 | $24 |
Eastchester | 36 Mill Rd. (Rte. 22) | 914-779-9006
"Genial" owner Peter will "make you feel at home" at this "cheap", "reliable" Eastchester Chinese that's "been there for years" offering "consistently good" renditions of "down-home" Sino classics; "eager-to-please" servers who are especially "accommodating" to children overcome the rather "basic" "traditional" surroundings.

Louie & Johnnies' Ristorante *Italian* | ▽ 22 | 16 | 20 | $31 |
Yonkers | 706 Central Park Ave. (Miles Square Rd.) | 914-423-3300
"It gets crowded" at this "affordable" Yonkers Southern Italian serving "huge portions" of "tasty" "down-home" fare in a "simple and airy" dining room; as for the "offbeat location" and the "old-world" vibe that's "straight out of *Goodfellas*" – well, that's all part of the charm.

Z Luca Ristorante Italiano **Ⓢ** *Italian* | 27 | 22 | 26 | $53 |
Wilton | 142 Old Ridgefield Rd. (Godfrey Pl.), CT | 203-563-9550 | www.lucaristoranteitaliano.com
Enthusiasts exclaim *molto bene!* over this small, "outstanding Italian" "in the heart of Wilton", with "dynamite food" and "home-

made pastas and desserts"; the chef-owner and staff are "delight-fully friendly and attentive", the "wine list is wonderful" and the earth-toned, low-lit room is "romantic"; it's also "packed and pricey but worth it."

Luce Restaurant Ⓜ *Italian* ▽ 22 | 20 | 22 | $47

Somers | 254 Rte. 100 (bet. Golden Bridge Rd. & Primrose St.) | 914-232-8080

"The owners" – a father and two sons – have done a "marvelous" job at this "elegant" "addition" to Somers that offers Northern Italian "classics" served by a "formal" tuxedo-clad staff; the "pretty" interior includes two Tuscan-inspired rooms (one the color of red wine, the other terra-cotta) each with white linens, candlelight and a fireplace.

Lucky's *Diner* 16 | 18 | 17 | $17

Stamford | 209 Bedford St. (bet. Broad & Spring Sts.), CT | 203-978-0268

This "retro '50s diner" dishing up burgers, fries and shakes in Downtown Stamford may provide "a flash from the past for baby boomers" and it's "fun for kids" too, (especially on weekends when the staff sings and dances); but while a few feel lucky to find "cheap eats", many lament the "mediocre" quality of the fare.

Luc's Café Ⓩ *French* 23 | 20 | 20 | $41

Ridgefield | 3 Big Shop Ln. (bet. Bailey Ave. & Main St.), CT | 203-894-8522

For "non-fussy, non-truffled" French fare you can't do better in Ridgefield than this "cozy, cellarlike space", where the mainstay is "croque monsieur" and "madame is the appellative norm"; surveyors say this "always-bustling" bistro gets its bonhomie from the" "spirited host" who is "always on hand" and "makes it the kind of place where you can comfortably hang out with friends."

Luna 61 Ⓜ *Vegetarian* ▽ 20 | 13 | 18 | $22

Tivoli | 55 Broadway (bet. Feroe Ave. & Montgomery St.) | 845-758-0061 | www.luna61.com

"Vegans rule!" at this Eclectic health-fooder that recently moved from Red Hook into posher digs in nearby Tivoli, and now delivers "delish" "veggie delights" in a modern, candlelit space with a spiral staircase (Decor ratings may not reflect the switch); somewhat "cranky service" doesn't deter even "meat eaters from coming back", and if you want to feel more "virtuous" still, there's "organic beer and wine too.

Ⓩ Lusardi's *Italian* 23 | 21 | 22 | $54

Larchmont | 1885 Palmer Ave. (bet. Chatsworth Ave. & Weaver St.) | 914-834-5555 | www.lusardislarchmont.com

"A neighborhood restaurant that knows how to please", this "bustling" Northern Italian in Larchmont (an offshoot of the NYC original) sets "the county standard" with "delicious" pastas and entrees, an "unbelievable wine list" and a staff of "seasoned professionals" that "treats you like a regular, even if you're not"; whether dining by the "cozy fireplace" or on "tables outside in the summer", it's a "clubby" "Manhattan" scene with "prices to match."

	FOOD	DECOR	SERVICE	COST

Lu Shane's Ⓜ *American*

	23	20	21	$49

Nyack | 8 N. Broadway (bet. Main & New Sts.) | 845-358-5556

"Kangaroo, ostrich, elk" – "there's always at least one exotic dish" on the "outstanding" Traditional American menu at this "trendy" little Nyack "Siamese twin to Heather's Open Cucina"; a "youngish crowd keeps the place hopping", and although the stylish "long copper bar and tin ceilings" do nothing to deaden "deafening" noise, the vibe is "festive", so dinner here feels like a "fun" "night out."

Mackenzie's Grill Room *Pub Food*

	16	13	18	$25

Old Greenwich | 148 Sound Beach Ave. (Webb Ave.), CT | 203-698-0223 | www.mackenziesgrillroom.com

"Commuters" gravitate to this Traditional American grill next to the train station for "a burger and a drink"; it's an "old-school pub" that's "a retreat from the ladies-who-lunch of Old Greenwich" and "one of the few reasonably priced options for simple food" in the area.

MacMenamin's Grill & ChefWorks *American*

	22	22	19	$51

New Rochelle | 115 Cedar St. (I-95, exit 16) | 914-632-4900 | www.macmenaminsgrill.com

"You feel like you're in a SoHo loft" at this New Rochelle New American set in an "airy", "atmospheric" former factory with exposed-brick walls and hardwood floors; the "well-presented", if "pricey", cuisine wins fans who call this "cool" spot "a terrific date place" (and "a nice surprise off of I-95 to boot"), but a few naysayers label it "inconsistent", with service that can be "spotty at best."

NEW Madalin's Table Ⓜ *American*

	▽ 19	23	19	$37

Tivoli | Madalin Hotel | 53 Broadway (Montgomery St.) | 845-757-2100 | www.madalinhotel.com

"A hit since it opened", this "trendy" Tivoli newcomer set in a "beautifully restored old hotel" is a "lively" "class act"; a "welcoming" staff serves a seasonal New American menu in either its dining room, where rich red walls top gray wainscot, the informal tavern or on the wraparound porch, where diners "sit and watch the street scene."

NEW Made In Asia *Asian*

	-	-	-	M

Armonk | 454 Main St. (bet. Annadale St. & Orchard Dr.) | 914-730-3663

Opening in the former Ginseng space, this Asian newcomer adorned with Beijing opera masks offers an extensive menu of sushi and sashimi as well as Malaysian, Thai and Chinese dishes; three tatami rooms allow patrons to kick off their shoes and sip passion fruit mai tais in private.

Maestro's *Italian*

	▽ 16	11	16	$28

New Rochelle | 1329 North Ave. (Quaker Ridge Rd.) | 914-636-6813

Maestro's II *Italian*

Jefferson Valley | Lourdes Shopping Ctr. | 3673 Hill Blvd. (Rte. 6) | 914-245-9241

A "favorite" take-out spot for families, these New Rochelle and Jefferson Valley "neighborhood Italians" dish up "reliable, though not inventive" takes on red-sauce classics; if service is "well-intentioned, but uneven" and the decor seems "a little tired", remember they're basically "glorified pizzerias."

Maggie's in the Alley ⓜ *American*
— | — | — | M

Chester | Bodles Opera Hse. | 39 Main St. (Bank St.) | 845-469-4595 | www.maggiesinthealley.com

Tucked under Bodles Opera House, this Chester New American incorporates wooden sleigh runners and other remains from the building's former incarnation as a carriage factory into the decor alongside recycled church pews and a repro tin ceiling; it all sets a mellow mood for boomers chowing down on cuisine that ranges from tapas to pecan-crusted venison and signature tuna tataki.

Maggie's Krooked Café *American*
— | — | — | I

Tannersville | 6000 Main St./Rte. 23A (bet. Church & Tompkins Sts.) | 518-589-6101

For "unbelievably good muffins and pancakes", a "fresh, healthy" breakfast or lunch, or the "best takeout in the area", locals and weekenders alike head straight to Maggie Landis' colorful, rustic BYO Tannersville New American, where the focus is on organic ingredients; it's now celebrating its 20th anniversary, and there's nothing crooked about that.

Main Course ⓜ *American*
23 | 12 | 18 | $28

New Paltz | 232 Main St./Rte. 299 (bet. Manheim Blvd. & N. Chestnut St.) | 845-255-2600 | www.maincourserestaurant.com

"Delicious", "seasonal" New American fare is the main reason to go to this "been-there-forever" New Paltz venue owned by caterer Bruce Kazan; "usually good" service is sometimes "a little neglectful", and "redecorated" digs "better" than before, but folks fretting that to them it's "still an old bank" in "an ugly shopping plaza" say it's "perfect for takeout" – and for kids under 12, who eat free.

Main Course at Alumnae House *American*
▽ 20 | 22 | 20 | $30

Poughkeepsie | Alumnae Hse. | 161 College View (bet. Fulton St. & Raymond Ave.) | 845-437-7153 | www.maincourserestaurant.com

"Worth a visit" for the "charming" "historic Vassar college inn setting" alone, this two-year-old Poughkeepsie outpost from chef Bruce Kazan got off to "a slow start", but now draws fans with "consistent", "attractively displayed" New American fare (plus "amazing" breakfasts and lunches for "cheap"); diners usually sit in the "handsome pub" room with its rafters, minstrel's balcony and 1940s murals, although there's additional seating in the library and living room.

Main Street Cafe ⓜ *American*
16 | 13 | 17 | $27

Tarrytown | 24 Main St. (Rte. 9) | 914-524-9770

Loyalists stand by this "family-run" "staple" in Tarrytown, finding it a "decent little place to meet friends" for "simple", "inexpensive" American chow served by a "friendly" staff; dissenters are turned off by the "dated" antique tchotchkes and "country-blue decor" –

FOOD DECOR SERVICE COST

though sidewalk seating makes it "fun" to "sit outside on a warm day" and "watch the world go by."

Malabar Hill Indian
23 | 16 | 19 | $32

Elmsford | 145 E. Main St. (Robbinson Ave.) | 914-347-7890 | www.fineindiandining.com

Get "an education in Indian cooking" in Elmsford from "eager-to-please" servers who guide you through "delicious" midpriced offerings, many "homestyle dishes not usually found" this side of the subcontinent as well as a "diverse" beer selection; foodwise, it's a "spice lover's paradise", but mal-contents argue the decor is "sparse" and could use something to spice up those saffron-colored walls.

Mamma Assunta Italian
19 | 15 | 19 | $36

Tuckahoe | 20 Columbus Ave. (Main St.) | 914-961-8142 | www.mammaassuntaristorante.com

Tuckahoe denizens count on this "reliable" "red-sauce" Italian for "hearty" dishes served by a "welcoming owner and staff"; a crackling fireplace adds to the "warm", "intimate" ambiance, but many still feel "Mamma needs to improve" the "tired"-looking digs.

Mamma Francesca Italian
19 | 15 | 19 | $33

New Rochelle | 414 Pelham Rd. (bet. Meadow Ln. & Town Dock Rd.) | 914-636-1229

Politicians power lunch at this "unassuming" New Rochelle Italian, which regales regulars with "traditional" dishes, a "comfortable" setting and "accommodating" service; add in "moderate" prices, a "view overlooking the harbor" and a "welcoming" owner who sometimes serenades the diners, and you get a "good local restaurant" no matter what your affiliation.

Mango Café Nuevo Latino
17 | 14 | 18 | $27

Mt. Kisco | 222 E. Main St./Rte. 117 (W. Hyatt Ave.) | 914-666-3238 | www.almangocafe.com

"Bring the kids" to this "friendly" "family place" in Mt. Kisco that serves up "large portions" of "dependable" Nuevo Latino fare at "reasonable prices"; if you find the "noisy" atmosphere a bit overwhelming, try to find a sidewalk table in season and remember that you "can always count on" the "fantastic" margaritas.

Manna Dew Cafe Ⓜ Eclectic
▽ 22 | 16 | 20 | $40

Millerton | 54 Main St. (Center St.) | 518-789-3500

Revolving art exhibits and live music lend this "lively" Millerton Eclectic the air "of a wine bar", but fans say it's been "evolving" into a "serious" restaurant that attracts locals and weekending "city folk" with "fine" fare like handmade pasta and "excellent desserts", all served by a "chatty" staff; N.B. open Thursday–Sunday.

Marcello's Italian
24 | 18 | 23 | $47

Suffern | 21 Lafayette Ave./Rte. 59 (Orange Ave.) | 845-357-9108 | www.marcellosgroup.com

All is *molto bene* purr pleased patrons at "renowned local chef" Marcello Russodivito's Suffern spot serving "superb" "updated"

Italian "classics with a light touch"; tabs may be "a little pricey" and "1970s decor" "less than elegant", but the "staff makes you feel at home" anyway; those who'd like tips from the "culinary genius" himself can sign up for one of the frequent cooking classes.

Marco ▯ American   ▽ 22 | 17 | 17 | $45

Lake Mahopac | 612 Main St./Rte. 6 (6 mi. south of I-684) | 845-621-1648 | www.marcoarestaurant.com

"Idiosyncratic, that's Marco" declare fans of Mark Donelli, the "ponytailed" chef-owner producing an equally "unusual" New American menu at his Putnam County eatery; two rooms, one wainscoted with a long bar, the other gussied up in purple and silver, serve as a backdrop for "very good" "exotic beef", "excellent game", seafood and the like, with a "nice wine list" as well.

Marianacci's ▯ Italian   21 | 13 | 18 | $41

Port Chester | 24 Sherman St. (S. Regent St.) | 914-939-3450 | www.marianaccis.com

An "old standby" for more than 50 years, this Port Chester Southern Italian is a "local landmark" that "old-timers continue to return to" for "excellent dishes" prepared with a "family touch"; though loyalists laud the "low-key" atmosphere as "comforting" and "quiet", most deem the "dreary setting" "tired" and call for it to be "updated."

Marion's Country Kitchen ▯ European   22 | 19 | 20 | $36

Woodstock | Woodstock Lodge | 20 Country Club Ln. (Rte. 375) | 845-679-3213 | www.marionscountrykitchen.com

Unlike the usual "Woodstock scene", this "hidden" European "jewel" feels more "like going to the home of a friend who's a great cook" say voters; "wonderful chef" Marion Maur's "interesting variety" of "top-notch" "German-inspired food" comes served by a "personable" staff in the casual, rustic cabin–style room, while "in good weather", you can enjoy the "woodsy setting" on the patio.

Martha's the Restaurant at Simmons' Way ▯ American   - | - | - | M

Millerton | Simmons' Way Village Inn | 53 Main St. (bet. Dutchess & N. Maple Aves.) | 518-789-6235 | www.simmonsway.com

"Friendly owners" "bend over backwards to welcome you" at this Millerton village inn, offering a "limited" but "well-prepared" seasonal menu of New American fare that might include signatures such as lobster bisque and fish in a macadamia nut crust; decor featuring antiques and oil lamps strikes some as "on the dowdy side" but suits the authentic Victorian setting.

Martindale Chief Diner Diner   ▽ 10 | 8 | 14 | $15

Craryville | 1000 Rte. 23 (Taconic Pkwy., Claverack-Hillsdale Rte. 23 exit) | 518-851-2525

It's "a diner – no more, no less" – decree travelers on the Taconic who trek into this "convenient" Columbia County spot "known for its pies", "homemade soups" and "cheap" "basics"; ok, it's "nothing to look at" and the "once grand sign of the chief is in disrepair" but it's still a "'50s" "classic."

Mary Ann's *Tex-Mex*

15 | 11 | 14 | $25

Port Chester | 275 Boston Post Rd. (bet. Olivia & S. Regent Sts.) | 914-939-8700

Keep your expectations low and you won't be disappointed at this "family-friendly" Port Chester Tex-Mex (an offshoot of the NYC-based mini-chain), which proffers "formulaic" (some say "taste-less") "homestyle" fare; sure, it's "nothing special", but the "parking is easy", "kids love the chips" and there are plenty of options for veg-etarians, making it a "decent" option for a "nice cheap night."

Maud's Tavern *American*

13 | 13 | 16 | $28

Hastings-on-Hudson | 149 Southside Ave. (Spring St.) | 914-478-2326 | www.maudstavern.com

During "prime times" "locals flock" to this "crowded" but "comfort-able" Hastings "saloon" whose "honest", "inexpensive" American fare is "a small step above standard" "pub grub"; regulars report it's "better for lunch" and toast the "burgers and brews" on tap but "its popularity escapes" those who find the cuisine "uninspired" and call the staff "affable" enough when "the service is on, but trying" when off.

Max's Memphis BBQ Ⓜ *BBQ*

20 | 17 | 17 | $29

Red Hook | 136 S. Broadway (Rokeby Rd.) | 845-758-6297 | www.maxsbbq.com

"Bravo!" cheer BBQ-heads of this "popular" Red Hook purveyor where the "tasty" "down-home" fare may not be "death-before-dishonor Texas-style", but the "pulled pork is close to Carolina per-fect", "sides are good", there's "tasty beer on tap" and it comes via a "spunky" staff; add "decent prices" and "cozy" surroundings with a "great bar", and it's no wonder it's a "local scene."

Mayflower Inn & Spa, The *American*

24 | 27 | 25 | $67

Washington | The Mayflower Inn & Spa | 118 Woodbury Rd./Rte. 47 (Rte. 199), CT | 860-868-9466 | www.mayflowerinn.com

"Not fortunate enough to have been born into royalty? no matter, save your pennies and splurge" at this "romantic" Relais & Châteaux inn set among "the serene sights and sounds" of a "lovely" Washington locale; "delectable" New American cuisine is "impec-cably served" in three "handsome" "formal dining rooms" that "shout special occasion"; a few critics complain the food "doesn't live up to the setting" and the prices are "ridiculous", but concede that following "an afternoon at their spa, you may be too blissed out" to care.

McArthur's American Grill *American*

– | – | – | M

Pleasantville | 14 Washington Ave. (Manville Rd.) | 914-773-4281

This Pleasantville tavern – convenient to the Jacob Burns Film Center – attracts filmgoers and a college crowd alike for burgers and brews and other basics from a lengthy American menu; though prices run high considering the casual vibe, it still works as a quick-bite neighborhood standby.

McKinney & Doyle
Fine Foods Cafe 🎬 *American*

| 23 | 18 | 21 | $39 |

Pawling | 10 Charles Colman Blvd. (Main St.) | 845-855-3875 |
www.mckinneyanddoyle.com

Shannon McKinney's "dependable" New American "fixture" in Pawling "manages to be down to earth" and "haute" at the same time, serving up "undeniably" good fare and "outrageous desserts" at "reasonable prices", all delivered by an "accommodating" staff in a "Norman Rockwell setting"; the "rib-sticking" brunch has "loyal clients" declaring it's "worth getting up and driving to."

NEW Med 15/35 🔯🎬 *Mediterranean*

| – | – | – | E |

Rye Brook | Hilton Rye Town | 699 Westchester Ave. (Lincoln Ave.) |
914-934-2550 | www.med1535.com

Chef Dominick Mancino, previously at New York's St. Regis and Four Seasons hotels, heads the kitchen at this dinner-only Mediterranean newcomer set in the Rye Hilton; diners can choose the rustic main dining room warmed up with red-and-brown accents or opt for a spot on the spacious terrace in season; N.B. chef's table seating is also available for reserved parties of five or more.

Mediterranean Grill *Mediterranean*

| 19 | 19 | 20 | $42 |

Wilton | Stop & Shop Plaza | 5 River Rd. (bet. Rte. 33 & Wolfpit Rd.), CT | 203-762-8484 | www.mediterraneangrillwilton.com

"The shopping-center locale is a minor detraction" say fans of this chef-owned Mediterranean in Wilton that garners praise for "delicious" dishes that range from Moroccan chicken to fish stew; "service is attentive", the setting is "bright and attractive" and there's "great outdoor seating in the summer."

Mediterraneo *Mediterranean*

| 22 | 19 | 19 | $46 |

Greenwich | 366 Greenwich Ave. (Grigg St.), CT | 203-629-4747 |
www.mediterraneoofgreenwich.com

Grab a "spot at the bar to watch the action in the open kitchen" or if you prefer to "people-watch" vie for an "outdoor table" at this Greenwich Med that serves "excellent" seafood and "attracts a Euro crowd"; "it's also well located for shopping", so "jetliner decibel-level" noise and "high prices" don't keep it from being "crowded."

Mediterraneo 🎬 *Italian/Mediterranean*

| 18 | 18 | 18 | $42 |

Pleasantville | 75 Cooley St. (Bedford Rd.) | 914-773-1020

"If you're in the neighborhood" this "unpretentious" Italian-Med in Pleasantville serves up "reliable if unspectacular" fare in a "large" space that can be as "noisy" and "crowded" as an old-world piazza (which the rustic decor resembles); service is "attentive" and the chef "a wonderful host", but now that it's "no longer the only game in town", some surveyors suggest that such "expensive" tabs "demand more."

Meera Cuisine of India *Indian*

| ▽ 16 | 10 | 17 | $29 |

Stamford | 227 Summer St. (bet. Broad & Main Sts.), CT | 203-975-0477

Supporters of this long-standing Stamford Indian give it credit for serving "reliable" "fare at a fair price" (like the $8.95 lunch buffet);

FOOD | DECOR | SERVICE | COST

but critics sniff at the "very tired" setting and contend that "if they brought something to the ambiance, like ambiance", perhaps "they'd have a crowd."

Meetinghouse Restaurant 🅼 *American*   17 | 14 | 15 | $38

Bedford Village | 635 Old Post Rd./Rte. 22 (Court Rd.) | 914-234-5656 | www.bedfordmeetinghouse.com

This "fun, neighborhood" New American eatery in Bedford Village is the "most convenient game in town" for "good casual food" (like burgers) and "a quick bite" "pre- or post-movie"; on the downside are "long waits", "cramped" tables and a menu that can feel "pricey for what it is."

Meli-Melo *French*   23 | 11 | 17 | $21

Greenwich | 362 Greenwich Ave. (Fawcett Pl.), CT | 203-629-6153

"Consistently delicious crêpes" – "both sweet and savory" – are what the crowds crave at this "good-value" French "gem" that offers "a welcome respite from the retail rip-off of Greenwich Avenue"; fans also favor the "excellent" "homemade ice creams" and "wonderful" "daily soup specials"; the only "downside" is the "shoebox-sized" "place is too small for the big attention it gets."

Melting Pot, The *Fondue*   20 | 20 | 19 | $44

Darien | 14 Grove St. (bet. Brook & Day Sts.), CT | 203-656-4774 | www.meltingpot.com

"Make sure not to eat for a week prior to going" to this Darien "fondue emporium" and "plan on a two-hour meal for one of the four-course dinners", "since you have to cook it yourself"; fans of such "feasts" say "it's great for socializing with friends", but foes forfend scarfing down "so much cheese and chocolate" "you'll feel like the Goodyear blimp", and add as "fun experiences" go, "it's "severely overpriced.""

NEW Memphis Mae's 🅼 *BBQ*   17 | 14 | 16 | $27

Croton-on-Hudson | Croton Commons | 173 S. Riverside Ave. (Municipal Pl.) | 914-271-0125 | www.memphismaes.com

This new barbecue joint "tucked into a small, strip-mall storefront" in Croton is able to "fancy up" "humongous" "smokehouse" specialties and "traditional" Southern sides while remaining "affordable"; it's "still finding its footing" with sometimes "haphazard" service, too few tables and "nondescript" decor, but those in need of a "rib fix" or a "hard-to-find beer" declare it a "positive addition to the Westchester dining scene."

NEW Mercato 🅼 *Italian*   – | – | – | M

Red Hook | 61 E. Market St. (Cherry St.) | 845-758-5879

Red curtains, yellow walls and wood floors in a 19th-century building set a mood of colorful country chic at this Red Hook Northern Italian newcomer where chef and co-owner Francesco Buitoni turns out signature risottos and other dishes of his native land; when all seats are full, patrons spill over to tables in the adjacent shop (where they can buy fresh pastas and other Italian specialties), or in summer dine on the large porch.

	FOOD	DECOR	SERVICE	COST

Meritage Ⓜ American
22 | 18 | 20 | $49

Scarsdale | Colonial Vlg. | 1505 Weaver St. (Wilmot Rd.) | 914-472-8484 | www.meritagerestaurant.net

"Don't let the strip-mall location" deter you from this "ambitious" Scarsdale New American with a "varied, seasonal menu" of "delicious", "beautifully presented" dishes; patrons find merit in the "talented" service and "elegant", understated dining room that's "quiet" enough for a "tête-à-tête", but many suggest it's "too pricey" and "uneven" and may need "a little push to get to the next level."

Meson Los Espanoles Spanish
▽ 20 | 17 | 19 | $46

White Plains | 135 E. Post Rd. (bet. Court St. & Mamaroneck Ave.) | 914-428-8445 | www.mesonlosespanoles.net

"Authentic" Spanish cuisine and a "cozy" atmosphere attract diners to this "undiscovered gem" in White Plains for "good paella, sangria" and tapas; "live music" on weekends is another "wonderful touch", which makes this "beautiful little place" simply "a pleasure."

Mexican Radio Mexican
19 | 20 | 17 | $31

Hudson | 537 Warren St. (bet. 5th & 6th Sts.) | 518-828-7770 | www.mexrad.com

A "delight amid the antiques shops" on Hudson's main drag, this "*muy bueno* Mexican" "packs them in" for "solid" "vittles" and "outtasight margaritas"; a "happy" "partylike atmosphere" prevails in the "cool room" done up with fruity hues and "mission flair" so it's easy to overlook "*mañana* service", but really, at these "Manhattan prices", "would it kill them to throw in free chips and salsa?"

NEW Mex-to-go Mexican
▽ 17 | 7 | 18 | $15

Croton-on-Hudson | 345 S. Riverside Ave. (Clinton St.) | 914-271-8646

Finally, a "funky", "fun" Mexican take-out taqueria in Croton say amigos who love the rotisserie chickens and find "great value" and "quality" in the other items at this newcomer from the folks behind nearby Ümami Café; it's "occasionally uneven" and there's no decor to speak of (and no table service, only a lunch counter), but it's "perfect for when you don't want to cook."

Michael's Tavern Pub Food
14 | 11 | 14 | $24

Pleasantville | 150 Bedford Rd. (Rte. 141) | 914-769-9849

"Fortysomething-football-fan guys" as well as "local college students" "crowd" into this "noisy" Pleasantville "sports bar" where "TVs" trump the "mediocre" American fare; though service is "flaky", it's still a good "place to watch the game" or refuel conveniently "after the movies", just "stick to the basics and you'll be fine."

Michele Michelle Ⓜ Italian
▽ 21 | 15 | 22 | $34

Valley Cottage | 40 Rte. 303 N. (bet Lake & Storms Rds.) | 845-358-3244 | www.michelemichelle.net

The Cappiello family have brightened up a Rockland County strip mall with this Italian restaurant that "aims to please"; daughter (and chef) Michele proffers "well-prepared", "homestyle fare" and "personal service" in a brick-arched, mirrored space complete with a

| | FOOD | DECOR | SERVICE | COST |

player piano, although things get most "entertaining when the matriarch sings in the dining room"; P.S. the Wednesday–Saturday "$9.95 prix fixe lunch is a steal."

NEW Mickey Spillane's *American*

| – | – | – | I |

Eastchester | 431 White Plains Rd. (bet. Crest & Fisher Aves.) | 914-395-3838 | www.mickeyspillanes.com

Hearty fare (like lamb chops and roasted chicken) as well as an eclectic salad selection make this Eastchester New American newcomer – with a classic pub look – an inclusive neighborhood spot; a mixture of barflies and bargain-hunters crowd in for sports events on the plasma TVs and special prix fixe dinners Monday–Wednesday.

Mighty Joe Young's *Steak*

| 20 | 21 | 18 | $44 |

White Plains | 610 W. Hartsdale Ave. (Dobbs Ferry Rd.) | 914-428-6868 | www.mightyjoeyoungs.com

Don't let the "taxidermied animals" scare you away from this "upbeat" White Plains steakhouse with "kitschy", "African-inspired" decor, a beef-centric menu and a rotating selection of "wild game" for more "adventurous" types; "if you arrive on the early side", the ambiance tends to be "child-friendly" (i.e. "noisy" "kids running around"), while late-nights and weekends, this "meat-eater's paradise" becomes a meet market with a "hopping bar scene."

Milan Roadhouse *Diner*

| – | – | – | I |

Milan | 1215 Rte. 199 (bet. Field Rd. & Morehouse Ln.) | 845-758-8333

Dutchess County dwellers hankering for hearty American coffeeshop classics find them at this authentic '50s diner dispensing old-fashioned specialties made from scratch, whether it's an eggy breakfast, burgers and sandwiches at lunch, baked goods 'round tea-time, or something more robust like open turkey with mashed potatoes or corned beef hash for dinner; just remember, they're open only Friday–Sunday in winter.

Millennio ⓜ *Italian*

| 21 | 17 | 20 | $38 |

Scarsdale | 808 Scarsdale Ave. (Lee Ave.) | 914-722-7022

Considering it's "a neighborhood restaurant across from the train tracks", this Scarsdale Italian is "surprisingly good" with "homey" fare served in "simple, yet pleasant" stucco'ed surroundings; if some find it too "predictable", with "warm service" and "reasonable" prices it's still "nice to have around."

Mill House Panda *Chinese*

| 17 | 13 | 16 | $25 |

Poughkeepsie | 289 Mill St. (Garden St.) | 845-454-2530
Rhinebeck | 19-21 W. Market St. (Garden St.) | 845-876-2399

Some dishes are "surprisingly good", and some simply "basic" at this Dutchess County Chinese duo, where service also wavers between "slow" and "efficient"; digs "aesthetically up from run-of-the-mill places" could nevertheless use "major TLC", but even former fans crying "come back little panda" admit these places are "convenient."

	FOOD	DECOR	SERVICE	COST

Miraggio *Italian*
19 | 13 | 18 | $29

Yorktown Heights | 90 Triangle Ctr. (Rte. 202) | 914-248-6200 | www.miraggiorestaurant.com

"Go hungry" to this "decent" Northern Italian restaurant set in a Yorktown Heights shopping center where "humongous", "family-style" portions reign and "family-style noise" dominates the rather "large" room; for such "huge" quantities of food, the tab is "remarkably small", just "be prepared for several days of leftovers."

Miss Lucy's Kitchen *American*
22 | 18 | 19 | $31

Saugerties | 90 Partition St. (bet. Jane & Main Sts.) | 845-246-9240 | www.misslucyskitchen.com

"Very good", "stick-to-the-ribs" Traditional American "home cooking" from a "chef using local produce" is the draw at this "wonderful" Saugerties spot (as are desserts so enticing "you always want four"); service is "above average", while gingham curtains and vintage cookware on the walls conjure such a "country-esque" "farmhouse feel" in the storefront space that it "looks just like it sounds."

Miss Saigon *Vietnamese*
▽ 18 | 9 | 15 | $20

Poughkeepsie | 25 Lagrange Ave. (Raymond Ave.) | 845-485-9706

There's "nothing to rave about" at this "tiny" Poughkeepsie Vietnamese near Vassar, just "faithful re-creations of authentic dishes" in an area where such fare is "hard to find"; that and "good prices" keep customers coming, but the "slowest service" and decor that "leaves much to be desired" make some suggest "takeout is best."

Modern Restaurant & Pizzeria *Italian*
23 | 10 | 18 | $24

New Rochelle | 12 Russell Ave. (Main St.) | 914-633-9479

Brick-oven pizza connoisseurs rave about this "secret" Southern Italian eatery "hidden" "in a maze of backstreets" in New Rochelle that serves up "fabulous" thin-crust pies and "delicious" renditions of "homestyle" dishes; throw in "inexpensive" prices and you'll forget all about the "drab" dining room that's kind of a "dump."

Mohonk Mountain House *American*
17 | 25 | 19 | $51

New Paltz | Mohonk Mountain Hse. | 1000 Mountain Rest Rd. (4 mi. north of Rte. 299) | 845-256-2056 | www.mohonk.com

It's "the one and only" proclaim proponents of New Paltz's "magnificent" mountaintop "château" resort "overlooking a lake" on one side and "a huge expanse of valley" on the other; "pricey" Traditional American prix fixe fare "has its moments" (especially the "good" breakfast and lunch, served buffet-style in the somewhat "daunting" dining room), but is still "secondary" to the whole "fabulous" peak "experience"; N.B. jackets at dinner, please.

Mojo Grill *American*
23 | 21 | 21 | $40

Wappingers Falls | Summerlin Plaza | 942 Rte. 376 (Robinson Ln.) | 845-226-1111 | www.mojogrill.net

"Love it! love it! love it!" gush groupies of this "casual" Wappingers Falls New American where Neuvo Latino accents prove the "chef

FOOD | DECOR | SERVICE | COST

isn't afraid to try something different"; "steak lovers are in heaven", "mix-and-match sides" are a "nice touch", and even if it's a "bit pretentious", a "welcoming staff", "colorful" digs, "funky cocktails" and "jazz" on Wednesdays and weekends add to the good mojo.

Momiji *Japanese*   ▽ 19 | 11 | 15 | $36

Harrison | 261 Halstead Ave. (Harrison Ave.) | 914-835-1078

A "mostly Japanese crowd" "squeezes in" to this "very small" somewhat "run-down" "family restaurant" in Harrison for a "variety" of sushi, "fusion" fare and other "izakaya-style" "cooked" dishes; the quality is "good", but beware of service that suffers "when it's busy."

Mona Lisa ⑤ *Italian*   24 | 18 | 22 | $42

Stamford | 133 Atlantic St. (I-95, exit 8), CT | 203-348-1070 | www.monalisarestaurant.org

At this chef-owned, family-run Italian in Downtown Stamford, respondents relish the "homestyle with a smile" cuisine and advise "try the tasting dinners, which pair regional foods with wines"; but with so "few tables", they advise "get there early", and as for looks, some call the brick-walled trattoria setting "cute", while others assert it's "cold."

⊿ Monteverde at   21 | 26 | 22 | $58
Oldstone Manor *Continental*

Cortlandt | 28 Bear Mountain Bridge Rd./Rte. 202 (2½ mi. southeast of Bear Mountain Bridge) | 914-739-5000 | www.monteverderestaurant.com

It's all about the "breathtaking views" of the Hudson at this "beautifully renovated" Cortlandt mansion whose "lovely location" (which includes three fireplaces and an outdoor terrace) and "attentive" service make it "wonderful" for "private parties" and "special occasions"; diners divide on the Continental cuisine ("delicious" vs. "ordinary"), even still, most think it's "worth the trip" for its "elegant" brunch; N.B. there's a spa and two luxury suites upstairs.

⊿ Morton's, The Steakhouse *Steak*   24 | 21 | 23 | $64

White Plains | The Source | 9 Maple Ave. (bet. S. B'way & Waller Ave.) | 914-683-6101

Stamford | UBS Investment Bank | 377 N. State St. (bet. Canal & Elm Sts.), CT | 203-324-3939

www.mortons.com

"Carnivores, start your engines" and rev up for prodigious porterhouse steaks "properly prepared" and "baked potatoes the size of small footballs" at this "very high-end" steakhouse chain; while most maintain the meats are "the best" and the "service is great", some surveyors balk at "overpriced, ogre-sized servings" and say they're "turned off by the Saran-wrapped" ingredient display – "do they really think we need to be shown a tomato and told what it is?"

Moscato *Italian/Mediterranean*   23 | 20 | 21 | $51

Scarsdale | 874 Scarsdale Ave. (Popham Rd.) | 914-723-5700

This "old-world" Italian-Mediterranean restaurant in Scarsdale is "noisy on a busy evening" no doubt due to "loyal regulars" "crowd"-ing in for "consistently good" fare, a "terrific wine list" and "solicitous service"; if a few critics carp it's "overrated" and "overpriced", they're overridden by those who deem the "formal" yet "comfortable" venue a "solid" "neighborhood" spot; N.B. it's under the same ownership as Lusardi's.

NEW Mo's New York Grill M *Steak* | 21 | 20 | 21 | $54 |

New Rochelle | 14 Memorial Hwy. (bet. Huguenot & Main Sts.) | 914-632-1442 | www.mosnewyorkgrill.com

Forget about hot dogs and dig in to some "quality" beef at this clubby New Rochelle steakhouse owned by All-Star relief pitcher Mariano Rivera (which might explain all the "Yankee memorabilia adorning the walls"); if the menu's a bit "pricey" and service "sometimes gets a walk", the "very good" desserts hit a home run, though the thrill of seeing "Mo" in the flesh is what really makes it "best for fans."

NEW Mountain Cow Cafe ⊅ *Diner* | - | - | - | I |

Pine Plains | 2987 Church St. (Rte. 199) | 518-398-0500

Yes, this coffee-shop newcomer on Pine Plains' main drag serves oatmeal, eggs and such for breakfast, but come lunchtime, things get a bit fancier (imagine a turkey sandwich reinvented as a Tex-Mex style panini, with house-smoked meat and chipotle aïoli); the sunlit space with its two bay windows is cozied up with recycled barn wood, a couch and loveseat, and a bar where patrons sip espresso or admire local artists' works on the walls.

Mountain Gate Indian M *Indian* | ∇ 15 | 14 | 17 | $27 |

Woodstock | 4 Deming St. (Rte. 212) | 845-679-5100

"Inexpensive" and certainly "not pretentious", this stalwart serves up "the only Indian food in Woodstock", which "arguably" makes it "the best" around; a sometimes "slow" kitchen delivers "standard" chicken korma, tandoori dishes and such, with a "fun" $10.95 all-you-can-eat buffet on Tuesdays, all served in "snug" surroundings decorated in traditional style.

Mount Fuji *Japanese/Steak* | 21 | 24 | 23 | $41 |

Hillburn | 296 Rte. 17 (Rte. 87N, exit 15A) | 845-357-4270 | www.mtfujisteakhouse.com

Long a "cult favorite for high schoolers", "fun" for birthday bashes or just to "introduce the kids to Japanese food", this "festive" Rockland County "landmark" "enthralls" with its "always amusing" hibachi chefs; even grown-ups who harrumph it's "a little hokey" enjoy "predictably good food", "impeccable service" and the "coolest views" from the "beautiful" "hilltop" location.

Mount Fuji Sushi *Japanese* | 19 | 12 | 16 | $27 |

Mt. Kisco | 176 N. Bedford Rd. (bet. Main St. & Victoria Dr.) | 914-666-2348

A "secret", some say "underrated", Japanese joint in Mt. Kisco that's a "family favorite" for "good" sushi, "delivery" and "birthdays and parties"; decor's rather spare, and service is slightly "disorganized" but "they try, especially with kids."

Mughal Palace *Indian* | 23 | 16 | 22 | $31 |

Valhalla | 16 Broadway (Cleveland St., across from Valhalla RR station) | 914-997-6090 | www.mughalpalace.com

"Weekends are noisier than a Delhi bazaar" at this Valhalla Indian whose convenient location "near the train station" and "outstanding" "high-quality" fare have made it a "solid" option for a "pleasant" meal; another plus: servers "who remember repeat customers."

☑ Mulino's of Westchester ●☑ *Italian* | 24 | 24 | 24 | $60 |

White Plains | 99 Court St. (Quarropas St.) | 914-761-1818

"If you want to be pampered" "in a *Godfather* setting", book a reservation at this "gorgeous" "old-time" Italian in White Plains known for "generous portions" of "superb" food, "excellent" wines and "top-notch" service that "makes you feel special" (the "gratis antipasto" is a "great touch"); in all, it sets "the standard" "for special-occasion" dining – just "make sure someone else is picking up the check"; N.B. the Christmas decor in the garden is legendary.

Myrna's Mediterranean Bistro ☑ *Mediterranean* | 22 | 10 | 20 | $21 |

Stamford | 866 E. Main St. (bet. N. State St. & Quintard Terr.), CT | 203-325-8736

"Marvelous" "mom-and-pop Mediterranean food" ranging from shish kebab to shrimp scampi is the draw at this "tiny", "inexpensive" Stamford spot run by "very helpful owners"; the only improvement surveyors seek is a "more comfortable setting" that doesn't include "luncheonettelike decor."

Nanuet Hotel *Italian* | 18 | 8 | 15 | $21 |

Nanuet | 132 S. Main St. (Rte. 59) | 845-623-9600 | www.nanuethotel.com

Rockland County residents craving "heavenly thin-crust pizza" register at this onetime hotel "hole-in-the-wall" Italian for "creative" pies (and "forget the rest"); "homey" if "somewhat dingy" digs are "comfortable", while a video arcade, crayons and games certainly suggest "bring the kids"; P.S. a tip: if you want "fast service, call ahead."

ℕ𝔼𝕎 Napa & Co. *American* | - | - | - | M |

Stamford | Courtyard Marriott Hotel | 75 Broad St. (Summer St.), CT | 203-353-3319 | www.napaandcompany.com

This New American newcomer brings together the former owners of Telluride with talented chef Bill Taibe, who continues his passion for combining unlikely ingredients (many of them organic) in dishes like duck breast braised in honey and thyme; located in Downtown Stamford's Courtyard Marriott Hotel, the dining room features 18-ft. ceilings, chandeliers and a wall of wine.

Neko Sushi *Japanese* | 20 | 17 | 20 | $28 |

New Paltz | 49 Main St./Rte. 299 (N. Chestnut St.) | 845-255-0162

Neko Sushi & Hibachi *Japanese*

Wappingers Falls | 1817 South Rd./Rte. 9 (Rte. 84) | 845-298-9869

Everyone "leaves happy" at these Japanese siblings, thanks to a wide variety of "very fresh", "well-seasoned" sushi in "healthy por-

| | FOOD | DECOR | SERVICE | COST |

tions", "good soups" and hot dishes – not to mention "quite the sake selection"; a "well-intentioned" staff works in rooms with "predictable" decor, while hibachi tables are a "fun" bonus at the Wappingers Falls branch.

NEW Nessa *Mediterranean*

– | – | – | M

Port Chester | 325 N. Main St. (Horton Ave.) | 914-939-0119

Dim lighting sets a sultry mood at this moderately priced Port Chester newcomer where Mediterranean dishes like oxtail gnocchi and monkfish puttanesca are paired with quartinos of Italian wines; come summer, patrons can opt for alfresco dining and people-watching in the adjacent garden.

Nestos Estiatorio *Mediterranean*

23 | 21 | 20 | $38

New City | Town Plaza | 191 S. Main St. (bet. Leona Ave. & Virginia St.) | 845-634-3456

Order the "fabulous fresh fish" "by the pound and you can really get hooked" declare Rockland County Grecophiles at this "lovely" Mediterranean whose "simple" yet "sophisticated" "Greek specialties" are "surprisingly good", and "a bargain" too; a "pleasant" staff serves in a "chic" setting with tin ceilings, wood floors and "big windows" or on the "delightful" "patio in summer", where, "except for passing traffic", you could almost be in the islands.

New World Home Cooking Co. M *American/Eclectic*

23 | 19 | 21 | $35

Saugerties | 1411 Rte. 212 (3½ mi. east of Woodstock) | 845-246-0900 | www.newworldhomecooking.com

It "still rocks!" cheer champions of "terrific" chef-owner Ric Orlando's "happening" Saugerties New American–Eclectic, where "truly imaginative" dishes with "lively spices" are rated on a "Ric-ter scale" for heat, and vegetarians get "treats" too (like "out-of-this-world seitan steak"); the "arty" (some say "gaudy") "decor is worth a look-see", and help is "friendly" and "efficient", so "go with a gang" for "a great night out."

Niko's Greek Taverna *Greek*

20 | 14 | 20 | $31

White Plains | 287 Central Ave. (Aqueduct Rd.) | 914-686-6456 | www.nikostaverna.com

"The owners try hard" to make you feel like "you're part of their Greek wedding" at this "friendly", "family-run" relative newcomer in White Plains that pleases patrons with "tasty" Hellenic specialties (psst – stick to the "ample" appetizers and it's a "great bang for the buck" too); the decor's a bit "dull", but come summer, ditch the "crowd" inside and "dine on the patio."

Nina *Eclectic*

24 | 21 | 22 | $48

Middletown | 27 W. Main St. (bet. Canal & North Sts.) | 845-344-6800 | www.nina-restaurant.com

"Friday nights", this Middletown Eclectic is "jammed with New Yorkers up for the weekend", feasting on chef-owner Franz Brendle's "fabulous", "original" fare and adding to the "almost" Manhattan-like vibe of the "old factory building"; a black-and-silver tin ceiling, brick walls and wood floors create "an inviting atmosphere", and the staff is "cheerful", so the only real complaint is it's a bit "pricey" for the area.

96 Main ⊠ Eclectic ▽ 21 | 16 | 19 | $30

Poughkeepsie | 96 Main St. (Clover St.) | 845-454-5200 | www.96main.org

"Surprisingly good food" is the main reason to check out Thomas Kacherski and Michael McCree's "casual" Poughkeepsie spot, where the chef duo's Eclectic menu mixes it up with signatures like ahi tuna taco, goat cheese won tons and filet mignon; if plain pub-style decor could use "a makeover", nobody notices when the place "morphs from fine dining" into a "college bar" later into the eve.

Nino's Italian 18 | 12 | 16 | $38

South Salem | 355 Rte. 123 (Glen Dr.) | 914-533-2671

Three brothers run this "reliable" "hometown" Italian spot set in a Colonial house in South Salem with "good value" Northern specialties; the menu and old-fashioned dining room "don't change much", but it's "comfortable and consistent" for diners living nearby where there are few other options; P.S. in summer, "eat out on the tiny porch."

Noda's Japanese Steakhouse Japanese 18 | 14 | 18 | $35

White Plains | White Plains Mall | 200 Hamilton Ave. (Martin Luther King Ave.) | 914-949-0990 | www.nodarestaurant.com

It's "always fun to watch the knife skills" in action at this "typical" Japanese hibachi in the White Plains Mall, where chefs put on a "great show" cooking up "good steak", seafood and veggies on the table in front of you (there's a selection of "delicious sushi" on the menu as well); despite "tired-looking" digs that "need an overhaul", "kids still love it" and even some adults find it "entertaining."

Northern Spy Cafe ⊠Ⓜ American 16 | 19 | 19 | $30

High Falls | Rte. 213 (bet. Lucas Tpke. & Mohonk Rd.) | 845-687-7298 | www.northernspycafe.com

A "charming" old "country farmhouse" with "lovely gardens" forms a backdrop for New American eats at this "nice" High Falls spot, where a "limited" menu that maybe "tries too hard" still offers something for "vegetarians, meat eaters" and whatever's "in between" – and it "doesn't cost much", either; "regular" spies say service is "attentive" and suggest dining on "the porch in summer."

North Star American ▽ 22 | 18 | 20 | $48

Pound Ridge | 85 Westchester Ave. (Pine Dr.) | 914-764-0200 | www.northstarny.com

"The chef's passion" comes across in the "creative", "excellently prepared" New American cuisine that "changes with the seasons" at this "tiny" "congenial" restaurant in Pound Ridge; a "warm atmosphere" and an "eager-to-please" staff makes this "hopping" "30-plus hang" a "cheerful" addition to the otherwise "stuffy" neighborhood; N.B. they have live bands on Thursday nights.

	FOOD	DECOR	SERVICE	COST

⊿ Ocean House 🛇 Ⓜ *New England/Seafood* | 27 | 17 | 23 | $41 |

Croton-on-Hudson | 49 N. Riverside Ave. (Rte. 9A) | 914-271-0702
The "cozy" "Cape Cod" setting suits this "boutique" New England-
style seafooder set in a "nautical-themed" renovated diner in
Croton-on-Hudson where chef-owner Brian Galvin and his wife,
Paula, "couldn't be friendlier" and their "lovingly prepared" cuisine
is "consistently" "enjoyable"; it's "worth the wait" "again and again",
but be advised there are "no reservations" and it's "BYOB", so "arrive early" with bottle in hand.

Ocean 211 🛇 *Seafood* | 24 | 19 | 21 | $52 |

Stamford | 211 Summer St. (bet. Broad & Main Sts.), CT | 203-973-0494 |
www.ocean211.com
"Non-seafood fans quickly see the light" at this Downtown Stamford
"ocean gem" serving "fantastically fresh fish" and "great oysters"
(20 types) in a "cute two-story townhouse" decorated to look like
the interior of a posh sailboat; the "owner takes great pride in his
food" and the staff often performs "tableside" preparations of
dishes like the signature Dover sole and Caesar salad, but "if you
aren't in the yachting set", the prices might produce a sinking feeling.

Off Broadway Restaurant Ⓜ *Continental* | 19 | 15 | 21 | $40 |

Dobbs Ferry | 17 Ashford Ave. (B'way) | 914-693-6170
The "warm, welcoming" staff offsets the somewhat "cold atmosphere" at this "quiet", "family-owned" restaurant in Dobbs Ferry
sending out "spot-on" Continental cuisine; if there are "no wows", it's
still a "consistently" "pleasant" experience and a "good value" as well.

Okinawa Japanese Restaurant *Japanese* | 15 | 13 | 14 | $33 |

Mt. Kisco | 39 S. Moger Ave. (Main St.) | 914-666-8188
"Hibachi heaven" for "kids and their wranglers", this "loud"
Japanese steak and sushi house in Mt. Kisco dazzles diners with an
"entertaining" show of "flipping knives" and "flaming food" – a good
thing, since the fare itself is rather "uninspiring"; in spite of that and
"rushed" service, it's still "birthday party" central.

Old Drovers Inn *American* | 23 | 25 | 22 | $57 |

Dover Plains | Old Drovers Inn | 196 E. Duncan Hill Rd. (Rte. 22) |
845-832-9311 | www.olddroversinn.com
"Escape into times past" at this "authentic" circa-1750s hostelry
in Dover Plains that just oozes "romantic" "atmosphere", with its
big stone fireplace and low ceilings ("watch out for beams"); the
"rather pricey" "top-drawer" New American fare includes long-
standing favorite cheddar cheese soup, and if "cocktails the size of
the national debt" leave you woozy, just head to one of the
refurbished rooms upstairs.

Olde Stone Mill, The *American* | 15 | 22 | 17 | $43 |

Tuckahoe | 2 Scarsdale Rd. (Main St.) | 914-771-7661 |
www.theoldestonemill.com
A "quaint" restored cotton mill overlooking the banks of the Bronx
River is the setting of this Tuckahoe Traditional American with a "de-

lightful outdoor terrace" that's "lovely" for a drink on a "summer day"; "spotty" cuisine and "unremarkable" service, unfortunately, are "not up to the decor", which is "too bad", because given the "wonderful space", the restaurant has "great potential."

Old '76 House American
15 | 22 | 17 | $41

Tappan | 110 Main St. (Palisades Pkwy., exit 5S) | 845-359-5476 | www.76house.com

Revolutionary War buffs believe "it's worth the trip" to this "landmark" Colonial Tappan hostelry for the "history oozing from its pores" despite "uneven" Traditional American eats that were "good in Major Andre's day"; optimists opine "stick to basics", "forget service" and just "admire the restored dining room."

Ole Mole ◪ Mexican
22 | 11 | 17 | $17

Stamford | 1030 High Ridge Rd. (Olga Dr.), CT | 203-461-9962 | www.ole-mole.com

"Ole cow!" rave reviewers of this "tiny", "mostly take-out" Stamford Mexican serving "supremely tasty" "housemade salsas and guac" and signature "enchiladas suizas"; not only is the food "fresh, good and cheap", "everything is cooked to order" and "served by a smiling staff"; some find the "prices high", but most enthusiasts urge it's "time to expand."

Oliva ◪ Mediterranean
23 | 18 | 20 | $43

New Preston | 18 E. Shore Rd./Rte. 45 (Rte. 202), CT | 860-868-1787

Litchfielders "make their standing reservations" at this "longtime" New Preston Mediterranean and even out-of-towners recommend it as "a great place to end a day of leaf-peeping" with "superb Moroccan-inflected cuisine"; "try to get a table upstairs" in the "lovely" "new dining area" or "eat outside" on the terrace if the weather's right – otherwise, you might find the seating "too tightly packed."

☑ Ondine ◪ French
26 | 24 | 25 | $62

Danbury | 69 Pembroke Rd./Rte. 37 (Wheeler Dr.), CT | 203-746-4900 | www.ondinerestaurant.com

"A treasure" "tucked away in Northern Danbury" is how surveyors sum up this "romantic", chef-owned "country French" stalwart serving dishes like "memorable venison" and "not-to-be-missed soufflés"; *amis* applaud the "expert service" and deem the five-course "$55 fixed-price menu a bargain"; N.B. no children allowed, and jackets are suggested for men.

NEW One American
▽ 27 | 24 | 24 | $58

Irvington | 1 Bridge St. (bet. N. Buckhout & River Sts.) | 914-591-2233

The owners of River City Grille up the street have warmed up the roomy bar and "pretty" dining room of the former Solera space for this expensive Irvington newcomer catering to "Westchester foodies" with New American and raw-bar selections; while few surveyors have found it so far, those who have seem smitten with this "welcome addition" to the "Hudson River scene."

121 Restaurant & Bar *American*

| 21 | 18 | 19 | $40 |

North Salem | 2-4 Dingle Ridge Rd. (Rte. 121) | 914-669-0121 | www.121restaurant.com

This "popular" North Salem New American "oasis on a country road" may be set in a "picturesque" location with a "wraparound porch", but inside it "feels like NYC" with a "chic", "upscale" ambiance and a "happening" bar scene; proponents praise the "excellent wines" and a "reliable", varied menu that spans "from pizza to gourmet", yet even they admit it's not just "lively", but "packed" and "noisy", and advise: go only if you can "stand the crowds."

122 Pizza Bistro *Italian/Pizza*

| 21 | 16 | 20 | $29 |

Stamford | 122 Broad St. (Bedford St.), CT | 203-348-1232

"In the heart of Downtown" Stamford, "across from the mall", this "more-than-a-pizza-joint" Italian offers a "great twist" on pies along with "unusual entrees" like pork osso buco; even though it can be a "little noisy", a "friendly staff", "hip decor" and "small but comfy bar" make this "reasonably priced" "casual place" a "great pre-movie choice" "for a quick bite."

Onyx Bar & Grill *Eclectic*

| 15 | 19 | 14 | $36 |

Stamford | 970 High Ridge Rd. (Cedar Heights Rd.), CT | 203-322-9888 | www.onyxbarandgrill.com

"They've changed their menu and staff more than I've changed my baby's diapers" sniff skeptics of this Stamford Eclectic "in a strip mall next to a Kinko's"; scenesters say the "sexy, hip" bar is a "cool place for oversized drinks", but foodies pan the only "adequate" eats.

Oporto 🅼 *Portuguese*

| 17 | 17 | 18 | $35 |

Hartsdale | 191 E. Hartsdale Ave. (bet. Bronx River Pkwy. & Central Park Ave.) | 914-722-6565

Surveyors report this "reasonably priced" Hartsdale Portuguese-Mediterranean has "improved" (it's up five Food points from last year) with "hearty", "well-prepared" fare, especially the wood-broiled chicken, which you can "pick up" for a "quick supper" (the "sides" still need work, though); "friendly service" and a "homey atmosphere" are two more reasons to "recommend it to friends."

Opus 465 *American*

| 18 | 17 | 17 | $39 |

Armonk | 465 Main St. (Orchard Dr.) | 914-273-4676 | www.opus465.com

At this "pleasant" bi-level New American cafe in Armonk, "dressed-down" insiders munch on "versatile" fare with "continental flair" (salads are a favorite); if it's "disappointing for dinner" and the decor's "a bit tired", there's still "something for everyone", including weekend music downstairs, a "great bar to hang out in", "full brunch" and outside dining in season.

Orem's Diner ◗ *Diner*

| 15 | 11 | 16 | $17 |

Wilton | 167 Danbury Rd./Rte. 7 (Rte. 33), CT | 203-762-7370

"Bring your grandparents or your kids but not your date" to this "large", "busy" "Wilton institution" (1921) where the "nothing-fancy" food doesn't stop "the entire town" from showing up "on weekends" for "reasonably priced" breakfasts; the less-supportive shrug "hey, it's a diner – period."

Oriental House 🅼 *Japanese/Korean* | – | – | – | M |
Pine Bush | 78 Main St. (New St.) | 845-744-8663

For "impeccably prepared" hot dishes grilled at table – as well as a selection of sushi – this Japanese-Korean hits the spot in under-served Pine Bush; no-frills digs are warmed by the Oh family's welcome, so even though it "takes a while for the food to be made", satisfied customers say it's "well worth" the wait.

🅽🅴🆆 Oriole 9 *European* | ▽ 19 | 17 | 13 | $23 |
Woodstock | 17 Tinker St. (bet. Mill Hill & Tannery Brook Rds.) | 845-679-5763 | www.oriole9.com

A roomier sibling of Saugerties' Café With Love, this Woodstock European newcomer serves "terrific breakfasts", "nice choices" at lunch and "innovative" dinnertime fare; customers sip coffee on couches in the lounge area, sink into pillows on a banquette or perch at plain wood tables in the richly hued room, and though naysayers find it "overpriced" for "locals" and many mention "spacey service", it probably just "needs time to find itself."

Osaka *Japanese* | 23 | 16 | 23 | $28 |
Rhinebeck | 22 Garden St. (W. Market St.) | 845-876-7338
Tivoli | 74 Broadway (Pine St.) | 845-757-5055
www.osakasushi.net

"Sweet owners" "make it a pleasure" for "Japanese food enthusiasts" to jam in at this "dependable" Duchess County duo dispensing "top-quality" "sushi and noodle dishes" as well as "great bento box specials" – and all at rates that seem "almost too reasonable"; "pleasant", "typical" digs are "tiny" in Rhinebeck, slightly "roomier" and "nicer" in the Tivoli branch.

Oscar *American* | – | – | – | M |
Kerhonkson | 5945 Rte. 44/55 (Lower Granite Rd.) | 845-626-9838 | www.oscarccc.com

Nestled in a onetime Ukrainian lodge left over from the region's Borscht Belt heyday, this Kerhonkson New American continues dishing up traditional comfort food like chicken pot pie and pierogi but with contemporary twists courtesy of chef Bart Greenbaum's California training; brother Jesse meets and greets in the cozy, ski-lodge style space with its raw-wood tables, retro '70s bar with pool table and pinball machine, and mini-lending-library next to couches by the fireplace.

O'Sho Japanese Steak House *Japanese* | ▽ 19 | 18 | 17 | $33 |
Poughkeepsie | 1988 South Rd./Rte. 9 (bet. Spring & Vassar Rds.) | 845-297-0540 | www.oshorestaurant.com

Sure, the hibachi chefs put on the "standard" display at Poughkeepsie's "traditional Japanese steakhouse" "but it's still enjoyable", and results in "such good food" too ("think Benihana only better"); patrons are less enthusiastic about sushi and Thai offerings served in the spacious rooms, and grouches grumble that tabs are "too much" and "waits excruciatingly long", yet it remains a "busy" "favorite" for a night out.

Osteria Applausi ⑤ *Italian* | 22 | 17 | 21 | $45 |

Old Greenwich | 199 Sound Beach Ave. (Arcadia Rd.), CT | 203-637-4447 | www.osteriaapplausi.com

The "homemade pastas are worth applause" at this "excellent" Old Greenwich Italian that's become "a local hangout for the BMW set" and "priced for the princely class"; but whether you find the atmosphere "peaceful and quiet" or the "storefront decor" "dull" will have to be your call.

Osteria Marietta *Italian*   ▽ | 19 | 17 | 20 | $35 |

Mamaroneck | 215 Halstead Ave. (Ward Ave.) | 914-777-2426

At this Northern Italian restaurant in Mamaroneck that bobs between a "neighborhood hangout" and a "more upscale" eatery, "homey pasta" "appeals to all ages" and "large portions provide treats for the next day"; a vineyard mural and terra-cotta tiles make for a "nice" interior although it lurks behind a "pizza parlor exterior."

⚡ Pacifico *Nuevo Latino/Seafood* | 22 | 19 | 20 | $45 |

Port Chester | 316 Boston Post Rd. (S. Regent St.) | 914-937-1610 | www.pacificony.com

Start with an "awesome" cocktail ("love those mojitos!") and then sample some seafood that "knocks your socks off" at this "noisy" Nuevo Latino in Port Chester (sister to Sonora) where chef Rafael Palomino dishes up "fusion" cuisine in a "cool", "colorful" environment; a rising chorus of critics, however, carps that "crowded" conditions and "uneven" food suggest a "chef who has spread himself too thin" and makes dining here a somewhat "disappointing" experience.

Pacific Restaurant *Chinese* | 16 | 11 | 12 | $31 |

Mt. Kisco | 222 E. Main St./Rte. 117 (W. Hyatt Ave.) | 914-666-7222

Fans find the fare's "declined" at this Mt. Kisco "Sunday night" Chinese "standby" (down five Food points from last year's Survey); still, it's "fine" for the "occasional convenience" "if you live nearby", though insiders insist on takeout to avoid the dining room "in need of a makeover" and "excruciatingly slow" service.

Pagoda *Chinese* | 22 | 13 | 19 | $26 |

Scarsdale | 694 Central Park Ave. (Old Army Rd.) | 914-725-8866

"Wonderful Shanghaiese" including "dim sum on weekends" and "healthful choices all over the menu" draw an "upscale clientele" to this Scarsdale Sino for "tasty", "authentic" Chinese fare; with an "affable host" and "friendly" staff, the only downside is the "shopping-plaza" location.

Painter's *Eclectic* | 19 | 19 | 19 | $30 |

Cornwall-on-Hudson | 266 Hudson St. (bet. Ave. A & Idlewild Ave.) | 845-534-2109 | www.painters-restaurant.com

"Lots of art" and "arty" "objects" adorn this "relaxed", "friendly" Orange County B&B-cum-"neighborhood bistro" where a "long, interesting menu" of Eclectic fare guarantees "something for everyone"; some bristle at "inconsistency", but most sketch it as a "fun place to grab a bite", especially if you indulge in "creative cocktails" in the well-stocked Gallery bar; "sidewalk seating in summer" is another "pleasure."

Palmer's Crossing *American*   17 | 15 | 18 | $36

Larchmont | 1957 Palmer Ave. (bet. East & West Aves.) | 914-833-3505
Larchmont locals head to this New American "neighborhood haunt" for "light dining" and Italian touches like "upscale pizza and pasta"; although some appreciate a "consistent" "place in town" with an "attentive young staff", many "wish the food were better", also noting that "prices keep going up."

Pamela's Traveling Feast   ▽ 18 | 21 | 16 | $40
on the Hudson *Continental*

Newburgh | Newburgh Yacht Club | 1 Park Pl. (N. Montgomery St.) | 845-562-4505 | www.pamelastravelingfeast.com
You can "enjoy the lovely view" of boats bobbing on the river from the nicely appointed dining room at this "quiet" venue "tucked away" at the Newburgh Yacht Club, but voters suggest caterer Pamela Resch's Continental fare (and "staff that has a hard time juggling tables") is "ok" but needs "to improve a little to match" the scenery.

Panda Pavilion *Chinese*   15 | 10 | 16 | $22

Greenwich | 420 W. Putnam Ave. (bet. Harold & Melrose Aves.), CT | 203-869-1111
Proponents propose "put on your slippers" and relax, because this "decent" Chinese has "the fastest delivery" in Greenwich; but even some couch potatoes take a pass, declaring that the "gone-downhill" spot offers only "ok" eats.

Pantanal Restaurant *Brazilian*   ▽ 22 | 12 | 21 | $39

Port Chester | 29 N. Main St. (Westchester Ave.) | 914-939-6894
At this Brazilian "beef eater's nirvana" in Port Chester, "you can eat the whole cow" skewered in "various cuts" and "served off swords" "rodizio"-style; though a "large" "eclectic" salad bar plays buffer to the "mountains of meat", with a staff circulating "BBQ" this "frequently", you'll likely "leave stuffed to the gills"; N.B. live music on weekends.

Pantry, The 🗷🅼 *American*   23 | 14 | 17 | $24

Washington Depot | 5 Titus Rd. (Rte. 47), CT | 860-868-0258
This "unique, little" chef-owned New American, with seating interspersed "amid the gourmet store's" produce and housewares, is a Washington Depot daytime "institution"; the "limited menu" includes an "impressive array of cheeses", "freshly prepared soups, salads", "interesting sandwich combinations" and "homemade desserts"; with food this "delicious", surveyors "wish they'd open for dinner."

Paradise Bar & Grille *American*   13 | 19 | 16 | $31

Stamford | Stamford Landing | 78 Southfield Ave. (I-95, exit 7), CT | 203-323-1116 | www.paradisebarandgrille.com
"Sitting outside with a Bloody Mary" "when the sun is out" at this New American looking over Stamford Harbor and the Long Island

Sound is "a bit of paradise"; but don't expect the food ("tastes like the samples at Costco") or "very spotty service" to come close to the view, especially when the "outdoor bar scene" is in full summertime swing.

Pascal's ⓜ *French* | 22 | 21 | 23 | $46 |

Larchmont | 141 Chatsworth Ave. (Palmer Ave.) | 914-834-6688
Regulars regard this "family-run", "well-kept secret" in Larchmont as "a great value" for "simple", "authentic" French "bistro" cooking in "quiet", "comfortable" surroundings; the "over-50 crowd" especially praises the "charming" owners who provide such "gracious" service, "it almost feels like you're going to their home" for dinner.

Pasquale Ristorante II ⓜ *Italian* | ▽ 19 | 13 | 21 | $40 |

Port Chester | 2 Putnam Ave. (N. Main St.) | 914-934-7770
This "old-style" Italian in Port Chester channels "Arthur Avenue" with "red-sauce" favorites in "large portions" that "deliver the goods"; the "staff goes out of its way" to be "warm" and "accommodating" ("special requests" are often no problem), and the "noisy" crowd adds to the fun, even with decor that needs a "spruce up"; P.S. "reservations a must!"

Passage to India *Indian* | 19 | 16 | 19 | $33 |

Mt. Kisco | 17 Main St. (Kisco Park Dr.) | 914-244-9595 | www.passagetoindia.us
Set in a former jazz club made more "open and airy" than its predecessor, this Indian newcomer "adds much needed variety" to Mt. Kisco dining options with "above average" fare that's "getting better over time"; service is "pleasant", and as usual, the lunch buffet is a "deal" and "takeout" is a plus.

Pasta Amore *Italian* | 16 | 16 | 16 | $34 |

Piermont | 200 Ash St. (Piermont Ave.) | 845-365-1911 | www.pasta-amore.com
"When you don't feel like cooking or spending too much" or just need a "late-night pasta fix", this "predictable" Piermont Northern Italian hits the spot; "cheerful" ambiance gets a boost from windows (and a patio) overlooking the Tappan Zee bridge spanning the Hudson River, so even if you don't "love the pasta", the view is "fabulous."

Pasta Cucina *Italian* | 20 | 16 | 19 | $30 |

New City | 253 S. Little Tor Rd. (Middletown Rd.) | 845-638-4729
Stony Point | 32 S. Liberty Dr. (Central Dr.) | 845-786-6060
Suffern | 8 N. Airmont Rd. (NY Thrwy., exit 14B) | 845-369-1313
www.pastacucina.com
These "cheap and cheerful", "family-friendly" Rockland County "neighborhood hot spots" dish up "humongous portions" of Italian eats and "bottomless salad bowls" via a staff that makes you "feel well taken care of"; no surprise, they're "always packed" (and "noisy"), although the New City branch's move to Beth Carrie's roomier old space is a "big step up" that "should cut the waiting time" some.

	FOOD	DECOR	SERVICE	COST

Pasta Vera *Italian* | 20 | 13 | 16 | $31

Greenwich | 48 Greenwich Ave. (W. Putnam Ave.), CT | 203-661-9705 | www.pastavera.com

Paesanos proclaim this "long-lived" Greenwich Italian with "huge portions" and "reasonable prices" "surprisingly good"; takeout is available for those who criticize the "charmless setting", but even they may pull up a chair and cheer the "warm" decor in the "recently renovated" dining room.

Pastina's Ristorante *Italian* | 18 | 12 | 16 | $28

Hartsdale | Hartsdale Plaza | 155 S. Central Ave. (S. Washington Ave.) | 914-997-7900

"Cramped is an understatement" at this "popular" Hartsdale strip-mall Italian that comforts carb-lovers with "hearty" "dependable" pasta in "huge portions" and "nice, big glasses of wine"; sure it "needs an overhaul" and the staff barely "stays sane" amid the "chaotic" environment, but with an "early-bird special" this "good" ($11.95 for two courses, Sunday–Thursday), who cares?

Pastorale Bistro & Bar Ⓜ *French* | 23 | 21 | 21 | $49

Lakeville | 223 Main St./Rte. 44 (Lincoln City Rd.), CT | 860-435-1011 | www.pastoralebistro.com

"For city flavors in the country", gourmets gravitate to chef Frederic Faveau's "excellent" bistro, a "wonderful respite" from the "Lakeville/Salisbury scene" for "delicious and bountiful" French cuisine; it's set in a "warm, cozy" Colonial near Lime Rock racetrack, and run by a "friendly and enthusiastic staff."

Patang Indian Restaurant *Indian* | 20 | 14 | 19 | $31

Yonkers | 2223 Central Park Ave. (Roxbury Dr.) | 914-793-8888 | www.patangcuisine.com

"Live sitar music" on Saturdays livens up this "traditional" Yonkers Indian with "affordable" food that's "well prepared", if "ordinary"; critics comment that the "shopping-center" location and "sparse" decor are on the "drab" side, but the "attentive" staff compensates.

Patrias Restaurant *Peruvian* | ▽ 22 | 15 | 21 | $31

Port Chester | 35½ N. Main St. (bet. Adee St. & Westchester Ave.) | 914-937-0177

"Surprises" abound at this "wonderful restaurant" in Port Chester that mixes Spanish and Peruvian cuisines to yield "interesting combinations of tastes" and especially "delicious seafood"; "reasonable prices", a "charming chef" and live music nightly make this "cute" place a "welcome addition" to the neighborhood.

Peekamoose *American* | ▽ 25 | 24 | 22 | $41

Big Indian | 8373 Rte. 28 (Lasher Rd.) | 845-254-6500 | www.peekamooserestaurant.com

What "a delightful surprise!" exclaim those who've stumbled upon the "truly fine" Traditional American fare dispensed at this Big Indian eatery in the middle of a "culinary wasteland"; the staff is "green" yet "gracious", while the 19th-century building's high ceilings, red walls and driftwood chandelier add up to a "cozy" yet "stunning setting" that's a "perfect spot to hunker down after a day in the Catskills."

Pellicci's *Italian*
20 | 11 | 20 | $28

Stamford | 96-98 Stillwater Ave. (bet. Alden & Spruce Sts.), CT | 203-323-2542 | www.pelliccisrestaurant.com

"You must try the baked chicken" order enthusiasts of this "old-school", family-run Stamford Italian that "never fails" to serve up "big portions" of "comfort food", making it "a favorite for families celebrating special occasions"; some say it "looks like a mausoleum", but that doesn't keep wallet-watchers from proclaiming "it's one of the best bangs for the buck."

Penang Grill *Pan-Asian*
23 | 14 | 20 | $27

Greenwich | 55 Lewis St. (Greenwich Ave.), CT | 203-861-1988

"It's all about the Pan-Asian food" at this BYO Greenwich "keeper" known for its "wonderful pad Thai" and other "treats"; it's a "tiny" operation offering "a lot of bang for the buck" and "always-smiling service" that's "as fast as a McDonald's drive-thru", which makes it a "refreshing change from the snobby scene" that surrounds it.

Peppino's Ristorante *Italian*
16 | 13 | 18 | $35

Katonah | 116 Katonah Ave. (Jay St.) | 914-232-3212 | www.peppinosristorante.com

"Set in an old railroad station", this "tried-and-true" Katonah spot "doesn't pretend to be" more than "solid" Northern Italian, though diners divide on whether this joint that's "popular" is "dependable" or just "boring"; though service is "friendly", it works best for "a quick pizza or hero"; N.B. the Decor score may not reflect a recent redo.

Peter Pratt's Inn Ⓜ *American*
23 | 21 | 20 | $52

Yorktown | 673 Croton Heights Rd. (Rte. 118) | 914-962-4090 | www.prattsinn.com

"Country dining as it should be!" proclaim proponents of this "elegant", "atmospheric" Yorktown inn where "imaginative" New American cuisine is "prepared to the highest standards", utilizing local ingredients; depending on the season, seating by the "roaring fireplace" or on the "splendid veranda" are equally "appealing", and even if a few feel decor could use a "spruce up", it's still considered a "place to impress" and a "splurge" that's "satisfying in every way."

Pete's Saloon & Restaurant ❶ *Pub Food*
16 | 14 | 17 | $27

Elmsford | 8 W. Main St. (Rte. 9A) | 914-592-9849 | www.petessaloon.com

After a redo in 2005, this "casual" Elmsford "bar and grill" has "gone up a few notches", making it a "solid" choice for "plentiful" "pub fare" like burgers; "live rock music" on weekends and "sports on TV" add to its "local" appeal.

Ⓩ P.F. Chang's *Chinese*
20 | 19 | 17 | $31

White Plains | Westchester Mall | 125 Westchester Ave. (bet. N. B'way & Paulding St.) | 914-997-6100 | www.pfchangs.com

"Always crowded and chaotic", this "glitzy", "high-end" Chinese chain in White Plains' Westchester mall assures a "diverse" – if "far

FOOD | DECOR | SERVICE | COST

from authentic" – "Asian-inspired" meal, which fans deem "reliable" for an "après-shopping" stop; despite "disorganized" service, the "wonderful" "lettuce wraps", "good drinks" and "vegan" and "gluten-free" options will keep everyone happy.

NEW Phoenix *American/Asian*
- | - | - | E

Mt. Tremper | Emerson Resort & Spa | 5340 Rte. 28 (Mt. Pleasant Rd.) | 845-688-7700 | www.emersonresort.com

Emerging from the ashes after a serious fire two years ago, this Mt. Tremper newcomer in the rebuilt Emerson Resort & Spa is resplendent with tapestries setting off deep jewel tones throughout its three dining areas (one family-friendly, an adult-only haven and a large bar with its own lighter menu); New American cuisine has exotic Indian and Thai touches in keeping with the Silk Road theme, but dining on the terrace overlooking the Esopus Creek in warm weather is pure Catskills.

Piccola Trattoria Ⓜ *Italian*
19 | 14 | 19 | $33

Dobbs Ferry | 41 Cedar St. (bet. Ashford Ave. & Main St.) | 914-674-8427

This "family-owned" Dobbs Ferry restaurant "does a lot in very little space", serving "solid" Italian "home cooking" "with personal attention" in a "warm", if too "brightly lit", space; despite a few grumbles about high prices, most are happy to have this "neighborhood" spot "in [their] own backyard."

Picolo Restaurant Ⓜ *Italian*
20 | 15 | 19 | $35

Millbrook | 3279 Franklin Ave. (Church St.) | 845-677-1005

Voters who "visit" this "solid" Millbrook spot "quite often" report they "love" the way the mainly Italian menu "mixes" it up with "tasty" "eclectic" offerings – and fin fans note "the chef has a way with fish" too; neither eats nor digs are "too fancy", and the "no-reservations policy is a downer", but a "professional" staff and a kid-friendly vibe help make up for any "shortcomings."

Piero's *Italian*
21 | 10 | 20 | $38

Mt. Kisco | 132 E. Main St. (Green St.) | 914-241-7940
Port Chester | 44 S. Regent St. (Franklin St.) | 914-937-2904 Ⓜ

"Everything tastes homemade" at this "tiny" "neighborhood" eatery in Port Chester (with a newer, roomier Mt. Kisco outpost) with "exceptionally good" "wholesome Italian" "and lots of it"; if the wood-paneled dining room seems "shabby", "marvelous service" and "good prices" keep it so "packed", you might not notice.

Piggy Bank *BBQ*
18 | 19 | 18 | $26

Beacon | 448 Main St. (bet. Schenck & Tioronda Aves.) | 845-838-0028 | www.piggybankrestaurant.com

Even "rib snobs give a thumbs-up" to the "tasty" "traditional" BBQ at this "pubby" Beacon spot (and suggest you "ask for seconds" of the "delicious cornbread"); though some say the other grub's just "so-so" and "service slow", the "old-time" bank setting with its high ceilings, columns and "clever wine cellar in the vault" is "pleasing", and tabs "cheap" – you'll "never go home hungry."

	FOOD	DECOR	SERVICE	COST

Pillars Carriage House Ⓜ *Continental/French*
| | - | 19 | - | M |

New Lebanon | 860 Rte. 20 (County Rte. 5) | 518-794-8007 | www.pillarsrestaurant.com

"Gentlemen and ladies" love the "fine country dining" at this Columbia County carriage house where Alan O'Brient (of the Berkshires' Once Upon a Table) recently took over the reins with ex-Swoon Kitchenbar chef James Parry at the stove; still on offer are "very good" French-Continental "standards" and signature "hot popovers that are sheer pleasure", although modernists hope for an update on a menu that seems "frozen in the 1970s" and decor likewise: "send these people a Crate & Barrel catalog!"

Pinocchio Ⓜ *Italian*
| | 23 | 18 | 22 | $46 |

Eastchester | 309 White Plains Rd. (Highland Ave.) | 914-337-0044

Owner Tarcisio Fava makes everyone "feel welcome" at this "friendly" Eastchester spot that supporters swear serves the "most excellent Italiano" in town; it's "expensive" (especially "specials"), but with such "wonderful" service and cuisine, "on a good night you wouldn't want to be anywhere else."

Piper's Kilt ⓓ *American*
| | 20 | 9 | 16 | $21 |

Eastchester | 433 White Plains Rd. (Mill Rd.) | 914-961-9815 | www.piperskilt.com

"Hands down", this "congenial" Eastchester American "hangout" that's been around "forever" (since 1979, actually) still serves one of the "best burgers" around exclaim enthusiasts who don't mind the "noise" or "dive"-y, "publike atmosphere" (and suggest you "pass on the rest" of the menu); favored by "families", it's "always busy", so be prepared to "wait."

Plateau *Asian Fusion*
| | 21 | 19 | 20 | $33 |

Stamford | 25 Bank St. (bet. Atlantic Ave. & Main St.), CT | 203-961-9875 | www.plateaurestaurant.com

This "always-good" Southeast Asian fusion restaurant in Downtown Stamford offers "nicely prepared" Malaysian, Thai and Vietnamese dishes and "interesting specials" in a "calm", "comfortable" setting; the cost-conscious also declare it reasonably priced "by Fairfield County standards."

Plates Ⓜ *American*
| | 24 | 20 | 19 | $56 |

Larchmont | 121 Myrtle Blvd. (Maple St.) | 914-834-1244 | www.platesonthepark.com

"Amiable chef-owner" Matthew Karp serves up "absolutely fantastic" "unusual" fare with a "personal touch" at this Larchmont New American "yuppie hangout" set in a converted landmark building that has "all the style of a city restaurant" while retaining the "charm" of a small town; despite "flawed" service and "small portions" that are deemed "expensive", it remains a "cute, bright spot" in the local dining scene and one that's certainly "different for Westchester."

	FOOD	DECOR	SERVICE	COST

Plumbush Inn *American* | 22 | 25 | 23 | $52 |

Cold Spring | Plumbush Inn | 1656 Rte. 9D (Rte. 301) | 845-265-3904 |
www.plumbushinn.net

Recently done up in "gorgeous" "Victorian splendor", this "quaint",
"secluded" Cold Spring inn's dining rooms set a "refined", "romantic"
mood perfect for "popping the question"; "traditional and avant-
garde" New American cuisine is delivered by "real waiters who know
how to serve", the wine list is "superior", the "gardens beautiful"
(don't miss the new veranda) – and "oh, yeah, the food's good too!"

Plum Tree *Japanese* | 20 | 18 | 19 | $36 |

New Canaan | 70 Main St. (Locust Ave.), CT | 203-966-8050 |
www.plumtreejapanese.com

This New Canaan Japanese tucked away in a "neat basement space"
across the street from Town Hall draws lots of "local families" with
"consistently good sushi" and the added attraction of a kid-friendly
"koi pond in the middle of the dining room"; however, some peace-
seeking patrons protest that raucous children "seem to rule" here.

Polpo *Italian* | 24 | 21 | 19 | $60 |

Greenwich | 554 Old Post Rd. No. 3 (W. Putnam Ave.), CT |
203-629-1999 | www.polporestaurant.com

If you can get past "the parade of Ferraris in the parking lot", you'll
find a "lively" "back-road Greenwich" Italian with a "great", albeit
"loud, bar" scene and "excellent seafood (killer angry lobster) and
veal dishes"; expect to pay "exorbitant prices" ("the wine list bor-
ders on extortion"), and surveyors suggest that you make "nice to
the maitre d'", as "the staff seems preoccupied with who's who and
caters to the celeb set."

NEW Pony Express 🚫🍸 *American* | - | - | - | I |

Pleasantville | 30 Wheeler Ave. (bet. Bedford & Manville Rds.) |
914-769-7669 | www.ponyexpresstogo.com

A gallop away from his Iron Horse Grill in Pleasantville, chef Philip
McGrath has opened this laid-back New American newcomer proffering health-conscious fast food with a menu that includes nitrate-free
hot dogs, hormone-free sliders and french fries without the trans
fats; given the limited space (eight seats), in-the-know patrons fax
or phone ahead their order and take advantage of curbside pickup.

Portobello Café 🔲 *Italian/Mexican* | ▽ 25 | 17 | 25 | $27 |

Montrose | 2081 Albany Post Rd. (Memorial Dr.) | 914-737-2244

Those in-the-know love this "cozy hideaway" in Montrose where
"charming" chef-owners "expertly" prepare "unusual" Mexican-Italian
fusion food full of "complex flavors"; though the "tiny" strip-mall
setting is deemed "uncomfortable" by some, it's still "worth seeking
out" for something that's "just a little different"; N.B. it's BYO.

Portofino Pizza & Pasta 🍸 *Italian* | 21 | 9 | 16 | $18 |

Goldens Bridge | A&P Shopping Ctr. | Rtes. 22 & 138 | 914-232-4363

"Unbelievably huge" slices as well as "irresistible" entrees like "the
best homemade pastas this side of Sicily" are the "draws" at this

"no-frills" "neighborhood place" in a Goldens Bridge shopping center; "friendly" service and kiddie appeal ensure this town's "one and only restaurant" is "usually crowded"; P.S the Decor score might not reflect a recent "upgrade" that added fishing village murals and comfy booths.

Portofino Ristorante ⓂItalian

▽ 22 | 16 | 21 | $31

Staatsburg | 57 Old Post Rd. (River Rd.) | 845-889-4711 | www.portofinorest.com

"If you can find the place", you'll discover "the star" at this "friendly" Staatsburg Italian is "just plain good", "well-prepared, tasty" food; decor is "like a home away from home", assuming your home is "without pretension", while the "value" is "hard to beat."

Portofino's II ⌷ Italian

20 | 17 | 19 | $35

Wilton | 10 Center St. (Rte. 106), CT | 203-761-9115

This "locally popular" "neighborhood watering hole" attracts lots of Wilton families with "consistently good" "Italian home cooking" like pizzas and "seasonally changing specials" served in a "charming Tuscan" setting; the less-enthused observe that when the "highly mobile children" come "untethered from their parents" the place "feels more like a playground than a restaurant", but what rankles respondents more is the "no-plastic" policy.

Post Corner Pizza Pizza

18 | 9 | 15 | $19

Darien | 847 Boston Post Rd. (Mansfield Ave.), CT | 203-655-7721

A Darien "favorite for over 35 years", this Greek-style pizzeria serves "thick, pan-crust" pies, "excellent gyros" "and huge salads"; they get you "in and out" quickly, which is a good thing, because it's "full of noisy kids at all hours" and as the Decor score suggests, the setting "could stand an upgrade in appearance."

Primavera Italian

23 | 22 | 23 | $50

Croton Falls | 592 Rte. 22 (Sun Valley Dr.) | 914-277-4580 | www.primaverarestaurantandbar.com

The "lovely countrified" home in Croton Falls that formerly housed the Finch Tavern has been transformed into this new Italian ("yes, another Italian") serving "phenomenal" cuisine of the North, with "tableside" preparation of fish and flambées; if the menu is "a little pricey", the staff is "hands-on" and "willing to please" and the "beautiful room" and "view" make it "worth a return visit"; P.S. the "cool" wine cellar is available for private parties.

Priya Ⓜ Indian

20 | 15 | 20 | $28

Suffern | 36 Lafayette Ave. (bet. Chestnut St. & Rte. 202) | 845-357-5700 | www.priyaindiancuisineny.com

"Great scott! good Indian in Suffern!" cry curry enthusiasts who like the "consistently" "terrific" tikka masala, tandoori and such at this Rockland County outpost, citing the "luncheon buffet" as an especially "good value"; the decorative touches in the plain room strike style mavens as "a bit tacky" but most concur, "overall, it's a nice experience."

Purdys Homestead ⓜ American | 23 | 25 | 24 | $56 |
North Salem | 100 Titicus Rd. (bet. Rtes. 22 & 116) | 914-277-2301
This "charming", "romantic destination" in North Salem continues to attract for "special occasions", "especially in winter" when "warmth from multiple fireplaces" makes this converted farmhouse "cozy inside"; the "delectable" New American cuisine is served by an "attentive" staff, though a number of naysayers feel the food is "lackluster" and "doesn't match up" with the "beautiful surroundings."

Q Restaurant & Bar BBQ | 23 | 11 | 16 | $24 |
Port Chester | 112 N. Main St. (bet. Adee St. & Willette Ave.) | 914-933-7427 | www.qrestaurantandbar.com
"There's no finer way to increase your cholesterol count" than by gorging on "down-home" "mouthwatering" 'cue that "rivals Texas" at this "affordable", order-at-the-counter "favorite" for "finger-licking ribs" in Port Chester; the decor is "spare", portions are "enormous" and the staff is "eager to please"; as an added bonus – the mason jars for beverages are "for keeping."

Quinta Steakhouse Portuguese/Steak | 18 | 15 | 17 | $42 |
Pearl River | 24 E. Central Ave. (bet. Main & William Sts.) | 845-735-5565
An on-the-premises butcher shop tips Rockland County carnivores craving steaks and burgers that they'll find them at this "popular" spot; maybe "it ain't NYC" quality, but "Portuguese-style dishes" perk up the menu, and the "$10 lunch is a bargain"; a "SoHo atmosphere" includes the "plus" of sidewalk seating, and if service is "uneven", owners Ricardo and Armando Cerdeira are always "hospitable."

Raccoon Saloon Pub Food | ▽ 19 | 16 | 18 | $32 |
Marlboro | 1330 Rte. 9W (Western Ave.) | 845-236-7872 | www.raccoonsaloon.com
Loyalists "miss the old owners'" "magic touch" at this Marlboro New American that changed hands a few years back, though unchanged is "decent, down-to-earth" pub grub, plus the "good" burgers (and signature basil ice cream) it's famous for; tavern-style decor includes a rustic, beamed-ceilinged bar, while there's still a "lovely view of the waterfall" in back from the balcony.

Rangoli Indian | ▽ 21 | 20 | 20 | $32 |
New Rochelle | 615 Main St. (Maple Ave.) | 914-235-1306 | www.rangoliindiancuisine.com
After a rockslide forced them out of their Pelham abode, this "very good" Indian eatery has taken up in "fancy new digs" in New Rochelle; surveyors happily report the "well-spiced" cuisine has "improved with location", and the "friendly" service from the "enthusiastic family staff" continues to make it a "nice place" no matter where they are.

NEW Rani Mahal Indian | - | - | - | M |
Mamaroneck | 322-323 Phillips Park Rd. (bet. E. Prospect Ave. & Spencer Pl.) | 914-835-9066 | www.ranimahalny.com
This Mamaroneck Indian newcomer, sibling to Mughal Palace in Valhalla, features upscale takes on multiregional offerings including

| | FOOD | DECOR | SERVICE | COST |

chicken makhani and lobster tandoori in addition to the usual kormas and masalas; the tranquil atmosphere comes via burgundy booths, linen tablecloths and fresh flowers on each table as well as a view that overlooks nearby Phillips Park.

Ray's Cafe *Chinese*
| | 19 | 7 | 16 | $26 |

Larchmont | 1995 Palmer Ave. (bet. Chatsworth Ave. & Glendale Dr.) | 914-833-2551
Rye Brook | Rye Ridge Shopping Ctr. | 176 S. Ridge St. (bet. Bowman Ave. & I-287) | 914-937-0747

"When the craving for Chinese hits", this Larchmont Shanghai "landmark" (with a newer Rye Brook sibling) "answers the call" with "no-fuss", "fresh" "favorites" "without the grease" or "heavy sauces" but with "no atmosphere" either; the "bland", scruffy luncheonette decor "is only a step up from the food court" – maybe that's why fans consider it the "take-out champ."

Reality Bites *American*
| | 20 | 17 | 19 | $24 |

Nyack | 100 Main St. (B'way) | 845-358-8800 | www.realitybites.net
You can lounge on a sofa at this "easygoing" Rockland County eatery-cum–screening room and "sample some independent movies" by local filmmakers while tucking into tapas, "well-prepared salads", sandwiches or other "good" Traditional American eats; it's certainly an "original concept", though non–couch potatoes are "so glad they added tables" too.

☑ Rebeccas 🚫Ⓜ *American*
| | 26 | 20 | 22 | $68 |

Greenwich | 265 Glenville Rd. (Riversville Rd.), CT | 203-532-9270 | www.rkateliers.com
This "classy, sophisticated" New American "is a gift to Greenwich" and a "foodie's delight" say supporters who are sold on chef/co-owner Reza Khorshidi's "perfectly executed" "imaginative" cuisine and his wife Rebecca's "warm and genuine welcome" (although some sniff that's reserved for "her coterie only"); some critics cite "atrocious acoustics", "too many tables" and a "too-big-for-its-britches" attitude and conclude it's "overpriced and underwhelming", but they're outvoted.

Red Barn, The Ⓜ *American*
| | ▽ 19 | 12 | 14 | $43 |

West Ghent | 47 Old Post Rd./Rte. 9H (2 mi. north of Rte. 66) | 518-828-6677 | www.redbarneats.com
Chef Bert Goldfinger's "home cooking" in "large portions" gets the nod at this "laid-back, come-as-you-are" Traditional American in an "out-of-the-way" location in West Ghent; the setting – a 1950s ice cream parlor within (yes) a red barn – "captures the Columbia County vibe", so the biggest problem is "service so slow, you forget what day it is"; N.B. open Thursday–Sunday in high season.

Red Dot Restaurant & Bar Ⓜ *Eclectic*
| | 16 | 16 | 16 | $29 |

Hudson | 321 Warren St. (bet. City Hall Pl. & 3rd St.) | 518-828-3657
"Hudson's answer to a neighborhood watering hole", this "boisterous", "Villagey" Eclectic keeps 'em coming with "bar food" and lights casting a "glow that makes everyone look great"; all gather for

vote at zagat.com   123 "people-watching" either inside or on the patio complete with pond, and ignore only "ok" fare (which slipped five points from last year) and "abrasive", "I'm-not-really-a-waiter" service.

Red Hat, The ⓂFrench

| 22 | 21 | 22 | $44 |

Irvington | 63 Main St. (bet. Dutcher & Eckar Sts.) | 914-591-5888 | www.redhatbistro.com

Francophiles favor this "swanky" "village" bistro "tucked away" in Irvington with "fabulous" New American–French fare and "wonderful cocktails"; the "friendly host" "makes sure everyone is comfortable" in the somewhat "cramped" room, which fills up even more when a Belgian chanteuse performs on two Wednesdays a month.

Red Lotus ⓈⓂ Thai

| 21 | 17 | 19 | $30 |

New Rochelle | 227 Main St. (Stephenson Blvd.) | 914-576-0444

"It's a little on the pricey side", but the "enticing", if "basic", Thai fare at this New Rochelle newcomer with "lovely" decor makes for a "marvelous" "post-movie meal"; if you can't decide what to order, your "best bet is to ask" the "friendly staff" for suggestions.

Red Onion American

| 22 | 18 | 18 | $41 |

Saugerties | 1654 Rte. 212 (Glasco Tpke.) | 845-679-1223 | www.redonionrestaurant.com

Fans of this New American "favorite" near Woodstock in Saugerties have "only nice things to say" about the "delectable" cuisine that's "ever changing"; foes complain of "curt" service, but most folks find there's "no better place for an informal meal" – or a glass of wine from the "superb list" – than the madeover farmhouse, with its coral walls and red laminate tables; "local entertainment" is another "plus."

Red Rooster Drive-In ⊅ Hamburgers

| 19 | 10 | 18 | $12 |

Brewster | 1566 Rte. 22 (Rte. 312) | 845-279-8046

"Droves" drive to this roadside "blast from the past" in Brewster for a taste of "what fast food was" back in the '50s: "burgers, dogs and fries that can't be beat", the "best ice cream" and "excellent" shakes; it's outdoor seating only and strictly "no-frills" unless you count the "miniature golf course next door", but it's a piece of "Americana" crow converts, so "don't change a thing!"

Reka's Thai

| 16 | 15 | 20 | $32 |

White Plains | 2 Westchester Ave. (Main St.) | 914-949-1440

Service shines at this "friendly" White Plains Thai where owner Reka Souwapawong will "entertain you with stories and recipes" "when she's there", which makes for a real "treat"; yet, despite a "staff that tries very hard to please", connoisseurs counter the food's "just average" and "much too expensive", as well; N.B. the Decor score may not reflect a recent renovation.

Relish Ⓜ American/Eclectic

| 25 | 16 | 21 | $50 |

Sparkill | 4 Depot Sq. (Main St.) | 845-398-2747 | www.relishsparkill.com

Once you discover this "amazing" American-Eclectic in not-yet-chic Sparkill, "you'll go back again and again" declare devotees, citing the "care taken with each course" on the "novel" menu, the "excellent" wine list and "effective team of staffers"; colorful recycled school chairs and plywood banquettes in the "tiny" onetime grocery store add up to a "cool", "downtown" setting that "doesn't have the flash" of some famous neighbors, but not many mind because it's all "super"; N.B. the Food score may not reflect a post-Survey chef change.

Restaurant M *Mediterranean*　　▽ 26 | 14 | 23 | $39

Germantown | 2 Church Ave. (Main St.) | 518-537-2160

It "gets better and better" at this Germantown newcomer coo the converted chowing down on chef-owner Marisa Scali's "exciting" Mediterranean menu of "delicious homemade" fare; signature dishes like warm fig pancake with prosciutto suit sophisticates and the sprinkling of celebs who drop into the simple space, while pizza straight from the wood-burning oven pleases kids; N.B. only open Thursdays–Sundays.

Z Restaurant X &　　　　　　27 | 26 | 26 | $58
Bully Boy Bar M *American*

Congers | 117 Rte. 303 (bet. Lake Rd. & Rte. 9W) | 845-268-6555 | www.xaviars.com

"More casual" than his flagship Xaviar's, this Congers New American is still just "what you'd expect from Peter Kelly": "lovingly prepared", "top-rate" dishes, a "well-trained", "highly professional" staff and "tastefully decorated" rooms in a "picturesque setting"; "while a bit pricey", all the "extra touches" mean "you really don't feel it", especially if you "indulge in glorious excess" at the "magnifico", "all-you-can-eat" Sunday brunch or go for the $20.07 prix fixe lunch; it's all "consistently superior" "and then some."

Ricky's Seafood Restaurant *Seafood*　　15 | 12 | 16 | $41

Yonkers | 1955 Central Park Ave. (Heights Dr.) | 914-961-8284

It's "hit-or-miss" at this "homestyle" Yonkers Italian seafood "joint" – in business since 1931 – which dropped three Food points from last year; if a few find it "dependable" for "inexpensive" "fresh fish", they're countered by critics who claim it "used to be better", citing "flavorless" fare and "tired" decor on recent visits.

Rigatoni *Italian*　　　　　　　　– | – | – | M

Pelham | 124 Fifth Ave. (bet. 2nd & 3rd Sts.) | 914-738-7373

This low-key Pelham Italian is no longer just about Neapolitan wood-fired pizza, but has expanded its menu to include more meat and seafood entrees like brick-oven shrimp and veal Michelangelo; a full interior renovation in late 2006 imparted a modern look.

River Bank *American*　　　　　▽ 25 | 29 | 23 | $31

Cornwall-on-Hudson | 3 River Ave. (Rte. 218) | 845-534-3046 | www.theriverbank.biz

Chef-owner Lucie Provencher sure "knows her stuff" admit acolytes at this "lovely" Cornwall newcomer off to "a strong start"; "marvelous decor" in the former bank includes a mural of the river, mahogany paneling, soaring ceilings, a copper bar and a vault room, so factor in an "efficient" staff serving "sophisticated, delicious" New American food (or "the best" brick-oven pizza if you want something simple) and the money's on this place as "worth a detour."

River Cafe *Spanish*
▽ 17 | 18 | 21 | $45

New Milford | 300 Kent Rd./Rte. 7 (Boardman Rd.), CT | 860-355-4466 | www.rivercafe.org

The "friendly" chef-owner sets the tone for the "down-home service" and "congenial atmosphere" of this New Milford Spanish and tapas specialist known for its "generous portions" of paella; the "pleasant and cozy" setting includes a water view and fireplace, plus once a month a flamenco dancer adds a little fuel to the fire.

River City Grille *American/Eclectic*
20 | 18 | 20 | $39

Irvington | 6 S. Broadway (bet. Main St. & Sycamore Ln.) | 914-591-2033 | www.rivercitygrille.com

A "friendly neighborhood" vibe prevails at this "solid" Irvington New American–Eclectic in a reclaimed diner where "imaginative" entrees and "nice wines by the glass" appease adults while "crayons on the table" mean it's "kid-friendly" too; the "informal setting" with "cozy bar" and a "large back room perfect for parties" "keep locals coming" despite a few who quibble it's "somewhat overpriced"; N.B. the same owners are also behind the recently opened One.

River Club, The *American*
16 | 17 | 17 | $34

Nyack | 11 Burd St. (bet. Hudson River & River St.) | 845-358-0220 | www.nyackriverclub.net

"Spectacular" views of the marina and the Tappan Zee bridge may be "the best offerings" at this "down-home", "riverside" Nyack American; otherwise it's "nothing glamorous", just a place for "dependable" seafood and BBQ, so some suggest "stick to the burgers", salads or wraps and gaze outwards – the "scenery will surely please."

River Grill, The *American*
21 | 21 | 18 | $39

Newburgh | 40 Front St. (2nd St.) | 845-561-9444 | www.therivergrill.com

You get "lovely river views" and "people-watching" all in one at chef-owner Mark Mallia's "popular" Newburgh spot "situated right on the Hudson"; a "varied menu" of "well-prepared" New American fare is best enjoyed on the "wonderful", "breezy" terrace in warm weather, where service is "slow" or just "unrushed", depending on your mood.

Riverview Ⓜ ⊅ *American*
24 | 20 | 25 | $38

Cold Spring | 45 Fair St. (Main St.) | 845-265-4778 | www.riverdining.com

"Full tables" at this Cold Spring "jewel" "testify" to its "really good" "seasonal" New American food, with Italian accents that include "terrific" pizzas; a staff characterized by "casual efficiency and genuine warmth" serves amid "bright, cheery" surroundings, but insiders recommend you "get a seat outside on the porch and gaze at Storm King"; it's cash only, but they "thoughtfully point you to the nearest ATM" before you're seated.

Roasted Garlic at
The Red Hook Inn *American* ▽ 14 | 19 | 17 | $34

Red Hook | Red Hook Inn | 7460 S. Broadway/Rte. 9 (bet. Fraleigh St. & Rte. 199) | 845-758-8445 | www.roastedgarlicrestaurant.com
A "cheerful atmosphere" infuses the "inviting" Victorian-style rooms at Red Hook's "lovely country inn", where the chef mixes up the New American menu with roasted garlic soup, fish 'n' chips, baba ghanoush and such (even vegans aren't forgotten); too bad it's marred by "slow service" and "mediocre" fare "that may overreach."

Rockwells ● *American* 12 | 11 | 14 | $23

Pelham | 105 Wolfs Ln. (Hutchinson Pkwy.) | 914-738-5881
"Those with young kids" patronize this "noisy" Pelham "standby" for American "burgers and basics" that rate pretty "average", "even by chain standards"; with "slow" service and beyond-"casual" digs, it works best "after Little League" or to "watch the game" on the many TVs with the "rousing" crowd at the bar; N.B. the Tuckahoe branch closed in May 2006.

Roger Sherman Inn *Continental* 23 | 26 | 23 | $62

New Canaan | Roger Sherman Inn | 195 Oenoke Ridge/Rte. 124 (Holmewood Ln.), CT | 203-966-4541 | www.rogershermaninn.com
"Bring your favorite aunt for a special occasion" to this "preppy" "charmer" in a "classic" New Canaan inn with "luxe dining rooms", "old-world waiters" who are "at your beck and call" and "excellent Continental cuisine"; "in the summer, eat outdoors and watch the sun set from the veranda"; of course, it's all very "New England" so you might find it "stodgy if you are under 65"; N.B. jacket suggested.

Roma Ⓜ *Pizza* 17 | 8 | 15 | $25

Tuckahoe | 29 Columbus Ave. (Main St.) | 914-961-3175
"Stick to the pies" with "thin crusts like paper" says "fans" of this "old-time" Tuckahoe pizza "establishment" run by the third generation of the Tavalillo family; other Italian "comfort food" is "serviceable" while decor in the "cavernous" dining room is "no great shakes" and service is of the "hurry, what would you like" variety.

Romolo's Ⓜ *Italian* 19 | 18 | 21 | $44

Congers | 77 Rte. 303 (Tremont St.) | 845-268-3770 | www.romolos.net
"Remember Caesar salad prepared at table, the way it's supposed to be?" - that's how chef-owner Anthony Mingone does it at his Congers "big-portion, red-sauce Italian" that's been dishing up "flavorful" fare for decades; the "staff welcomes you" in a "classic" space with archways, large windows and deep-orange walls, so though critics aver it's "average across the board", most declare it's "an oldie, but still a goodie."

Rosendale Cafe *Vegetarian* ▽ 18 | 15 | 17 | $21

Rosendale | 434 Main St./Rte. 213 (bet. Central & Keator Aves.) | 845-658-9048 | www.rosendalecafe.com
This "well-meaning" Rosendale "'70s throwback" keeps it true with "vegetarian comfort food" (plus turkey dogs and tuna sandwiches

for non-veggies), "good microbrew beers on tap" and organic wines; in keeping with the vibe, storefront digs are yard-sale "funky" and the staff "laid-back", even on weekends when crowds crush in for "great performances" of folk, blues and "red-hot jazz."

☑ Rosie's Bistro Italiano *Italian*

23	19	21	$42

Bronxville | 10 Palmer Ave. (Paxton Ave.) | 914-793-2000

It's "a hit" proclaim proponents of this relatively new "upscale Italian bistro" in Bronxville, where a "hopping bar", "creative" cuisine and "wonderful service" make it an "extremely pleasant" experience "from beginning to end"; if "lousy parking" and "crowded" conditions deter some diners, you wouldn't know it from the masses that "fill up" this "popular" spot, especially on "weekends."

Route 22 *Pub Food*

15	18	14	$27

Armonk | 55 Old Rte. 22 (Kaysal Ct.) | 914-765-0022
NEW **Stamford** | 1980 W. Main St. (Alvord Ln.), CT | 203-323-2229
www.rt22restaurant.com

These "basic American burger joints" in Armonk and Stamford with "overcluttered" "vintage repair shop" decor serve "decent" "pub food" that's "good enough", but what really keeps them "jammed" with "families" are the kiddie meals served in classic muscle cars; "teenage" servers who are "inconsistent" do nothing to alleviate the "chaotic" feel.

Royal Palace *Indian*

▽ 18	9	18	$30

White Plains | 77 Knollwood Rd. (Dobbs Ferry Rd.) | 914-289-1988 |
www.royalindiapalace.com

"The Indian community flocks" to this White Plains standby for "authentic" and "satisfying" fare, including "buffet" options at lunch and dinner; the "spice and heat are on the mark", but "no awards" go to the decor of the large, generic, wedding hall–style dining room, which surveyors say has "no atmosphere."

Ruby's Hotel ⊠ Ⓜ *Eclectic/French*

–	–	–	M

Freehold | Ruby's Hotel | 3689 CR-67 (Rte. 32) | 518-634-7790 |
www.rubyshotel.com

Open for dinner only on Fridays and Saturdays, chef-owner Anna Sporer's Eclectic–French in the boonies of Greene County "suffers from its part-time status", but it's still a "shining star" for local "foodies" who "love" the "small" menu, "tiny, restored" art deco hotel, "accommodating staff" and "bonus of an art gallery upstairs"; another plus: "delightful creekside dining in summer", when it's open Thursdays too.

Ruby's Oyster Bar & Bistro *Seafood*

21	20	19	$48

Rye | 45 Purchase St. (Purdy Ave.) | 914-921-4166 |
www.rubysoysterbar.net

"It's impossible to have a bad time" at this "noisy" seafood "brasserie" in Rye that offers a "wide variety" of fin fare (including oysters "that can't be beat"), "excellent brunch" and 200 wines in a "surprisingly hip" and "sexy atmosphere"; the "lively bar scene" spills out onto the sidewalk in the summer, making it a "gem" for "people-watching."

Rustico *Italian*

| | 20 | 17 | 19 | $40 |

Scarsdale | 753 Central Park Ave. (Mt. Joy Ave.) | 914-472-4005
"Consistently good pasta", "pleasant" servers and a "downtown", though still "child-friendly", atmosphere make this "spacious" Italian "hangout" in a Scarsdale shopping center a "solid" choice for "casual dining"; though it's "popular with the locals", comfort-hounds call it "cramped" and say "conversation is impossible" given how "loud" it is.

☒ Ruth's Chris Steak House *Steak*

| | 23 | 19 | 22 | $59 |

Tarrytown | Marriott Westchester | 670 White Plains Rd. (bet. I-287 & Old White Plains Rd.) | 914-631-3311 | www.ruthschris.com
"It may be a chain", but "this is why God made us carnivores" claim proponents of "consistent, good-quality" "steaks drenched in butter" "that sizzle so much you can hear (and smell) them from across the room"; but cynics snipe that it's "under-decorated and overpriced" – "what's with everything being à la carte? for the $$$, throw in some carrots."

Sabatiello's *Italian*

| | 18 | 18 | 18 | $37 |

Stamford | 269 Bedford St. (Broad St.), CT | 203-353-3300 | www.sabatiellos.com
Fans of this Stamford Italian say the "friendly" chef-owner ensures the "reasonably priced" "Italian food stays consistently *delizioso*", plus they praise the upstairs "lounge", with "the best views" of Downtown and "live music on weekends"; however, the less-jazzed jape about the "bland fare" and "schizoid layout."

Sabroso *Nuevo Latino/Spanish*

| | ▽ 26 | 22 | 23 | $45 |

Rhinebeck | 22 Garden St. (W. Market St./Rte. 308) | 845-876-8688 | www.sabrosoplatos.com
"Perfectly delicious", "spot-on" Spanish and "imaginative" Nuevo Latino dishes come "beautifully presented" (like "the fish standing up") at this Rhinebeck two-year-old set "a wee bit off the main street"; the "food is exciting" for sure, but the vibe in the "very attractive" room is "soothing" and "calm" even when the crowd's indulging in "awesome margaritas", leading local sophisticates to "linger for hours" attended by the "welcoming" staff.

Saigon Café ⊄ *Vietnamese*

| | ▽ 18 | 5 | 21 | $16 |

Poughkeepsie | 6A LaGrange Ave. (Raymond Ave.) | 845-473-1392 | www.saigoncafe.net
It's certainly "not about ambiance" at this Poughkeepsie "husband-and-wife operation" where fans hunker down at "one of the few tables" for Vietnamese food and an "enjoyable chat" "with charming host" Hung Truong; it's "good value" too, so those who don't dig the digs simply say: "carry out."

Sakura *Japanese*

| | 18 | 13 | 20 | $30 |

Scarsdale | 56 Garth Rd. (Popham Rd.) | 914-723-7767
"Solid sushi" and "other traditional favorites" at "respectable prices" make this "small-town" Scarsdale Japanese an "easy" choice

for "locals"; "dreary" decor is offset by "caring" servers who "welcome everyone like old friends."

Salsa ⓂⒻ Southwestern   ▽ 19 | 8 | 19 | $21

New Milford | 54 Railroad St. (Bank St.), CT | 860-350-0701
"Come as you are" to this small New Milford spot, an "unlikely outpost of innovative but not fancy" Southwestern cooking, where the chef-owner makes "his food very spicy (unless you request it tamer)"; respondents praise the "friendly service", but give the open-kitchen, "bare-bones" setting a "zero for ambiance."

Sal's Pizza Ⓕ Pizza   25 | 6 | 13 | $12

Mamaroneck | 316 Mamaroneck Ave. (Palmer Ave.) | 914-381-2022
"Perfection in sauce and crust" defines this Mamaroneck "institution" that's "short on atmosphere", but serves pizza among "the best" "outside of NYC" to a steady stream of "teenagers", families and folks who "drive in from Connecticut" and line up "outside", "even in the winter"; "attitude" from "the counter guys" and "shabby" decor are "all part of the fun" for regulars who gladly "suffer" both, for another "sublime" slice.

Samba Na' Brasa Brazilian/Steak   ▽ 18 | 21 | 23 | $38

Mt. Vernon | 42 W. Broad St. (Fleetwood. Ave.) | 914-668-1112
"Make sure you don't fill up" on salads, sides or "freshly made" caipirinhas at this "enormous" Mt. Vernon Brazilian steakhouse that's "good for groups" and the main event is a "carnivore's dream" where "all-you-can-eat" "freshly grilled meats" ($27.95 at dinner) are sliced and served by "attentive" servers working the room; a few find the fare "uneven", but overall, it's a "fun experience"; N.B. there's live samba on Fridays and Saturdays.

Sam's Italian   18 | 10 | 18 | $29

Dobbs Ferry | 126-128 Main St. (Oak St.) | 914-693-9724
It's the "same ol' reliable", "red-sauce" fare and pizza at this Dobbs Ferry Italian that families find a "dependable" neighborhood "joint" with "friendly" service that's "good" "for a cheap night out"; despite a redo in 2005 (which included a paint job and improved lighting), critics call decor "unworthy", and prefer "takeout."

Sam's of Gedney Way American   18 | 15 | 19 | $35

White Plains | 52 Gedney Way (bet. Mamaroneck Ave. &
Old Mamaroneck Rd.) | 914-949-0978 | www.samsofgedneyway.com
This White Plains "neighborhood institution" has "been here forever" (over 70 years, in fact) serving "solid" American "comfort" foods including an especially "tasty" burger; most find the meals "dependable" and the staff "attentive", but the brass-rail tavern decor is "worn out" and needs an "update", despite a pleasant "new outdoor area."

Santa Fe Mexican/Southwestern   17 | 15 | 18 | $29

Tarrytown | 5 Main St. (Rte. 9) | 914-332-4452 |
www.santaferestaurant.com
The food's "a bit tame" at this Southwestern-Mexican in Tarrytown, but a mix of "light fare as well as cheese-covered favorites" and "in-

expensive" tabs still keep it "crowded"; the "happy atmosphere" comes courtesy of "pitchers of margaritas", a "friendly staff" plus earthy colors and "cute decorations" adorning the walls.

Santa Fe Ⓜ *Mexican* | 21 | 17 | 19 | $29 |

Tivoli | 52 Broadway (Montgomery St.) | 845-757-4100 | www.santafetivoli.com

"Always jumping", this "funky" Tivoli "favorite" dishes up "deftly prepared" "Mexican with a twist" in "colorful" quarters, where "attractive young waitresses" may be part of the draw for the "high-energy Bard students" who flock there; if you "don't mind" "lively acoustics", it's a "great place to linger over" "the best margaritas" or mojitos.

ⓩ Sapore *Seafood/Steak* | 26 | 23 | 23 | $48 |

Fishkill | 1108 Main St. (North St.) | 845-897-3300 | www.saporesteakhouse.com

"First rate and a bit of a surprise" in less than fancy Fishkill, this two-year-old cousin to Newburgh's Il Cenàcolo is a "New York City steakhouse wannabe" that succeeds with "superb beef and chops", game, seafood and a long wine list; "good service" plus rooms done up with mahogany paneling, soft colors and leather couches add a touch of traditional "class", so the only downside is "Manhattan prices" – "bring your piggy bank."

NEW Sardegna Ⓜ *Italian* | – | – | – | M |

Larchmont | 154 Larchmont Ave. (Addison St.) | 914-833-3399

A "splendid surprise", this Larchmont newcomer serves "sophisticated" Italian cuisine that's "enjoyable", though diners are "disappointed" not to find "more Sardinian" dishes on the menu; the warmly lit dining room makes a "relaxed" setting, and locals "hope" it's "here to stay."

NEW Savvy Restaurant *Mediterranean* | 18 | 18 | 15 | $51 |

New Canaan | 26 Locust Ave. (Forest St.), CT | 203-972-3303 | www.savvy-restaurant.com

Diners are divided over this new, "trying-hard" New Canaan Mediterranean: some say the "accomplished" cooking and patio seating make it "a welcome addition" to the area, but critics counter that "overpriced", "unimpressive" food and "marginal service" make for a "disappointing" experience.

Sazan *Japanese* | 24 | 12 | 18 | $39 |

Ardsley | 729 Saw Mill River Rd. (Center St.) | 914-674-6015

"Skillfully prepared", "beautifully presented sushi" wins raves from "executive guests from Japan" (especially those with "expense accounts") at this minimalist Ardsley eatery where the focus is on "traditional", "authentic" fare; service is formal (some call it "stiff"), and though decor is "understated", it's still "pleasant."

Scaramella's *Italian* | 21 | 13 | 19 | $40 |

Dobbs Ferry | 1 Southfield Ave. (Ashford Ave.) | 914-693-6024

"Skip the menu and go straight to the specials" instruct insiders of this Dobbs Ferry Italian where an "out-of-the-way" "strip-mall" location doesn't deter devotees of "massive portions" of "lip-smacking" "classics"; it's just like "the old neighborhood in the Bronx", down to "dated" decor, slightly "standoffish" waiters and a "colorful host."

Seaside Johnnie's *Seafood*   11 16 13 $35

Rye | 94 Dearborn Ave. (Forrest Ave.) | 914-921-6104 | www.seasidejohnnies.com

You "pay for" the "unbeatable view" at this "beachside" Rye seafooder that's "great fun with the kids pre-Playland" and a "nice place" to "sit outside" on a "hot day"; stick to a "summer cocktail or two", as the "spotty" service and only "tolerable" fare may leave you wishing it was "BYOF (bring your own food)."

Seasons American Bistro & Lounge *American*   20 19 19 $40

Somers | 289 Rte. 100 (Rte. 202) | 914-276-0600 | www.seasonsatsomers.com

A "sophisticated" spot "seemingly in the middle of nowhere", this Somers sophomore serves "surprisingly good" fare from a "varied" New American menu (the signature house-smoked ribs are "first-rate"); though some surveyors report it's still "a little wobbly", an "efficient" staff and an "airy" low-lit room and seasonal patio seating make it a pleasant "local dining experience."

Seasons Japanese Bistro *Japanese*   21 13 18 $34

White Plains | 105 Mamaroneck Ave. (Quarropas St.) | 914-421-1163

"Tasty sushi" "and "fair" prices prove a perfect match at this "convenient" Japanese in White Plains with "accommodating" servers; if it doesn't offer "much in the way of decor", the large portions are a "good value" and the sake selection (with more than 20 available by the glass) "is incredible."

☑ Serevan *Mediterranean*   25 20 23 $47

Amenia | 6 Autumn Ln. (Rte. 44, west of Rte. 22) | 845-373-9800 | www.serevan.com

"A master at flavor and texture", "ambitious" chef Serge Madikians honed his skills at swank NYC spots like Jean Georges and Bouley, then headed to Amenia to open this "unique" restaurant that's a "great addition to the area"; a simple sage-and-slate-blue "farmhouse setting" forms a backdrop for "imaginative", "delicious" Mediterranean dishes, "perfumed with subtlety", that reflect his Armenian heritage, all served by "an expert staff."

Sesame Seed ☒ *Mideastern*   19 15 16 $24

Danbury | 68 W. Wooster St. (bet. Division & Pleasant Sts.), CT | 203-743-9850

This chef-owned Middle Eastern "staple" is considered an "offbeat" "local treasure" by Danbury's "earthy granola" types that tout the "inexpensive" "tasty vegetarian dishes" like hummus; but while some find the decor – "shelf upon shelf of antique toys, photographs and kitsch" – "charming", others assert it's "overly funky" and needs a "makeover."

	FOOD	DECOR	SERVICE	COST

Seven Woks *Chinese* | 15 | 11 | 19 | $24 |

Scarsdale | 1122 Wilmot Rd. (Heathcote Rd.) | 914-472-4774
"They haven't changed the menu since the Ming Dynasty", but that doesn't deter "lazy Scarsdale folk" from frequenting this strip-mall Sino where the fare is "inexpensive" and "reliable" and "you can always find a friend in the dining room"; add in "hospitable" service, and it's a "decent" meal with "no surprises" – "favorable or otherwise."

NEW **Shadows on the Hudson** *American* | – | – | – | M |

Poughkeepsie | 176 Rinaldi Blvd. (bet. Church & Main Sts.) |
845-486-9500 | www.shadowsonthehudson.com
Everything's big at this ritzy Poughkeepsie newcomer perched on the banks of the Hudson, from the broad New American menu with its focus on steaks and seafood, to the huge windows overlooking the river; five themed dining areas suit any mood, but come happy hour, most gather at the long serpentine bar in the cocktail lounge, or in warm weather, head to the bar on the deck.

Ship Lantern Inn **M** *American/Continental* | ▽ 25 | 24 | 27 | $46 |

Milton | 1725 Rte. 9W (Old Indian Rd.) | 845-795-5400 |
www.shiplanterninn.com
"The staff, the style and the menu haven't changed since the '60s" at this "lovely" Milton New American–Continental, and loyalists hope it stays that way; "outstanding" "professional old-time service", "marvelous food" and "comfortable" surroundings in the beamed Revolutionary War–era building with its sea-faring motif make it an "utmost favorite" for "special occasions", while the "bargain" $16.95 Twilight menu has folks setting a course midweek too.

Ship to Shore *American/Seafood* | 23 | 19 | 21 | $38 |

Kingston | 15 W. Strand St. (B'way) | 845-334-8887 |
www.shiptoshorehudsonvalley.com
It's "smooth sailing" at chef-owner Samir Hrichi's "honest, hardworking" New American "hideaway" in Kingston's Rondout district, what with "tasty morsels" of "first-rate food", a "competent" staff and "a waterfront location that's all the atmosphere you need"; at night, a "fun crowd" creates a "hopping" "scene" at the bar, while quieter types "stick to the more intimate setting in the back room."

Siam Orchid *Thai* | 20 | 12 | 20 | $29 |

Scarsdale | 750 Central Park Ave. (Mt. Joy Ave.) | 914-723-9131
"Tame, but reliable" is the consensus about this Scarsdale Thai "with a nice variety of dishes" but which could use a little "more oomph" in terms of spicing; decor's a bit "shopworn", but the "warm" staff that "really lets you take your time" makes the atmosphere "easygoing and relaxed."

Siena **S** *Italian* | 23 | 18 | 21 | $41 |

Stamford | 519 Summer St. (bet. Broad & Spring Sts.), CT |
203-351-0898 | www.sienaristorante.net
The owner "will welcome you with open arms" at this "sophisticated" Northern Italian in Downtown Stamford, which surveyors salute for

its "outstanding homemade pastas", "superb specials" and "great wine list"; service "could not be more accommodating", though some reviewers recommend that to combat "the decibel level" of the "loud, clangy interior" "they should teach the staff sign language."

Smokey Joe's *BBQ*

| 19 | 7 | 10 | $19 |

Stamford | 1308 E. Main St./Rte. 1 (Weed Ave.), CT | 203-406-0605 | www.waiterontherun.com

"Go for the ribs and get dirty" at this "surprisingly good" Stamford barbecue "joint" where the "cheap" eatin' can be done at the "upstairs bar" "with beer on tap" or "downstairs with the kiddies" at "redwood picnic tables"; if "cafeteria-style service" and a "decrepit setting" "feel too backcountry to be comfortable", "get takeout."

Solaia *Italian*

| ▽ 20 | 20 | 18 | $48 |

Greenwich | Greenwich Financial Ctr. | 363 Greenwich Ave. (Fawcett Pl.), CT | 203-622-6400 | www.solaiaenoteca.com

Oenophiles who admire this "great wine bar" come for the "incredible selection" of vinos (400 by the bottle, 55 by the glass), but "stay for the tasty small plates" of Italian eats, which fans favor as a "less formal alternative to the big-deal dinner places in Greenwich"; however, just because the portions are petite, don't expect the prices to be.

Solé Ristorante *Italian*

| 21 | 18 | 18 | $45 |

New Canaan | 105 Elm St. (bet. Park St. & South Ave.), CT | 203-972-8887 | www.soleofnewcanaan.com

"Watching the chefs prepare wonderful" cuisine like "excellent pizzas" "is always a highlight" at this "lively" New Canaan Northern Italian with "lovely" decor; but opponents opine the "submarinelike acoustics" will have you rushing to "Times Square to get some peace and quiet" and add they find the "indifferent" staff "arrogant."

NEW Sonoma California Cafe *Californian*

| - | - | - | M |

Brewster | 90 Independent Way (Rte. 312) | 845-278-5261

Brewster gets a blast of California at this trendy newcomer serving up quesadillas, spring rolls with shredded duck and mildly spicy crab cakes as well as burgers, steaks, chicken and sandwiches; large windows lend an airy feel to the cheery space done up with faux stone, tilework behind the bar and art deco–style murals, so noshers can pretend they're on the other coast whether seated in a booth or at a table in the back.

Z Sonora *Nuevo Latino*

| 25 | 22 | 21 | $47 |

Port Chester | 179 Rectory St. (Willett Ave.) | 914-933-0200 | www.sonorany.com

"Brilliant", "well-presented" Nuevo Latino fare and "killer cocktails" make dinner at "fantastically creative" chef Rafael Palomino's "off-the-beaten-path" Port Chester restaurant (sister to Pacifico) like a "sophisticated" "vacation in South America"; the atmosphere is "festive", making it a "new favorite" for "special occasions", and if the dining room is occasionally "too noisy", "start with the biggest mojito you can get" and you may not "care."

Soul Dog 🗷 *Hot Dogs* ▽ 21 | 17 | 23 | $12

Poughkeepsie | 107 Main St. (bet. Clover & Perry Sts.) | 845-454-3254 |
www.souldog.biz

They "make 'em like you want 'em" at this "friendly" Poughkeepsie
purveyor known for "excellent hot dogs" with "awesome toppings", as
well as other American lunch favorites such as homemade soups and
chili; lots of "gluten-free options" and veggie choices please anyone
with "special dietary needs", while all like the "reasonable rates"
and "welcoming", colorful digs; N.B. they now offer beer and wine.

Southbound Bar-B-Que 🅼 *BBQ* 17 | 11 | 16 | $25

Valhalla | 301 Columbus Ave. (Highclere Ln.) | 914-644-7427 |
www.southboundbbq.com

When "the mood for ribs or pulled pork" strikes, this BBQ set in a
"funky" Valhalla "roadhouse" delivers with "slow-cooked" hickory-
smoked meat "that's a beautiful pink" say cue connoisseurs who
confide, "if it's not the real thing, it's close"; "bare-bones decor" is
"none too pretty", but the "unpretentious" staff, "modest prices"
and live music on weekends make it a "fun night out"; N.B. there's an
all-you-can-eat buffet Tuesday–Thursday.

Southport Brewing Co. *Pub Food* 16 | 17 | 16 | $26

Stamford | 131 Summer St. (Broad St.), CT | 203-327-2337 |
www.southportbrewing.com

"There's a beer to fit every mood" at this "loud" Stamford chain link
that features pub grub, Italian-American dishes and a "good children's
menu"; fans view this "comfy fallback" as a "faithful friend", but foes
file it as a "relic of the in-house brewer boom."

Southwest Cafe *New Mexican* 20 | 17 | 21 | $27

Ridgefield | 109 Danbury Rd. (bet. Copps Hill Rd. & South St.), CT |
203-431-3398 | www.culinarymenus.com

Amigos insist you'll "ease your ride off into the sunset" by eating at
this 20-year-old Ridgefield New Mexican with "good" cooking and a
"very colorful setting" that's enhanced by authentic Navajo artwork
and a "warm, welcoming staff"; but enimigos assert: "I don't get it –
it's in a shopping center and the food is only ok."

Spaccarelli's 🅼 *Italian* 22 | 20 | 21 | $45

Millwood | Millwood Town Plaza | 238 Saw Mill River Rd./Rte. 100
(Rte. 133) | 914-941-0105 | www.spaccarellisrestaurant.com

"Hearty" fare with a "refined" touch is the draw at this "high-end"
Millwood Italian that's "still good after all these years", even if wallet-
watchers say it's "getting pricey"; the setting, with sunny yellow walls
and alfresco dining in season, is "sophisticated", and while the staff is
"accommodating", a few suspect "pet customers" are "better served."

Spiga *Italian* 17 | 17 | 17 | $34

Scarsdale | 718 Central Park Ave. (Mt. Joy Ave.) | 914-725-8240 |
www.racanellirestaurants.com

"It's not exactly haute cuisine", but this family-style Scarsdale
Italian moves "*molto*" mounds of "standard" fare making it "a great

| | FOOD | DECOR | SERVICE | COST |

value for the money" (and a "good place to feed hungry teenagers"); the "large" dining room has a "festive" air that works well with "group dinners", and if sensitive sorts "wish the acoustics were better", others opine that "being loud is part of the fun."

Spiritoso *Italian* ▽ 22 | 17 | 20 | $38

Yonkers | 811 McLean Ave. (Aqueduct St.) | 914-237-4075 | www.spiritosoristorante.com

An open kitchen pumps out "well-prepared" fare at this Yonkers Italian that caters to "families" with portions that "could serve an army" and prices that are "a good value"; add in a "respectful staff" and "live music" on Fridays and it's one of the more "enjoyable" places in town.

NEW Spring Asian Cuisine *Pan-Asian* - | - | - | M

Mt. Vernon | 545 Gramatan Ave. (Broad St.) | 914-699-2828

"Not your run-of-the-mill Chinese restaurant", this Mt. Vernon relative newcomer now includes "all things Asian" on the menu (including Japanese, Thai, Malaysian and Indonesian elements) and "live jazz on Saturdays"; "excellent" service, seasonal sidewalk seating and "takeout" are also appealing.

Squires of Briarcliff *American* 18 | 9 | 15 | $22

Briarcliff Manor | 94 N. State Rd. (Briarcliff-Peekskill Pkwy.) | 914-762-3376

It's "basically a bar", but this Briarcliff Traditional American "classic" is a "favorite for locals" for "terrific burgers", fries, onion rings and other pub grub; the wood-heavy, tavern decor "hasn't changed much in over a quarter of a century", but it's still the "Friday scene for middle-aged couples" stopping in for a "reasonable", "quick" bite.

St. Andrew's Cafe Ⓢ *American* 24 | 21 | 22 | $38

Hyde Park | Culinary Institute of America | 1946 Campus Dr. (Rte. 9) | 845-471-6608 | www.ciachef.edu

"Stellar cuisine for the nutrition conscious" is the goal at the most "relaxed" of the Hyde Park culinary school's restaurants, which explains the "many heart healthy" choices on its "interesting" New American menu; there's a "cheerful atmosphere" in the "spacious dining room", so try to overlook "nervous" student servers who sometimes get "tangled up", because they "really want you to enjoy" the experience.

Steakhouse 22 Ⓜ *American/Steak* ▽ 17 | 16 | 15 | $38

Patterson | 2693 Rte. 22 (Haviland Hollow Rd.) | 845-878-9877 | www.steakhouse22.com

As the name suggests, this "relaxed" Traditional American in Patterson plies "simply prepared", "solid comfort food" like prime rib, homemade pies and other robust repasts; the "homey" decor in the three dining rooms is "much more pleasant than the exterior" suggests, so "request a fireside table" or head to the deck in warm weather and wait for slow but "solicitous service."

	FOOD	DECOR	SERVICE	COST

Sterling Inn, The M *American/French* | 20 | 19 | 18 | $54 |

New Rochelle | 1279 North Ave. (Quaker Ridge Rd.) | 914-636-2400 |
www.thesterlinginnrestaurant.com

Chef-owner Sterling Smith brings "NYC gourmet to the 'burbs" with his "classy and elegant" New American–French eatery in New Rochelle that's "warm and welcoming" with exposed-brick walls and a polished wood bar; though the "creative" fare reflects his "high aspirations", prices are even "higher" and a few take issue with service that can be "pretentious"; N.B. there's occasional live music and a Sunday jazz brunch.

Stissing House *French/Italian* | 19 | 21 | 18 | $46 |

Pine Plains | 7801 S. Main St./ Rte. 199 (Rte. 82) | 518-398-8800 |
www.stissinghouse.com

After going "through so many incarnations" in recent years, this "grand, old" 1782 hostelry in "the middle of nowhere" (aka Pine Plains) is now in the hands of ex-NYC's Provence team Patricia and Michel Jean, who are offering "tantalizing" French-Italian entrees, "amazing pizzas" and other fare "worthy" of the setting; rooms in the "restored" inn are "very pretty" ("a seat by the fireplace is heaven"), so some say the "only shortcoming is the service"; N.B. movies are screened upstairs on weeknights.

Stonehenge S *Continental/French* | 23 | 23 | 23 | $61 |

Ridgefield | Stonehenge Inn | 35 Stonehenge Rd. (Rte. 7), CT |
203-438-6511 | www.stonehengeinn-ct.com

Staunch traditionalists say you "can't go to Ridgefield and not visit" this "high-end" inn situated on 11 acres with views of a "charming duck pond"; they tout its "well-crafted", "if not terribly imaginative", French-Continental cuisine like medallions of elk with huckleberry sauce and "excellent service", but modernists maintain its "overpriced" "old-school food" and decor are "disappointing."

Stoneleigh Creek M *Eclectic* | 23 | 17 | 21 | $47 |

Croton Falls | 166 Stoneleigh Ave. (Rte. 100) | 845-276-0000 |
www.stoneleighcreek.com

"Tiny, remote" and totally "worth it" (especially the "bargain" $14.95 prix fixe lunch), this "romantic" "little spot" in a "quaint" "old house" in Croton Falls pairs "delicious", "imaginative" Eclectic cuisine with a "wonderful" selection of wines; add in "top-notch hospitality" and you've got a "gem" that's "extremely popular, and deservedly so."

Strega *Italian* | - | - | - | M |

Pleasantville | 2 Broadway (Bedford Rd.) | 914-769-4040 |
www.strega-restaurant.com

Reopened in February after a five-month renovation, this Pleasantville restaurant is roomier now, with 94 seats, wood floors and a Tuscan-Mediterranean vibe; new chef Carmelo D'Aprile (formerly of Grappolo Locando in Chappaqua) turns out dishes like signature panzanella (bread salad) and veal chop Milanese from an Italian menu.

	FOOD	DECOR	SERVICE	COST

Striped Bass *Seafood* — 16 | 15 | 14 | $35

Tarrytown | Tarrytown Bow Club | 236 W. Main St. (Green St.) |
914-366-4455 | www.stripedbassny.com

You can "enjoy the tremendous views" of the "glorious Hudson" at
this Tarrytown seafooder that locals liken to a "mini-vacation", especially in summer when the outdoor Cabana Bar & Grill "grills" up
burgers and other offerings in a "party" atmosphere; fare, unfortunately, "can't quite compete" with the "terrific location", but even
critics concede it's "good for drinks" or "watching the sunset."

Sue & Hai *Chinese/Japanese* — ▽ 19 | 8 | 15 | $22

Yorktown Heights | 2038 Saw Mill River Rd. (Crompond Rd.) |
914-962-7996

Yorktown Heights denizens declare this "decent" Chinese-Japanese
among "the better" "local" choices for "fresh" Asian fare "in an area
with few other options"; with decor on the "depressing" side, "takeout" or "delivery" is preferred.

Sukhothai Ⓜ *Thai* — ▽ 24 | 20 | 21 | $25

Beacon | 516 Main St. (bet. North & South Sts.) | 845-790-5375 |
www.sukhothainy.com

"Wow", "Thai food to rave about" boast Beaconites of this two-year-
old dispensing "surprisingly good" dishes spiced to your taste and
"enhanced" by "sauces that don't overpower" – plus "if you want
something special, just ask" the accommodating chef-owner; the
"simple setting" with its exposed brick and temple rubbings is "nice-
looking", service is "classy" and prices "cheap", though it's no
longer BYO, which the cost rating may not reflect.

Sunset Cove *Continental* — 15 | 18 | 15 | $35

Tarrytown | Washington Irving Boat Club | 238 Green St. (W. Main St.) |
914-366-7889 | www.sunsetcove.net

"Sunday brunch" is your best bet at this Tarrytown Continental where
the "expansive" view of the Hudson River and Tappan Zee Bridge
somewhat "makes up for uneven fare" that's especially "mediocre" at
"dinner"; despite that, and "harried" service it's still "lovely" "when
the weather is warm" and you can "relax" on the outdoor deck.

Sunset Grille Ⓜ *Mexican* — 22 | 17 | 20 | $36

White Plains | 68 Gedney Way (Gedney Terr.) | 914-227-9353 |
www.sunsetgrilleny.com

"Authentic" "gourmet" Mexican "that stands above" "sticky-melted-
jack-cheese" fare makes this "imaginative" White Plains addition a
"new favorite" (especially for its "homemade tortillas" and "superb
tamales"); "quality" ingredients mean it's "a little pricey", but numbers
are easy to overlook with a "welcoming" host and "pleasant" decor.

Susan's *American* — 18 | 15 | 17 | $37

Peekskill | 12 N. Division St. (bet. Main & Park Sts.) | 914-737-6624 |
www.susansinpeekskill.com

"Live music" (Tuesday–Saturday) has "spiced up" this "comfortable"
Peekskill New American that's a stone's throw from the Paramount

Theatre; "eclectic" "home cooking" and a "helpful" staff make it a "pleasant local spot" that's "great for lunch" too.

Sushi Man Ⓜ Japanese   23 | 15 | 21 | $40

Ardsley | 724 Saw Mill River Rd. (Center St.) | 914-693-8800
"Sit at the bar" and "put yourself in the chef's hands" at this "costly" Ardsley "oasis" "for grown-ups", which charms connoisseurs with "pristine", "beautiful sushi" "of the highest quality", even "in an area with stiff competition"; add in "accommodating" servers, and you have devotees dubbing it "nirvana", despite the "casual" quality of the "Zen-like" decor.

⊿ Sushi Mike's Japanese   25 | 14 | 21 | $33

Dobbs Ferry | 146 Main St. (Cedar St.) | 914-591-0054 | www.sushimikes.com
Fin fans "come in droves" to this "tiny", "always-packed" Dobbs Ferry Japanese for "delish fish with a twist" that wins "nothing but raves" from both the "risk taker and novice" alike for "adventurous rolls" and "tasty" "chef's specials"; "great hospitality" comes via the owner who "should run for mayor" because even when it's "rushed" and "tight", he makes the less-than-"restful" atmosphere "part of the fun."

Sushi Nanase Japanese   ▽ 28 | 14 | 20 | $65

White Plains | 522 Mamaroneck Ave. (DeKalb Ave.) | 914-285-5351 | www.sushinanase.com
The chef-owner at this "tiny" "no frills" Japanese "inn" in White Plains may strike some as "fussy", but come here for "nothing else" but "exquisite" sushi "delicately" prepared with "special touches" and you'll be in "heaven"; many find it "exorbitantly overpriced" with a $30 minimum per person, but keep in mind "your dinner was in Japan 18 hours earlier", so if "it feels like you're paying to fly in your meals, you are!"

Sushi Niji Japanese   ▽ 23 | 16 | 22 | $28

Dobbs Ferry | 73 Main St. (Chestnut St.) | 914-693-8838
"Incredibly fresh sushi" has Dobbs Ferry denizens dubbing this Japanese "addition" a "consistently good" "alternative" to the "famous competition" nearby, and a few even find it "better" (and more "moderate" in price to boot); "friendly" service and "simple but attractive" decor are additional appeasements.

Swaddee House of Thai Food Thai   20 | 10 | 17 | $28

Thornwood | 886 Franklin Ave. (Marble Ave.) | 914-769-8007
"Considering the lack of Thai food" in Northern Westchester, this "authentic" Thornwood restaurant is recognized for its "virtues" (namely, an "extensive menu selection" and "reliable" fare); service is "friendly", if "slow", and "booths with triangle pillows" are a "comfortable" bright spot in the otherwise "drab setting."

Sweet Sue's ⊘ American   24 | 15 | 17 | $16

Phoenicia | 49 Main St. (bet. Jay St. & Rte. 212) | 845-688-7852
"People line up outside" this "informal" Phoenicia breakfast and lunch fave for the "huge selection" of "famous pancakes" "as big as

magic carpets", "great French toast" and "tasty sandwiches and salads"; it gets "crazy busy" on weekends, when locals, tourists and low-key celebs "crowd" into the "warm, country cozy" space (complete with pancake portraits on the walls).

Swiss Hütte ⓂⓂ Continental/Swiss
20 | 18 | 21 | $44

Hillsdale | Swiss Hütte Country Inn | Rte. 23 (3 mi. east of Rte. 22) | 518-325-3333 | www.swisshutte.com

Weight watchers worry about "carbs galore", but "meat and potato" heads "crave" the "rich" Swiss-Continental cuisine (like Wiener schnitzel and "yummy" rosti potatoes) at this Columbia County inn overlooking Catamount's slopes; the "ski-lodge" look "needs work" but is made up for by a staff "that makes you feel welcome and important", as well as a "magnificent garden" for summer dining.

Swoon Kitchenbar · American
24 | 20 | 20 | $40

Hudson | 340 Warren St. (bet. 3rd & 4th Sts.) | 518-822-8938 | www.swoonkitchenbar.com

"Sounds like a silly name" until you taste the "sumptuous" fare coo Columbia County's "'in'-crowd", "swooning" over chef-owner Jeffrey Gimmel's "first-class" New American food and spouse Nina's desserts "beyond your wildest dreams"; there's plenty of "studied elegance" and "arty flair" in the "fabulously lit", flower-bedecked Hudson space, so the one flaw is sometimes "haphazard service" from a "staff that could stand some coaching."

Takayama Japanese
19 | 12 | 17 | $34

Chappaqua | 95 King St. (bet. N. Greeley Ave. & Prospect Dr.) | 914-238-5700

"Quality sushi" that's "solid", if "nothing to write home about", keeps this "reasonable" Chappaqua Japanese "bustling" with "neighborhood" families; "cafeteria"-like decor isn't helped by the "recent addition of noisy hibachi tables", say surveyors who sigh, "if only they delivered."

T&J Villaggio Trattoria ⓂⓂ Italian
∇ 21 | 12 | 20 | $31

Port Chester | 223-225 Westchester Ave. (bet. Grove & Oak Sts.) | 914-937-6665 | www.tandjs.net

"Old-fashioned" Italian "home cooking", "just like mama would make", pleases patrons at this "busy" Port Chester offspring of the "hole-in-the-wall" pizzeria next door; though both are favored by "families" for "large portions" and reasonable tabs, unlike the "checkered-tablecloth feel" of the original, this establishment offers "a little more" in the way of service and decor.

Tandoori Taste of India Indian
23 | 15 | 21 | $30

Port Chester | 163 N. Main St. (bet. Highland & Mill Sts.) | 914-937-2727 | www.tandooritasteofindia.com

"Delicious spices" and "excellent preparation" are "perfectly meshed" at this Port Chester Indian, where the "helpful staff" will ensure your "water glass is never empty" (important when you're "enjoying a spicy vindaloo") and the "typical decor" with rosewood accents is "nice enough; wallet-watchers also call the lunch buffet a "great buy."

☑ Tango Grill *Argentinean/Italian*   23 | 19 | 20 | $58

White Plains | 128 E. Post Rd. (Court St.) | 914-946-6222 |
www.tangogrillny.com

"Fanciful twists on Argentinean and Italian food" fill the "huge menu" of "luxurious", "well-executed" choices at this newly expanded eatery in White Plains, which caters to a "yuppie crowd", with "excellent" cuts of meat and a "superb wine list"; it's a "happening scene", for sure, but with "prices dancing on the high end" ("beware of the specials!"), it's one some surveyors have relegated to "special-occasion" dining only.

Tanjore *Indian*   ▽ 25 | 19 | 23 | $23

Fishkill | 992 Main St. (bet. Blodgett Rd. & Luyster Pl.) | 845-896-6659 |
www.tanjoreindiancuisine.com

"Not your everyday Indian fare" by a long shot, this Fishkill outpost serves "sophisticated", "intensely flavored" "dishes with flair", "at bargain prices" – although the "best buy" may be the "fabulous" "lunch buffet", which novices note is "a good way to try" the cuisine, as well; the "strip-mall frontage" gives way to a colorful Bollywood-style interior that strikes some as "a bit over the top, but fun"; N.B. it's now fully licensed for alcohol.

Taro's ⊘ *Italian/Pizza*   19 | 10 | 20 | $21

Millerton | 18 Main St. (N. Center St.) | 518-789-6630

"Proof that good things come in small packages", this little "family-run" Millerton pizza and pasta joint is a "favorite pit stop" among locals and weekenders wanting "good, honest, unpretentious Italian favorites" served by a staff that stays "eager" "even when they're frantic."

Tavern at Highlands Country Club *American*   ▽ 23 | 24 | 23 | $40

Garrison | Highlands Country Club | 955 Rte. 9D (Rte. 403) |
845-424-3254 | www.highlandscountryclub.net

It's "like eating in the kitchen of a hunting lodge" in the "cozy" tavern at this Garrison venue overlooking the ninth hole of the Highlands' golf course; the "delicious" American "comfort food" is also served in the "romantically lit ballroom", where couches face "tremendously inviting fireplaces" at each end of the room; parents "pleasantly surprised to see it's kid-friendly" are made even happier by the $5 children's menu; N.B. the Food score may not reflect the departure of chef Peter Kielec.

Telluride *Southwestern*   24 | 22 | 21 | $45

Stamford | 245 Bedford St. (bet. Broad & Spring Sts.), CT | 203-357-7679 |
www.tellurliderestaurant.com

"This cool bit of Colorado" in Downtown Stamford is the place to go for "great eclectic Southwestern fare" (made mostly from organic ingredients) complemented by "an excellent wine list" (40 selections by the glass); "romantic lighting", "big wooden tables and a mellow bar" give it such "good buzz", "it's harder to get into than an audience with the pope" despite its "pricey" tabs.

	FOOD	DECOR	SERVICE	COST

Temptations Cafe *Eclectic*

21	15	18	$21

Nyack | 80½ Main St. (B'way) | 845-353-3355 |
www.temptationscafe.com

"Delicious desserts" and "homemade" "ice cream are the lure" at this "low-key" Nyack Eclectic "hangout", but once inside, the sweet-toothed also discover less sinful, "wholesome" fare and "good sandwiches" for "cheap"; "college-age servers text messaging their friends" are a modern touch in the "tiny" "deja-vu '60s" space with its "Villagey vibe"; in summer, "try the garden."

Temptation Tea House *Asian*

21	18	19	$30

Mt. Kisco | 11A S. Moger Ave. (Main St.) | 914-666-8808

"Delicately presented" Asian small plates are washed down with bubble teas and fruit smoothies at this "informal" cafe in Mt. Kisco done up in festive reds and golds; though a few quibble with "skimpy portions" and "expensive" tabs, most are willing to overlook both for a find this "unusual" "in a land of slim pickin's."

Tenampa *Mexican*

▽ 14	17	18	$29

Croton-on-Hudson | 2011 Albany Post Rd. (Memorial Dr.) |
914-271-2920 | www.tenampamexican.com

A "friendly atmosphere" prevails at this relatively new Croton Mexican with "cheerful", "hacienda"-like decor, mariachis on weekends and servers who make an "effort"; cuisine, however, is not "up to snuff", with patrons pleading them to "spice up the food"; until then – "forget dinner and just relax with a margarita at the bar."

☑ Tengda Asian Bistro *Pan-Asian*

23	20	19	$40

NEW Katonah | Katonah Shopping Ctr. | 286 Katonah Ave. (Rte. 117) |
914-232-3900 Ⓜ

Greenwich | 21 Field Point Rd. (bet. W. Elm St. & W. Putnam Ave.),
CT | 203-625-5338 | www.tengdaasianbistro.com

"Enjoy a gastronomic journey from Thailand to China to Japan all in one stop" at these Pan-Asian bistros that boosters boast are almost the equivalent of "Nobu north" for their "deliciously fresh exotic rolls"; they are also "noisy", "hip" hangouts with "chic modern decor" where the after-work crowd congregates for "lots of crazy drinks" and "great sake flights."

Ten Railroad Ave. *Italian/Spanish*

▽ 16	15	19	$43

Warwick | 10 Railroad Ave. (Rte. 94) | 845-986-1509 |
www.tenrailroad.com

Voters vary on this Italian-Spanish in Warwick, with pros who "keep going back" praising it as a "neighborhood favorite" dispensing "good food" in a "quaint" setting, and cons complaining that despite soaring ceilings and a fireplace, the courtyard room and casual dining room are "short on atmosphere" and the cooking "just ok."

Tequila Mockingbird *Mexican*

16	18	18	$30

New Canaan | 6 Forest St. (East Ave.), CT | 203-966-2222

"Who can resist the name?" of this "extremely family-friendly" New Canaan Mexican ask amigos who agree that "their margaritas are

FOOD | DECOR | SERVICE | COST

muy bueno" and the "festive" "folk art" decor make it "a fun place to go" with kids; but foodies feel "this bird should be tequilad" for serving such "generic" fare.

Tequila Sunrise *Mexican*
17 | 18 | 18 | $32

Larchmont | 145 Larchmont Ave. (bet. Boston Post Rd. & Cherry St.) | 914-834-6378 | www.tequilasunrisenewyork.com

"Mariachis and margaritas" are the attractions at this spacious Larchmont cantina that draws "frazzled parents" for "family birthday celebrations" early on, and then morphs into a "lively bar" later in the evening; despite dishes that aren't quite "authentic", it's still a "noisy", "cheerful" spot that's "a lot of fun"; N.B. live music Thursday–Sunday.

❷ Terrapin *American*
24 | 23 | 20 | $43

Rhinebeck | 6426 Montgomery St./Rte. 9 (Livingston St.) | 845-876-3330 | www.terrapinrestaurant.com

"Once a church, now a sanctuary for gourmands", chef Josh Kroner's "delightful" Rhinebeck two-fer packs in "hip locals and touristas" for "heavenly" New American on the "lovely" "tablecloth side" or "snazzy choices" like "inventive tapas" and "choose-your-own sandwiches" in the "terrific", "bargain" bistro; though service is "hit-or-miss", the "staff looks good" and so does the food: "you can almost hear the hosannas when the beautiful dishes arrive."

Terra Ristorante *Italian*
20 | 18 | 18 | $44

Greenwich | 156 Greenwich Ave. (bet. Elm & Lewis Sts.), CT | 203-629-5222 | www.terraofgreenwich.com

"Watch the celebs and ladies who lunch" while dining on "wonderful" wood-roasted pizzas and chicken at this "always-busy" Northern Italian "on trendy Greenwich Avenue"; "eating on the terrace is fine" when the weather allows, but indoors can be "as noisy as Grand Central Station", and "sometimes service is a little on the laid-back Euro side."

Terra Rustica *Italian*
20 | 20 | 19 | $41

Briarcliff Manor | 550 N. State Rd. (Ryder Ave.) | 914-923-8300

"A surprise" in Briarcliff Manor, this Italian "neighborhood haunt" charms customers with "consistently solid" cuisine paired with "great wines" at "reasonable prices"; though a few critics carp it's "rather ordinary", "warm surroundings" and convenience go a long way to make it a "successful" "family favorite"; N.B. there's deck dining in season.

Thai Garden ▥ *Thai*
24 | 17 | 20 | $29

Sleepy Hollow | 128 Cortlandt St. (College Ave.) | 914-524-5003 | www.thethaigarden.com

"Exceptionally good" Thai soups, stir-fries, noodles and curries (as well as "lots of vegetarian choices") are served in "large portions" at this Sleepy Hollow venue that's "tucked away on a side street"; the "charming" atmosphere comes via lime-green walls and "attentive" servers who make each visit "a delight."

	FOOD	DECOR	SERVICE	COST

Thai House *Thai* | 22 | 17 | 20 | $29 |

Ardsley | 466 Ashford Ave. (Rte. 9A) | 914-674-6633 |
www.thaihouserestaurant.com **M**
Nyack | 12 Park St. (bet. High Ave. & Main St.) | 845-358-9100 |
www.thaihousenyack.com

"Delicious" Siamese fare spiced "hot" and served in "generous portions" "does the job" at these "tasty" twin Thai "hideaways" in Nyack (set in a converted diner) and Ardsley (with "a long climb up a narrow staircase"); both branches have a "pleasant", "homey" feel accentuated by "helpful" servers who are happy to "order for you."

Thai Pearl *Thai* | 20 | 16 | 19 | $28 |

Ridgefield | Copps Hill Common | 113 Danbury Rd. (Farmingville Rd.),
CT | 203-894-1424 | www.thaipearlrestaurant.com

The "tasty dishes" at this Ridgefield Thai "hidden in the corner of a shopping center" offer a "balance of flavors" "at a great low price" (the $7.95 "lunch specials are a bargain with soup, soda and dessert included"); no wonder diners have dubbed this "unassuming spot" with "friendly service" a "welcome addition to the area."

◪ Thali *Indian* | 24 | 21 | 22 | $37 |

New Canaan | 87 Main St. (bet. East & Locust Aves.), CT |
203-972-8332
Ridgefield | Ridgefield Motor Inn | 296 Ethan Allen Hwy./Rte. 7
(Florida Hill Rd.), CT | 203-894-1080
www.thali.com

"Awesome" is what admirers say about the "Konkan crab appetizer" and "rack of cardamom lamb chops", both signature dishes at this "expensive" duo of chef-owned Indians; the decor varies widely with the location (Ridgefield is in a "no-tell motel" and New Canaan boasts a "way-cool overhead waterfall"), but the food is "consistently outstanding"; P.S. the $16.95 Sunday brunch buffet is a "fantastic deal."

Thataway Cafe *American* | 15 | 14 | 15 | $28 |

Greenwich | 409 Greenwich Ave. (bet. Grigg St. & Railroad Ave.),
CT | 203-622-0947 | www.thatawaycafe.com

Frugal sorts favor this "friendly, neighborhood" Traditional American eatery "for a casual bite without attitude" "before the movies" or while "waiting for the train" and credit it for "quick, inexpensive eats", considering its "upscale" competition on Greenwich Avenue; the "outdoor patio area" is a big draw "when the weather is right", but foodies who fume the fare is only "ok" contend "you can't eat location."

That Little Italian Restaurant **M** *Italian* | 18 | 13 | 17 | $29 |

Greenwich | 228-230 Mill St. (Henry St.), CT | 203-531-7500 |
www.tlirgreenwich.com

This "not-so-little-anymore" "neighborhood institution" in Greenwich serves "generous portions" of "down-home Italian food"; it's "casual" and "caters to young families" that are looking for "good value for what you get."

	FOOD	DECOR	SERVICE	COST

☑ Thomas Henkelmann ⌧ *French* | 29 | 28 | 28 | $80 |

Greenwich | Homestead Inn | 420 Field Point Rd. (bet. Bush Ave. & Merica Ln.), CT | 203-869-7500 | www.thomashenkelmann.com

Once again, chef Thomas Henkelmann and his wife, Theresa, achieve "the peak of perfection" with their "truly exceptional" New French restaurant – housed in "an absolutely gorgeous" Greenwich inn; considered the culinary "Matterhorn north of Manhattan", it "pampers" its clientele with a "beautiful" setting, "impeccable service", "sublime entrees, ethereal desserts" and a "superb" wine selection, albeit at prices that "would make J.P. Morgan wince"; N.B. jacket required.

Thomas Moran's Forsythia *American* | 22 | 20 | 19 | $43 |

New Milford | 31 Bank St. (bet. Main & Railroad Sts.), CT | 860-355-3266

Supporters say the "personable" chef-owner of this New Milford New American "can do no wrong" with his "exceptional flavorful" cuisine, which is served by a "wonderful" staff in "stylish" split-level surroundings; they declare it's "definitely worth a visit", but a growing number of less-flowery folks feel "both the food and the service can be uneven."

☑ Thomas Moran's Petite Syrah *American* | 25 | 20 | 23 | $61 |

New Preston | 223 Litchfield Tpke./Rte. 202 (Wilbur Rd.), CT | 860-868-7763

This "intimate" New Preston New American destination "manages to be a high-end and neighborhood place simultaneously"; chef-owner Thomas Moran's "top-notch" cuisine (which includes small-plate selections) combined with "incredibly attentive service" and an "unpretentious", "quaint" candlelit dining room makes for a "wonderful experience" and "one of the better choices" in the county.

NEW Tokushin Ⓜ *Japanese* | - | - | - | M |

Greenwich | 28 W. Putnam Ave. (Greenwich Ave.), CT | 203-661-1600

There's "no reason to go anywhere else for sushi in Greenwich" say the few who've found this new chef-owned Japanese with "ultra-fresh, ridiculously tasty" raw fish, along with "enough creative hot dishes to keep things interesting"; "stunning" "modern decor" adds to the overall experience.

Tollgate Hill Inn & Restaurant Ⓜ *American* | ▽ 20 | 24 | 23 | $52 |

Litchfield | 571 Torrington Rd./Rte. 202 (bet. Tollgate & Wilson Rds.), CT | 860-567-1233 | www.tollgatehill.com

The fortunate few who've found this wood-paneled Traditional American eatery housed in a "charming" 1745 Litchfield inn that boasts a working fireplace say it's just "right for cold snowy nights"; still, some modernists muse that "eating in a Colonial museum is not for everyone."

Tollgate Steakhouse *Steak*

24 | 16 | 21 | $57

Mamaroneck | 974 E. Boston Post Rd. (Keeler Ave.) | 914-381-7233 | www.tollgatesteakhouse.com

Carnivores craving "superior" steak and all the "familiar trappings" settle in to this Mamaroneck restaurant for some of the "finest porterhouses on the planet", "fired to perfection"; consider it "Luger's on the Sound", but "without the attitude", where "very friendly service" overcomes "gloomy", turn-of-the-century, gaslight decor.

Tomatillo Ⓜ *Mexican*

21 | 16 | 19 | $22

Dobbs Ferry | 13 Cedar St. (Rte. 9) | 914-478-2300 | www.mexchester.com

"You can taste the difference" "locally grown produce" and "organic ingredients" make in the "fresh"-flavored fare at this Dobbs Ferry relative newcomer that emphasizes "innovative" and "health conscious" takes on Mexican standards; "funky" orange-and-yellow decor and "friendly" servers add to the "lively" feel of the dining room that's "packed", though "festive"; add in "inexpensive" tabs and it's a "bargain" that "lives up to the hype."

Tombolino's Ⓜ *Italian*

▽ 21 | 17 | 23 | $38

Yonkers | 356 Kimball Ave. (Yonkers Ave.) | 914-237-1266 | www.tombolinorestaurant.com

"They treat you like family" at this "traditional" Yonkers Italian where the food is "consistent", though slightly "undistinguished"; if a few find it on the "boring" side, moderate prices and a "lovely" atmosphere (and live piano on Fridays) make it a "good neighborhood place", especially for "parties and special events."

NEW Tonique *American*

- | - | - | M

Beacon | 240 Main St. (bet. Elm & Walnut Sts.) | 845-831-0003 | www.toniquerestaurant.com

Despite the name, there's nothing French about this Beacon newcomer from Pascal Graff (owner of Cold Spring's Le Bouchon); here he meets and greets in the former OII space, now with silver accents and mobiles forming a retro-modern backdrop for a thoroughly up-to-date New American menu featuring the likes of chile-seared big eye tuna and pistachio-crusted lamb, as well as some fun specialty drinks.

Tony La Stazione *Italian*

16 | 12 | 18 | $38

Elmsford | 15 Saw Mill River Rd. (W. Main St.) | 914-592-5980

"Eat hearty, but keep your eyes closed" declare diners who find this Elmsford Italian "joint" – open since 1975 – is showing its age with "checkered-tablecloth" decor that's gotten "shabby" "after all these years"; "red-sauce" fare is deemed "decent", but "diehards" are holding out that the "caring owner" will return this "stalwart" to the former glory of its "better days."

Torches on The Hudson *American*

15 | 23 | 16 | $36

Newburgh | 120 Front St. (4th St.) | 845-568-0100 | www.torchesonthehudson.com

Soak up "showstopping river views" or get "hypnotized" by the "phenomenal fish tank" between the bar and dining room at this

Newburgh "singles mix-and-meet" "watering hole" because Traditional American eats are only "so-so"; "service could be better" too, although if you "have a cocktail" on the terrace on a summer's night, it'll seem "all's right with the world."

Torchia's Ristorante *Italian*   16 | 11 | 15 | $30

Briarcliff Manor | 518 N. State Rd. (bet. Blue Lantern & Chappaqua Rds.) | 914-762-2963

"Good pizza" and pasta are "safe bets" at this "basic" Briarcliff Manor Italian that's a "local hangout" for "casual dining"; service can be "very slow" to the extent that you might be able to squeeze in "a nap before you're served."

Toscana *Italian*   19 | 20 | 21 | $46

Ridgefield | 43 Danbury Rd. (bet. Grove St. & Mountain View Ave.), CT | 203-894-8995

Surveyors send mixed messages when it comes to this airy, expansive Ridgefield Tuscan: some find the "hard-working" chef-owner's dishes "delicious", the "staff welcoming" and the "lively" atmosphere "festive", but protesters point out that "air-kissing and far too much noise make for a less-than-winning combination."

Toscani's 🅜 *Italian/Mediterranean*   ▽ 17 | 17 | 13 | $37

New Paltz | 119 Main St. (Prospect St.) | 845-255-3800

"If only they'd serve what they used to sell in their deli" pine patrons at this New Paltz Italian-Mediterranean run by the "friendly" family known for its neighboring shop; despite "weak" aspects, "lots of large (read: loud) groups" convene in the "modern" dining room to tuck into "homestyle" eats or "enjoy the piano" in the adjacent bar.

Totonho's Pizzeria Napolitano *Pizza*   ▽ 18 | 6 | 10 | $21

Yonkers | Ramada Inn | 125 Tuckahoe Rd. (bet. Bushey & Touissant Aves.) | 914-476-4446 | www.totonnos.com

Intrepid eaters seek out this Yonkers offshoot of the 80-year-old Coney Island pizzeria that's set in a "weird location" in the lobby of the Ramada Inn; diners divide on the "variable" brick-oven pies ("fabulous" vs. "terrible") and say the "dive"-like ambiance and downright "terrible" service are not up to the "original's high standards."

Town Dock *American*   18 | 14 | 19 | $35

Rye | 15 Purdy Ave. (bet. Boston Post Rd. & Purchase St.) | 914-967-2497

A "no-frills" "neighborhood spot", this Rye Traditional American offers fare (like burgers and seafood) that's "better than average", though "overpriced" for the "casual" "pub"-like surroundings; still, "friendly bartenders" and "comfortable" wooden booths make all feel "welcome."

Towne Crier Cafe 🅜 *American*   17 | 17 | 16 | $35

Pawling | 130 Rte. 22 (¼ mi. north of Rte. 311) | 845-855-1300 | www.townecrier.com

This "jumping" Pawling "haunt" is a "local institution" for "great live music" and "country-priced" drinks; the New American menu includes burgers big enough "to choke a horse" among the "better

	FOOD	DECOR	SERVICE	COST

than ok" eclectic entrees and desserts, but even if "the fiddles are better than the vittles", you'll still "have a great night."

Toyo Sushi *Japanese* — 22 | 17 | 19 | $33

Mamaroneck | 253 Mamaroneck Ave. (Prospect Ave.) | 914-777-8696 | www.toyosushi.com

"Nouvelle" twists on sushi and "creative" "cooked" dishes surface at this "very popular" Japanese relative newcomer in Mamaroneck; "bargain prices" also mean you may "wait for a table" in the sleek wood-paneled dining room that exudes a "cool" "Manhattan vibe."

Traditions 118 *American/Italian* — ▽ 19 | 18 | 19 | $34

Somers | 11 Old Tomahawk St. (Rte. 202) | 914-248-7200 | www.traditions118restaurant.com

The "owners aim to please" at this "friendly" Somers Italian-American that's blossoming into a "neighborhood fave" with a "good menu with plenty to choose from" (including a lengthy martini list), served in a "nice", "roomy" space with patio dining in season; live music on Fridays and moderate tabs add to its appeal.

Tramonto *Italian* — 19 | 17 | 19 | $40

Hawthorne | 27 Saw Mill River Rd. (Saw Mill River Pkwy., exit 25) | 914-347-8220

Filmgoers find this Hawthorne Italian – "convenient to the multiplex" – a "dependable" "little place" for a "solid" meal "before a movie"; the less-enthused, however, protest prices that are "too high" for an "unpretentious" spot in a "local setting."

Traphagen *American* — 22 | 23 | 21 | $40

Rhinebeck | Beekman Arms Hotel | 6387 Mill St./Rte. 9 (Rte. 308) | 845-876-1766

"Rhinebeck's grand old restaurant" in the circa-1766 Beekman Arms, this American's "historic setting" makes the "enjoyable food" even "better" claim customers chowing down in either the tavern with its fireplace and beamed ceiling, one of the "gorgeous" Colonial-style rooms or in the "delightful greenhouse"; the staff is "attentive", so even if it's all "a wee bit sleepy", there's really "nothing to dislike."

NEW Trattoria Lucia *Italian* — ▽ 14 | 16 | 15 | $34

Bedford | 454 Old Post Rd. (Vinton Ave.) | 914-234-7600 | www.trattorialuciany.com

Restaurant-starved Bedford locals "welcomed" this "casual Italian" eatery to the neighborhood, but they're generally "underwhelmed" by "pastas and other casual fare" that rate "a step above a pizzeria"; service is "spotty" and "families with children" "rule the roost" here, so expect some "noise."

Trattoria Vivolo *Italian* — 22 | 14 | 22 | $36

Harrison | 301 Halstead Ave. (Rte. 127) | 914-835-6199

"Hearty ", "unpretentious" Italian "basics" and "delightful wines" await in this 1950s-style "refurbished diner" in Harrison, where the host and staff are "always trying to please" with "warm, gracious" service; add in "nice-sized" portions and moderate prices and it succeeds in "satisfying"; N.B. there's a pretty greenhouse room as well.

Travelers Rest Ⓜ️ *Continental*

| 18 | 21 | 20 | $47 |

Ossining | Rte. 100 (bet. Random Farms Rd. & Rte. 134) | 914-941-7744 | www.thetravelersrest.com

"Classic Continental fare" with "German flair" charms champions of this "old-fashioned" (some say "stuffy") Ossining "special-occasion" restaurant set in a converted coach house with four fireplaces and a dining room that's especially "beautifully decorated during the holidays"; a "lovely garden" and "accommodating" service are additional "nice" touches.

Tre Angelina Ⓢ️ *Italian*

| 22 | 19 | 23 | $44 |

White Plains | 478 Mamaroneck Ave. (Bloomingdale Rd.) | 914-686-0617 | www.treangelina.com

"Nicely presented", "authentic" "Italian" cuisine drives diners to this White Plains eatery where "free bruschetta" sets the tone for a "reliable" meal; the "subdued" warm-hued interior "oozes romance" and an "attentive, but not intrusive", staff makes it "perfect for a date."

Trinity Grill & Bar *American*

| 16 | 14 | 17 | $34 |

Harrison | 7-9 Purdy St. (Halstead Ave.) | 914-835-5920

Look no further than this Harrison "standby" for a "casual", "convenient" "meeting place" with New American eats; the "gigantic" bar draws a "neighborhood" crowd, but "fuddy duddies" beware, the noise level can be "loud."

Trotters Ⓢ️ *Mediterranean*

| 24 | 22 | 21 | $57 |

White Plains | 175 Main St. (Court St.) | 914-421-5012 | www.trottersny.com

This "chic" White Plains boîte draws an "upscale" crowd including "expense-account" types and "political powerhouses" for a "sophisticated" Mediterranean menu that's "constantly changing" with the seasons; plush seating and silver candelabras add to the "grown-up" room that "strives for a Manhattan vibe", though a few critics complain of prices "that can be a shock" in spite of "royal treatment."

Troutbeck Ⓜ️ *American*

| ▽ 18 | 28 | 20 | $55 |

Amenia | Troutbeck Estate & Resort | 515 Leedsville Rd./Rte. 2 (Rte. 343) | 845-373-9681 | www.troutbeck.com

"The setting is worth every penny" you might spend at this Dutchess County inn, resort and conference center housed in a stone "manor in a parklike setting"; the "garden is spectacular, even in snow", the interior all "sophisticated" "country charm" as many "brides and grooms" will attest, and if the New American "banquet-style food" is sometimes only "so-so", service is "lovely."

Tsuru *Japanese*

| 23 | 14 | 19 | $35 |

Hartsdale | Square Shopping Mall | 259 N. Central Ave. (bet. Harvard Dr. & Laurel St.) | 914-761-0057 | www.tsururestaurant.net

"Reliably high-quality sushi" and "authentic dishes you don't see" elsewhere keep this "nondescript" Japanese set in a Hartsdale strip mall frequently "packed"; "fair prices" and a "warm welcome" from the chefs overcome the "average-looking" decor.

Tulip Tree *Continental* — | — | — | I
Rye Brook | Hilton Rye Town | 699 Westchester Ave. (I-287, exit 10) | 914-939-6300 | www.ryetown.hilton.com
"Pleasant" and "airy", this "very pretty" Colonial-style lobby coffee shop with a terrace in the Hilton Rye Town offers Continental "hotel fare", notably a lunch buffet Monday–Friday and a jazz brunch on Sunday.

Tung Hoy *Chinese* 15 | 11 | 18 | $23
Mamaroneck | 1160 W. Boston Post Rd. (Richbell Rd.) | 914-381-0190
"Like dining in a 1970s time warp", this "old-school" Mamaroneck Chinese "decorated with Buddhas" may be "ordinary", but those "nostalgic" for the Cantonese cuisine of their "youth" (spareribs and won ton soup) feel it "holds its own"; but the less starry-eyed snipe "it just isn't what it used to be."

Turkish Meze *Mediterranean/Turkish* 23 | 18 | 21 | $34
Mamaroneck | 409 Mt. Pleasant Ave. (Stanley Ave.) | 914-777-3042 | www.turkishmeze.com
"Marvelous meze" (including "delicious dips") and other "impecca-bly fresh", "authentic" Mediterranean-Turkish dishes have made this Mamaroneck spot a "neighborhood favorite"; even if the decor "could be nicer", a "warm" staff and "reasonable prices" ensure it's a "real" "delight."

Turning Point Ⓜ *American* 14 | 13 | 17 | $29
Piermont | 468 Piermont Ave. (bet. Ash St. & Tate Ave.) | 845-359-1089 | www.turningpointcafe.com
"Go for the music, stay for the music" advise wags unimpressed by the New American "grub" at this "comfortable" Piermont institu-tion, best known for "showcasing local and national" jazz, folk and blues acts; "sandwiches, burgers, soups" and such are deemed "fine", so even if the "wonderful downstairs club" far outranks re-pasts, the "combo works just fine."

Turquoise *Mediterranean/Turkish* 20 | 17 | 20 | $33
Larchmont | 1895 Palmer Ave. (Chatsworth Ave.) | 914-834-9888 | www.turqmed.com
"The owners are always happy to see you" at this "lively" Larchmont Med-Turkish ("a nice change from Italian food") where "ample por-tions" of "consistently" "good" cuisine are served under "colorful glass lamps" in the "exoticly" appointed dining room; outdoor dining in summer and "belly dancing" on Saturday are additional draws.

Tuscano Ⓩ *Italian* ▽ 18 | 17 | 17 | $32
Danbury | 275 Main St. (bet. Library Pl. & White St.), CT | 203-743-0004
This relatively new Northern Italian in Downtown Danbury has a "great bar" and "good food" like dry-aged steaks and fresh seafood dishes, but it's "difficult to park" here and the "local college kids" have adopted it as their "pre-clubbing hangout."

Tuscan Oven Trattoria *Italian*   19 | 17 | 18 | $39

Mt. Kisco | 360 N. Bedford Rd. (bet. Foxwood Circle & Park Dr.) | 914-666-7711 | www.tuscanoven.com

Though it's "set in a strip mall", this "good" Mt. Kisco Italian with an "extensive menu" is "warm and homey" inside with a Tuscan farmhouse vibe, wood-burning oven and terra-cotta tiled floors; diners divide on service ("professional" vs "indifferent"), but most agree it's "reliable", if "a little pricey."

Twist 🖪 Ⓜ *American*   25 | 18 | 23 | $42

Hyde Park | 4290 Albany Post Rd. (Pine Woods Rd.) | 845-229-7094 | www.letstwist.com

It can be "tough to snag a table" at this "fabulous" Hyde Park New American, where "talented" chef-owner Benjamin Mauk "lives up to" his reputation with "original presentations" of "superb" food; an "unusual menu format" lets you "choose sides" and meat portion size, pleasing "large or small appetites", so add "marvelous service" and a colorful space that offsets the "dubious strip-mall" locale, and no wonder this is a "favorite new-ish" spot.

Two Steps
Downtown Grille *Southwestern*   15 | 17 | 17 | $24

Danbury | 5 Ives St. (White St.), CT | 203-794-0032 | www.ciaocafetwosteps.com

This Danbury Southwestern "is soooo much fun" if you like a "loud, raucous" watering hole housed in a former firehouse that's "decorated with cowboy boots hanging from the rafters"; big eaters are enthused about "more-than-ample portions" of "fall-off-the-bone ribs", but picky pardners say "the food is but two steps above bar fare" so maybe you should "take two steps back."

Ugly Gus Cafe & Bar 🖪 *American*   ▽ 18 | 16 | 20 | $29

Kingston | 11 Main St. (Clinton Ave.) | 845-331-5100 | www.uglygus.com

"Convenient" for the suit set in Kingston's Uptown business district, this "dependable" "neighborhood place" pleases with a varied Traditional American menu, so you can either "eat light or have a prime rib" – all "good for the price"; yellow walls, wood floors and a cherry bar make for a plain, "comfortable" setting and service is "friendly", so just "sit back and relax."

Ümami Café *Eclectic*   21 | 13 | 18 | $31

Croton-on-Hudson | 325 S. Riverside Ave. (Oneida Ave.) | 914-271-5555 | www.umamicafe.com

The "magic" "truffled mac 'n' cheese" alone is "worth a visit" to this "upbeat" Croton Eclectic "that really shines" with a "winning" formula of "reasonably priced" tabs and "imaginative", "delicious" food (though a few boosters beg them to "vary the menu" once in a while); "despite "sparse furnishings", it's still a "cute" place with a "nice", "kid-friendly" atmosphere and outdoor seating that's "great in summer"; N.B. the Fishkill location has been re-born as Jackalope BBQ.

	FOOD	DECOR	SERVICE	COST

Underhills Crossing *American*

21 | 20 | 20 | $47

Bronxville | 74½ Pondfield Rd. (bet. Midland & Palmer Aves.) | 914-337-1200 | www.underhillscrossing.com

This "sophisticated" New American is "abuzz" in "sleepy Bronxville" with a "smart-looking" crowd packing into the "lively" (some say "noisy") space for a "wide and varied menu" that will "please even the pickiest palate"; tabs are on the "borderline-pricey" side, no surprise given the "haute", "NYC"-style atmosphere that it strives for.

☑ Valbella *Italian*

25 | 23 | 25 | $67

NEW **Scarsdale** | 754 White Plains Rd. (New Wilmot Rd.) | 914-725-0566

Riverside | 1309 E. Putnam Ave./Rte. 1 (Sound Beach Ave.), CT | 203-637-1155 ⑤

www.valbellact.com

There are "celebrity sightings nightly" at this *"magnifico"* Riverside Northern Italian where "Tony the maitre d' is always ready with tricky trivia questions for customers" and the "fantastic" dishes include seasonal seafood and a "special Napoleon for two that's worth the money"; service is "solicitous" and the ambiance throughout is "memorable", but "for a real treat, eat in the wine cellar" amid the vinous treasure trove of "great" bottles; there's only one caveat: "make sure your credit limit can handle the bill"; N.B. the Scarsdale branch opened in early 2007 and focuses on steak and seafood.

Valentino's *Italian*

23 | 11 | 21 | $37

Yonkers | 132 Bronx River Rd. (bet. McLean & Wakefield Aves.) | 914-776-6731

A touch of "Arthur Avenue" in a Yonkers strip mall, this "cozy" Italian is still pleasing patrons "after all these years" dishing out "heaping helpings" of "homemade fare" (including "chicken parm that sets a new standard") in a dining room full of "regulars" and "lots of big hair"; despite "nonexistent" decor, there's "always a scene" with "personable" waiters from "another era" adding to the "old-world" vibe.

☑ Valley Restaurant at the Garrison ⑤ Ⓜ *American*

26 | 25 | 25 | $56

Garrison | Garrison Resort | 2015 Rte. 9 (Snake Hill Rd.) | 845-424-2339 | www.thegarrison.com

"Pssst, keep this one a secret" whisper the wowed who want this New American "find" at the Garrison Resort for themselves; "phenomenal", "country fresh" food is "tops", "service impeccable" and the space done up in "fabulous taste"; add "magnificent views" of "the mountains and river" from "comfortable outdoor seating" and in all, it's "almost perfect"; those who "can't wait to return" sigh "sadly, they're open only April–November", and then just on Friday and Saturdays.

Velvet Monkey *American*

▽ 20 | 17 | 19 | $50

Monroe | 46 Millpond Pkwy. (bet. Lake St. & Smithfield Ct.) | 845-781-7762 | www.thevmonkey.com

There's not much variety for diners in Monroe, so this New American overlooking a pond fills a need; admirers declare the menu "enjoyable" and the atmosphere "comfortable" in the "attractive enough" room paneled in pine with a wrought-iron divider; detractors declare there's "too much noise" and it's "overpriced for what it is", though maybe the only real problem is "inconsistency."

Versailles *Bakery/French*

22 | 15 | 12 | $34

Greenwich | 315 Greenwich Ave. (Arch St.), CT | 203-661-6634

"You won't mind widening your waistline" on "delicious European pastries and cakes" at this "first-class French bakery", which is also a "petite" bistro where Greenwich "ladies who lunch" go for duck confit and warm goat cheese salads; though the "setting is spartan" and the "service is sour, slow and unhelpful", the "wonderful desserts" keep some things sweet.

⬛ Vertigo *American*

18 | 25 | 18 | $48

Nyack | 91 Main St. (bet. B'way & Cedar St.) | 845-358-3202 | www.vertigonyack.com

Some say it's like a "nightclub", others a "strip club", but all agree the "eye-popping" deco-influenced decor is an "ornate" "sight to see" at this Nyack New American, where a staircase spirals through three levels, each with its own bar and balcony "overlooking scenic Downtown"; too bad "awkward service" and "food don't match up", though the twinkle-toed don't mind on weekends, when dining gives way to dancing after 10 PM.

Via Appia *Italian*

19 | 11 | 20 | $32

White Plains | 9 E. Taylor Sq. (Lake St.) | 914-949-5810

"Just what every neighborhood needs", this White Plains Italian has been serving up "old-fashioned" food "like mom's" for over 30 years (though the "thin, crisp and hot" pizzas draw the most salutations from surveyors); as for the decor, locals say it's "time to update."

Via Nove *Italian*

19 | 19 | 20 | $37

Fishkill | 1166 Main St. (Rte. 9) | 845-896-2255 | www.via-nove.com

A "gregarious owner" sets the tone for "pleasant service" at this "dependable" Fishkill Italian with a "large repertoire" of "solid" fare and a wide "selection of wines" to match; the red, green and gold dining room "caters to families", while the "fun bar/lounge" offers "fabulous drinks" making it a "good place for a night out."

NEW Viansa *Italian*

- | - | - | E

Yorktown | 345 Kear St. (bet. Commerce St. & Rte. 118) | 914-455-3900

Sage-green walls, low lighting, white tablecloths and semiformal service create an understated, yet upscale, atmosphere despite the Yorktown strip-mall location of this Italian newcomer; the menu is equally restrained with traditional takes on pasta, chicken and veal dishes; N.B. live jazz on weekends is another elegant touch.

NEW Vico *Italian*

- | - | - | M

Hudson | 136 Warren St. (bet. 1st & 2nd Sts.) | 518-828-6529 | www.vico-restaurant.com

Vico means village in the Tuscan dialect, and it's a community vibe that chef-owner Mark Ganem and co-owner Adam Klersfeld are aiming for at this homey Hudson newcomer dressed up with glowing golden yellow walls, abstract art and white tablecloths; locals are already lining up for Northern Italian classics based on seasonal, regional produce as well as a lighter bar menu.

Victor's Steakhouse *Steak*   ▽ 21 | 20 | 19 | $51
(fka Opus Terrace Steakhouse)
Monroe | 355 Rte. 17M (bet. Orchard Dr. & Snoop St.) | 845-783-5990 | www.opussteakhouse.net

Co-owner Victor Chavez changed the name of his Orange County meatery, but all else remains the same: "almost NYC quality" beef and "excellent sides" served in a classic steakhouse setting that reflects the chef's Smith & Wollensky background; now all that remains is to restore the "original staff's passion" and "find a good sommelier"; N.B. plans are in the works to add a butcher shop.

Villa Del Sol *Mexican*   16 | 16 | 17 | $28
Mt. Kisco | 20 S. Moger Ave. (W. Main St.) | 914-244-1908 | www.villadelsolrestaurants.com

Surveyors single out the "bathtub-sized margaritas" and "festive" atmosphere at this "decent" Mexican in Mt. Kisco; but they balk at "fare that lacks imagination" and "tastes mass-produced."

NEW Village Café, The *American*   15 | 17 | 16 | $36
Bronxville | 143 Parkway Rd. (bet. Milburn St. & Palmer Ave.) | 914-337-3351

"Formerly a casual diner", this Bronxville New American has gone "upscale" with a new look and "fancier" menu offerings while still retaining some of the dishes (like omelets and burgers) of its "greasy spoon" past; though they're "making an effort", the "food and service" still "need to improve", and neither "measure up to the great music" in the form of live jazz on weekend nights.

Village Grille Ⓜ *American/Mideastern*   ▽ 21 | 15 | 20 | $43
Tappan | 65 Old Tappan Rd. (Brandt Ave.) | 845-398-3232

"People love" this "gem in the little town" of Tappan, where the "tasty" organic American fare gets a "spark" from "Middle Eastern accents" courtesy of "gracious" chef-owner Khaled Elkady, while the "small", "cozy" room sometimes gets one from a belly dancer; most nights, though, the mood's more like being "treated well" "in someone's home."

Village TeaRoom Ⓜ *Tea Room*   21 | 20 | 22 | $25
New Paltz | 10 Plattekill Ave. (Main St.) | 845-255-3434 | www.thevillagetearoom.com

"You feel you should be wearing a petticoat and bonnet" at this "lovely little" all-organic American that offers a "perfect respite from Downtown New Paltz"; it's "a tea lover's paradise", with the "tastiest scones", "yummy cream puffs", pastries and "baked goods to die for", but also serves "scrumptious entrees" (like signature pot pies) in a "very relaxed", "inviting" "restored carriage house" whose only flaw is that it's "a bit cramped."

	FOOD	DECOR	SERVICE	COST

Villa Nova E. Ⓜ *American/Italian*   ▽ 19 | 13 | 18 | $32

Pelham | 6 First St. (4th Ave.) | 914-738-1444

Family-owned and -operated, this "reliable" Pelham Italian-American, "convenient to the train station", has been dishing out "large portions" of "working-class" "red-sauce" fare for over 36 years; if the "traditional" cooking "reminds you of a simpler time", so does the "1970s-style" decor, which isn't exactly "romantic."

Vinny's Backyard *Pub Food*   ▽ 17 | 13 | 18 | $18

Stamford | 1078 Hope St. (Camp Ave.), CT | 203-461-9003 | www.culinarymenus.com

For inexpensive Italian-accented pub fare, Stamford families head to this "basic" bar, with a dining room decorated like a yard and filled with booths, for "thin-crust pizzas", pastas and a "delicious" "Rice Krispy treat dessert"; but "the funny thing is, no one knows who Vinny is."

Vintage Restaurant & Bar Ⓢ *American/Eclectic*   ▽ 16 | 14 | 16 | $33

White Plains | 171 Main St. (bet. Court & William Sts.) | 914-328-5803 | www.vintagebar.net

"Singles" and "business" folks "meet and eat", especially at "happy hour", at this White Plains New American–Eclectic eatery done up in a 1920s speakeasy setting that can be "upscale" and "noisy" or "deserted" and "boring", depending on the night; though service is "lackluster", if you stick to "decent bar food" and drinks, it's a "good value."

Violette *American*   ▽ 22 | 21 | 20 | $38

Woodstock | 85 Mill Hill Rd./ Rte 212 (Playhouse Ln.) | 845-679-5300 | www.violettewoodstock.com

Just as the name's pronounced "vee-oh-let", this Woodstock New American has a French accent, offering "simple, elegant" signature dishes like chicken paillard as well as "wonderful tuna" with an Asian touch – all "at a fair price" and with "nice wines by the glass" too; everything's served by a "youthful, energetic staff", that bops around in the Provençal-style room or on the "delightful" patio in summer.

Vox Ⓜ *American/French*   21 | 21 | 21 | $52

North Salem | 721 Titicus Rd. (bet. Rtes. 116 & 121) | 914-669-5450 | www.voxnorthsalem.com

"The dining room is buzzing" with "movers and shakers" at this decidedly "unstuffy" film-themed North Salem New American–New French decorated with vintage "movie theater" seats, where a dinner of "good bistro fare" begins with a "basket of seasoned popcorn"; with a staff that's "friendly" and an outdoor terrace that's "lovely in season", the only objection is a "pricey" wine list that "needs more selections."

Vuli Ⓢ *Italian*   17 | 23 | 19 | $54

Stamford | Marriott Hotel | 2 Stamford Forum, 17th fl. (Town Center Dr.), CT | 203-323-5300 | www.vulirestaurant.com

"On a clear night", there are "great views of Manhattan" to be had from the "revolving" dining room of this chef-owned Northern

FOOD | DECOR | SERVICE | COST

Italian with floor-to-ceiling windows that's perched atop the Marriott in Downtown Stamford; but dizzy detractors declare the "overpriced" "food tastes like stereotypical hotel fare" that isn't made any better by "having the floor rotate beneath one's feet."

Walter's ᗡ *Hot Dogs* | 21 | 8 | 14 | $9

Mamaroneck | 937 Palmer Ave. (bet. Fulton & Richbell Rds.) | www.waltershotdogs.com

"One of the American greats" declare devotees of this "legendary" Mamaroneck hot dog stand (once again rated the No. 1 Bang for the Buck in Westchester/HV) where "addictive" "split-griddled" franks are slathered with "incredible homemade mustard" and peddled with "thick milkshakes" and "curly fries" from a "kitchy" "roadside" pagoda; if a minority deems it "overrated" and overcrowded, aficionados attest they're happy to "wait on line" at this "fast-food" "heaven."

Ward's Bridge Inn Ⓜ *American* | ▽ 19 | 17 | 20 | $33

Montgomery | 135 Ward St./Rte. 17K (Rte. 211) | 845-457-1300 | www.wardsbridgeinn.com

Montgomery denizens descend on this family-friendly American "old country inn" for repasts ranging from burgers to prime rib, lasagna and zuppa de pesce; though some suggest the "menu could use a refresher course" and one diner's "romantic atmosphere" is "too dark" for another in the rustic, woody interior, the consensus is it's a "good neighborhood" spot.

Wasabi *Japanese* | 20 | 15 | 21 | $27

Hudson | 807 Warren St. (bet. 8th St. & Prospect Ave.) | 518-822-1888

"Those in the hinterlands know sushi is hard to come by", so this two-year-old Hudson Japanese "hits the spot" with "darn good", "straightforward" "fresh" fish and "tasty" tempura; "typical decor" is "spartan" and "well-lit", and the "hard-working" "young" servers "are anxious to please."

Ⓩ Wasabi *Japanese* | 27 | 24 | 22 | $51

Nyack | 110 Main St. (Park St.) | 845-358-7977 | www.wasabinyack.com

"All the beautiful people of Nyack go to be seen" at this "upscale", "jumping Japanese" dubbed "Nobu north", where chef-owner Doug Nguyen is "a master artist" proffering "perfectly sculpted" "pristine sushi" and sashimi, "phenomenal ceviche" and such "unusual" dishes that the "entire menu is a treasure"; "chic" modern decor sets a "cool" vibe, but "Manhattan prices" can "sting", so it's even more enjoyable "if someone else is paying."

Watercolor Cafe *American* | 19 | 16 | 19 | $38

Larchmont | 2094 Boston Post Rd. (Larchmont Ave.) | 914-834-2213 | www.watercolorcafe.net

The staff "tries its best" at this "intimate" (read: "cramped") New American cafe in Larchmont where the food is "creative", if sometimes "off the mark"; it's best known as an "excellent" "music venue" and "great jazz", folk and blues keep a "well-dressed clientele" squishing in nightly and "staying late."

Z Watermoon *Pan-Asian* | 24 | 19 | 17 | $39 |

Rye | 66 Purchase St. (Purdy Ave.) | 914-921-8880 |
www.watermooncafe.com

"A beautiful spot", as long as you can "ignore the deafening" din,
this "upscale" Rye Pan-Asian with black lacquer furniture and an in-
door waterfall is one "hip joint" where "modern", "palate-pleasing"
dishes win raves ("the sushi is superb") from the "tony" "young"
crowd; "service can be slow", but even "long waits" don't deter fusion fans who say "the food is worth it."

West Street Grill *American* | 21 | 19 | 20 | $50 |

Litchfield | 43 West St. (bet. Meadow & North Sts.), CT | 860-567-3885

"See and be seen on the Litchfield green" at this pricey, "always-
packed" "celebrity loaded" New American where the "interesting
menu changes frequently" and the "very good chow" is "comforting"; less-nurturing is the "snooty service", which surveyors say "is
so valuable that it's a real favor when they give you any."

White Hart, The *American* | 18 | 20 | 20 | $40 |

Salisbury | White Hart Inn | 15 Undermountain Rd./Rte. 41 (Rte. 44),
CT | 860-435-0030 | www.whitehartinn.com

"Rub elbows with the horsey set" at this Salisbury Traditional
American where the Tap Room (as opposed to the Garden Room)
with its "warm fireplace" and original 1806 hardwood flooring "is
the best seat" in the "quaint inn", although "the wraparound porch"
is also appealing "in season"; foodwise, "it ain't France" – so stick to
"the basics" like burgers and berry cobblers – but it is "what New
England hospitality is all about."

Wildfire Grill *Eclectic* | ▽ 23 | 17 | 22 | $42 |

Montgomery | 74 Clinton St. (Rte. 211) | 845-457-3770

Chef-owner Krista Wild's Montgomery Eclectic may not "knock
your socks off", but "very fine" fare that includes a dash of out-of-
the-ordinary offerings like ostrich, plus "good service" and a colorful, "casual setting", complete with wood-burning stove, paintings
of animals and African touches, combine to make this "a nice find."

Wild Ginger *Pan-Asian* | 23 | 19 | 19 | $44 |

Greenwich | The Mill | 328 Pemberwick Rd. (Glenville Rd.), CT |
203-531-3322 | www.wildginger-ct.com

This "pricey" Pan-Asian, a "hidden treasure" in Greenwich's "beautiful and quiet" Glenville neighborhood, serves "inventive"
"Manhattan-quality sushi" and "superior cooked dishes"; the
"sleek" setting is stylish but "noisy" so the preferred seating is out
on the patio "overlooking the old mill's dam."

Wild Ginger Cafe *Pan-Asian* | 23 | 15 | 16 | $29 |

Ridgefield | 461 Main St. (Prospect St.), CT | 203-431-4588 |
www.chingsrestaurant.com

There's "almost always a line" at this "as-good-as-it-gets-for-
Ridgefield" Pan-Asian, which is favored for its "delicious" curry
dishes and "anything with mango sauce"; though a recent "expan-

FOOD DECOR SERVICE COST

sion created a lot more room", it remains a "bustling", "noisy" place with waiters who "rush you out the door", so many recommend getting it to go.

Willett House, The *Steak*

23 | 21 | 22 | $63

Port Chester | 20 Willett Ave. (Abendroth Ave.) | 914-939-7500 | www.thewilletthouse.com

"Excellent prime cuts" and sides (including "to-die-for spinach") are the hallmarks of this Port Chester restaurant, which perfects the "classic" steakhouse formula, but without the requisite "snootiness" from the staff; "clubby" decor adds to the appeal for "corporate" types, though "the experience" is best "when someone else is footing the bill" (it's not nicknamed "The Wallet House" for nothing).

Willy Nick's *American*

18 | 15 | 15 | $38

Katonah | 17 Katonah Ave. (Edgemont Rd.) | 914-232-8030 | www.willynicks.com

"NYC hip" meets "neighborhood" joint at this "bustling" Katonah Traditional American "near the train station" that "keeps reinventing" itself, recently adding a long attractive bar and sidewalk tables and upgrading the menu to fit with a "more upscale concept"; despite somewhat "crummy" service and "high" prices, it's a "popular spot" that "works", though a smattering of surveyors say they "enjoyed it more" in its previous less "fancy" incarnation; N.B. it's now open for both lunch and dinner.

Wobble Café 🅼 *Eclectic*

21 | 14 | 20 | $20

Ossining | 21 Campwoods Rd. (Stone Ave.) | 914-762-3459 | www.wobblecafe.com

"It's a keeper!" gush groupies of this "offbeat" Ossining breakfast and lunch spot where the Eclectic "comfort-food" menu includes "strong lattes", "pancakes with creative additions" and plenty of "veg-friendly" options; a husband-and-wife team preside over the "quirky", "thrift-store"-style surroundings where toys and a "play area" mean it's "kid-friendly" too; N.B. there's dinner service Thursday–Saturday.

Woodland, The 🅼 *American/Continental*

22 | 18 | 21 | $40

Lakeville | 192 Sharon Rd./Rte. 41 (bet. Rtes. 44 & 112), CT | 860-435-0578

This "solid", "oh-so-crowded" "ribs to sushi" American Continental is a "deservedly popular spot" among Lakeville locals; "enormous portions", a "wonderful", "reasonably priced" wine list and "friendly service" help patrons "ignore the '70s decor."

NEW Woody's on Main *American*

– | – | – | M

Mt. Kisco | 251 E. Main St. (E. Hyatt Ave.) | 914-242-5151

Simple, hearty fare like prime steaks, roasted chicken and brick-oven pizzas make a perfect pre- or post-movie meal at this Mt. Kisco New American newcomer, located a block from the multiplex in the former Luna space; an open kitchen, copper-topped bar and soaring ceilings lend a contemporary feel, while the outdoor seating in warmer months is an additional enticement.

	FOOD	DECOR	SERVICE	COST

Would, The ⓈⓂ *American* | 23 | 19 | 20 | $41 |

Highland | Inn at Applewood | 120 North Rd. (Rte. 9W) | 845-691-9883 |
www.thewould.com

It's "quite surprising" to discover this "quirky" New American
among the "backwoods orchards of Highland" admit admirers,
noshing on "nicely done", "imaginative choices" on the seasonal
menu, washed down with "good wines" from the "extensive list";
one "relaxing" dining area is airy, one more like "your grandma's rec
room", so whether you want a "rousing time, an intimate dinner" "or
just conversation at the bar", there's "something for everyone."

Wunderbar | ▽ 15 | 11 | 19 | $22 |
and Bistro Ⓩ *American*

Hudson | 744 Warren St. (bet. 7th & 8th Sts.) | 518-828-0555 |
www.wunderbarandbistro.com

Maybe it's "non-gourmet", but the American grub offered by "affable" owner Imre Vilaghy at his "casual" Hudson "bar/restaurant" is
"hearty", while "home-cooking" entries with "Austrian flair" (like
"the best wurst") are a nod to his homeland; "slightly scruffy" digs
don't deter those who "count on seeing friends" when they go, and
all enjoy "unbelievably inexpensive" tabs.

Ⓩ Xaviar's at Piermont Ⓜ *American* | 29 | 25 | 27 | $79 |

Piermont | 506 Piermont Ave. (Ash St.) | 845-359-7007 | www.xaviars.com

It's "the epitome of excellence" swoon smitten surveyors voting
"brilliant" chef Peter Kelly's Piermont New American No. 1 for Food
and Service; "glorious" cuisine, "magnificent presentation", a "thoroughly professional staff" and "marked attention to detail" including
"impeccable tableware" in the "teensy", "pretty" room add up to
something "memorable", so never mind the "hefty price tag" ($70
prix fixe, $38 for lunch), "put on your best" duds, and "be a king or
queen for an evening"; even with the cash-only (or Amex) policy and
"parking hassle", "it's worth it all."

Yama Sushi *Japanese* | 24 | 15 | 21 | $33 |

Briarcliff Manor | 1914 Pleasantville Rd. (Chappaqua Rd.) |
914-941-3100 | www.yamasushimenu.com

"Fresh, creative, beautifully presented" sushi and rolls "could compete" with "the best" of them in Westchester or Manhattan swear
supporters of this Briarcliff Manor Japanese; the staff is "friendly and
efficient" so even if the "storefront" strip-mall setting is "blank and uninspired", the overall experience has enthusiasts exclaiming: "wow."

Yobo *Pan-Asian* | 19 | 19 | 18 | $33 |

Newburgh | 1297 Rte. 300 (Rte. 84, exit 7S) | 845-564-3848 |
www.yoborestaurant.com

Expect a "wide array" of "good" fare at this "busy" Newburgh "stalwart" serving Japanese, Indonesian, Thai and Korean dishes that
have fans yelling "yummo"; "Asian Disneyland" decor includes a
"babbling brook" in the dining room that's "fun", so though stylists
say it all "needs a refurb", at least it takes your mind off "slow" service, as do "well-made drinks."

	FOOD	DECOR	SERVICE	COST

Yvonne's Southern Cuisine ⓜ *Southern* | 22 | 17 | 23 | $30 |
Pelham | 503 Fifth Ave. (6th St.) | 914-738-2005
Fans of "down-home cooking" are "glad to have" chef-owner Yvonne Parker's Pelham Southern that serves as a "suburban alternative to NYC's Sylvia's" with "lip-smacking ribs", "hot fried chicken" and the kind of "sides you'd only see in Georgia"; moderate tabs and live jazz on weekends mean it can get "crowded"; P.S. Tuesday and Thursday there's an all-you-can-eat buffet – just "don't forget to take your Lipitor."

Zafrán ⓜ *European/Indian* ▽ 21 | 17 | 18 | $31 |
Yonkers | 1550 Central Park Ave. (Tuckahoe Rd.) | 914-395-3186
A "cool menu" of "intriguing" Indian-European fusion dishes (think pastas with "spicy sauces" and steak tandoori) "done just right" makes this Yonkers "storefront spot" a "pleasant" night out (and the option to BYO with no corkage fee makes it "even better"); with an "affable owner" and a "warm" saffron-colored room, the only downside is its "lousy location" in a local strip mall.

Zanaro's *Italian* | 14 | 19 | 15 | $33 |
White Plains | 1 Mamaroneck Ave. (Main St.) | 914-397-9400 | www.zanaros.com
"Hearty helpings" of "decent" "Italian staples" plus an "atmospheric" setting in a "converted bank" make this White Plains eatery work well for "cheap dates", "family gatherings" or a "post-movie" meal; critics cite "formulaic" fare and say service can be "less-than-attentive", but "it does the job."

Zen Tango ⓢ *Asian Fusion/Pan-Latin* ▽ 21 | 20 | 20 | $38 |
New Rochelle | Radisson Hotel | 1 Radisson Plaza (Huguenot St.) | 914-576-4141 | www.radisson.com
Bright orange walls and white leather banquettes set a "stylish" mood at this restaurant "hidden" in the Radisson Hotel New Rochelle, where the "inventive" Asian–Pan-Latin fusion fare is "fresh and delicious", if "pricey"; "tasty" cocktails can be imbibed here or in The City Martini Lounge next door.

ⓩ Zephs' ⓜ *American/Eclectic* | 26 | 18 | 23 | $53 |
Peekskill | 638 Central Ave. (bet. Nelson Ave. & Water St.) | 914-736-2159
"Attentive" brother-and-sister-team Vicky and Michael Zeph turn out "homegrown" yet "elegant" New American–Eclectic dishes from an "imaginative" (if "limited") menu at their "off-the-beaten-path" Peekskill perch set in an old charcoal factory; if a smattering of surveyors say they're "underwhelmed" by "less than exceptional" cuisine and service, they're outnumbered by those who claim it's a "charming" spot that lives up to its "high reputation."

Zinc Bistro & Bar *American/French* | 19 | 16 | 17 | $35 |
Stamford | 222 Summer St. (Broad St.), CT | 203-252-2352 | www.zincstamford.com
This Downtown Stamford bistro in a "prime location" near the theater serves "a mix of American and French fare" that ranges from

	FOOD	DECOR	SERVICE	COST

burgers to escargots; while a number criticize the "uncaring service" and "cold" interior, extroverts extol the "excellent people-watching" perks from the "great sidewalk tables."

NEW Zitoune *Moroccan* | - | - | - | M |

Mamaroneck | 1127 W. Boston Post Rd. (Richbell Rd.) | 914-835-8350

A "warm and inviting" dining room draped with fabric and decorated with North African knickknacks heralds something "new and different" at this Mamaroneck Moroccan that channels Marrakesh with "creative", brightly spiced dishes from the chef-owner's native country; "the whole experience", from the "great food" and "friendly service" to "belly dancing" on Fridays and Saturdays, has locals lauding it as "an outstanding addition" to the neighborhood.

NEW Zody *Italian* | - | - | - | M |

Stamford | 21 Atlantic St. (Broad St.), CT | 203-359-9639 | www.zodycafe.com

The few surveyors who've discovered this moderately priced "newcomer to the Stamford scene" cite "delicious" Italian-American fare, "friendly, helpful service" and a "pleasant", "welcoming" atmosphere; just note that "parking can be difficult", given the "excellent" Downtown location.

Zuppa Restaurant & Lounge *Italian* | 23 | 24 | 23 | $50 |

Yonkers | 59 Main St. (bet. Buena Vista & Riverdale Aves.) | 914-376-6500 | www.zupparestaurant.com

Like a "SoHo lounge without the pretentiousness", this "sleek, sophisticated" boîte in "aspiring" Downtown Yonkers proffers Northern Italian cuisine with "deft and creative touches" that "rarely disappoints"; service is "stellar", so the biggest drawbacks are "high prices" and a room that gets "noisy", thanks in part to a "festive bar" and live jazz Thursday–Saturday; P.S. there's an "intimate" "wine cellar" for private dining and events.

WESTCHESTER/ HUDSON VALLEY WITH NEIGHBORING CONNECTICUT TOWNS INDEXES

Cuisines

Includes restaurant names, neighborhoods and Food ratings. ☑ indicates places with the highest ratings, popularity and importance.

AMERICAN (NEW)

Adrienne | **New Milford**	23
☑ American Bounty | **Hyde Pk**	26
☑ An American Bistro | **Tuck**	22
Andrew's | **Elmsford**	18
Aroma Thyme | **Ellenville**	20
NEW Artist's Palate | **Poughkp**	24
Aux Délices | **multi. loc.**	22
NEW Backals | **Scarsdale**	16
NEW Backyard | **Montgomery**	–
Bailey's Backyard | **multi. loc.**	20
Basement Bistro | **Earlton**	29
☑ Bear Cafe | **Bearsville**	23
Beebs | **Newburgh**	22
Beech Tree Grill | **Poughkp**	20
Beehive | **Armonk**	17
Belvedere | **Staatsburg**	17
Bird and Bottle | **Garrison**	21
Bistro 22 | **Bedford**	23
Black Goose | **Darien**	17
NEW Bloom | **Hastings/Hud**	21
Blu | **Hastings/Hud**	18
Blue | **White Pl**	19
☑ Blue Hill/Stone | **Poc Hills**	27
Blue Plate | **Chatham**	18
Boulders Inn | **New Preston**	21
☑ Busy Bee | **Poughkp**	26
NEW Bywater | **Rosendale**	18
Cafe Tamayo | **Saugerties**	24
Calico | **Rhinebeck**	25
Catskill Rose | **Mt. Tremper**	–
Chefs On Fire | **High Falls**	22
Citrus Grille | **Airmont**	24
Comfort | **Hastings/Hud**	20
NEW Copper Rest. | **Fishkill**	–
Country Inn | **Krumville**	–
☑ Crabtree's | **Chappaqua**	24
Creek | **Purchase**	15
Crew | **Poughkp**	20
Deer Park Tavern | **Katonah**	19
☑ DePuy Canal | **High Falls**	25
Division St. Grill | **Peekskill**	19
Emerson | **Woodstock**	18
☑ Equus | **Tarrytown**	26
Flying Pig | **Mt. Kisco**	21
Foundry Cafe | **Cold Spring**	18
Four Doors Down | **Buchanan**	–
☑ Freelance Café | **Piermont**	28
Frodo's | **P'ville**	23
Gaia | **Greenwich**	24
Globe B&G | **Larch**	16
Grand | **Stamford**	21
Granite Springs | **Granite Spr**	20
Halstead Ave. Bistro | **Harrison**	22
Harvest/Brookfield | **Brookfield**	21
Harvest Café | **New Paltz**	24
Haymaker | **Poughkp**	23
Heights Bistro | **Yorktown Hts**	24
Hillsdale Hse. | **Hillsdale**	13
Hudson Hse. Nyack | **Nyack**	20
Hudson Hse. Inn | **Cold Spring**	21
Iron Forge Inn | **Warwick**	21
☑ Iron Horse Grill | **P'ville**	27
Jack & Dyls | **Tarrytown**	18
Jackson & Wheeler | **P'ville**	17
Julianna's | **Cortlandt Man**	–
Kraft Bistro | **Bronxville**	19
Landau Grill | **Woodstock**	12
Lexington Sq. Café | **Mt. Kisco**	18
NEW Local 111 | **Philmont**	–
MacMenamin's | **New Roch**	22
NEW Madalin's Table | **Tivoli**	19
Maggie's in the Alley | **Chester**	–
Maggie's Krooked | **Tanners**	–
Main Course | **New Paltz**	23
Main Course/Alum. | **Poughkp**	20
Marco | **Lake Mahopac**	22
Martha's | **Millerton**	–
Mayflower Inn | **Washington**	24
McKinney & Doyle | **Pawling**	23
Meetinghouse | **Bedford Vill**	17
Meritage | **Scarsdale**	22

NEW Mickey Spill. | **Eastchester**	–
Mojo Grill | **Wapp Falls**	23
NEW Napa & Co. | **Stamford**	–
New World | **Saugerties**	23
Northern Spy Cafe | **High Falls**	16
North Star | **Pound Ridge**	22
Old Drovers Inn | **Dover Plains**	23
NEW One | **Irvington**	27
121 Rest./Bar | **N Salem**	21
Opus 465 | **Armonk**	18
Oscar | **Kerhonkson**	–
Palmer's Crossing | **Larch**	17
Pantry | **Wash Depot**	23
Paradise B&G | **Stamford**	13
Peter Pratt's Inn | **Yorktown**	23
NEW Phoenix | **Mt. Tremper**	–
Plates | **Larch**	24
Plumbush Inn | **Cold Spring**	22
NEW Pony Express | **P'ville**	–
Purdys Homestead | **N Salem**	23
Raccoon Saloon | **Marlboro**	19
☑ Rebeccas | **Greenwich**	26
Red Hat | **Irvington**	22
Red Onion | **Saugerties**	22
Relish | **Sparkill**	25
☑ Rest. X/Bully | **Congers**	27
River Bank | **Cornwall/Hud**	25
River City Grille | **Irvington**	20
River Grill | **Newburgh**	21
Riverview | **Cold Spring**	24
Roasted Garlic | **Red Hook**	14
Seasons American | **Somers**	20
NEW Shadows | **Poughkp**	–
Ship Lantern | **Milton**	25
Ship to Shore | **Kingston**	23
St. Andrew's Cafe | **Hyde Pk**	24
Sterling Inn | **New Roch**	20
Strega | **P'ville**	–
Susan's | **Peekskill**	18
Swoon Kitchenbar | **Hudson**	24
☑ Terrapin | **Rhinebeck**	24
☑ Thomas Moran's | **New Preston**	25
Thomas Moran's | **New Milford**	22
NEW Tonique | **Beacon**	–

Towne Crier Cafe | **Pawling**	17
Trinity Grill | **Harrison**	16
Troutbeck | **Amenia**	18
Turning Point | **Piermont**	14
Twist | **Hyde Pk**	25
Underhills Crossing | **Bronxville**	21
☑ Valley/Garrison | **Garrison**	26
Velvet Monkey | **Monroe**	20
☑ Vertigo | **Nyack**	18
NEW Village Café | **Bronxville**	15
Vintage | **White Pl**	16
Violette | **Woodstock**	22
Vox | **N Salem**	21
Watercolor Cafe | **Larch**	19
West St. Grill | **Litchfield**	21
NEW Woody's | **Mt. Kisco**	–
Would | **Highland**	23
☑ Xaviar's | **Piermont**	29
☑ Zephs' | **Peekskill**	26

AMERICAN (TRADITIONAL)

American Pie Co. | **Sherman**	19
NEW Anna Maria's | **Larch**	20
B4 Bistro | **Valhalla**	18
Boathouse | **Lakeville**	16
Bobby Valentine's | **Stamford**	14
Briar's | **Briarcliff Manor**	15
NEW Brick House | **Stamford**	15
Bull's Bridge Inn | **Kent**	16
Bull's Head Inn | **Campbell Hall**	19
Cascade Mtn. Winery | **Amenia**	22
Catherine's | **Goshen**	22
Chat 19 | **Larch**	17
☑ Cheesecake Fac. | **White Pl**	18
NEW Chelsea's | **Pelham**	–
Cobble Stone | **Purchase**	16
Copper Bottom | **Florida**	19
Cutillo's | **Carmel**	–
NEW DABA | **Hudson**	19
NEW De La Vergne | **Amenia**	21
Doubleday's | **Dobbs Ferry**	13
Egg's Nest | **High Falls**	18
Elms | **Ridgefield**	21
NEW Fifty Coins | **Ridgefield**	14
59 Bank | **multi. loc.**	18

NEW Gail's | **Ridgefield**	‑
Gentleman Jim's | **Poughkp**	17
Gianna's | **Yonkers**	21
Ginger Man | **Greenwich**	17
Grandma's | **Yorktown**	16
Granite Springs | **Granite Spr**	20
Greenbaum | **Wapp Falls**	16
G.W. Tavern | **Wash Depot**	18
Horse & Hound | **S Salem**	16
Horsefeathers | **Tarrytown**	17
Horseman Rest. | **Sleepy Hollow**	13
J.J. Mannion's | **Yonkers**	15
Justin Thyme | **Croton/Hud**	16
Landmark Inn | **Warwick**	17
Larchmont Tavern | **Larch**	15
Last Chance | **Tanners**	21
Lighthouse/Hudson | **Piermont**	16
Long Ridge Tavern | **Stamford**	15
Lu Shane's | **Nyack**	23
Mackenzie's | **Old Greenwich**	16
Main St. Cafe | **Tarrytown**	16
Martindale Chief | **Craryville**	10
Maud's Tavern | **Hastings/Hud**	13
McArthur's | **P'ville**	‑
Michael's Tavern | **P'ville**	14
Milan Roadhouse | **Milan**	‑
Miss Lucy's | **Saugerties**	22
Mohonk Mtn. Hse. | **New Paltz**	17
Olde Stone Mill | **Tuck**	15
Old '76 House | **Tappan**	15
Peekamoose | **Big Indian**	25
Piper's Kilt | **Eastchester**	20
Reality Bites | **Nyack**	20
Red Barn | **W Ghent**	19
Red Rooster | **Brewster**	19
River Club | **Nyack**	16
Rockwells | **Pelham**	12
Sam's/Gedney | **White Pl**	18
Soul Dog | **Poughkp**	21
Southport Brewing | **Stamford**	16
Squires | **Briarcliff Manor**	18
Steakhouse 22 | **Patterson**	17
Sweet Sue's | **Phoenicia**	24
Tavern at Highlands | **Garrison**	23
Thataway Cafe | **Greenwich**	15

Tollgate Hill Inn | **Litchfield**	20
Torches on Hudson | **Newburgh**	15
Town Dock | **Rye**	18
Traditions 118 | **Somers**	19
Traphagen | **Rhinebeck**	22
Ugly Gus Cafe | **Kingston**	18
Village Grille | **Tappan**	21
Village Tea. | **New Paltz**	21
Villa Nova E. | **Pelham**	19
Ward's Bridge | **Montgomery**	19
White Hart | **Salisbury**	18
Willy Nick's | **Katonah**	18
Woodland | **Lakeville**	22
Wunderbar | **Hudson**	15
Zinc Bistro & Bar | **Stamford**	19
NEW Zody | **Stamford**	‑

ARGENTINEAN

Z Tango Grill | **White Pl**	23

ASIAN

NEW Made In Asia | **Armonk**	‑
Temptation Tea | **Mt. Kisco**	21

ASIAN FUSION

Ace Asian-French | **Thornwood**	24
NEW Euro Asian | **Port Chester**	‑
Plateau | **Stamford**	21
Zen Tango | **New Roch**	21

AUSTRIAN

Hopkins Inn | **New Preston**	18

BAKERIES

American Pie Co. | **Sherman**	19
Apple Pie | **Hyde Pk**	24
Bread Alone | **multi. loc.**	20
Chiboust | **Tarrytown**	23
Corner Bakery | **Pawling**	25
Jackson & Wheeler | **P'ville**	17
Jean Claude's | **Warwick**	26
Versailles | **Greenwich**	22

BARBECUE

NEW Big W's | **Wingdale**	‑
Casa Miguel | **Mt. Kisco**	14
Cookhouse | **multi. loc.**	19
Hickory BBQ | **Kingston**	18
Holy Smoke | **Mahopac**	18

NEW Jackalope BBQ | **Fishkill** | – |
Max's Memphis | **Red Hook** | 20 |
NEW Memphis Mae's | **Croton/Hud** | 17 |
Piggy Bank | **Beacon** | 18 |
Q Rest. | **Port Chester** | 23 |
Smokey Joe's | **Stamford** | 19 |
Southbound BBQ | **Valhalla** | 17 |

BRAZILIAN

Caravela | **Tarrytown** | 20 |
Pantanal | **Port Chester** | 22 |
Samba | **Mt. Vernon** | 18 |

CAJUN

Bayou | **Mt. Vernon** | 21 |
Big Easy Bistro | **Newburgh** | 17 |
High St. Road. | **Rye** | 18 |

CALIFORNIAN

Gates | **New Canaan** | 18 |
NEW Sonoma | **Brewster** | – |

CARIBBEAN

NEW Lejends | **Yonkers** | – |

CHINESE

(* dim sum specialist)
Aberdeen* | **White Pl** | 24 |
China Rose | **multi. loc.** | 21 |
David Chen | **Armonk** | 19 |
East Harbor | **Yonkers** | 16 |
Empire Hunan | **Yorktown Hts** | 16 |
Golden House | **Jeff Valley** | 20 |
Hunan Larchmont | **Larch** | 17 |
Hunan Ritz | **Thornwood** | 19 |
Hunan Village | **Yonkers** | 23 |
Imperial Wok | **multi. loc.** | 18 |
K. Fung's | **Hartsdale** | 20 |
Lotus King | **Eastchester** | 18 |
Mill House Panda | **multi. loc.** | 17 |
Pacific | **Mt. Kisco** | 16 |
Pagoda* | **Scarsdale** | 22 |
Panda Pavilion | **Greenwich** | 15 |
Z P.F. Chang's | **White Pl** | 20 |
Ray's Cafe | **multi. loc.** | 19 |
Seven Woks | **Scarsdale** | 15 |
Sue & Hai | **Yorktown Hts** | 19 |
Tung Hoy | **Mamaro** | 15 |

COFFEEHOUSES

Cafe Mozart | **Mamaro** | 15 |
Dragonfly Caffé | **P'ville** | 15 |

COFFEE SHOPS/DINERS

Bread Alone | **multi. loc.** | 20 |
Brooklyn's Famous | **White Pl** | 16 |
Z City Limits Diner | **multi. loc.** | 19 |
Daily Planet | **LaGrangeville** | 18 |
Eveready Diner | **Hyde Pk** | 17 |
Lucky's | **Stamford** | 16 |
Martindale Chief | **Craryville** | 10 |
Milan Roadhouse | **Milan** | – |
NEW Mtn. Cow | **Pine Plains** | – |
Orem's Diner | **Wilton** | 15 |

CONTINENTAL

Alpine Inn | **Patterson** | – |
Canterbury | **Cornwall/Hud** | 23 |
Chateau Hathorn | **Warwick** | 22 |
Copper Bottom | **Florida** | 19 |
Friends & Family | **Accord** | 21 |
Grande Centrale | **Congers** | 19 |
Hoffman Hse. | **Kingston** | 19 |
Jennifer's | **Yorktown Hts** | 19 |
John's Harvest | **Middletown** | 19 |
L'Europe | **S Salem** | 24 |
Lipperas' | **Chatham** | 19 |
Z Monteverde | **Cortlandt** | 21 |
Off Broadway | **Dobbs Ferry** | 19 |
Pamela's Traveling | **Newburgh** | 18 |
Pillars | **New Lebanon** | – |
Roger Sherman | **New Canaan** | 23 |
Ship Lantern | **Milton** | 25 |
Stonehenge | **Ridgefield** | 23 |
Sunset Cove | **Tarrytown** | 15 |
Swiss Hütte | **Hillsdale** | 20 |
Travelers | **Ossining** | 18 |
Tulip Tree | **Rye Brook** | – |
Woodland | **Lakeville** | 22 |

CREOLE

Bayou | **Mt. Vernon** | 21 |
High St. Road. | **Rye** | 18 |

CUBAN

NEW Belle Havana | **Yonkers** | – |
NEW Coco Rumba | **Mt. Kisco** | 17 |

Karamba | **White Pl**	22
Latin Am. Cafe | **White Pl**	20

DELIS

Bagels & More | **multi. loc.**	18
Bloom's Deli | **Yorktown Hts**	19
Epstein's Deli | **multi. loc.**	16
Kisco Kosher | **White Pl**	18
Lange's Deli | **Scarsdale**	18

DESSERT

American Pie Co. | **Sherman**	19
Apple Pie | **Hyde Pk**	24
Aux Délices | **multi. loc.**	22
Cafe Mozart | **Mamaro**	15
Calico | **Rhinebeck**	25
Z Cheesecake Fac. | **White Pl**	18
Corner Bakery | **Pawling**	25
Grandma's | **Yorktown**	16
Jean Claude's | **Warwick**	26
McKinney & Doyle | **Pawling**	23
Pantry | **Wash Depot**	23
Temptations Cafe | **Nyack**	21
Versailles | **Greenwich**	22
Village Tea. | **New Paltz**	21

ECLECTIC

Arch | **Brewster**	25
Aroma Thyme | **Ellenville**	20
Beehive | **Armonk**	17
Beso | **New Paltz**	25
Cafe Mirage | **Port Chester**	20
Calico | **Rhinebeck**	25
Division St. Grill | **Peekskill**	19
Down by the Bay | **Mamaro**	16
NEW Dragonfly Grille | **Woodstock**	-
NEW Dragonfly Lounge | **Stamford**	18
Earth Foods | **Hudson**	-
Gigi's Folderol II | **Westtown**	24
Global Gatherings | **Hartsdale**	20
Hamilton Inn | **Millerton**	19
Luna 61 | **Tivoli**	20
Manna Dew Cafe | **Millerton**	22
New World | **Saugerties**	23
Nina | **Middletown**	24

96 Main | **Poughkp**	21
Onyx B&G | **Stamford**	15
Painter's | **Cornwall/Hud**	19
Red Dot | **Hudson**	16
Relish | **Sparkill**	25
River City Grille | **Irvington**	20
Ruby's Hotel | **Freehold**	-
Stoneleigh Creek | **Crot Falls**	23
Temptations Cafe | **Nyack**	21
Ümami Café | **Croton/Hud**	21
Vintage | **White Pl**	16
Wildfire Grill | **Montgomery**	23
Wobble Café | **Ossining**	21
Z Zephs' | **Peekskill**	26

EUROPEAN

Café with Love | **Saugerties**	19
NEW Charlotte's | **Millbrook**	-
Cutillo's | **Carmel**	-
NEW Duo | **Stamford**	-
Lena's | **Nyack**	21
Locust Tree | **New Paltz**	21
Marion's Country | **Woodstock**	22
NEW Oriole 9 | **Woodstock**	19
Zafrán | **Yonkers**	21

FONDUE

Brasserie Swiss | **Ossining**	19
Melting Pot | **Darien**	20

FRENCH

NEW A'Tavola | **Harrison**	-
Aux Délices | **multi. loc.**	22
NEW Belle Havana | **Yonkers**	-
Z Bernard's | **Ridgefield**	26
Z Buffet/Gare | **Hastings/Hud**	26
Capriccio | **Brewster**	21
Z Equus | **Tarrytown**	26
Z Escoffier | **Hyde Pk**	26
French Corner | **Stone Ridge**	25
Z Jean-Louis | **Greenwich**	27
La Bretagne | **Stamford**	23
Z La Crémaillère | **Bedford**	27
Z La Panetière | **Rye**	27
La Salière | **Ridgefield**	21
Le Chambord | **Hopewell Jct**	22
Z Le Château | **S Salem**	25

🅩 Le Pavillon | **Poughkp**	27
L'Escale | **Greenwich**	21
Meli-Melo | **Greenwich**	23
🅩 Ondine | **Danbury**	26
Pillars | **New Lebanon**	–
Ruby's Hotel | **Freehold**	–
Sterling Inn | **New Roch**	20
Stissing House | **Pine Plains**	19
Stonehenge | **Ridgefield**	23

FRENCH (BISTRO)

Bistro Bonne Nuit | **New Canaan**	24
Bistro 22 | **Bedford**	23
🅩 Café Les Baux | **Millbrook**	25
Chez Jean-Pierre | **Stamford**	22
Chiboust | **Tarrytown**	23
Encore Bistro | **Larch**	21
Figaro Bistro | **Greenwich**	19
Jackie's Bistro | **Eastchester**	20
La Duchesse | **Mt. Tremper**	–
Le Canard Enchaîné | **Kingston**	24
Le Jardin du Roi | **Chappaqua**	20
🅩 Le Petit Bistro | **Rhinebeck**	26
Le Provençal | **Mamaro**	23
Luc's Café | **Ridgefield**	23
Pascal's | **Larch**	22
Pastorale | **Lakeville**	23
Red Hat | **Irvington**	22
Versailles | **Greenwich**	22
Zinc Bistro & Bar | **Stamford**	19

FRENCH (BRASSERIE)

Le Bouchon | **Cold Spring**	22

FRENCH (NEW)

Gaia | **Greenwich**	24
🅩 Thomas Henkelmann | **Greenwich**	29
Vox | **N Salem**	21

GERMAN

Jennifer's | **Yorktown Hts**	19

GREEK

Diasporas | **Rhinebeck**	20
🅩 Lefteris Gyro | **multi. loc.**	21
Niko's Greek | **White Pl**	20
Post Corner Pizza | **Darien**	18

HAMBURGERS

Blazer Pub | **Purdys**	21
Brooklyn's Famous | **White Pl**	16
Cobble Stone | **Purchase**	16
Doubleday's | **Dobbs Ferry**	13
Horsefeathers | **Tarrytown**	17
Horseman Rest. | **Sleepy Hollow**	13
Landau Grill | **Woodstock**	12
Lucky's | **Stamford**	16
Mackenzie's | **Old Greenwich**	16
Pete's Saloon | **Elmsford**	16
Piper's Kilt | **Eastchester**	20
🆕 Pony Express | **P'ville**	–
Raccoon Saloon | **Marlboro**	19
Red Rooster | **Brewster**	19
Route 22 | **multi. loc.**	15
Sam's/Gedney | **White Pl**	18
Town Dock | **Rye**	18
Towne Crier Cafe | **Pawling**	17

HEALTH FOOD

Aroma Thyme | **Ellenville**	20
Luna 61 | **Tivoli**	20
Tomatillo | **Dobbs Ferry**	21

HOT DOGS

🆕 Pony Express | **P'ville**	–
Soul Dog | **Poughkp**	21
Walter's | **Mamaro**	21

ICE CREAM PARLORS

Temptations Cafe | **Nyack**	21

INDIAN

Agra Tandoor | **Rhinebeck**	17
🅩 Bengal Tiger | **White Pl**	23
🆕 Bollywood | **P'ville**	24
🆕 Bukhara Grill | **Yonkers**	25
Café Tandoor | **Tarrytown**	21
Chola | **Greenwich**	22
🅩 Coromandel | **multi. loc.**	26
Dakshin | **Stamford**	23
India Cafe | **Armonk**	20
India House | **Montrose**	23
Jaipore Indian | **Brewster**	24
Malabar Hill | **Elmsford**	23
Meera Cuisine | **Stamford**	16

WEST/HV/CT

CUISINES

Mountain Gate	**Woodstock**	15
Mughal Palace	**Valhalla**	23
Passage to India	**Mt. Kisco**	19
Patang Indian	**Yonkers**	20
Priya	**Suffern**	20
Rangoli	**New Roch**	21
NEW Rani Mahal	**Mamaro**	-
Royal Palace	**White Pl**	18
Tandoori Taste	**Port Chester**	23
Tanjore	**Fishkill**	25
Z Thali	**multi. loc.**	24
Zafrán	**Yonkers**	21

IRISH

NEW Chelsea's	**Pelham**	-
Finn McCool's	**White Pl**	16
Garth Road Inn	**Scarsdale**	16

ITALIAN

(N=Northern; S=Southern)

Abatino's	**N White Plains**	20
Abruzzi Trattoria	**Patterson**	20
Alba's	N	**Port Chester**	23
Aloi	N	**New Canaan**	24
Amalfi	**Briarcliff Manor**	20
A' Mangiare	S	**multi. loc.**	-
Amarone's	**Sugar Loaf**	21
Angelina's	**Tuck**	19
NEW Anna Maria's	**Larch**	20
Z Aroma Osteria	**Wapp Falls**	27
NEW A'Tavola	**Harrison**	-
Aurora	N	**Rye**	19
Babbone	**Bronxville**	22
Bacio Trattoria	**Cross River**	19
Bastones Italian	**New Roch**	18
Bella Vita	**Mohegan Lake**	20
Bellizzi	**multi. loc.**	14
Bel Paese	**Hawthorne**	17
Bertucci's	**multi. loc.**	15
Blue Dolphin	S	**Katonah**	22
Blue Fountain	**Hopewell Jct**	20
Brothers Trattoria	**Beacon**	23
Buon Amici	**White Pl**	20
Cafe Livorno	N	**Rye**	19
Cafe on the Green	N	**Danbury**	23
Cafe Portofino	**Piermont**	20

Ca'Mea	N	**Hudson**	21
Capriccio	N	**Brewster**	21
Casa Rina	**Thornwood**	17
Z Caterina de Medici	**Hyde Pk**	26
Cathryn's	N	**Cold Spring**	22
Cava Wine	N	**New Canaan**	22
Cena 2000	N	**Newburgh**	24
Centro	N	**multi. loc.**	19
Chef Antonio	S	**Mamaro**	14
Ciao!	N	**Eastchester**	18
Ciao! Cafe	**Danbury**	21
Z Columbus Park	**Stamford**	24
Coppola's	**Poughkp**	18
Cosimo's Brick	**multi. loc.**	20
Cosimo's Tratt.	**Poughkp**	19
NEW DaVinci's	**New Roch**	-
DiNardo's	**Pound Ridge**	17
Doc's	N	**New Preston**	22
Downtown Cafe	**Kingston**	21
Eclisse	N	**Stamford**	19
Z Emilio Rist.	**Harrison**	25
Enzo's	**Mamaro**	18
Ernesto	**White Pl**	20
Fortuna	N	**Croton/Hud**	22
Fratelli	**New Roch**	21
Fuffi 2000	N	**New Roch**	17
Gaudio's	**Yorktown Hts**	17
Gavi	**Armonk**	18
Gianna's	**Yonkers**	21
Z Gigi Trattoria	**Rhinebeck**	23
Gina Marie's	**Eastchester**	19
Giorgio's	N	**Port Chester**	23
Giulio's of Tappan	**Tappan**	18
Grande Centrale	**Congers**	19
Grappolo Locanda	**Chappaqua**	19
Graziellas	**White Pl**	19
Heather's Cucina	**Nyack**	21
Hostaria Mazzei	**Port Chester**	21
Il Bacio Tratt.	**Bronxville**	23
Z Il Barilotto	**Fishkill**	26
Z Il Cenàcolo	N	**Newburgh**	27
Il Continori	N	**Wapp Falls**	-
Il Falco	**Stamford**	22
Il Forno	**Somers**	20

Restaurant	Rating
Il Portico | **Tappan**	22
Il Sorriso | **Irvington**	20
NEW Il Teatro | N | **Mamaro**	21
Il Tesoro | N | **Goshen**	26
Insieme | **Ridgefield**	24
Z Johnny's | S | **Mt. Vernon**	25
La Fontanella | N | **Pelham**	25
Lago di Como | N | **Tarrytown**	21
Laguna | N | **White Pl**	20
La Lanterna | **Yonkers**	19
La Manda's | **White Pl**	18
Lanterna Tuscan | N | **multi. loc.**	21
La Piccola Casa | N | **Mamaro**	21
La Riserva | **Larch**	21
La Scala | **Armonk**	20
La Stazione | **New Paltz**	19
La Trattoria | **New Roch**	23
La Villetta | **Larch**	24
Le Fontane | S | **Katonah**	21
Lia's | **Hartsdale**	21
Lia's Mtn. View | **Pine Plains**	16
Little Sorrento | **Cortlandt**	18
NEW Locanda | S | **Fishkill**	–
Louie & Johnnies' | S | **Yonkers**	22
Z Luca Rist. | **Wilton**	27
Luce Rest. | N | **Somers**	22
Z Lusardi's | N | **Larch**	23
Maestro's | **multi. loc.**	16
Mamma Assunta | **Tuck**	19
Mamma Francesca | **New Roch**	19
Marcello's | **Suffern**	24
Marianacci's | S | **Port Chester**	21
Mediterraneo | **P'ville**	18
NEW Mercato | N | **Red Hook**	–
Michele | **Valley Cott**	21
Millennio | **Scarsdale**	21
Miraggio | N | **Yorktown Hts**	19
Modern | S | **New Roch**	23
Mona Lisa | **Stamford**	24
Moscato | **Scarsdale**	23
Z Mulino's | **White Pl**	24
Nanuet Hotel | **Nanuet**	18
Nino's | N | **S Salem**	18
122 Pizza Bistro | **Stamford**	21
Osteria Applausi | **Old Greenwich**	22
Osteria Marietta | N | **Mamaro**	19
Pasquale Rist. | **Port Chester**	19
Pasta Amore | N | **Piermont**	16
Pasta Cucina | **multi. loc.**	20
Pasta Vera | **Greenwich**	20
Pastina's | **Hartsdale**	18
Pellicci's | **Stamford**	20
Peppino's | N | **Katonah**	16
Piccola Tratt. | **Dobbs Ferry**	19
Picolo | **Millbrook**	20
Piero's | **multi. loc.**	21
Pinocchio | **Eastchester**	23
Polpo | **Greenwich**	24
Portobello Café | **Montrose**	25
Portofino | **Goldens Bridge**	21
Portofino Rist. | **Staatsburg**	22
Portofino's II | **Wilton**	20
Primavera | N | **Crot Falls**	23
Ricky's Seafood | **Yonkers**	15
Rigatoni | **Pelham**	–
Roma | **Tuck**	17
Romolo's | **Congers**	19
Z Rosie's Bistro | **Bronxville**	23
Rustico | **Scarsdale**	20
Sabatiello's | **Stamford**	18
Sam's | **Dobbs Ferry**	18
NEW Sardegna | **Larch**	–
Scaramella's | **Dobbs Ferry**	21
Siena | N | **Stamford**	23
Solaia | **Greenwich**	20
Solé Rist. | N | **New Canaan**	21
Southport Brewing | **Stamford**	16
Spaccarelli's | **Millwood**	22
Spiga | **Scarsdale**	17
Spiritoso | **Yonkers**	22
Stissing House | **Pine Plains**	19
Strega | N | **P'ville**	–
T&J Villaggio | **Port Chester**	21
Z Tango Grill | **White Pl**	23
Taro's | **Millerton**	19
Ten Railroad | **Warwick**	16
Terra Rist. | N | **Greenwich**	20
Terra Rustica | **Briarcliff Manor**	20

WEST/HV/CT

CUISINES

That Little Italian	**Greenwich**	18	Imperial Wok	**multi. loc.**	18
Tombolino's	**Yonkers**	21	Japan Inn*	**Bronxville**	22
Tony La Stazione	**Elmsford**	16	Kang Suh	**Yonkers**	22
Torchia's	**Briarcliff Manor**	16	Karuta*	**New Roch**	19
Toscana	N	**Ridgefield**	19	Kazu Japanese*	**Hartsdale**	21
Toscani's	**New Paltz**	17	Kicho*	**Bedford Hills**	19
Traditions 118	**Somers**	19	Kirari*	**Scarsdale**	20
Tramonto	**Hawthorne**	19	Kira Steak	**Armonk**	17
NEW Trattoria Lucia	**Bedford**	14	Kira Sushi*	**Armonk**	23
Tratt. Vivolo	**Harrison**	22	Z Koo*	**multi. loc.**	24
Tre Angelina	N	**White Pl**	22	Kotobuki*	**Stamford**	23
Tuscano	N	**Danbury**	18	Kujaku*	**Stamford**	20
Tuscan Oven	N	**Mt. Kisco**	19	Kyoto Sushi*	**Kingston**	24
Z Valbella	N	**multi. loc.**	25	Momiji	**Harrison**	19
Valentino's	**Yonkers**	23	Mount Fuji	**Hillburn**	21
Via Appia	**White Pl**	19	Mount Fuji Sushi*	**Mt. Kisco**	19
Via Nove	**Fishkill**	19	Neko Sushi*	**multi. loc.**	20
NEW Viansa	**Yorktown**	–	Noda's Steak*	**White Pl**	18
NEW Vico	N	**Hudson**	–	Okinawa*	**Mt. Kisco**	15
Villa Nova E.	**Pelham**	19	Oriental House*	**Pine Bush**	–
Vinny's Backyard	**Stamford**	17	Osaka*	**multi. loc.**	23
Vuli	N	**Stamford**	17	O'Sho Japanese	**Poughkp**	19
Zanaro's	**White Pl**	14	Plum Tree*	**New Canaan**	20
NEW Zody	**Stamford**	–	Sakura*	**Scarsdale**	18
Zuppa	N	**Yonkers**	23	Sazan*	**Ardsley**	24

JAPANESE

(* sushi specialist)

Abis*	**multi. loc.**	17
Z Azuma Sushi*	**Hartsdale**	27
Cherry Blossom*	**Fishkill**	22
Don bo*	**New Windsor**	17
NEW Duo	**Stamford**	–
East Harbor*	**Yonkers**	16
Egane*	**Stamford**	20
Empire Hunan*		16
Yorktown Hts		
NEW Flirt Sushi*	**Irvington**	20
Fuji Mountain	**Larch**	15
Gasho of Japan	**multi. loc.**	17
NEW Haiku*	**multi. loc.**	23
Hajime*	**Harrison**	24
Hanada Sushi*	**P'ville**	20
Hokkaido*	**New Paltz**	24
Hunan Ritz	**Thornwood**	19
Ichi Riki*	**Elmsford**	21

Seasons Jap.*	**White Pl**	21
Sue & Hai*	**Yorktown Hts**	19
Sushi Man*	**Ardsley**	23
Z Sushi Mike's*	**Dobbs Ferry**	25
Sushi Nanase*	**White Pl**	28
Sushi Niji*	**Dobbs Ferry**	23
Takayama*	**Chappaqua**	19
Z Tengda*	**Greenwich**	23
NEW Tokushin*	**Greenwich**	–
Toyo Sushi*	**Mamaro**	22
Tsuru*	**Hartsdale**	23
Wasabi*	**Hudson**	20
Z Wasabi*	**Nyack**	27
Yama Sushi*	**Briarcliff Manor**	24

KOREAN

(* barbecue specialist)

Egane*	**Stamford**	20
Kang Suh*	**Yonkers**	22
Oriental House	**Pine Bush**	–

KOSHER

Bloom's Deli | **Yorktown Hts** — 19

Epstein's Deli | **multi. loc.** — 16

Kisco Kosher | **White Pl** — 18

LEBANESE

Hanna's | **Danbury** — 20

MEDITERRANEAN

Aspen Garden | **Litchfield** — 13

Azzurri | **Thornwood** — 17

Bacio Trattoria | **Cross River** — 19

B4 Bistro | **Valhalla** — 18

Centro | **multi. loc.** — 19

Chiboust | **Tarrytown** — 23

Diasporas | **Rhinebeck** — 20

🆕 F.I.S.H. | **Port Chester** — 23

Gates | **New Canaan** — 18

🆕 Gigi Trattoria | **Rhinebeck** — 23

Globe B&G | **Larch** — 16

🆕 Harvest/Hud. | **Hastings/Hud** — 22

Kraft Bistro | **Bronxville** — 19

NEW Med 15/35 | **Rye Brook** — —

Mediterr. Grill | **Wilton** — 19

Mediterraneo | **Greenwich** — 22

Mediterraneo | **P'ville** — 18

Moscato | **Scarsdale** — 23

Myrna's | **Stamford** — 22

NEW Nessa | **Port Chester** — —

Nestos Estiatorio | **New City** — 23

Oliva | **New Preston** — 23

Oporto | **Hartsdale** — 17

Restaurant | **Germantown** — 26

NEW Savvy | **New Canaan** — 18

🆕 Serevan | **Amenia** — 25

Toscani's | **New Paltz** — 17

Trotters | **White Pl** — 24

Turkish Meze | **Mamaro** — 23

Turquoise | **Larch** — 20

MEXICAN

Blue Moon | **Bronxville** — 17

Cafe Maya/Maya | **multi. loc.** — 23

Casa Maya | **Scarsdale** — 14

Coyote Flaco | **multi. loc.** — 20

El Danzante | **Kingston** — 19

El Tio | **Port Chester** — —

Guadalajara | **Briarcliff Manor** — 20

Gusano Loco | **Mamaro** — 18

Gypsy Wolf | **Woodstock** — 16

La Hacienda | **Stamford** — 13

La Mexicana | **Red Hook** — 17

NEW La Puerta Azul | **Salt Pt** — 16

Little Mex. Cafe | **New Roch** — 23

Mexican Radio | **Hudson** — 19

NEW Mex-to-go | **Croton/Hud** — 17

Ole Mole | **Stamford** — 22

Portobello Café | **Montrose** — 25

Santa Fe | **Tarrytown** — 17

Santa Fe | **Tivoli** — 21

Sunset Grille | **White Pl** — 22

Tenampa | **Croton/Hud** — 14

Tequila Mocking. | **New Canaan** — 16

Tequila Sunrise | **Larch** — 17

Tomatillo | **Dobbs Ferry** — 21

Villa Del Sol | **Mt. Kisco** — 16

MIDDLE EASTERN

Sesame Seed | **Danbury** — 19

MOROCCAN

NEW Zitoune | **Mamaro** — —

NEW ENGLAND

🆕 Ocean Hse. | **Croton/Hud** — 27

NEW MEXICAN

Southwest Cafe | **Ridgefield** — 20

NUEVO LATINO

Mango Café | **Mt. Kisco** — 17

🆕 Pacifico | **Port Chester** — 22

Sabroso | **Rhinebeck** — 26

🆕 Sonora | **Port Chester** — 25

PAN-ASIAN

Asiana Cafe | **Greenwich** — 23

NEW Asian Tempt. | **White Pl** — —

🆕 Baang Cafe | **Riverside** — 24

🆕 Ching's | **multi. loc.** — 25

Golden Rod | **New Roch** — 20

NEW Haiku | **multi. loc.** — 23

Penang Grill | **Greenwich** — 23

NEW Spring Asian | **Mt. Vernon** — —

🆕 Tengda | **multi. loc.** — 23

🆕 Watermoon | **Rye** — 24

Wild Ginger | **Greenwich**	23
Wild Ginger Cafe | **Ridgefield**	23
Yobo | **Newburgh**	19

PAN-LATIN

NEW Coco Rumba | **Mt. Kisco**	17
Karamba | **White Pl**	22
Zen Tango | **New Roch**	21

PERUVIAN

Patrias | **Port Chester**	22

PIZZA

Abatino's | **N White Plains**	20
Abruzzi Trattoria | **Patterson**	20
Amalfi | **Briarcliff Manor**	20
A' Mangiare | **multi. loc.**	-
Angelina's | **Tuck**	19
Aurora | **Rye**	19
Baba Louie's | **Hudson**	23
Bellizzi | **multi. loc.**	14
Bertucci's | **multi. loc.**	15
Brothers Trattoria | **Beacon**	23
California Pizza | **Scarsdale**	16
Chefs On Fire | **High Falls**	22
Ciao! | **Eastchester**	18
Cosimo's Brick | **multi. loc.**	20
Cosimo's Tratt. | **Poughkp**	19
NEW DaVinci's | **New Roch**	-
DiNardo's | **Pound Ridge**	17
Ernesto | **White Pl**	20
Gaudio's | **Yorktown Hts**	17
Horseman Rest. | **Sleepy Hollow**	13
Il Bacio Tratt. | **Bronxville**	23
Il Forno | **Somers**	20
☑ Johnny's | **Mt. Vernon**	25
La Manda's | **White Pl**	18
Maestro's | **multi. loc.**	16
Modern | **New Roch**	23
Nanuet Hotel | **Nanuet**	18
122 Pizza Bistro | **Stamford**	21
Portofino | **Goldens Bridge**	21
Portofino's II | **Wilton**	20
Post Corner Pizza | **Darien**	18
Restaurant | **Germantown**	26
Rigatoni | **Pelham**	-
River Bank | **Cornwall/Hud**	25

Riverview | **Cold Spring**	24
Roma | **Tuck**	17
Sal's Pizza | **Mamaro**	25
Stissing House | **Pine Plains**	19
Taro's | **Millerton**	19
Terra Rist. | **Greenwich**	20
Totonno's | **Yonkers**	18
Via Appia | **White Pl**	19
NEW Woody's | **Mt. Kisco**	-

PORTUGUESE

Aquario | **W Harrison**	23
Caravela | **Tarrytown**	20
Docas | **Ossining**	-
Oporto | **Hartsdale**	17
Quinta Steak | **Pearl River**	18

PUB FOOD

Blazer Pub | **Purdys**	21
Candlelight Inn | **Scarsdale**	21
Finn McCool's | **White Pl**	16
Garth Road Inn | **Scarsdale**	16
Justin Thyme | **Croton/Hud**	16
Landau Grill | **Woodstock**	12
Lazy Boy Saloon | **White Pl**	17
Mackenzie's | **Old Greenwich**	16
Michael's Tavern | **P'ville**	14
Pete's Saloon | **Elmsford**	16
Raccoon Saloon | **Marlboro**	19
Route 22 | **multi. loc.**	15
Southport Brewing | **Stamford**	16
Vinny's Backyard | **Stamford**	17

PUERTO RICAN

El Coqui | **Kingston**	15

SANDWICHES

Apple Pie | **Hyde Pk**	24
Bagels & More | **multi. loc.**	18
Bloom's Deli | **Yorktown Hts**	19
Bread Alone | **multi. loc.**	20
Brooklyn's Famous | **White Pl**	16
Corner Bakery | **Pawling**	25
Così | **multi. loc.**	16
Dragonfly Caffé | **P'ville**	15
Epstein's Deli | **multi. loc.**	16
Harney & Sons | **Millerton**	-
Irving Farm | **Millerton**	18

Kisco Kosher | **White Pl**	18
NEW Mtn. Cow | **Pine Plains**	-
Pantry | **Wash Depot**	23
Reality Bites | **Nyack**	20
Sweet Sue's | **Phoenicia**	24
Temptations Cafe | **Nyack**	21

SCANDINAVIAN

NEW DABA | **Hudson**	19

SEAFOOD

Aquario | **W Harrison**	23
Bennett's Steak | **Stamford**	20
NEW Big B's | **Stamford**	-
Caffe Regatta | **Pelham**	19
Caravela | **Tarrytown**	20
Chart House | **Dobbs Ferry**	16
Conte's Fishmkt. | **Mt. Kisco**	22
Cornetta's Seafood | **Piermont**	13
Down by the Bay | **Mamaro**	16
Downtown Cafe | **Kingston**	21
Z Eastchester Fish | **Scarsdale**	24
Ebb Tide | **Port Chester**	20
Z Elm St. Oyster | **Greenwich**	24
Z F.I.S.H. | **Port Chester**	23
Fish Cellar | **Mt. Kisco**	21
Gadaleto's | **New Paltz**	19
NEW Goldfish | **Ossining**	22
Gus's Franklin Park | **Harrison**	21
Harry's | **Hartsdale**	19
Hudson's Ribs | **Fishkill**	18
La Salière | **Ridgefield**	21
La Villetta | **Larch**	24
Z Legal Sea Foods | **multi. loc.**	19
Z Ocean Hse. | **Croton/Hud**	27
Ocean 211 | **Stamford**	24
Z Pacifico | **Port Chester**	22
Ricky's Seafood | **Yonkers**	15
River Club | **Nyack**	16
Ruby's Oyster Bar | **Rye**	21
Z Sapore | **Fishkill**	26
Seaside Johnnie's | **Rye**	11
Ship to Shore | **Kingston**	23
Striped Bass | **Tarrytown**	16
Town Dock | **Rye**	18
Z Valbella | **Scarsdale**	25

SMALL PLATES

(See also Spanish tapas specialist)

NEW Dragonfly Lounge | Eclectic | **Stamford**	18
Maggie's in the Alley | New American | **Chester**	-
Reality Bites | American | **Nyack**	20
Solaia | Italian | **Greenwich**	20
Temptation Tea | Asian | **Mt. Kisco**	21
Z Thomas Moran's | Amer. | **New Preston**	25

SOUP

Crew | **Poughkp**	20
Irving Farm | **Millerton**	18
Martindale Chief | **Craryville**	10
Pantry | **Wash Depot**	23
Soul Dog | **Poughkp**	21

SOUTHERN

Cookhouse | **multi. loc.**	19
NEW Lejends | **Yonkers**	-
NEW Memphis Mae's | **Croton/Hud**	17
Yvonne's | **Pelham**	22

SOUTHWESTERN

Boxcar Cantina | **Greenwich**	19
Salsa | **New Milford**	19
Santa Fe | **Tarrytown**	17
Telluride | **Stamford**	24
Two Steps | **Danbury**	15

SPANISH

(* tapas specialist)

Barcelona* | **Greenwich**	22
La Camelia* | **Mt. Kisco**	21
Meson Espanoles* | **White Pl**	20
Patrias | **Port Chester**	22
River Cafe* | **New Milford**	17
Sabroso | **Rhinebeck**	26
Ten Railroad | **Warwick**	16

STEAKHOUSES

Alpine Inn | **Patterson**	-
Bennett's Steak | **Stamford**	20
NEW Big B's | **Stamford**	-
Chart House | **Dobbs Ferry**	16
Chuck's Steak | **multi. loc.**	17
NEW Croton Creek | **Crot Falls**	-

Edo Japanese | **multi. loc.**	21
Flames Steak | **Briarcliff Manor**	20
Frankie & Johnnie's | **Rye**	22
Giovanni's | **Darien**	19
Harry's | **Hartsdale**	19
Hudson's Ribs | **Fishkill**	18
Mighty Joe | **White Pl**	20
🄰 Morton's Steak | **multi. loc.**	24
🄽🄴🅆 Mo's NY | **New Roch**	21
Mount Fuji | **Hillburn**	21
Okinawa | **Mt. Kisco**	15
O'Sho Japanese | **Poughkp**	19
Pantanal | **Port Chester**	22
Quinta Steak | **Pearl River**	18
🄰 Ruth's Chris | **Tarrytown**	23
Samba | **Mt. Vernon**	18
🄰 Sapore | **Fishkill**	26
Steakhouse 22 | **Patterson**	17
Tollgate Steak | **Mamaro**	24
🄰 Valbella | **Scarsdale**	25
Victor's | **Monroe**	21
Willett House | **Port Chester**	23

SWISS

Brasserie Swiss | **Ossining**	19
Canterbury | **Cornwall/Hud**	23
Swiss Hütte | **Hillsdale**	20

TEAROOMS

Harney & Sons | **Millerton**	-
Village Tea. | **New Paltz**	21

TEX-MEX

Armadillo B&G | **Kingston**	22
Casa Miguel | **Mt. Kisco**	14
Mary Ann's | **Port Chester**	15

THAI

Bangkok Thai | **Mamaro**	21
Don bo | **New Windsor**	17
King & I | **Nyack**	19
Kit's Thai | **Stamford**	23
🄽🄴🅆 Little Thai | **multi. loc.**	22
Red Lotus | **New Roch**	21
Reka's | **White Pl**	16
Siam Orchid | **Scarsdale**	20
Sukhothai | **Beacon**	24
Swaddee Hse. | **Thornwood**	20
Thai Garden | **Sleepy Hollow**	24
Thai House | **multi. loc.**	22
Thai Pearl | **Ridgefield**	20

TURKISH

Turkish Meze | **Mamaro**	23
Turquoise | **Larch**	20

VEGETARIAN
(* vegan)

Aroma Thyme* | **Ellenville**	20
Dakshin | **Stamford**	23
Earth Foods* | **Hudson**	-
Foundry Cafe | **Cold Spring**	18
K. Fung's | **Hartsdale**	20
Luna 61* | **Tivoli**	20
Northern Spy Cafe | **High Falls**	16
🄰 P.F. Chang's* | **White Pl**	20
Rosendale Cafe* | **Rosendale**	18
Soul Dog | **Poughkp**	21
Thai Garden | **Sleepy Hollow**	24
Wobble Café | **Ossining**	21

VIETNAMESE

Miss Saigon | **Poughkp**	18
Saigon Café | **Poughkp**	18

Locations

Includes restaurant names, cuisines and Food ratings. ☑ indicates places with the highest ratings, popularity and importance.

Westchester County

ARDSLEY

Sazan | *Jap.* 24
Sushi Man | *Jap.* 23
Thai House | *Thai* 22

ARMONK

Beehive | *Amer./Eclectic* 17
David Chen | *Chinese* 19
Gavi | *Italian* 18
India Cafe | *Indian* 20
Kira Steak | *Jap.* 17
Kira Sushi | *Jap.* 23
La Scala | *Italian* 20
NEW Made In Asia | *Asian* ‒
Opus 465 | *Amer.* 18
Route 22 | *Pub* 15

BEDFORD

Bistro 22 | *Amer./French* 23
☑ La Crémaillère | *French* 27
NEW Trattoria Lucia | *Italian* 14

BEDFORD HILLS

Kicho | *Jap.* 19

BEDFORD VILLAGE

Meetinghouse | *Amer.* 17

BRIARCLIFF MANOR

Amalfi | *Italian* 20
Briar's | *Amer.* 15
Flames Steak | *Steak* 20
Guadalajara | *Mex.* 20
Squires | *Amer.* 18
Terra Rustica | *Italian* 20
Torchia's | *Italian* 16
Yama Sushi | *Jap.* 24

BRONXVILLE

A' Mangiare | *Italian* ‒
Babbone | *Italian* 22
Blue Moon | *Mex.* 17
NEW Haiku | *Pan-Asian* 23
Il Bacio Tratt. | *Italian* 23

Japan Inn | *Jap.* 22
Kraft Bistro | *Amer./Med.* 19
☑ Rosie's Bistro | *Italian* 23
Underhills Crossing | *Amer.* 21
NEW Village Café | *Amer.* 15

BUCHANAN

Four Doors Down | *Amer.* ‒

CHAPPAQUA

☑ Crabtree's | *Amer.* 24
Grappolo Locanda | *Italian* 19
Le Jardin du Roi | *French* 20
Takayama | *Jap.* 19

CORTLANDT

Little Sorrento | *Italian* 18
☑ Monteverde | *Continental* 21

CORTLANDT MANOR

Julianna's | *Amer.* ‒

CROSS RIVER

Bacio Trattoria | *Italian/Med.* 19
NEW Haiku | *Pan-Asian* 23

CROTON FALLS

NEW Croton Creek | *Steak* ‒
Primavera | *Italian* 23
Stoneleigh Creek | *Eclectic* 23

CROTON-ON-HUDSON

Fortuna | *Italian* 22
Justin Thyme | *Pub Food* 16
NEW Memphis Mae's | *BBQ* 17
NEW Mex-to-go | *Mex.* 17
☑ Ocean Hse. | 27
    New Eng./Seafood
Tenampa | *Mex.* 14
Ümami Café | *Eclectic* 21

DOBBS FERRY

Chart House | *Seafood/Steak* 16
Doubleday's | *Amer.* 13
Off Broadway | *Continental* 19
Piccola Tratt. | *Italian* 19
Sam's | *Italian* 18

Scaramella's | *Italian* | 21
☑ Sushi Mike's | *Jap.* | 25
Sushi Niji | *Jap.* | 23
Tomatillo | *Mex.* | 21

EASTCHESTER

Ciao! | *Italian* | 18
Gina Marie's | *Italian* | 19
Jackie's Bistro | *French* | 20
Lotus King | *Chinese* | 18
NEW Mickey Spill. | *Amer.* | -
Pinocchio | *Italian* | 23
Piper's Kilt | *Amer.* | 20

ELMSFORD

A' Mangiare | *Italian* | -
Andrew's | *Amer.* | 18
Ichi Riki | *Jap.* | 21
Malabar Hill | *Indian* | 23
Pete's Saloon | *Pub Food* | 16
Tony La Stazione | *Italian* | 16

GOLDENS BRIDGE

Portofino | *Italian* | 21

GRANITE SPRINGS

Granite Springs | *Amer.* | 20

HARRISON

NEW A'Tavola | *French/Italian* | -
☑ Emilio Rist. | *Italian* | 25
Gus's Franklin Park | *Seafood* | 21
Hajime | *Jap.* | 24
Halstead Ave. Bistro | *Amer.* | 22
Momiji | *Jap.* | 19
Tratt. Vivolo | *Italian* | 22
Trinity Grill | *Amer.* | 16

HARTSDALE

☑ Azuma Sushi | *Jap.* | 27
Bagels & More | *Deli* | 18
Epstein's Deli | *Deli* | 16
Global Gatherings | *Eclectic* | 20
Harry's | *Seafood/Steak* | 19
Kazu Japanese | *Jap.* | 21
K. Fung's | *Chinese* | 20
Lia's | *Italian* | 21
Oporto | *Portug.* | 17
Pastina's | *Italian* | 18
Tsuru | *Jap.* | 23

HASTINGS-ON-HUDSON

NEW Bloom | *Amer.* | 21
Blu | *Amer.* | 18
☑ Buffet/Gare | *French* | 26
Comfort | *Amer.* | 20
☑ Harvest/Hud. | *Med.* | 22
Maud's Tavern | *Amer.* | 13

HAWTHORNE

Bel Paese | *Italian* | 17
Gasho of Japan | *Jap.* | 17
Tramonto | *Italian* | 19

IRVINGTON

NEW Flirt Sushi | *Jap.* | 20
Il Sorriso | *Italian* | 20
NEW One | *Amer.* | 27
Red Hat | *French* | 22
River City Grille | *Amer./Eclectic* | 20

JEFFERSON VALLEY

Golden House | *Chinese* | 20
Maestro's | *Italian* | 16

KATONAH

Blue Dolphin | *Italian* | 22
Deer Park Tavern | *Amer.* | 19
Le Fontane | *Italian* | 21
Peppino's | *Italian* | 16
☑ Tengda | *Pan-Asian* | 23
Willy Nick's | *Amer.* | 18

LARCHMONT

NEW Anna Maria's | *Italian* | 20
Bellizzi | *Italian* | 14
Chat 19 | *Amer.* | 17
Così | *Sandwiches* | 16
Encore Bistro | *French* | 21
Fuji Mountain | *Jap.* | 15
Globe B&G | *Amer./Med.* | 16
Hunan Larchmont | *Chinese* | 17
Lanterna Tuscan | *Italian* | 21
Larchmont Tavern | *Amer.* | 15
La Riserva | *Italian* | 21
La Villetta | *Italian/Seafood* | 24
☑ Lusardi's | *Italian* | 23
Palmer's Crossing | *Amer.* | 17
Pascal's | *French* | 22
Plates | *Amer.* | 24

Ray's Cafe	*Chinese*	19
NEW Sardegna	*Italian*	-
Tequila Sunrise	*Mex.*	17
Turquoise	*Med./Turkish*	20
Watercolor Cafe	*Amer.*	19

MAMARONECK

Abis	*Jap.*	17
Bangkok Thai	*Thai*	21
Cafe Mozart	*Coffee*	15
Chef Antonio	*Italian*	14
Down by the Bay	*Eclectic*	16
Enzo's	*Italian*	18
Gusano Loco	*Mex.*	18
NEW Il Teatro	*Italian*	21
La Piccola Casa	*Italian*	21
Le Provençal	*French*	23
Osteria Marietta	*Italian*	19
NEW Rani Mahal	*Indian*	-
Sal's Pizza	*Pizza*	25
Tollgate Steak	*Steak*	24
Toyo Sushi	*Jap.*	22
Tung Hoy	*Chinese*	15
Turkish Meze	*Med./Turkish*	23
Walter's	*Hot Dogs*	21
NEW Zitoune	*Moroccan*	-

MILLWOOD

Spaccarelli's	*Italian*	22

MOHEGAN LAKE

Bella Vita	*Italian*	20

MONTROSE

India House	*Indian*	23
Portobello Café	*Italian*	25

MT. KISCO

Bellizzi	*Italian*	14
Casa Miguel	*BBQ/Tex-Mex*	14
NEW Coco Rumba	*Cuban/Pan-Latin*	17
Conte's Fishmkt.	*Seafood*	22
Così	*Sandwiches*	16
Fish Cellar	*Seafood*	21
Flying Pig	*Amer.*	21
La Camelia	*Spanish*	21
☑ Lefteris Gyro	*Greek*	21
Lexington Sq. Café	*Amer.*	18

Mango Café	*Nuevo Latino*	17
Mount Fuji Sushi	*Jap.*	19
Okinawa	*Jap.*	15
Pacific	*Chinese*	16
Passage to India	*Indian*	19
Piero's	*Italian*	21
Temptation Tea	*Asian*	21
Tuscan Oven	*Italian*	19
Villa Del Sol	*Mex.*	16
NEW Woody's	*Amer.*	-

MT. VERNON

Bayou	*Cajun/Creole*	21
☑ Johnny's	*Pizza*	25
Samba	*Brazilian/Steak*	18
NEW Spring Asian	*Pan-Asian*	-

NEW ROCHELLE

Bastones Italian	*Italian*	18
☑ Coromandel	*Indian*	26
Così	*Sandwiches*	16
Coyote Flaco	*Mex.*	20
NEW DaVinci's	*Italian*	-
Fratelli	*Italian*	21
Fuffi 2000	*Italian*	17
Golden Rod	*Pan-Asian*	20
Karuta	*Jap.*	19
La Trattoria	*Italian*	23
Little Mex. Cafe	*Mex.*	23
MacMenamin's	*Amer.*	22
Maestro's	*Italian*	16
Mamma Francesca	*Italian*	19
Modern	*Italian*	23
NEW Mo's NY	*Steak*	21
Rangoli	*Indian*	21
Red Lotus	*Thai*	21
Sterling Inn	*Amer./French*	20
Zen Tango	*Asian Fusion/Pan-Latin*	21

NORTH SALEM

121 Rest./Bar	*Amer.*	21
Purdys Homestead	*Amer.*	23
Vox	*Amer./French*	21

OSSINING

Brasserie Swiss	*Swiss*	19
Docas	*Portug.*	-

NEW Goldfish	*Seafood*	22
Travelers	*Continental*	18
Wobble Café	*Eclectic*	21

PEEKSKILL

Division St. Grill	*Amer./Eclectic*	19
Susan's	*Amer.*	18
Z Zephs'	*Amer./Eclectic*	26

PELHAM

Caffe Regatta	*Seafood*	19
NEW Chelsea's	*Amer./Irish*	-
Edo Japanese	*Jap./Steak*	21
La Fontanella	*Italian*	25
Rigatoni	*Italian*	-
Rockwells	*Amer.*	12
Villa Nova E.	*Amer./Italian*	19
Yvonne's	*Southern*	22

PLEASANTVILLE

A' Mangiare	*Italian*	-
NEW Bollywood	*Indian*	24
Dragonfly Caffé	*Coffee*	15
Frodo's	*Amer.*	23
Hanada Sushi	*Jap.*	20
Z Iron Horse Grill	*Amer.*	27
Jackson & Wheeler	*Amer.*	17
McArthur's	*Amer.*	-
Mediterraneo	*Italian/Med.*	18
Michael's Tavern	*Pub Food*	14
NEW Pony Express	*Amer.*	-
Strega	*Italian*	-

POCANTICO HILLS

Z Blue Hill/Stone	*Amer.*	27

PORT CHESTER

Alba's	*Italian*	23
Cafe Mirage	*Eclectic*	20
Coyote Flaco	*Mex.*	20
Ebb Tide	*Seafood*	20
Edo Japanese	*Jap./Steak*	21
El Tio	*Mex.*	-
NEW Euro Asian	*Asian Fusion*	-
Z F.I.S.H.	*Med./Seafood*	23
Giorgio's	*Italian*	23
Hostaria Mazzei	*Italian*	21
Marianacci's	*Italian*	21
Mary Ann's	*Tex-Mex*	15

NEW Nessa	*Med.*	-
Z Pacifico		22
Nuevo Latino/Seafood		
Pantanal	*Brazilian*	22
Pasquale Rist.	*Italian*	19
Patrias	*Peruvian*	22
Piero's	*Italian*	21
Q Rest.	*BBQ*	23
Z Sonora	*Nuevo Latino*	25
T&J Villaggio	*Italian*	21
Tandoori Taste	*Indian*	23
Willett House	*Steak*	23

POUND RIDGE

DiNardo's	*Italian*	17
North Star	*Amer.*	22

PURCHASE

Cobble Stone	*Amer.*	16
Creek	*Amer.*	15

PURDYS

Blazer Pub	*Pub Food*	21

RYE

Aurora	*Italian*	19
Cafe Livorno	*Italian*	19
Così	*Sandwiches*	16
Frankie & Johnnie's	*Steak*	22
High St. Road.	*Cajun/Creole*	18
Z Koo	*Jap.*	24
Z La Panetière	*French*	27
Ruby's Oyster Bar	*Seafood*	21
Seaside Johnnie's	*Seafood*	11
Town Dock	*Amer.*	18
Z Watermoon	*Pan-Asian*	24

RYE BROOK

NEW Med 15/35	*Med.*	-
Ray's Cafe	*Chinese*	19
Tulip Tree	*Continental*	-

SCARSDALE

NEW Backals	*Amer.*	16
California Pizza	*Pizza*	16
Candlelight Inn	*Pub*	21
Casa Maya	*Mex.*	14
Z Eastchester Fish	*Seafood*	24
Garth Road Inn	*Pub Food*	16
Kirari	*Jap.*	20

Lange's Deli | *Deli*	18
Meritage | *Amer.*	22
Millennio | *Italian*	21
Moscato | *Italian/Med.*	23
Pagoda | *Chinese*	22
Rustico | *Italian*	20
Sakura | *Jap.*	18
Seven Woks | *Chinese*	15
Siam Orchid | *Thai*	20
Spiga | *Italian*	17
☑ Valbella | *Italian*	25

SLEEPY HOLLOW

Horseman Rest. | *Amer./Pizza*	13
Thai Garden | *Thai*	24

SOMERS

Il Forno | *Italian*	20
Imperial Wok | *Chinese/Jap.*	18
Luce Rest. | *Italian*	22
Seasons American | *Amer.*	20
Traditions 118 | *Amer./Italian*	19

SOUTH SALEM

Horse & Hound | *Amer.*	16
☑ Le Château | *French*	25
L'Europe | *Continental*	24
Nino's | *Italian*	18

TARRYTOWN

Café Tandoor | *Indian*	21
Caravela | *Brazilian/Portug.*	20
Chiboust | *French/Med.*	23
☑ Equus | *Amer./French*	26
Horsefeathers | *Amer.*	17
Jack & Dyls | *Amer.*	18
Lago di Como | *Italian*	21
☑ Lefteris Gyro | *Greek*	21
Main St. Cafe | *Amer.*	16
☑ Ruth's Chris | *Steak*	23
Santa Fe | *Mex./SW*	17
Striped Bass | *Seafood*	16
Sunset Cove | *Continental*	15

THORNWOOD

Abis | *Jap.*	17
Ace Asian-French | *Asian Fusion*	24
Azzurri | *Med.*	17
Casa Rina | *Italian*	17

Hunan Ritz | *Chinese/Jap.*	19
Swaddee Hse. | *Thai*	20

TUCKAHOE

☑ An American Bistro | *Amer.*	22
Angelina's | *Amer./Italian*	19
Mamma Assunta | *Italian*	19
Olde Stone Mill | *Amer.*	15
Roma | *Pizza*	17

VALHALLA

B4 Bistro | *Amer./Med.*	18
Mughal Palace | *Indian*	23
Southbound BBQ | *BBQ*	17

WEST HARRISON

Aquario | *Portug./Seafood*	23

WHITE PLAINS/N. WHITE PLAINS

Abatino's | *Italian*	20
Aberdeen | *Chinese*	24
A' Mangiare | *Italian*	-
NEW Asian Tempt. | *Pan-Asian*	-
☑ Bengal Tiger | *Indian*	23
Blue | *Amer.*	19
Brooklyn's Famous | *Diner*	16
Buon Amici | *Italian*	20
☑ Cheesecake Fac. | *Amer.*	18
☑ City Limits Diner | *Diner*	19
Ernesto | *Italian*	20
Finn McCool's | *Pub Food*	16
Graziellas | *Italian*	19
Imperial Wok | *Chinese/Jap.*	18
Karamba | *Cuban/Pan-Latin*	22
Kisco Kosher | *Deli*	18
Laguna | *Italian*	20
La Manda's | *Italian*	18
Latin Am. Cafe | *Cuban*	20
Lazy Boy Saloon | *Pub Food*	17
☑ Legal Sea Foods | *Seafood*	19
Meson Espanoles | *Spanish*	20
Mighty Joe | *Steak*	20
☑ Morton's Steak | *Steak*	24
☑ Mulino's | *Italian*	24
Niko's Greek | *Greek*	20
Noda's Steak | *Jap.*	18
☑ P.F. Chang's | *Chinese*	20
Reka's | *Thai*	16

Royal Palace	*Indian*	18
Sam's/Gedney	*Amer.*	18
Seasons Jap.	*Jap.*	21
Sunset Grille	*Mex.*	22
Sushi Nanase	*Jap.*	28
🆕 Tango Grill	*Argent./Italian*	23
Tre Angelina	*Italian*	22
Trotters	*Med.*	24
Via Appia	*Italian*	19
Vintage	*Amer./Eclectic*	16
Zanaro's	*Italian*	14

YONKERS

🆕 Belle Havana	*Cuban/French*	-
🆕 Bukhara Grill	*Indian*	25
East Harbor	*Chinese/Jap.*	16
Epstein's Deli	*Deli*	16
Gianna's	*Amer./Italian*	21
Hunan Village	*Chinese*	23
J.J. Mannion's	*Amer.*	15
Kang Suh	*Korean*	22
La Lanterna	*Italian*	19
🆕 Lejends	*Carib./Southern*	-
Louie & Johnnies'	*Italian*	22
Patang Indian	*Indian*	20
Ricky's Seafood	*Seafood*	15
Spiritoso	*Italian*	22
Tombolino's	*Italian*	21
Totonno's	*Pizza*	18
Valentino's	*Italian*	23
Zafrán	*Euro./Indian*	21
Zuppa	*Italian*	23

YORKTOWN

Grandma's	*Amer.*	16
Peter Pratt's Inn	*Amer.*	23
🆕 Viansa	*Italian*	-

YORKTOWN HEIGHTS

Bagels & More	*Deli*	18
Bloom's Deli	*Deli*	19
Empire Hunan	*Chinese/Jap.*	16
Gaudio's	*Italian*	17
Heights Bistro	*Amer.*	24
Jennifer's	*German*	19
Miraggio	*Italian*	19
Sue & Hai	*Chinese/Jap.*	19

Hudson Valley

ACCORD
Friends & Family	*Continental*	21

AIRMONT
Citrus Grille	*Amer.*	24

AMENIA
Cascade Mtn. Winery	*Amer.*	22
🆕 De La Vergne	*Amer.*	21
🆕 Serevan	*Med.*	25
Troutbeck	*Amer.*	18

BEACON
Brothers Trattoria	*Italian*	23
Cafe Maya/Maya	*Mex.*	23
Piggy Bank	*BBQ*	18
Sukhothai	*Thai*	24
🆕 Tonique	*Amer.*	-

BIG INDIAN
Peekamoose	*Amer.*	25

BOICEVILLE
Bread Alone	*Bakery/Coffee*	20

BREWSTER
Arch	*Eclectic*	25
Capriccio	*French/Italian*	21
Jaipore Indian	*Indian*	24
Red Rooster	*Hamburgers*	19
🆕 Sonoma	*Calif.*	-

CAMPBELL HALL
Bull's Head Inn	*Amer.*	19

CARMEL
Cutillo's	*Euro.*	-

CENTRAL VALLEY
Gasho of Japan	*Jap.*	17

CHATHAM
Blue Plate	*Amer.*	18
Lipperas'	*Continental*	19

CHESTER
Maggie's in the Alley	*Amer.*	-

COLD SPRING
Cathryn's	*Italian*	22
Foundry Cafe	*Amer.*	18
Hudson Hse. Inn	*Amer.*	21
Le Bouchon	*French*	22

Plumbush Inn	*Amer.*	22
Riverview	*Amer.*	24

CONGERS

Grande Centrale	*Continental/Italian*	19
🇿 Rest. X/Bully	*Amer.*	27
Romolo's	*Italian*	19

CORNWALL-ON-HUDSON

Canterbury	*Continental/Swiss*	23
Painter's	*Eclectic*	19
River Bank	*Amer.*	25

CRARYVILLE

Martindale Chief	*Diner*	10

DOVER PLAINS

Old Drovers Inn	*Amer.*	23

EARLTON

Basement Bistro	*Amer.*	29

ELLENVILLE

Aroma Thyme	*Amer.*	20

FISHKILL

Cafe Maya/Maya	*Mex.*	23
Cherry Blossom	*Jap.*	22
NEW Copper Rest.	*Amer.*	-
Hudson's Ribs	*Seafood/Steak*	18
🇿 Il Barilotto	*Italian*	26
NEW Jackalope BBQ	*BBQ*	-
NEW Locanda	*Italian*	-
🇿 Sapore	*Seafood/Steak*	26
Tanjore	*Indian*	25
Via Nove	*Italian*	19

FLORIDA

Copper Bottom	*Amer.*	19

FREEHOLD

Ruby's Hotel	*Eclectic/French*	-

GARRISON

Bird and Bottle	*Amer.*	21
Tavern at Highlands	*Amer.*	23
🇿 Valley/Garrison	*Amer.*	26

GERMANTOWN

Restaurant	*Med.*	26

GOSHEN

Catherine's	*Amer.*	22
Il Tesoro	*Italian*	26

HIGH FALLS

Chefs On Fire	*Amer.*	22
🇿 DePuy Canal	*Amer.*	25
Egg's Nest	*Amer.*	18
Northern Spy Cafe	*Amer.*	16

HIGHLAND

Would	*Amer.*	23

HILLBURN

Mount Fuji	*Jap./Steak*	21

HILLSDALE

Hillsdale Hse.	*Amer.*	13
Swiss Hütte	*Continental/Swiss*	20

HOPEWELL JUNCTION

Blue Fountain	*Italian*	20
Le Chambord	*French*	22

HUDSON

Baba Louie's	*Pizza*	23
Ca'Mea	*Italian*	21
NEW DABA	*Amer./Scan.*	19
Earth Foods	*Eclectic/Veg.*	-
Mexican Radio	*Mex.*	19
Red Dot	*Eclectic*	16
Swoon Kitchenbar	*Amer.*	24
NEW Vico	*Italian*	-
Wasabi	*Jap.*	20
Wunderbar	*Amer.*	15

HYDE PARK

🇿 American Bounty	*Amer.*	26
Apple Pie	*Bakery/Sandwiches*	24
🇿 Caterina de Medici	*Italian*	26
🇿 Escoffier	*French*	26
Eveready Diner	*Diner*	17
St. Andrew's Cafe	*Amer.*	24
Twist	*Amer.*	25

KERHONKSON

Oscar	*Amer.*	-

KINGSTON

Armadillo B&G	*Tex-Mex*	22
Bread Alone	*Bakery/Coffee*	20
China Rose	*Chinese*	21

Cosimo's Brick	*Italian*	20
Downtown Cafe	*Italian*	21
El Coqui	*Puerto Rican*	15
El Danzante	*Mex.*	19
Hickory BBQ	*BBQ*	18
Hoffman Hse.	*Continental*	19
Kyoto Sushi	*Jap.*	24
Le Canard Enchainé	*French*	24
Ship to Shore	*Amer./Seafood*	23
Ugly Gus Cafe	*Amer.*	18

KRUMVILLE
Country Inn	*Amer.*	–

LAGRANGEVILLE
Daily Planet	*Diner*	18

LAKE MAHOPAC
Marco	*Amer.*	22

MAHOPAC
Holy Smoke	*BBQ*	18

MARLBORO
Raccoon Saloon	*Pub*	19

MIDDLETOWN
Cosimo's Brick	*Italian*	20
John's Harvest	*Continental*	19
Nina	*Eclectic*	24

MILAN
Milan Roadhouse	*Diner*	–

MILLBROOK
🅉 Café Les Baux	*French*	25
NEW Charlotte's	*Euro.*	–
Picolo	*Italian*	20

MILLERTON
Hamilton Inn	*Eclectic*	19
Harney & Sons	*Tea*	–
Irving Farm	*Sandwiches/Soup*	18
Manna Dew Cafe	*Eclectic*	22
Martha's	*Amer.*	–
Taro's	*Italian/Pizza*	19

MILTON
Ship Lantern	*Amer./Continental*	25

MONROE
Velvet Monkey	*Amer.*	20
Victor's	*Steak*	21

MONTGOMERY
NEW Backyard	*Amer.*	–
Ward's Bridge	*Amer.*	19
Wildfire Grill	*Eclectic*	23

MT. TREMPER
Catskill Rose	*Amer.*	–
La Duchesse	*French*	–
NEW Phoenix	*Amer.*	–

NANUET
Nanuet Hotel	*Italian*	18

NEWBURGH
Beebs	*Amer.*	22
Big Easy Bistro	*Cajun*	17
Cena 2000	*Italian*	24
Cosimo's Brick	*Italian*	20
🅉 Il Cenàcolo	*Italian*	27
Pamela's Traveling	*Continental*	18
River Grill	*Amer.*	21
Torches on Hudson	*Amer.*	15
Yobo	*Pan-Asian*	19

NEW CITY
Nestos Estiatorio	*Med.*	23
Pasta Cucina	*Italian*	20

NEW LEBANON
Pillars	*Continental/French*	–

NEW PALTZ
Beso	*Eclectic*	25
Gadaleto's	*Seafood*	19
Harvest Café	*Amer.*	24
Hokkaido	*Jap.*	24
La Stazione	*Italian*	19
Locust Tree	*Euro.*	21
Main Course	*Amer.*	23
Mohonk Mtn. Hse.	*Amer.*	17
Neko Sushi	*Jap.*	20
Toscani's	*Italian/Med.*	17
Village Tea.	*Tea*	21

NEW WINDSOR
Don bo	*Jap./Thai*	17

NYACK
Heather's Cucina	*Italian*	21
Hudson Hse. Nyack	*Amer.*	20
King & I	*Thai*	19

Lanterna Tuscan | *Italian* 21
Lena's | *Euro.* 21
Lu Shane's | *Amer.* 23
Reality Bites | *Amer.* 20
River Club | *Amer.* 16
Temptations Cafe | *Eclectic* 21
Thai House | *Thai* 22
🔲 Vertigo | *Amer.* 18
🔲 Wasabi | *Jap.* 27

PATTERSON

Abruzzi Trattoria | *Italian* 20
Alpine Inn | *Continental/Steak* -
Steakhouse 22 | *Amer./Steak* 17

PAWLING

Corner Bakery | *Bakery* 25
McKinney & Doyle | *Amer.* 23
Towne Crier Cafe | *Amer.* 17

PEARL RIVER

Quinta Steak | *Portug./Steak* 18

PHILMONT

NEW Local 111 | *Amer.* -

PHOENICIA

Sweet Sue's | *Amer.* 24

PIERMONT

Cafe Portofino | *Italian* 20
Cornetta's Seafood | *Seafood* 13
🔲 Freelance Café | *Amer.* 28
Lighthouse/Hudson | *Amer.* 16
Pasta Amore | *Italian* 16
Turning Point | *Amer.* 14
🔲 Xaviar's | *Amer.* 29

PINE BUSH

Oriental House | *Jap./Korean* -

PINE PLAINS

Lia's Mtn. View | *Italian* 16
NEW Mtn. Cow | *Diner* -
Stissing House | *French/Italian* 19

POUGHKEEPSIE

NEW Artist's Palate | *Amer.* 24
Beech Tree Grill | *Amer.* 20
🔲 Busy Bee | *Amer.* 26
Coppola's | *Italian* 18
Cosimo's Tratt. | *Italian* 19

Crew | *Amer.* 20
Gentleman Jim's | *Amer.* 17
Haymaker | *Amer.* 23
🔲 Le Pavillon | *French* 27
Main Course/Alum. | *Amer.* 20
Mill House Panda | *Chinese* 17
Miss Saigon | *Viet.* 18
96 Main | *Eclectic* 21
O'Sho Japanese | *Jap.* 19
Saigon Café | *Viet.* 18
NEW Shadows | *Amer.* -
Soul Dog | *Hot Dogs* 21

RED HOOK

La Mexicana | *Mex.* 17
Max's Memphis | *BBQ* 20
NEW Mercato | *Italian* -
Roasted Garlic | *Amer.* 14

RHINEBECK

Agra Tandoor | *Indian* 17
Bread Alone | *Bakery/Coffee* 20
Calico | *Amer./Eclectic* 25
Diasporas | *Greek/Med.* 20
🔲 Gigi Trattoria | *Italian/Med.* 23
🔲 Le Petit Bistro | *French* 26
Mill House Panda | *Chinese* 17
Osaka | *Jap.* 23
Sabroso | *Nuevo Latino/Spanish* 26
🔲 Terrapin | *Amer.* 24
Traphagen | *Amer.* 22

RHINECLIFF

China Rose | *Chinese* 21

ROSENDALE

NEW Bywater | *Amer.* 18
Rosendale Cafe | *Veg.* 18

SALT POINT

NEW La Puerta Azul | *Mex.* 16

SAUGERTIES

Cafe Tamayo | *Amer.* 24
Café with Love | *Euro.* 19
Miss Lucy's | *Amer.* 22
New World | *Amer./Eclectic* 23
Red Onion | *Amer.* 22

SPARKILL

Relish | *Amer./Eclectic* 25

STAATSBURG

Belvedere | *Amer.*	17
Portofino Rist. | *Italian*	22

STONE RIDGE

French Corner | *French*	25

STONY POINT

Pasta Cucina | *Italian*	20

SUFFERN

Marcello's | *Italian*	24
Pasta Cucina | *Italian*	20
Priya | *Indian*	20

SUGAR LOAF

Amarone's | *Italian*	21

TANNERSVILLE

Last Chance | *Amer.*	21
Maggie's Krooked | *Amer.*	-

TAPPAN

Giulio's of Tappan | *Italian*	18
Il Portico | *Italian*	22
Old '76 House | *Amer.*	15
Village Grille | *Amer.*	21

TIVOLI

Luna 61 | *Veg.*	20
NEW Madalin's Table | *Amer.*	19
Osaka | *Jap.*	23
Santa Fe | *Mex.*	21

VALLEY COTTAGE

Michele | *Italian*	21

WAPPINGERS FALLS

Z Aroma Osteria | *Italian*	27
Greenbaum | *Amer.*	16
Il Continori | *Italian*	-
Mojo Grill | *Amer.*	23
Neko Sushi | *Jap.*	20

WARWICK

Chateau Hathorn | *Continental*	22
Iron Forge Inn | *Amer.*	21
Jean Claude's | *Dessert*	26
Landmark Inn | *Amer.*	17
Ten Railroad | *Italian/Spanish*	16

WEST GHENT

Red Barn | *Amer.*	19

WEST NYACK

Z Legal Sea Foods | *Seafood*	19

WESTTOWN

Gigi's Folderol II | *Eclectic*	24

WINGDALE

NEW Big W's | *BBQ*	-

WOODSTOCK
(Including Bearsville)

Z Bear Cafe | *Amer.*	23
Bread Alone | *Bakery/Coffee*	20
NEW Dragonfly Grille | *Eclectic*	-
Emerson | *Amer.*	18
Gypsy Wolf | *Mex.*	16
Landau Grill | *Pub Food*	12
Marion's Country | *Euro.*	22
Mountain Gate | *Indian*	15
NEW Oriole 9 | *Euro.*	19
Violette | *Amer.*	22

Connecticut

BROOKFIELD

Bailey's Backyard | *Amer.*	20
Harvest/Brookfield | *Amer.*	21

DANBURY

Bertucci's | *Italian*	15
Cafe on the Green | *Italian*	23
Chuck's Steak | *Steak*	17
Ciao! Cafe | *Italian*	21
Hanna's | *Lebanese*	20
Z Ondine | *French*	26
Sesame Seed | *Mideast.*	19
Tuscano | *Italian*	18
Two Steps | *SW*	15

DARIEN

Aux Délices | *Amer./French*	22
Bertucci's | *Italian*	15
Black Goose | *Amer.*	17
Centro | *Italian/Med.*	19
Z Ching's | *Pan-Asian*	25
Chuck's Steak | *Steak*	17
Cookhouse | *BBQ*	19
Z Coromandel | *Indian*	26
Così | *Sandwiches*	16

Giovanni's | *Steak*	19
NEW Little Thai | *Thai*	22
Melting Pot | *Fondue*	20
Post Corner Pizza | *Pizza*	18

GREENWICH

Abis | *Jap.*	17
Asiana Cafe | *Pan-Asian*	23
Aux Délices | *Amer./French*	22
Barcelona | *Spanish*	22
Boxcar Cantina | *SW*	19
Centro | *Italian/Med.*	19
Chola | *Indian*	22
Così | *Sandwiches*	16
Z Elm St. Oyster | *Seafood*	24
Figaro Bistro | *French*	19
Gaia | *Amer./French*	24
Ginger Man | *Amer.*	17
Z Jean-Louis | *French*	27
L'Escale | *French*	21
NEW Little Thai | *Thai*	22
Mediterraneo | *Med.*	22
Meli-Melo | *French*	23
Panda Pavilion | *Chinese*	15
Pasta Vera | *Italian*	20
Penang Grill | *Pan-Asian*	23
Polpo | *Italian*	24
Z Rebeccas | *Amer.*	26
Solaia | *Italian*	20
Z Tengda | *Pan-Asian*	23
Terra Rist. | *Italian*	20
Thataway Cafe | *Amer.*	15
That Little Italian | *Italian*	18
Z Thomas Henkelmann | *French*	29
NEW Tokushin | *Jap.*	-
Versailles | *Bakery/French*	22
Wild Ginger | *Pan-Asian*	23

KENT

Bull's Bridge Inn | *Amer.*	16

LAKEVILLE

Boathouse | *Amer.*	16
Pastorale | *French*	23
Woodland | *Amer./Continental*	22

LITCHFIELD

Aspen Garden | *Med.*	13
Tollgate Hill Inn | *Amer.*	20
West St. Grill | *Amer.*	21

NEW CANAAN

Aloi | *Italian*	24
Bistro Bonne Nuit | *French*	24
Cava Wine | *Italian*	22
Z Ching's | *Pan-Asian*	25
Gates | *Calif./Med.*	18
Plum Tree | *Jap.*	20
Roger Sherman | *Continental*	23
NEW Savvy | *Med.*	18
Solé Rist. | *Italian*	21
Tequila Mocking. | *Mex.*	16
Z Thali | *Indian*	24

NEW MILFORD

Adrienne | *Amer.*	23
Cookhouse | *BBQ*	19
59 Bank | *Amer.*	18
River Cafe | *Spanish*	17
Salsa | *SW*	19
Thomas Moran's | *Amer.*	22

NEW PRESTON

Boulders Inn | *Amer.*	21
Doc's | *Italian*	22
Hopkins Inn | *Austrian*	18
Oliva | *Med.*	23
Z Thomas Moran's | *Amer.*	25

OLD GREENWICH

Mackenzie's | *Pub Food*	16
Osteria Applausi | *Italian*	22

RIDGEFIELD

Bailey's Backyard | *Amer.*	20
Z Bernard's | *French*	26
Elms | *Amer.*	21
NEW Fifty Coins | *Amer.*	14
59 Bank | *Amer.*	18
NEW Gail's | *Amer.*	-
Insieme | *Italian*	24
Z Koo | *Jap.*	24
La Salière | *French*	21
Luc's Café | *French*	23
Southwest Cafe | *New Mex.*	20

Stonehenge | *Continental/French* 23

Thai Pearl | *Thai* 20

Z Thali | *Indian* 24

Toscana | *Italian* 19

Wild Ginger Cafe | *Pan-Asian* 23

RIVERSIDE

Aux Délices | *Amer./French* 22

Z Baang Cafe | *Pan-Asian* 24

Z Valbella | *Italian* 25

SALISBURY

White Hart | *Amer.* 18

SHERMAN

American Pie Co. | *Amer.* 19

STAMFORD

Bennett's Steak | *Seafood/Steak* 20

NEW Big B's | *Seafood/Steak* –

Bobby Valentine's | *Amer.* 14

NEW Brick House | *Amer.* 15

Chez Jean-Pierre | *French* 22

Z City Limits Diner | *Diner* 19

Z Columbus Park | *Italian* 24

Dakshin | *Indian* 23

NEW Dragonfly Lounge | *Eclectic* 18

NEW Duo | *Euro./Jap.* –

Eclisse | *Italian* 19

Egane | *Korean* 20

Grand | *Amer.* 21

Il Falco | *Italian* 22

Kit's Thai | *Thai* 23

Kotobuki | *Jap.* 23

Kujaku | *Jap.* 20

La Bretagne | *French* 23

La Hacienda | *Mex.* 13

Long Ridge Tavern | *Amer.* 15

Lucky's | *Diner* 16

Meera Cuisine | *Indian* 16

Mona Lisa | *Italian* 24

Z Morton's Steak | *Steak* 24

Myrna's | *Med.* 22

NEW Napa & Co. | *Amer.* –

Ocean 211 | *Seafood* 24

Ole Mole | *Mex.* 22

122 Pizza Bistro | *Italian/Pizza* 21

Onyx B&G | *Eclectic* 15

Paradise B&G | *Amer.* 13

Pellicci's | *Italian* 20

Plateau | *Asian Fusion* 21

Route 22 | *Pub* 15

Sabatiello's | *Italian* 18

Siena | *Italian* 23

Smokey Joe's | *BBQ* 19

Southport Brewing | *Pub Food* 16

Telluride | *SW* 24

Vinny's Backyard | *Pub* 17

Vuli | *Italian* 17

Zinc Bistro & Bar | *Amer./French* 19

NEW Zody | *Italian* –

WASHINGTON

Mayflower Inn | *Amer.* 24

WASHINGTON DEPOT

G.W. Tavern | *Amer.* 18

Pantry | *Amer.* 23

WILTON

Z Luca Rist. | *Italian* 27

Mediterr. Grill | *Med.* 19

Orem's Diner | *Diner* 15

Portofino's II | *Italian* 20

Special Features

Listings cover the best in each category and include restaurant names, locations and Food ratings. Multi-location restaurants' features may vary by branch. ☑ indicates places with the highest ratings, popularity and importance.

BREAKFAST

(See also Hotel Dining)

American Pie Co. | **Sherman**	19
Apple Pie | **Hyde Pk**	24
Aux Délices | **multi. loc.**	22
Bread Alone | **multi. loc.**	20
Cafe Mozart | **Mamaro**	15
Calico | **Rhinebeck**	25
☑ City Limits Diner | **White Pl**	19
Corner Bakery | **Pawling**	25
Così | **multi. loc.**	16
☑ Equus | **Tarrytown**	26
Foundry Cafe | **Cold Spring**	18
Grandma's | **Yorktown**	16
Irving Farm | **Millerton**	18
Karamba | **White Pl**	22
Le Jardin du Roi | **Chappaqua**	20
Maggie's Krooked | **Tanners**	–
Meli-Melo | **Greenwich**	23
Orem's Diner | **Wilton**	15
Pantry | **Wash Depot**	23
Sweet Sue's | **Phoenicia**	24
Versailles | **Greenwich**	22
Wobble Café | **Ossining**	21

BRUNCH

Arch | **Brewster**	25
Beech Tree Grill | **Poughkp**	20
Beehive | **Armonk**	17
☑ Bernard's | **Ridgefield**	26
Calico | **Rhinebeck**	25
Capriccio | **Brewster**	21
Cathryn's | **Cold Spring**	22
☑ City Limits Diner | **White Pl**	19
☑ Crabtree's | **Chappaqua**	24
Dakshin | **Stamford**	23
☑ DePuy Canal | **High Falls**	25
☑ Equus | **Tarrytown**	26
French Corner | **Stone Ridge**	25
Gates | **New Canaan**	18
Jackson & Wheeler | **P'ville**	17

Jaipore Indian | **Brewster**	24
La Duchesse | **Mt. Tremper**	–
Lanterna Tuscan | **multi. loc.**	21
Le Canard Enchainé | **Kingston**	24
Le Provençal | **Mamaro**	23
L'Europe | **S Salem**	24
Locust Tree | **New Paltz**	21
Maggie's Krooked | **Tanners**	–
Main Course | **New Paltz**	23
Main Course/Alum. | **Poughkp**	20
Marion's Country | **Woodstock**	22
McKinney & Doyle | **Pawling**	23
Miss Lucy's | **Saugerties**	22
New World | **Saugerties**	23
Nina | **Middletown**	24
☑ Ondine | **Danbury**	26
☑ Pacifico | **Port Chester**	22
Paradise B&G | **Stamford**	13
Red Hat | **Irvington**	22
☑ Rest. X/Bully | **Congers**	27
River Grill | **Newburgh**	21
Roasted Garlic | **Red Hook**	14
Roger Sherman | **New Canaan**	23
Thataway Cafe | **Greenwich**	15
Traphagen | **Rhinebeck**	22
Troutbeck | **Amenia**	18
Tulip Tree | **Rye Brook**	–
Underhills Crossing | **Bronxville**	21
Versailles | **Greenwich**	22
Violette | **Woodstock**	22
Watercolor Cafe | **Larch**	19
Yvonne's | **Pelham**	22

BUFFET

(Check availability)

Abis | **multi. loc.**	17
Agra Tandoor | **Rhinebeck**	17
Alpine Inn | **Patterson**	–
☑ Bengal Tiger | **White Pl**	23
Blue Moon | **Bronxville**	17
NEW Bollywood | **P'ville**	24

NEW Bukhara Grill | **Yonkers**	25
Z Coromandel | **multi. loc.**	26
Dakshin | **Stamford**	23
Frodo's | **P'ville**	23
India Cafe | **Armonk**	20
India House | **Montrose**	23
Jaipore Indian | **Brewster**	24
Lighthouse/Hudson | **Piermont**	16
Lipperas' | **Chatham**	19
MacMenamin's | **New Roch**	22
Malabar Hill | **Elmsford**	23
Meera Cuisine | **Stamford**	16
Mohonk Mtn. Hse. | **New Paltz**	17
Mountain Gate | **Woodstock**	15
Mughal Palace | **Valhalla**	23
Passage to India | **Mt. Kisco**	19
Patang Indian | **Yonkers**	20
Rangoli | **New Roch**	21
NEW Rani Mahal | **Mamaro**	-
Royal Palace | **White Pl**	18
Samba | **Mt. Vernon**	18
Southbound BBQ | **Valhalla**	17
Spiga | **Scarsdale**	17
Sunset Cove | **Tarrytown**	15
Swaddee Hse. | **Thornwood**	20
Tandoori Taste | **Port Chester**	23
Tanjore | **Fishkill**	25
Tulip Tree | **Rye Brook**	-
Two Steps | **Danbury**	15
Vintage | **White Pl**	16
Yvonne's | **Pelham**	22

BUSINESS DINING

Abis | **Greenwich**	17
Alba's | **Port Chester**	23
NEW Artist's Palate | **Poughkp**	24
Azzurri | **Thornwood**	17
Z Baang Cafe | **Riverside**	24
Bennett's Steak | **Stamford**	20
Bird and Bottle | **Garrison**	21
Bistro 22 | **Bedford**	23
Z Caterina de Medici | **Hyde Pk**	26
Centro | **multi. loc.**	19
Chez Jean-Pierre | **Stamford**	22
Ciao! Cafe | **Danbury**	21
Dakshin | **Stamford**	23

Division St. Grill | **Peekskill**	19
Z Elm St. Oyster | **Greenwich**	24
Z Equus | **Tarrytown**	26
Z Escoffier | **Hyde Pk**	26
Figaro Bistro | **Greenwich**	19
French Corner | **Stone Ridge**	25
Gaia | **Greenwich**	24
Gigi's Folderol II | **Westtown**	24
Giovanni's | **Darien**	19
Graziellas | **White Pl**	19
Harry's | **Hartsdale**	19
Z Harvest/Hud. | **Hastings/Hud**	22
Hoffman Hse. | **Kingston**	19
Z Il Barilotto | **Fishkill**	26
Il Continori | **Wapp Falls**	-
Il Falco | **Stamford**	22
Il Portico | **Tappan**	22
Z Jean-Louis | **Greenwich**	27
Z Koo | **Ridgefield**	24
Kotobuki | **Stamford**	23
La Bretagne | **Stamford**	23
Le Canard Enchaîné | **Kingston**	24
Z Le Château | **S Salem**	25
L'Europe | **S Salem**	24
Locust Tree | **New Paltz**	21
Z Lusardi's | **Larch**	23
Lu Shane's | **Nyack**	23
NEW Med 15/35 | **Rye Brook**	-
Mediterraneo | **Greenwich**	22
Mona Lisa | **Stamford**	24
Z Morton's Steak | **Stamford**	24
Z Mulino's | **White Pl**	24
Nestos Estiatorio | **New City**	23
Nino's | **S Salem**	18
Ocean 211 | **Stamford**	24
NEW One | **Irvington**	27
122 Pizza Bistro | **Stamford**	21
Onyx B&G | **Stamford**	15
Osteria Applausi | **Old Greenwich**	22
Pinocchio | **Eastchester**	23
Z Rest. X/Bully | **Congers**	27
River Grill | **Newburgh**	21
Rustico | **Scarsdale**	20
Z Ruth's Chris | **Tarrytown**	23

St. Andrew's Cafe | **Hyde Pk** _24_
Swoon Kitchenbar | **Hudson** _24_
🔃 Tango Grill | **White Pl** _23_
🔃 Thomas Henkelmann | _29_
 Greenwich
Tony La Stazione | **Elmsford** _16_
Tramonto | **Hawthorne** _19_
Trinity Grill | **Harrison** _16_
Troutbeck | **Amenia** _18_
Tulip Tree | **Rye Brook** _–_
🔃 Valbella | **multi. loc.** _25_
🔃 Valley/Garrison | **Garrison** _26_
Victor's | **Monroe** _21_
Vuli | **Stamford** _17_
Willett House | **Port Chester** _23_
Zanaro's | **White Pl** _14_
Zen Tango | **New Roch** _21_
Zinc Bistro & Bar | **Stamford** _19_

BYO

Abis | **Greenwich** _17_
Agra Tandoor | **Rhinebeck** _17_
NEW A'Tavola | **Harrison** _–_
NEW Big W's | **Wingdale** _–_
NEW Bollywood | **P'ville** _24_
NEW Bukhara Grill | **Yonkers** _25_
Cafe Maya/Maya | **Beacon** _23_
Café Tandoor | **Tarrytown** _21_
Café with Love | **Saugerties** _19_
Comfort | **Hastings/Hud** _20_
Conte's Fishmkt. | **Mt. Kisco** _22_
🔃 Coromandel | **multi. loc.** _26_
Doc's | **New Preston** _22_
NEW Duo | **Stamford** _–_
NEW Gail's | **Ridgefield** _–_
Jean Claude's | **Warwick** _26_
John's Harvest | **Middletown** _19_
Julianna's | **Cortlandt Man** _–_
Kira Sushi | **Armonk** _23_
🔃 Le Château | **S Salem** _25_
NEW Little Thai | **Greenwich** _22_
NEW Local 111 | **Philmont** _–_
Maggie's Krooked | **Tanners** _–_
NEW Med 15/35 | **Rye Brook** _–_
Meli-Melo | **Greenwich** _23_
Michele | **Valley Cott** _21_

NEW Mtn. Cow | **Pine Plains** _–_
NEW Napa & Co. | **Stamford** _–_
🔃 Ocean Hse. | **Croton/Hud** _27_
Ole Mole | **Stamford** _22_
Penang Grill | **Greenwich** _23_
Peter Pratt's Inn | **Yorktown** _23_
Portobello Café | **Montrose** _25_
River City Grille | **Irvington** _20_
NEW Savvy | **New Canaan** _18_
NEW Shadows | **Poughkp** _–_
Solaia | **Greenwich** _20_
Solé Rist. | **New Canaan** _21_
Stoneleigh Creek | **Crot Falls** _23_
Telluride | **Stamford** _24_
Temptations Cafe | **Nyack** _21_
That Little Italian | **Greenwich** _18_
🔃 Thomas Moran's | _25_
 New Preston
Thomas Moran's | **New Milford** _22_
Tollgate Hill Inn | **Litchfield** _20_
Tomatillo | **Dobbs Ferry** _21_
NEW Tonique | **Beacon** _–_
Trotters | **White Pl** _24_
Tuscano | **Danbury** _18_
Velvet Monkey | **Monroe** _20_
NEW Viansa | **Yorktown** _–_
West St. Grill | **Litchfield** _21_
Wild Ginger | **Greenwich** _23_
Wobble Café | **Ossining** _21_
Woodland | **Lakeville** _22_
NEW Woody's | **Mt. Kisco** _–_
Zafrán | **Yonkers** _21_
Zinc Bistro & Bar | **Stamford** _19_

CATERING

🔃 An American Bistro | **Tuck** _22_
Aroma Thyme | **Ellenville** _20_
Aux Délices | **multi. loc.** _22_
Basement Bistro | **Earlton** _29_
🔃 Bernard's | **Ridgefield** _26_
Blue | **White Pl** _19_
🔃 Busy Bee | **Poughkp** _26_
Cafe Mirage | **Port Chester** _20_
Cathryn's | **Cold Spring** _22_
Catskill Rose | **Mt. Tremper** _–_
Cena 2000 | **Newburgh** _24_

Coromandel | **New Roch**	26
Crabtree's | **Chappaqua**	24
DePuy Canal | **High Falls**	25
Downtown Cafe | **Kingston**	21
Eastchester Fish | **Scarsdale**	24
Equus | **Tarrytown**	26
F.I.S.H. | **Port Chester**	23
Flying Pig | **Mt. Kisco**	21
Frankie & Johnnie's | **Rye**	22
Freelance Café | **Piermont**	28
Gadaleto's | **New Paltz**	19
Gigi Trattoria | **Rhinebeck**	23
Giulio's of Tappan | **Tappan**	18
Golden Rod | **New Roch**	20
Grand | **Stamford**	21
Harvest/Hud. | **Hastings/Hud**	22
Hunan Village | **Yonkers**	23
Il Barilotto | **Fishkill**	26
Il Cenàcolo | **Newburgh**	27
Il Tesoro | **Goshen**	26
Kira Sushi | **Armonk**	23
Koo | **Rye**	24
La Camelia | **Mt. Kisco**	21
La Fontanella | **Pelham**	25
Lanterna Tuscan | **Nyack**	21
Le Canard Enchainé | **Kingston**	24
Le Chambord | **Hopewell Jct**	22
Lu Shane's | **Nyack**	23
MacMenamin's | **New Roch**	22
Main Course | **New Paltz**	23
Main Course/Alum. | **Poughkp**	20
Malabar Hill | **Elmsford**	23
Marcello's | **Suffern**	24
McKinney & Doyle | **Pawling**	23
Moscato | **Scarsdale**	23
Mughal Palace | **Valhalla**	23
New World | **Saugerties**	23
Nina | **Middletown**	24
Ole Mole | **Stamford**	22
Opus 465 | **Armonk**	18
Pacifico | **Port Chester**	22
Pantry | **Wash Depot**	23
Plates | **Larch**	24
Portofino Rist. | **Staatsburg**	22

Purdys Homestead | **N Salem**	23
Q Rest. | **Port Chester**	23
Rangoli | **New Roch**	21
Rest. X/Bully | **Congers**	27
River Cafe | **New Milford**	17
River Grill | **Newburgh**	21
Riverview | **Cold Spring**	24
Sabatiello's | **Stamford**	18
Santa Fe | **Tarrytown**	17
Ship to Shore | **Kingston**	23
Sonora | **Port Chester**	25
Strega | **P'ville**	-
Sushi Mike's | **Dobbs Ferry**	25
Tango Grill | **White Pl**	23
Telluride | **Stamford**	24
Thali | **multi. loc.**	24
Thomas Moran's | **New Preston**	25
Trotters | **White Pl**	24
Ümami Café | **Croton/Hud**	21
Underhills Crossing | **Bronxville**	21
Valley/Garrison | **Garrison**	26
Village Grille | **Tappan**	21
Violette | **Woodstock**	22
Watermoon | **Rye**	24
Wild Ginger | **Greenwich**	23
Willett House | **Port Chester**	23
Would | **Highland**	23
Xavier's | **Piermont**	29
Yvonne's | **Pelham**	22
Zafrán | **Yonkers**	21

CHILD-FRIENDLY

(Alternatives to the usual fast-food places; * children's menu available)

Abatino's* | **N White Plains**	20
Amalfi* | **Briarcliff Manor**	20
American Pie Co.* | **Sherman**	19
Apple Pie | **Hyde Pk**	24
Armadillo B&G* | **Kingston**	22
Aroma Osteria | **Wapp Falls**	27
Aroma Thyme* | **Ellenville**	20
Asiana Cafe | **Greenwich**	23
Baba Louie's* | **Hudson**	23
Bacio Trattoria | **Cross River**	19
Bagels & More | **Hartsdale**	18
Bailey's Backyard* | **Ridgefield**	20

Bastones Italian*	**New Roch**	18
☑ Bear Cafe	**Bearsville**	23
Beehive*	**Armonk**	17
Bellizzi*	**multi. loc.**	14
Bel Paese	**Hawthorne**	17
Bertucci's*	**multi. loc.**	15
Blazer Pub	**Purdys**	21
Blue Dolphin	**Katonah**	22
Blue Fountain*	**Hopewell Jct**	20
Bread Alone	**multi. loc.**	20
Brooklyn's Famous*	**White Pl**	16
☑ Busy Bee	**Poughkp**	26
California Pizza	**Scarsdale**	16
Casa Maya*	**Scarsdale**	14
Casa Miguel*	**Mt. Kisco**	14
Catskill Rose	**Mt. Tremper**	–
☑ Cheesecake Fac.	**White Pl**	18
Chefs On Fire	**High Falls**	22
China Rose	**multi. loc.**	21
Chuck's Steak*	**multi. loc.**	17
☑ City Limits Diner*	**multi. loc.**	19
Comfort*	**Hastings/Hud**	20
Corner Bakery	**Pawling**	25
Così*	**multi. loc.**	16
Cosimo's Brick*	**multi. loc.**	20
Cosimo's Tratt.*	**Poughkp**	19
Coyote Flaco*	**multi. loc.**	20
Crew*	**Poughkp**	20
David Chen	**Armonk**	19
Deer Park Tavern*	**Katonah**	19
DiNardo's	**Pound Ridge**	17
Doubleday's*	**Dobbs Ferry**	13
Dragonfly Caffé	**P'ville**	15
Earth Foods	**Hudson**	–
East Harbor	**Yonkers**	16
Edo Japanese*	**Pelham**	21
Egg's Nest*	**High Falls**	18
Epstein's Deli*	**multi. loc.**	16
Foundry Cafe*	**Cold Spring**	18
Four Doors Down*	**Buchanan**	–
Friends & Family*	**Accord**	21
Fuffi 2000*	**New Roch**	17
Fuji Mountain*	**Larch**	15
Gadaleto's*	**New Paltz**	19
Gasho of Japan*	**Central Valley**	17

Gates*	**New Canaan**	18
☑ Gigi Trattoria	**Rhinebeck**	23
Golden Rod	**New Roch**	20
Grandma's*	**Yorktown**	16
Gus's Franklin Park*	**Harrison**	21
Hanna's	**Danbury**	20
Hickory BBQ*	**Kingston**	18
Horse & Hound*	**S Salem**	16
Hunan Larchmont	**Larch**	17
Il Portico	**Tappan**	22
Jennifer's	**Yorktown Hts**	19
☑ Johnny's*	**Mt. Vernon**	25
K. Fung's	**Hartsdale**	20
Kit's Thai	**Stamford**	23
Laguna	**White Pl**	20
Lange's Deli	**Scarsdale**	18
La Piccola Casa	**Mamaro**	21
Lexington Sq. Café*	**Mt. Kisco**	18
Lipperas'*	**Chatham**	19
Locust Tree	**New Paltz**	21
Main Course/Alum.	**Poughkp**	20
Main St. Cafe*	**Tarrytown**	16
Mamma Francesca*	**New Roch**	19
Mango Café*	**Mt. Kisco**	17
Marianacci's	**Port Chester**	21
Mary Ann's*	**Port Chester**	15
McKinney & Doyle*	**Pawling**	23
Meetinghouse*	**Bedford Vill**	17
Melting Pot	**Darien**	20
Michael's Tavern*	**P'ville**	14
Miss Lucy's*	**Saugerties**	22
Modern*	**New Roch**	23
Mojo Grill	**Wapp Falls**	23
Mount Fuji*	**Hillburn**	21
Mughal Palace	**Valhalla**	23
New World*	**Saugerties**	23
Nino's	**S Salem**	18
Northern Spy Cafe*	**High Falls**	16
Okinawa*	**Mt. Kisco**	15
Ole Mole	**Stamford**	22
Orem's Diner*	**Wilton**	15
Painter's*	**Cornwall/Hud**	19
Panda Pavilion	**Greenwich**	15
Pantry	**Wash Depot**	23
☑ P.F. Chang's	**White Pl**	20

Portofino | **Goldens Bridge**	21
Q Rest.* | **Port Chester**	23
Raccoon Saloon* | **Marlboro**	19
Ray's Cafe | **multi. loc.**	19
Red Barn* | **W Ghent**	19
Relish* | **Sparkill**	25
☑ Rest. X/Bully | **Congers**	27
Riverview | **Cold Spring**	24
Rockwells* | **Pelham**	12
Route 22* | **Armonk**	15
Sal's Pizza | **Mamaro**	25
Santa Fe* | **Tivoli**	21
Sesame Seed | **Danbury**	19
Seven Woks | **Scarsdale**	15
Southbound BBQ* | **Valhalla**	17
Southport Brewing* | **Stamford**	16
St. Andrew's Cafe | **Hyde Pk**	24
Striped Bass* | **Tarrytown**	16
Sukhothai | **Beacon**	24
Susan's* | **Peekskill**	18
Swaddee Hse. | **Thornwood**	20
Sweet Sue's | **Phoenicia**	24
Temptations Cafe* | **Nyack**	21
Tequila Mocking.* | **New Canaan**	16
Thai Garden | **Sleepy Hollow**	24
Thai Pearl | **Ridgefield**	20
☑ Thali* | **multi. loc.**	24
Tollgate Steak | **Mamaro**	24
Totonno's* | **Yonkers**	18
Town Dock* | **Rye**	18
Travelers* | **Ossining**	18
Tung Hoy | **Mamaro**	15
Turkish Meze | **Mamaro**	23
Tuscan Oven | **Mt. Kisco**	19
Twist* | **Hyde Pk**	25
Two Steps* | **Danbury**	15
Velvet Monkey | **Monroe**	20
Via Nove* | **Fishkill**	19
Villa Del Sol* | **Mt. Kisco**	16
Village Tea.* | **New Paltz**	21
Vinny's Backyard* | **Stamford**	17
Violette* | **Woodstock**	22
Wild Ginger | **Greenwich**	23
Wild Ginger Cafe | **Ridgefield**	23

Wobble Café* | **Ossining**	21
Would | **Highland**	23
Wunderbar | **Hudson**	15
Yvonne's | **Pelham**	22
Zanaro's* | **White Pl**	14

DANCING

Brooklyn's Famous | **White Pl**	16
Cafe Maya/Maya | **Beacon**	23
Chat 19 | **Larch**	17
El Coqui | **Kingston**	15
Globe B&G | **Larch**	16
High St. Road. | **Rye**	18
Horse & Hound | **S Salem**	16
Le Canard Enchaîné | **Kingston**	24
NEW Mickey Spill. | **Eastchester**	-
Mohonk Mtn. Hse. | **New Paltz**	17
Mount Fuji | **Hillburn**	21
Route 22 | **Stamford**	15
☑ Vertigo | **Nyack**	18
Vintage | **White Pl**	16

DELIVERY

Abatino's | **N White Plains**	20
Aux Délices | **multi. loc.**	22
Bertucci's | **Darien**	15
Blue | **White Pl**	19
Bobby Valentine's | **Stamford**	14
Brooklyn's Famous | **White Pl**	16
Candlelight Inn | **Scarsdale**	21
Casa Maya | **Scarsdale**	14
Coyote Flaco | **multi. loc.**	20
Epstein's Deli | **multi. loc.**	16
Gadaleto's | **New Paltz**	19
Golden Rod | **New Roch**	20
NEW Haiku | **Cross River**	23
Hunan Ritz | **Thornwood**	19
Imperial Wok | **N White Plains**	18
K. Fung's | **Hartsdale**	20
Kit's Thai | **Stamford**	23
Kotobuki | **Stamford**	23
Kujaku | **Stamford**	20
☑ Lefteris Gyro | **Tarrytown**	21
Maggie's Krooked | **Tanners**	-
Modern | **New Roch**	23
Noda's Steak | **White Pl**	18
Panda Pavilion | **Greenwich**	15

Pasta Vera	**Greenwich**	20
Pellicci's	**Stamford**	20
Plateau	**Stamford**	21
Polpo	**Greenwich**	24
Post Corner Pizza	**Darien**	18
Reality Bites	**Nyack**	20
Royal Palace	**White Pl**	18
Sesame Seed	**Danbury**	19
Smokey Joe's	**Stamford**	19
Thai Garden	**Sleepy Hollow**	24
Totonno's	**Yonkers**	18
Two Steps	**Danbury**	15
Vintage	**White Pl**	16

EARLY-BIRD MENUS

Amarone's	**Sugar Loaf**	21
Bull's Bridge Inn	**Kent**	16
Buon Amici	**White Pl**	20
Caffe Regatta	**Pelham**	19
Casa Rina	**Thornwood**	17
Chuck's Steak	**Darien**	17
Citrus Grille	**Airmont**	24
Deer Park Tavern	**Katonah**	19
☑ Eastchester Fish	**Scarsdale**	24
East Harbor	**Yonkers**	16
Epstein's Deli	**Hartsdale**	16
Eveready Diner	**Hyde Pk**	17
Fuffi 2000	**New Roch**	17
Golden Rod	**New Roch**	20
Grande Centrale	**Congers**	19
Harry's	**Hartsdale**	19
Heights Bistro	**Yorktown Hts**	24
India Cafe	**Armonk**	20
Lia's	**Hartsdale**	21
NEW Mickey Spill.	**Eastchester**	–
NEW Mo's NY	**New Roch**	21
Pasta Cucina	**multi. loc.**	20
Pastina's	**Hartsdale**	18
Ricky's Seafood	**Yonkers**	15
Route 22	**Stamford**	15
Ship Lantern	**Milton**	25
☑ Sonora	**Port Chester**	25
Ten Railroad	**Warwick**	16
NEW Tonique	**Beacon**	–
☑ Vertigo	**Nyack**	18
NEW Zitoune	**Mamaro**	–

ENTERTAINMENT

(Call for days and times of performances)

☑ Bernard's	varies	**Ridgefield**	26
Black Goose	guitar/vocals	**Darien**	17
Bobby Valentine's	karaoke	**Stamford**	14
Caffe Regatta	jazz	**Pelham**	19
☑ Crabtree's	blues/jazz	**Chappaqua**	24
Division St. Grill	jazz	**Peekskill**	19
Downtown Cafe	varies	**Kingston**	21
☑ Equus	jazz	**Tarrytown**	26
Gadaleto's	varies	**New Paltz**	19
Harry's	cover bands	**Hartsdale**	19
High St. Road.	blues	**Rye**	18
Jackson & Wheeler	varies	**P'ville**	17
Le Canard Enchaîné	piano bar	**Kingston**	24
Luc's Café	gypsy jazz	**Ridgefield**	23
Mojo Grill	jazz	**Wapp Falls**	23
New World	blues/rock	**Saugerties**	23
Opus 465	bands	**Armonk**	18
Red Hat	vocals	**Irvington**	22
Rosendale Cafe	varies	**Rosendale**	18
Southbound BBQ	blues	**Valhalla**	17
Southport Brewing	varies	**Stamford**	16
Thataway Cafe	varies	**Greenwich**	15
Towne Crier Cafe	varies	**Pawling**	17
Troutbeck	bands	**Amenia**	18
Turning Point	varies	**Piermont**	14
Vintage	bands/DJs	**White Pl**	16
Watercolor Cafe	jazz	**Larch**	19
Yvonne's	jazz	**Pelham**	22

FIREPLACES

| Adrienne | **New Milford** | 23 |
| Alba's | **Port Chester** | 23 |

Andrew's | **Elmsford**	18
Angelina's | **Tuck**	19
Arch | **Brewster**	25
NEW Backals | **Scarsdale**	16
☑ Bear Cafe | **Bearsville**	23
Belvedere | **Staatsburg**	17
☑ Bernard's | **Ridgefield**	26
Bird and Bottle | **Garrison**	21
Black Goose | **Darien**	17
Blu | **Hastings/Hud**	18
☑ Blue Hill/Stone | **Poc Hills**	27
Boathouse | **Lakeville**	16
Boulders Inn | **New Preston**	21
Boxcar Cantina | **Greenwich**	19
Brothers Trattoria | **Beacon**	23
Bull's Bridge Inn | **Kent**	16
Bull's Head Inn | **Campbell Hall**	19
Cafe Maya/Maya | **Fishkill**	23
Cafe Tamayo | **Saugerties**	24
Canterbury | **Cornwall/Hud**	23
Capriccio | **Brewster**	21
NEW Charlotte's | **Millbrook**	–
Chart House | **Dobbs Ferry**	16
Chateau Hathorn | **Warwick**	22
Citrus Grille | **Airmont**	24
NEW Coco Rumba | **Mt. Kisco**	17
Cornetta's Seafood | **Piermont**	13
Country Inn | **Krumville**	–
☑ Crabtree's | **Chappaqua**	24
NEW De La Vergne | **Amenia**	21
☑ DePuy Canal | **High Falls**	25
Diasporas | **Rhinebeck**	20
Elms | **Ridgefield**	21
☑ Equus | **Tarrytown**	26
Frankie & Johnnie's | **Rye**	22
Friends & Family | **Accord**	21
Gaia | **Greenwich**	24
Gentleman Jim's | **Poughkp**	17
Gigi's Folderol II | **Westtown**	24
Ginger Man | **Greenwich**	17
Giorgio's | **Port Chester**	23
Giulio's of Tappan | **Tappan**	18
Granite Springs | **Granite Spr**	20
G.W. Tavern | **Wash Depot**	18
Hamilton Inn | **Millerton**	19
Harvest/Brookfield | **Brookfield**	21
☑ Harvest/Hud. | **Hastings/Hud**	22
Hickory BBQ | **Kingston**	18
Hillsdale Hse. | **Hillsdale**	13
Hoffman Hse. | **Kingston**	19
Hopkins Inn | **New Preston**	18
Horse & Hound | **S Salem**	16
Hudson Hse. Inn | **Cold Spring**	21
Hudson's Ribs | **Fishkill**	18
India Cafe | **Armonk**	20
Iron Forge Inn | **Warwick**	21
Irving Farm | **Millerton**	18
La Camelia | **Mt. Kisco**	21
☑ La Crémaillère | **Bedford**	27
La Duchesse | **Mt. Tremper**	–
Landmark Inn | **Warwick**	17
Last Chance | **Tanners**	21
La Villetta | **Larch**	24
Le Bouchon | **Cold Spring**	22
Le Chambord | **Hopewell Jct**	22
☑ Le Château | **S Salem**	25
L'Escale | **Greenwich**	21
L'Europe | **S Salem**	24
Lia's Mtn. View | **Pine Plains**	16
Lighthouse/Hudson | **Piermont**	16
Lipperas' | **Chatham**	19
Locust Tree | **New Paltz**	21
Long Ridge Tavern | **Stamford**	15
Luce Rest. | **Somers**	22
☑ Lusardi's | **Larch**	23
MacMenamin's | **New Roch**	22
Main Course/Alum. | **Poughkp**	20
Mamma Assunta | **Tuck**	19
Marion's Country | **Woodstock**	22
Mayflower Inn | **Washington**	24
Michele | **Valley Cott**	21
NEW Mickey Spill. | **Eastchester**	–
Mighty Joe | **White Pl**	20
Mill House Panda | **Poughkp**	17
Mohonk Mtn. Hse. | **New Paltz**	17
☑ Monteverde | **Cortlandt**	21
Northern Spy Cafe | **High Falls**	16
Old Drovers Inn | **Dover Plains**	23
Olde Stone Mill | **Tuck**	15

Deer Park Tavern | **Katonah**	19
☑ DePuy Canal | **High Falls**	25
Docas | **Ossining**	–
Elms | **Ridgefield**	21
Emerson | **Woodstock**	18
☑ Emilio Rist. | **Harrison**	25
☑ Equus | **Tarrytown**	26
☑ Escoffier | **Hyde Pk**	26
Figaro Bistro | **Greenwich**	19
Flames Steak | **Briarcliff Manor**	20
Flying Pig | **Mt. Kisco**	21
Fortuna | **Croton/Hud**	22
Frankie & Johnnie's | **Rye**	22
☑ Freelance Café | **Piermont**	28
French Corner | **Stone Ridge**	25
Gaia | **Greenwich**	24
Gigi's Folderol II | **Westtown**	24
☑ Gigi Trattoria | **Rhinebeck**	23
Grand | **Stamford**	21
Granite Springs | **Granite Spr**	20
G.W. Tavern | **Wash Depot**	18
Hamilton Inn | **Millerton**	19
Harvest/Brookfield | **Brookfield**	21
Heather's Cucina | **Nyack**	21
Heights Bistro | **Yorktown Hts**	24
Hopkins Inn | **New Preston**	18
Hostaria Mazzei | **Port Chester**	21
Hudson Hse. Nyack | **Nyack**	20
Hudson Hse. Inn | **Cold Spring**	21
☑ Il Barilotto | **Fishkill**	26
☑ Il Cenàcolo | **Newburgh**	27
Il Falco | **Stamford**	22
Il Forno | **Somers**	20
Il Tesoro | **Goshen**	26
Iron Forge Inn | **Warwick**	21
☑ Iron Horse Grill | **P'ville**	27
Jack & Dyls | **Tarrytown**	18
Jackie's Bistro | **Eastchester**	20
Jackson & Wheeler | **P'ville**	17
☑ Jean-Louis | **Greenwich**	27
Kraft Bistro | **Bronxville**	19
La Bretagne | **Stamford**	23
La Camelia | **Mt. Kisco**	21
☑ La Crémaillère | **Bedford**	27
La Duchesse | **Mt. Tremper**	–
Landmark Inn | **Warwick**	17
Lanterna Tuscan | **multi. loc.**	21
☑ La Panetière | **Rye**	27
La Riserva | **Larch**	21
La Salière | **Ridgefield**	21
Le Bouchon | **Cold Spring**	22
Le Canard Enchainé | **Kingston**	24
Le Chambord | **Hopewell Jct**	22
Le Fontane | **Katonah**	21
Le Jardin du Roi | **Chappaqua**	20
☑ Le Pavillon | **Poughkp**	27
Le Provençal | **Mamaro**	23
L'Europe | **S Salem**	24
Lia's | **Hartsdale**	21
Locust Tree | **New Paltz**	21
Luce Rest. | **Somers**	22
☑ Lusardi's | **Larch**	23
Lu Shane's | **Nyack**	23
MacMenamin's | **New Roch**	22
Maggie's in the Alley | **Chester**	–
Main Course | **New Paltz**	23
Main Course/Alum. | **Poughkp**	20
Manna Dew Cafe | **Millerton**	22
Marco | **Lake Mahopac**	22
Mayflower Inn | **Washington**	24
Mediterraneo | **P'ville**	18
Meritage | **Scarsdale**	22
Mighty Joe | **White Pl**	20
Mohonk Mtn. Hse. | **New Paltz**	17
Mojo Grill | **Wapp Falls**	23
Moscato | **Scarsdale**	23
NEW Napa & Co. | **Stamford**	–
New World | **Saugerties**	23
Old '76 House | **Tappan**	15
☑ Ondine | **Danbury**	26
121 Rest./Bar | **N Salem**	21
Oporto | **Hartsdale**	17
Pascal's | **Larch**	22
Pastorale | **Lakeville**	23
Peter Pratt's Inn | **Yorktown**	23
Piggy Bank | **Beacon**	18
Pinocchio | **Eastchester**	23
Plates | **Larch**	24
Polpo | **Greenwich**	24
Portobello Café | **Montrose**	25

Purdys Homestead | N Salem 23
Quinta Steak | Pearl River 18
Raccoon Saloon | Marlboro 19
☑ Rebeccas | Greenwich 26
Red Hat | Irvington 22
Relish | Sparkill 25
Roger Sherman | New Canaan 23
Ship Lantern | Milton 25
Spaccarelli's | Millwood 22
St. Andrew's Cafe | Hyde Pk 24
Stonehenge | Ridgefield 23
Stoneleigh Creek | Crot Falls 23
Strega | P'ville ⌐
Swiss Hütte | Hillsdale 20
Telluride | Stamford 24
☑ Tengda | Greenwich 23
☑ Terrapin | Rhinebeck 24
☑ Thomas Henkelmann | Greenwich 29
☑ Thomas Moran's | New Preston 25
NEW Tonique | Beacon ⌐
Toscana | Ridgefield 19
Traphagen | Rhinebeck 22
Tratt. Vivolo | Harrison 22
Travelers | Ossining 18
Trinity Grill | Harrison 16
Trotters | White Pl 24
Troutbeck | Amenia 18
Tuscan Oven | Mt. Kisco 19
Twist | Hyde Pk 25
Underhills Crossing | Bronxville 21
NEW Vico | Hudson - ⌐
Vuli | Stamford 17
White Hart | Salisbury 18
Wildfire Grill | Montgomery 23
Willett House | Port Chester 23
☑ Xaviar's | Piermont 29
Zuppa | Yonkers 23

HISTORIC PLACES
(Year opened; * building)
1668 | Old '76 House* | Tappan 15
1678 | Village Tea.* | New Paltz 21
1687 | Hoffman Hse.* | Kingston 19

1700 | Canterbury* | Cornwall/Hud 23
1700 | Dragonfly Grille* | Woodstock ⌐
1730 | Old Drovers Inn* | Dover Plains 23
1732 | Monteverde* | Cortlandt 21
1749 | Horse & Hound* | S Salem 16
1754 | La Salière* | Ridgefield 21
1759 | Locust Tree* | New Paltz 21
1760 | Iron Forge Inn* | Warwick 21
1760 | Peter Pratt's Inn* | Yorktown 23
1761 | Bird and Bottle* | Garrison 21
1762 | Bull's Bridge Inn* | Kent 16
1766 | Traphagen* | Rhinebeck 22
1770 | Le Pavillon* | Poughkp 27
1774 | Adrienne* | New Milford 23
1775 | Purdys Homestead* | N Salem 23
1778 | Landmark Inn* | Warwick 17
1782 | Stissing House* | Pine Plains 19
1783 | Roger Sherman* | New Canaan 23
1786 | Bull's Head Inn* | Campbell Hall 19
1790 | Crabtree's* | Chappaqua 24
1790 | La Camelia* | Mt. Kisco 21
1792 | Down by the Bay* | Mamaro 16
1797 | Chefs On Fire* | High Falls 22
1797 | DePuy Canal* | High Falls 25
1799 | Elms* | Ridgefield 21
1799 | Thomas Henkelmann* | Greenwich 29
1800 | Peekamoose* | Big Indian 25
1803 | Olde Stone Mill* | Tuck 15
1806 | White Hart* | Salisbury 18
1813 | Hillsdale Hse. | Hillsdale 13

1820 | Gentleman Jim's* | **Poughkp**	17
1824 | Terrapin* | **Rhinebeck**	24
1827 | Le Bouchon* | **Cold Spring**	22
1830 | Artist's Palate* | **Poughkp**	24
1834 | Pillars* | **New Lebanon**	–
1838 | China Rose* | **Rhinecliff**	21
1841 | Roasted Garlic* | **Red Hook**	14
1850 | G.W. Tavern* | **Wash Depot**	18
1850 | La Duchesse* | **Mt. Tremper**	–
1850 | La Panetière* | **Rye**	27
1850 | Swiss Hütte* | **Hillsdale**	20
1854 | Martha's* | **Millerton**	–
1855 | Hudson Hse. Nyack* | **Nyack**	20
1855 | Maggie's in the Alley* | **Chester**	–
1855 | Red Hat* | **Irvington**	22
1859 | Lipperas'* | **Chatham**	19
1860 | Gigi's Folderol II* | **Westtown**	24
1860 | Northern Spy Cafe* | **High Falls**	16
1863 | Le Chambord* | **Hopewell Jct**	22
1864 | Cafe Tamayo* | **Saugerties**	24
1869 | Mohonk Mtn. Hse.* | **New Paltz**	17
1870 | Il Barilotto* | **Fishkill**	26
1870 | La Stazione* | **New Paltz**	19
1876 | Travelers* | **Ossining**	18
1880 | Mayflower Inn* | **Washington**	24
1880 | Relish* | **Sparkill**	25
1881 | Q Rest.* | **Port Chester**	23
1882 | Harney & Sons* | **Millerton**	–
1890 | Boulders Inn* | **New Preston**	21
1890 | Main St. Cafe* | **Tarrytown**	16
1892 | Nanuet Hotel* | **Nanuet**	18
1892 | Zuppa* | **Yonkers**	23

1897 | Mercato* | **Red Hook**	–
1898 | Restaurant* | **Germantown**	26
1900 | Belvedere* | **Staatsburg**	17
1900 | MacMenamin's* | **New Roch**	22
1900 | Marco* | **Lake Mahopac**	22
1900 | 96 Main* | **Poughkp**	21
1900 | Painter's* | **Cornwall/Hud**	19
1900 | Polpo* | **Greenwich**	24
1902 | Plates* | **Larch**	24
1904 | Iron Horse Grill* | **P'ville**	27
1905 | Ugly Gus Cafe* | **Kingston**	18
1906 | Strega* | **P'ville**	–
1907 | Le Château* | **S Salem**	25
1910 | Julianna's* | **Cortlandt Man**	–
1915 | Arch* | **Brewster**	25
1917 | Cobble Stone* | **Purchase**	16
1919 | Walter's | **Mamaro**	21
1920 | Modern* | **New Roch**	23
1920 | Red Barn* | **W Ghent**	19
1920 | Troutbeck* | **Amenia**	18
1921 | Aloi* | **New Canaan**	24
1921 | Orem's Diner | **Wilton**	15
1924 | Main Course/Alum.* | **Poughkp**	20
1925 | Ship Lantern | **Milton**	25
1929 | Steakhouse 22* | **Patterson**	17
1930 | Finn McCool's* | **White Pl**	16
1930 | Granite Springs* | **Granite Spr**	20
1930 | Route 22* | **Armonk**	15
1930 | Would* | **Highland**	23
1931 | Gus's Franklin Park | **Harrison**	21
1931 | Ricky's Seafood | **Yonkers**	15
1931 | Roma | **Tuck**	17
1932 | Sam's/Gedney | **White Pl**	18
1933 | Larchmont Tavern | **Larch**	15
1934 | Blazer Pub | **Purdys**	21

1940 | Blue Dolphin | **Katonah** 22

1940 | River City Grille* | **Irvington** 20

1940 | Stoneleigh Creek* | **Crot Falls** 23

1942 | Johnny's | **Mt. Vernon** 25

1945 | Alpine Inn* | **Patterson** ⌐

1946 | Hopkins Inn | **New Preston** 18

1947 | La Crémaillère | **Bedford** 27

1947 | La Manda's | **White Pl** 18

1947 | Mickey Spill.* | **Eastchester** ⌐

1947 | Pellicci's | **Stamford** 20

1949 | Sam's | **Dobbs Ferry** 18

1950 | Marianacci's | **Port Chester** 21

1952 | Epstein's Deli | **Yonkers** 16

1955 | Candlelight Inn | **Scarsdale** 21

1955 | Made In Asia* | **Armonk** ⌐

HOTEL DINING

Beekman Arms Hotel

Traphagen | **Rhinebeck** 22

Bird and Bottle Inn

Bird and Bottle | **Garrison** 21

Courtyard Marriott Hotel

NEW Napa & Co. | **Stamford** ⌐

Crabtree's Kittle House Inn

☑ Crabtree's | **Chappaqua** 24

Delamar Hotel

L'Escale | **Greenwich** 21

Emerson Resort & Spa

NEW Phoenix | **Mt. Tremper** ⌐

Esplanade White Plains Hotel

Graziellas | **White Pl** 19

Hilton Rye Town

Tulip Tree | **Rye Brook** ⌐

Homestead Inn

☑ Thomas Henkelmann | **Greenwich** 29

Inn at Applewood

Would | **Highland** 23

Inn at Ca'Mea

Ca'Mea | **Hudson** 21

La Duchesse Anne

La Duchesse | **Mt. Tremper** ⌐

Le Chambord

Le Chambord | **Hopewell Jct** 22

Madalin Hotel

NEW Madalin's Table | **Tivoli** 19

Marriott Hotel

Vuli | **Stamford** 17

Marriott Residence Inn

Aberdeen | **White Pl** 24

Marriott Westchester

☑ Ruth's Chris | **Tarrytown** 23

Mayflower Inn & Spa

Mayflower Inn | **Washington** 24

Mohonk Mountain Hse.

Mohonk Mtn. Hse. | **New Paltz** 17

Old Drovers Inn

Old Drovers Inn | **Dover Plains** 23

Plumbush Inn

Plumbush Inn | **Cold Spring** 22

Radisson Hotel

Zen Tango | **New Roch** 21

Ramada Inn

Totonno's | **Yonkers** 18

Red Hook Inn

Roasted Garlic | **Red Hook** 14

Ridgefield Motor Inn

☑ Thali | **Ridgefield** 24

Roger Sherman Inn

Roger Sherman | **New Canaan** 23

Ruby's Hotel

Ruby's Hotel | **Freehold** ⌐

Simmons' Way Village Inn

Martha's | **Millerton** ⌐

Stonehenge Inn

Stonehenge | **Ridgefield** 23

Swiss Hütte Country Inn

Swiss Hütte | **Hillsdale** 20

Troutbeck Estate & Resort

Troutbeck | **Amenia** 18

White Hart Inn
White Hart | **Salisbury** 18

Woodstock Lodge
Marion's Country | 22
Woodstock

Hudson Hse. Nyack	**Nyack**	20
Jackson & Wheeler	**P'ville**	17
Kraft Bistro	**Bronxville**	19
La Hacienda	**Stamford**	13
Lazy Boy Saloon	**White Pl**	17
Le Canard Enchainé	**Kingston**	24
Lexington Sq. Café	**Mt. Kisco**	18
Lipperas'	**Chatham**	19
NEW Local 111	**Philmont**	–
Long Ridge Tavern	**Stamford**	15
Lu Shane's	**Nyack**	23
Mackenzie's	**Old Greenwich**	16
MacMenamin's	**New Roch**	22
NEW Madalin's Table	**Tivoli**	19
Mango Café	**Mt. Kisco**	17
Mediterraneo	**Greenwich**	22
Melting Pot	**Darien**	20
Mexican Radio	**Hudson**	19
Michael's Tavern	**P'ville**	14
NEW Mickey Spill.	**Eastchester**	–
Mighty Joe	**White Pl**	20
Miss Lucy's	**Saugerties**	22
Mojo Grill	**Wapp Falls**	23
Z Mulino's	**White Pl**	24
NEW Napa & Co.	**Stamford**	–
Northern Spy Cafe	**High Falls**	16
Off Broadway	**Dobbs Ferry**	19
NEW One	**Irvington**	27
121 Rest./Bar	**N Salem**	21
122 Pizza Bistro	**Stamford**	21
Onyx B&G	**Stamford**	15
Oscar	**Kerhonkson**	–
Palmer's Crossing	**Larch**	17
Paradise B&G	**Stamford**	13
Raccoon Saloon	**Marlboro**	19
Red Onion	**Saugerties**	22
Z Rest. X/Bully	**Congers**	27
Rockwells	**Pelham**	12
Sabatiello's	**Stamford**	18
Santa Fe	**Tarrytown**	17
Santa Fe	**Tivoli**	21
Seasons American	**Somers**	20
Z Sonora	**Port Chester**	25
Southwest Cafe	**Ridgefield**	20
Squires	**Briarcliff Manor**	18

Strega	**P'ville**	–
Sunset Grille	**White Pl**	22
Z Tango Grill	**White Pl**	23
Telluride	**Stamford**	24
Temptation Tea	**Mt. Kisco**	21
Ten Railroad	**Warwick**	16
Tequila Mocking.	**New Canaan**	16
Towne Crier Cafe	**Pawling**	17
Traditions 118	**Somers**	19
Tramonto	**Hawthorne**	19
Traphagen	**Rhinebeck**	22
Trotters	**White Pl**	24
Turning Point	**Piermont**	14
Ugly Gus Cafe	**Kingston**	18
Z Vertigo	**Nyack**	18
Via Nove	**Fishkill**	19
Vinny's Backyard	**Stamford**	17
Violette	**Woodstock**	22
Vox	**N Salem**	21
Watercolor Cafe	**Larch**	19
Zanaro's	**White Pl**	14
Zen Tango	**New Roch**	21
Zinc Bistro & Bar	**Stamford**	19
Zuppa	**Yonkers**	23

NATURAL/ORGANIC

(These restaurants often or always use organic, local ingredients)

Abruzzi Trattoria	**Patterson**	20
Agra Tandoor	**Rhinebeck**	17
Amarone's	**Sugar Loaf**	21
Z American Bounty	**Hyde Pk**	26
Arch	**Brewster**	25
Aroma Thyme	**Ellenville**	20
NEW Artist's Palate	**Poughkp**	24
Baba Louie's	**Hudson**	23
NEW Backyard	**Montgomery**	–
Basement Bistro	**Earlton**	29
Beebs	**Newburgh**	22
Belvedere	**Staatsburg**	17
Beso	**New Paltz**	25
Big Easy Bistro	**Newburgh**	17
Bird and Bottle	**Garrison**	21
NEW Bloom	**Hastings/Hud**	21
Z Blue Hill/Stone	**Poc Hills**	27
Bread Alone	**multi. loc.**	20

☑ Thomas Moran's | **New Preston**	25
Tomatillo | **Dobbs Ferry**	21
Tony La Stazione | **Elmsford**	16
Tramonto | **Hawthorne**	19
Trotters | **White Pl**	24
Tsuru | **Hartsdale**	23
Turquoise | **Larch**	20
☑ Valbella | **Riverside**	25
☑ Valley/Garrison | **Garrison**	26
Village Grille | **Tappan**	21
Village Tea. | **New Paltz**	21
☑ Wasabi | **Nyack**	27
Willett House | **Port Chester**	23
NEW Woody's | **Mt. Kisco**	–
Would | **Highland**	23
☑ Xaviar's | **Piermont**	29

NOTEWORTHY
NEWCOMERS

Anna Maria's | **Larch**	20
Artist's Palate | **Poughkp**	24
Asian Tempt. | **White Pl**	–
A'Tavola | **Harrison**	–
Backals | **Scarsdale**	16
Backyard | **Montgomery**	–
Belle Havana | **Yonkers**	–
Big B's | **Stamford**	–
Big W's | **Wingdale**	–
Bloom | **Hastings/Hud**	21
Bollywood | **P'ville**	24
Brick House | **Stamford**	15
Bukhara Grill | **Yonkers**	25
Bywater | **Rosendale**	18
Charlotte's | **Millbrook**	–
Chelsea's | **Pelham**	–
Coco Rumba | **Mt. Kisco**	17
Copper Rest. | **Fishkill**	–
Croton Creek | **Crot Falls**	–
DABA | **Hudson**	19
DaVinci's | **New Roch**	–
De La Vergne | **Amenia**	21
Dragonfly Grille | **Woodstock**	–
Dragonfly Lounge | **Stamford**	18
Duo | **Stamford**	–
Euro Asian | **Port Chester**	–

Fifty Coins | **Ridgefield**	14
Flirt Sushi | **Irvington**	20
Gail's | **Ridgefield**	–
Goldfish | **Ossining**	22
Haiku | **multi. loc.**	23
Il Teatro | **Mamaro**	21
Jackalope BBQ | **Fishkill**	–
La Puerta Azul | **Salt Pt**	16
Lejends | **Yonkers**	–
Little Thai | **multi. loc.**	22
Local 111 | **Philmont**	–
Locanda | **Fishkill**	–
Madalin's Table | **Tivoli**	19
Made In Asia | **Armonk**	–
Med 15/35 | **Rye Brook**	–
Memphis Mae's | **Croton/Hud**	17
Mercato | **Red Hook**	–
Mex-to-go | **Croton/Hud**	17
Mickey Spill. | **Eastchester**	–
Mo's NY | **New Roch**	21
Mtn. Cow | **Pine Plains**	–
Napa & Co. | **Stamford**	–
Nessa | **Port Chester**	–
One | **Irvington**	27
Oriole 9 | **Woodstock**	19
Phoenix | **Mt. Tremper**	–
Pony Express | **P'ville**	–
Rani Mahal | **Mamaro**	–
Sardegna | **Larch**	–
Savvy | **New Canaan**	18
Shadows | **Poughkp**	–
Sonoma | **Brewster**	–
Spring Asian | **Mt. Vernon**	–
Tokushin | **Greenwich**	–
Tonique | **Beacon**	–
Trattoria Lucia | **Bedford**	14
Viansa | **Yorktown**	–
Vico | **Hudson**	–
Village Café | **Bronxville**	15
Woody's | **Mt. Kisco**	–
Zitoune | **Mamaro**	–
Zody | **Stamford**	–

OFFBEAT

Aux Délices | **multi. loc.**	22
☑ Azuma Sushi | **Hartsdale**	27

Basement Bistro | **Earlton**	29
Cafe Mirage | **Port Chester**	20
Cascade Mtn. Winery | **Amenia**	22
Chefs On Fire | **High Falls**	22
Conte's Fishmkt. | **Mt. Kisco**	22
Country Inn | **Krumville**	-
Earth Foods | **Hudson**	-
Egane | **Stamford**	20
Egg's Nest | **High Falls**	18
Flying Pig | **Mt. Kisco**	21
Fuffi 2000 | **New Roch**	17
Global Gatherings | **Hartsdale**	20
Gusano Loco | **Mamaro**	18
Hanna's | **Danbury**	20
High St. Road. | **Rye**	18
NEW Jackalope BBQ | **Fishkill**	-
Kit's Thai | **Stamford**	23
La Mexicana | **Red Hook**	17
Last Chance | **Tanners**	21
Lucky's | **Stamford**	16
Max's Memphis | **Red Hook**	20
Melting Pot | **Darien**	20
Miss Saigon | **Poughkp**	18
NEW Mtn. Cow | **Pine Plains**	-
New World | **Saugerties**	23
Oriental House | **Pine Bush**	-
Oscar | **Kerhonkson**	-
O'Sho Japanese | **Poughkp**	19
Painter's | **Cornwall/Hud**	19
Pantry | **Wash Depot**	23
Pasta Vera | **Greenwich**	20
Ray's Cafe | **multi. loc.**	19
Reality Bites | **Nyack**	20
Restaurant | **Germantown**	26
Rosendale Cafe | **Rosendale**	18
Salsa | **New Milford**	19
Sesame Seed | **Danbury**	19
Smokey Joe's | **Stamford**	19
Southbound BBQ | **Valhalla**	17
Temptation Tea | **Mt. Kisco**	21
Tratt. Vivolo | **Harrison**	22
Two Steps | **Danbury**	15
Would | **Highland**	23
Yobo | **Newburgh**	19
☑ Zephs' | **Peekskill**	26

OUTDOOR DINING

(G=garden; P=patio; S=sidewalk; T=terrace; W=waterside)

Ace Asian-French | P | **Thornwood**	24
Adrienne | P | **New Milford**	23
Arch | P | **Brewster**	25
Armadillo B&G | P | **Kingston**	22
Aspen Garden | P | **Litchfield**	13
☑ Bear Cafe | G, W | **Bearsville**	23
Blu | T, W | **Hastings/Hud**	18
☑ Blue Hill/Stone | P | **Poc Hills**	27
Boulders Inn | P | **New Preston**	21
Bull's Head Inn | G, T | **Campbell Hall**	19
Cafe on the Green | P, T | **Danbury**	23
Canterbury | P, W | **Cornwall/Hud**	23
Capriccio | T | **Brewster**	21
☑ Caterina de Medici | T | **Hyde Pk**	26
Cathryn's | G | **Cold Spring**	22
Catskill Rose | G, P | **Mt. Tremper**	-
Cena 2000 | P, W | **Newburgh**	24
Chart House | P, T, W | **Dobbs Ferry**	16
Chez Jean-Pierre | S | **Stamford**	22
Ciao! Cafe | P, S | **Danbury**	21
☑ Crabtree's | G | **Chappaqua**	24
Elms | P | **Ridgefield**	21
Encore Bistro | S | **Larch**	21
☑ Equus | T | **Tarrytown**	26
Figaro Bistro | P | **Greenwich**	19
Fish Cellar | P | **Mt. Kisco**	21
Flying Pig | P | **Mt. Kisco**	21
☑ Gigi Trattoria | P | **Rhinebeck**	23
Gina Marie's | P | **Eastchester**	19
G.W. Tavern | T, W | **Wash Depot**	18
☑ Harvest/Hud. | G, P, W | **Hastings/Hud**	22
Heather's Cucina | S | **Nyack**	21
Hopkins Inn | P, T | **New Preston**	18
Hudson Hse. Inn | P, T, W | **Cold Spring**	21
Il Bacio Tratt. | S | **Bronxville**	23

Il Sorriso | P | **Irvington**	20
Ⓩ Iron Horse Grill | P | **P'ville**	27
La Camelia | P | **Mt. Kisco**	21
Lazy Boy Saloon | S | **White Pl**	17
Le Bouchon | G | **Cold Spring**	22
Le Fontane | G | **Katonah**	21
Ⓩ Lefteris Gyro | S | **Tarrytown**	21
Le Jardin du Roi | G | **Chappaqua**	20
L'Escale | T, W | **Greenwich**	21
Marion's Country | T | **Woodstock**	22
Mayflower Inn | P | **Washington**	24
Mediterr. Grill | P | **Wilton**	19
Mediterraneo | P | **Greenwich**	22
Niko's Greek | P | **White Pl**	20
Nina | P | **Middletown**	24
Northern Spy Cafe | P | **High Falls**	16
Old Drovers Inn | P | **Dover Plains**	23
Oliva | T | **New Preston**	23
NEW One | P, W | **Irvington**	27
121 Rest./Bar | P, T | **N Salem**	21
122 Pizza Bistro | S | **Stamford**	21
Opus 465 | P | **Armonk**	18
Pastorale | T | **Lakeville**	23
Portofino's II | P | **Wilton**	20
Raccoon Saloon | T, W | **Marlboro**	19
Red Barn | P | **W Ghent**	19
Red Dot | G | **Hudson**	16
River Grill | P, W | **Newburgh**	21
Riverview | P | **Cold Spring**	24
Roger Sherman | P, T | **New Canaan**	23
Ruby's Hotel | P | **Freehold**	–
Santa Fe | S | **Tivoli**	21
Seaside Johnnie's | T, W | **Rye**	11
NEW Shadows | P | **Poughkp**	–
Stissing House | T | **Pine Plains**	19
Stoneleigh Creek | P | **Crot Falls**	23
Striped Bass | P, W | **Tarrytown**	16
Sunset Cove | P, W | **Tarrytown**	15
Terra Rist. | P | **Greenwich**	20
Thataway Cafe | P | **Greenwich**	15
Troutbeck | T, W | **Amenia**	18

Two Steps | P | **Danbury**	15
Ümami Café | T | **Croton/Hud**	21
Underhills Crossing | S | **Bronxville**	21
Ⓩ Valley/Garrison | T, W | **Garrison**	26
White Hart | P | **Salisbury**	18
Wild Ginger | P, W | **Greenwich**	23
Zinc Bistro & Bar | P | **Stamford**	19

PEOPLE-WATCHING

NEW Asian Tempt. | **White Pl**	–
Ⓩ Baang Cafe | **Riverside**	24
NEW Backals | **Scarsdale**	16
Ⓩ Bear Cafe | **Bearsville**	23
Beebs | **Newburgh**	22
Beech Tree Grill | **Poughkp**	20
Blue | **White Pl**	19
Boathouse | **Lakeville**	16
Chart House | **Dobbs Ferry**	16
NEW Coco Rumba | **Mt. Kisco**	17
Emerson | **Woodstock**	18
NEW Euro Asian | **Port Chester**	–
Figaro Bistro | **Greenwich**	19
NEW Flirt Sushi | **Irvington**	20
Frankie & Johnnie's | **Rye**	22
Ⓩ Freelance Café | **Piermont**	28
Gaia | **Greenwich**	24
Ⓩ Gigi Trattoria | **Rhinebeck**	23
Ginger Man | **Greenwich**	17
Grand | **Stamford**	21
G.W. Tavern | **Wash Depot**	18
Harry's | **Hartsdale**	19
Ⓩ Harvest/Hud. | **Hastings/Hud**	22
Ⓩ Il Cenàcolo | **Newburgh**	27
Ⓩ Jean-Louis | **Greenwich**	27
Ⓩ Koo | **Rye**	24
Landau Grill | **Woodstock**	12
Le Canard Enchainé | **Kingston**	24
NEW Lejends | **Yonkers**	–
Ⓩ Le Petit Bistro | **Rhinebeck**	26
Lexington Sq. Café | **Mt. Kisco**	18
Ⓩ Lusardi's | **Larch**	23
MacMenamin's | **New Roch**	22
NEW Madalin's Table | **Tivoli**	19

Mayflower Inn | **Washington**	24
Mediterraneo | **P'ville**	18
Mighty Joe | **White Pl**	20
☑ Mulino's | **White Pl**	24
New World | **Saugerties**	23
North Star | **Pound Ridge**	22
Oliva | **New Preston**	23
☑ Pacifico | **Port Chester**	22
Pastina's | **Hartsdale**	18
Pastorale | **Lakeville**	23
Polpo | **Greenwich**	24
☑ Rebeccas | **Greenwich**	26
Red Dot | **Hudson**	16
☑ Rest. X/Bully | **Congers**	27
Ruby's Oyster Bar | **Rye**	21
Sabroso | **Rhinebeck**	26
☑ Sonora | **Port Chester**	25
Swoon Kitchenbar | **Hudson**	24
☑ Tango Grill | **White Pl**	23
Temptation Tea | **Mt. Kisco**	21
Torches on Hudson | **Newburgh**	15
Trotters | **White Pl**	24
Underhills Crossing | **Bronxville**	21
☑ Vertigo | **Nyack**	18
West St. Grill | **Litchfield**	21
Zen Tango | **New Roch**	21
Zuppa | **Yonkers**	23

POWER SCENES

Alba's | **Port Chester**	23
☑ Baang Cafe | **Riverside**	24
NEW Backals | **Scarsdale**	16
☑ Bear Cafe | **Bearsville**	23
Boathouse | **Lakeville**	16
Citrus Grille | **Airmont**	24
☑ Crabtree's | **Chappaqua**	24
☑ Equus | **Tarrytown**	26
Gaia | **Greenwich**	24
Graziellas | **White Pl**	19
Il Falco | **Stamford**	22
Il Portico | **Tappan**	22
☑ Jean-Louis | **Greenwich**	27
☑ Koo | **multi. loc.**	24
☑ Lusardi's | **Larch**	23
Mayflower Inn | **Washington**	24
☑ Morton's Steak | **Stamford**	24

Moscato | **Scarsdale**	23
☑ Mulino's | **White Pl**	24
Polpo | **Greenwich**	24
☑ Ruth's Chris | **Tarrytown**	23
☑ Tango Grill | **White Pl**	23
☑ Thomas Henkelmann | **Greenwich**	29
☑ Valbella | **Riverside**	25
West St. Grill | **Litchfield**	21
Willett House | **Port Chester**	23
☑ Xaviar's | **Piermont**	29
Zuppa | **Yonkers**	23

PRIVATE ROOMS

(Restaurants charge less at off times; call for capacity)

☑ Bernard's | **Ridgefield**	26
Centro | **Greenwich**	19
Eclisse | **Stamford**	19
Elms | **Ridgefield**	21
Gaia | **Greenwich**	24
Ginger Man | **Greenwich**	17
Grand | **Stamford**	21
Graziellas | **White Pl**	19
Il Falco | **Stamford**	22
Kujaku | **Stamford**	20
Mayflower Inn | **Washington**	24
Ocean 211 | **Stamford**	24
Plum Tree | **New Canaan**	20
Polpo | **Greenwich**	24
River Cafe | **New Milford**	17
Roger Sherman | **New Canaan**	23
Stonehenge | **Ridgefield**	23
☑ Tengda | **Greenwich**	23
☑ Thali | **New Canaan**	24
☑ Thomas Henkelmann | **Greenwich**	29
Vuli | **Stamford**	17

PRIX FIXE MENUS

(Call for prices and times)

Arch | **Brewster**	25
☑ Bengal Tiger | **White Pl**	23
☑ Bernard's | **Ridgefield**	26
Blue Hill/Stone | **Poc Hills**	27
☑ Crabtree's | **Chappaqua**	24
DePuy Canal | **High Falls**	25
French Corner | **Stone Ridge**	25

subscribe to zagat.com

Gaia | **Greenwich** 24

☑ Gigi Trattoria | **Rhinebeck** 23

Halstead Ave. Bistro | **Harrison** 22

Hudson Hse. Inn | **Cold Spring** 21

☑ Jean-Louis | **Greenwich** 27

☑ La Crémaillère | **Bedford** 27

☑ La Panetière | **Rye** 27

Le Canard Enchainé | **Kingston** 24

☑ Le Pavillon | **Poughkp** 27

Marion's Country | **Woodstock** 22

New World | **Saugerties** 23

☑ Ondine | **Danbury** 26

☑ Pacifico | **Port Chester** 22

Pascal's | **Larch** 22

Pastina's | **Hartsdale** 18

☑ Rest. X/Bully | **Congers** 27

Roger Sherman | **New Canaan** 23

Stoneleigh Creek | **Crot Falls** 23

☑ Terrapin | **Rhinebeck** 24

Traphagen | **Rhinebeck** 22

Trotters | **White Pl** 24

Troutbeck | **Amenia** 18

☑ Xavier's | **Piermont** 29

Zen Tango | **New Roch** 21

Zuppa | **Yonkers** 23

ROMANTIC PLACES

Adrienne | **New Milford** 23

Arch | **Brewster** 25

NEW Backals | **Scarsdale** 16

Bella Vita | **Mohegan Lake** 20

Belvedere | **Staatsburg** 17

☑ Bengal Tiger | **White Pl** 23

☑ Bernard's | **Ridgefield** 26

Bird and Bottle | **Garrison** 21

Bistro Bonne Nuit | **New Canaan** 24

Bistro 22 | **Bedford** 23

Boulders Inn | **New Preston** 21

☑ Buffet/Gare | **Hastings/Hud** 26

Bull's Head Inn | **Campbell Hall** 19

Canterbury | **Cornwall/Hud** 23

Caravela | **Tarrytown** 20

☑ Caterina de Medici | **Hyde Pk** 26

Chez Jean-Pierre | **Stamford** 22

☑ Crabtree's | **Chappaqua** 24

☑ DePuy Canal | **High Falls** 25

Division St. Grill | **Peekskill** 19

Down by the Bay | **Mamaro** 16

☑ Eastchester Fish | **Scarsdale** 24

Elms | **Ridgefield** 21

☑ Emilio Rist. | **Harrison** 25

Encore Bistro | **Larch** 21

☑ Equus | **Tarrytown** 26

☑ Escoffier | **Hyde Pk** 26

NEW Flirt Sushi | **Irvington** 20

Frankie & Johnnie's | **Rye** 22

Fuffi 2000 | **New Roch** 17

Gaudio's | **Yorktown Hts** 17

Giulio's of Tappan | **Tappan** 18

NEW Goldfish | **Ossining** 22

Granite Springs | **Granite Spr** 20

Harry's | **Hartsdale** 19

Hopkins Inn | **New Preston** 18

Horse & Hound | **S Salem** 16

Il Portico | **Tappan** 22

Il Sorriso | **Irvington** 20

☑ Iron Horse Grill | **P'ville** 27

Jackie's Bistro | **Eastchester** 20

☑ Jean-Louis | **Greenwich** 27

Julianna's | **Cortlandt Man** –

La Bretagne | **Stamford** 23

La Camelia | **Mt. Kisco** 21

☑ La Crémaillère | **Bedford** 27

La Duchesse | **Mt. Tremper** –

La Fontanella | **Pelham** 25

Lago di Como | **Tarrytown** 21

☑ La Panetière | **Rye** 27

La Piccola Casa | **Mamaro** 21

Le Canard Enchainé | **Kingston** 24

Le Chambord | **Hopewell Jct** 22

☑ Le Château | **S Salem** 25

Lena's | **Nyack** 21

☑ Le Pavillon | **Poughkp** 27

L'Europe | **S Salem** 24

Locust Tree | **New Paltz** 21

Mamma Assunta | **Tuck** 19

Mayflower Inn | **Washington** 24

Moscato | **Scarsdale** 23

☑ Mulino's | **White Pl** 24

NEW Napa & Co. | **Stamford** –

Northern Spy Cafe | **High Falls** 16

WEST/HV/CT

SPECIAL FEATURES

Ocean 211	**Stamford**	24
Old Drovers Inn	**Dover Plains**	23
Oliva	**New Preston**	23
☑ Ondine	**Danbury**	26
NEW One	**Irvington**	27
121 Rest./Bar	**N Salem**	21
Opus 465	**Armonk**	18
Osteria Marietta	**Mamaro**	19
Pascal's	**Larch**	22
Pastorale	**Lakeville**	23
Peter Pratt's Inn	**Yorktown**	23
Plumbush Inn	**Cold Spring**	22
Purdys Homestead	**N Salem**	23
☑ Rest. X/Bully	**Congers**	27
Roger Sherman	**New Canaan**	23
NEW Sardegna	**Larch**	–
Sazan	**Ardsley**	24
☑ Sonora	**Port Chester**	25
Sterling Inn	**New Roch**	20
Stonehenge	**Ridgefield**	23
Sunset Cove	**Tarrytown**	15
Susan's	**Peekskill**	18
Swaddee Hse.	**Thornwood**	20
☑ Tango Grill	**White Pl**	23
Thai House	**multi. loc.**	22
☑ Thomas Henkelmann	**Greenwich**	29
☑ Thomas Moran's	**New Preston**	25
Town Dock	**Rye**	18
Traphagen	**Rhinebeck**	22
Tratt. Vivolo	**Harrison**	22
Travelers	**Ossining**	18
Trinity Grill	**Harrison**	16
Troutbeck	**Amenia**	18
Vuli	**Stamford**	17
Ward's Bridge	**Montgomery**	19
Watercolor Cafe	**Larch**	19
☑ Xaviar's	**Piermont**	29
☑ Zephs'	**Peekskill**	26
NEW Zitoune	**Mamaro**	–

SENIOR APPEAL

American Pie Co.	**Sherman**	19
NEW Big B's	**Stamford**	–
Bistro 22	**Bedford**	23

Blue Fountain	**Hopewell Jct**	20
☑ Buffet/Gare	**Hastings/Hud**	26
Bull's Bridge Inn	**Kent**	16
Bull's Head Inn	**Campbell Hall**	19
Cafe Portofino	**Piermont**	20
Canterbury	**Cornwall/Hud**	23
NEW Charlotte's	**Millbrook**	–
Coppola's	**Poughkp**	18
☑ Crabtree's	**Chappaqua**	24
Division St. Grill	**Peekskill**	19
Encore Bistro	**Larch**	21
Epstein's Deli	**multi. loc.**	16
☑ Equus	**Tarrytown**	26
59 Bank	**Ridgefield**	18
NEW Gail's	**Ridgefield**	–
Gigi's Folderol II	**Westtown**	24
Giorgio's	**Port Chester**	23
Giovanni's	**Darien**	19
Graziellas	**White Pl**	19
Hoffman Hse.	**Kingston**	19
Il Sorriso	**Irvington**	20
NEW Il Teatro	**Mamaro**	21
Insieme	**Ridgefield**	24
☑ Iron Horse Grill	**P'ville**	27
Jackie's Bistro	**Eastchester**	20
John's Harvest	**Middletown**	19
Kisco Kosher	**White Pl**	18
La Camelia	**Mt. Kisco**	21
☑ La Crémaillère	**Bedford**	27
☑ La Panetière	**Rye**	27
Le Chambord	**Hopewell Jct**	22
☑ Le Château	**S Salem**	25
☑ Le Pavillon	**Poughkp**	27
☑ Le Petit Bistro	**Rhinebeck**	26
Le Provençal	**Mamaro**	23
L'Europe	**S Salem**	24
Long Ridge Tavern	**Stamford**	15
Marcello's	**Suffern**	24
Melting Pot	**Darien**	20
Michele	**Valley Cott**	21
Mohonk Mtn. Hse.	**New Paltz**	17
☑ Mulino's	**White Pl**	24
Nino's	**S Salem**	18
Old Drovers Inn	**Dover Plains**	23
Pantry	**Wash Depot**	23

Pascal's	**Larch**	22	Casa Miguel	**Mt. Kisco**	14
Pellicci's	**Stamford**	20	China Rose	**Rhinecliff**	21
Plumbush Inn	**Cold Spring**	22	Cobble Stone	**Purchase**	16
Portofino	**Goldens Bridge**	21	NEW Coco Rumba	**Mt. Kisco**	17
Portofino Rist.	**Staatsburg**	22	Cosimo's Tratt.	**Poughkp**	19
Portofino's II	**Wilton**	20	NEW Duo	**Stamford**	-
Purdys Homestead	**N Salem**	23	El Coqui	**Kingston**	15
Roger Sherman	**New Canaan**	23	NEW Euro Asian	**Port Chester**	-
Romolo's	**Congers**	19	Finn McCool's	**White Pl**	16
☑ Ruth's Chris	**Tarrytown**	23	Frankie & Johnnie's	**Rye**	22
Ship Lantern	**Milton**	25	Grand	**Stamford**	21
Stonehenge	**Ridgefield**	23	High St. Road.	**Rye**	18
Swiss Hütte	**Hillsdale**	20	Hudson Hse. Nyack	**Nyack**	20
T&J Villaggio	**Port Chester**	21	La Hacienda	**Stamford**	13
Thai Pearl	**Ridgefield**	20	Lazy Boy Saloon	**White Pl**	17
☑ Thomas Henkelmann	**Greenwich**	29	Lexington Sq. Café	**Mt. Kisco**	18
			Long Ridge Tavern	**Stamford**	15
Tollgate Hill Inn	**Litchfield**	20	Mackenzie's	**Old Greenwich**	16
Tony La Stazione	**Elmsford**	16	MacMenamin's	**New Roch**	22
Toscani's	**New Paltz**	17	NEW Madalin's Table	**Tivoli**	19
Traphagen	**Rhinebeck**	22	Mary Ann's	**Port Chester**	15
Travelers	**Ossining**	18	Max's Memphis	**Red Hook**	20
Tuscano	**Danbury**	18	Mediterraneo	**Greenwich**	22
Underhills Crossing	**Bronxville**	21	Mexican Radio	**Hudson**	19
Valentino's	**Yonkers**	23	Michael's Tavern	**P'ville**	14
Via Appia	**White Pl**	19	Mighty Joe	**White Pl**	20
Victor's	**Monroe**	21	NEW One	**Irvington**	27
West St. Grill	**Litchfield**	21	121 Rest./Bar	**N Salem**	21
White Hart	**Salisbury**	18	Paradise B&G	**Stamford**	13
Woodland	**Lakeville**	22	Sabatiello's	**Stamford**	18
			Sam's	**Dobbs Ferry**	18

SINGLES SCENES

Armadillo B&G	**Kingston**	22	Santa Fe	**Tarrytown**	17
NEW Asian Tempt.	**White Pl**	-	Southport Brewing	**Stamford**	16
☑ Baang Cafe	**Riverside**	24	Telluride	**Stamford**	24
Bayou	**Mt. Vernon**	21	☑ Tengda	**Katonah**	23
Beebs	**Newburgh**	22	Tequila Sunrise	**Larch**	17
Beech Tree Grill	**Poughkp**	20	Terra Rist.	**Greenwich**	20
Big Easy Bistro	**Newburgh**	17	Thataway Cafe	**Greenwich**	15
Black Goose	**Darien**	17	Trotters	**White Pl**	24
Blue	**White Pl**	19	Turning Point	**Piermont**	14
Boathouse	**Lakeville**	16	Underhills Crossing	**Bronxville**	21
Bobby Valentine's	**Stamford**	14	☑ Vertigo	**Nyack**	18
NEW Brick House	**Stamford**	15	Vintage	**White Pl**	16
NEW Bywater	**Rosendale**	18	Zen Tango	**New Roch**	21
			Zuppa	**Yonkers**	23

WEST/HV/CT

SPECIAL FEATURES

SLEEPERS

(Good to excellent food,
but little known)

Abruzzi Trattoria | **Patterson**	20
Amarone's | **Sugar Loaf**	21
Babbone | **Bronxville**	22
Basement Bistro | **Earlton**	29
Beebs | **Newburgh**	22
Bella Vita | **Mohegan Lake**	20
NEW Bloom | **Hastings/Hud**	21
Blue Fountain | **Hopewell Jct**	20
NEW Bollywood | **P'ville**	24
Brothers Trattoria | **Beacon**	23
NEW Bukhara Grill | **Yonkers**	25
Canterbury | **Cornwall/Hud**	23
Cascade Mtn. Winery | **Amenia**	22
Chateau Hathorn | **Warwick**	22
Cherry Blossom | **Fishkill**	22
Comfort | **Hastings/Hud**	20
Corner Bakery | **Pawling**	25
Crew | **Poughkp**	20
NEW De La Vergne | **Amenia**	21
Diasporas | **Rhinebeck**	20
Downtown Cafe | **Kingston**	21
Ernesto | **White Pl**	20
NEW Flirt Sushi | **Irvington**	20
Fortuna | **Croton/Hud**	22
Friends & Family | **Accord**	21
Gianna's | **Yonkers**	21
Gigi's Folderol II | **Westtown**	24
Golden House | **Jeff Valley**	20
Hokkaido | **New Paltz**	24
NEW Il Teatro | **Mamaro**	21
Il Tesoro | **Goshen**	26
Iron Forge Inn | **Warwick**	21
Jean Claude's | **Warwick**	26
Karamba | **White Pl**	22
Kazu Japanese | **Hartsdale**	21
Kyoto Sushi | **Kingston**	24
La Piccola Casa | **Mamaro**	21
Last Chance | **Tanners**	21
Little Mex. Cafe | **New Roch**	23
Louie & Johnnies' | **Yonkers**	22
Luce Rest. | **Somers**	22
Main Course/Alum. | **Poughkp**	20
Manna Dew Cafe | **Millerton**	22

Marco | **Lake Mahopac**	22
Meson Espanoles | **White Pl**	20
Michele | **Valley Cott**	21
96 Main | **Poughkp**	21
North Star | **Pound Ridge**	22
NEW One | **Irvington**	27
Pantanal | **Port Chester**	22
Patrias | **Port Chester**	22
Peekamoose | **Big Indian**	25
Portobello Café | **Montrose**	25
Portofino Rist. | **Staatsburg**	22
Rangoli | **New Roch**	21
Restaurant | **Germantown**	26
River Bank | **Cornwall/Hud**	25
Ship Lantern | **Milton**	25
Solaia | **Greenwich**	20
Soul Dog | **Poughkp**	21
Spiritoso | **Yonkers**	22
Sukhothai | **Beacon**	24
Sushi Nanase | **White Pl**	28
Sushi Niji | **Dobbs Ferry**	23
T&J Villaggio | **Port Chester**	21
Tanjore | **Fishkill**	25
Tavern at Highlands | **Garrison**	23
Tollgate Hill Inn | **Litchfield**	20
Tombolino's | **Yonkers**	21
Velvet Monkey | **Monroe**	20
Victor's | **Monroe**	21
Village Grille | **Tappan**	21
Violette | **Woodstock**	22
Wildfire Grill | **Montgomery**	23
Zafrán | **Yonkers**	21
Zen Tango | **New Roch**	21

TRENDY

Alba's | **Port Chester**	23
NEW Artist's Palate | **Poughkp**	24
NEW Asian Tempt. | **White Pl**	-
Aurora | **Rye**	19
Z Azuma Sushi | **Hartsdale**	27
Z Baang Cafe | **Riverside**	24
NEW Backals | **Scarsdale**	16
Z Bear Cafe | **Bearsville**	23
NEW Belle Havana | **Yonkers**	-
NEW Bloom | **Hastings/Hud**	21
Blue | **White Pl**	19

🔲 Blue Hill/Stone | **Poc Hills**	27
Cafe Mozart | **Mamaro**	15
Chat 19 | **Larch**	17
🔲 Ching's | **Darien**	25
NEW Coco Rumba | **Mt. Kisco**	17
NEW Croton Creek | **Crot Falls**	—
NEW DABA | **Hudson**	19
Deer Park Tavern | **Katonah**	19
🔲 Eastchester Fish | **Scarsdale**	24
🔲 Elm St. Oyster | **Greenwich**	24
NEW Euro Asian | **Port Chester**	—
Figaro Bistro | **Greenwich**	19
NEW Flirt Sushi | **Irvington**	20
Flying Pig | **Mt. Kisco**	21
🔲 Freelance Café | **Piermont**	28
Gaia | **Greenwich**	24
🔲 Gigi Trattoria | **Rhinebeck**	23
Global Gatherings | **Hartsdale**	20
Halstead Ave. Bistro | **Harrison**	22
Harry's | **Hartsdale**	19
🔲 Harvest/Hud. | **Hastings/Hud**	22
🔲 Koo | **multi. loc.**	24
Kotobuki | **Stamford**	23
Kraft Bistro | **Bronxville**	19
Lanterna Tuscan | **multi. loc.**	21
NEW La Puerta Azul | **Salt Pt**	16
Le Canard Enchaîné | **Kingston**	24
NEW Lejends | **Yonkers**	—
Lexington Sq. Café | **Mt. Kisco**	18
NEW Local 111 | **Philmont**	—
Lu Shane's | **Nyack**	23
MacMenamin's | **New Roch**	22
NEW Madalin's Table | **Tivoli**	19
Mediterr. Grill | **Wilton**	19
Mediterraneo | **Greenwich**	22
Mediterraneo | **P'ville**	18
Mexican Radio | **Hudson**	19
Mighty Joe | **White Pl**	20
Mojo Grill | **Wapp Falls**	23
NEW Napa & Co. | **Stamford**	—
New World | **Saugerties**	23
Oliva | **New Preston**	23
NEW One | **Irvington**	27
NEW Oriole 9 | **Woodstock**	19

🔲 Pacifico | **Port Chester**	22
Painter's | **Cornwall/Hud**	19
Pastorale | **Lakeville**	23
Peter Pratt's Inn | **Yorktown**	23
Reality Bites | **Nyack**	20
🔲 Rebeccas | **Greenwich**	26
Red Dot | **Hudson**	16
Red Hat | **Irvington**	22
Red Onion | **Saugerties**	22
Relish | **Sparkill**	25
🔲 Rest. X/Bully | **Congers**	27
🔲 Rosie's Bistro | **Bronxville**	23
Ruby's Oyster Bar | **Rye**	21
Sabroso | **Rhinebeck**	26
Solé Rist. | **New Canaan**	21
🔲 Sonora | **Port Chester**	25
Swoon Kitchenbar | **Hudson**	24
🔲 Tango Grill | **White Pl**	23
Temptation Tea | **Mt. Kisco**	21
🔲 Tengda | **Katonah**	23
🔲 Terrapin | **Rhinebeck**	24
🔲 Thomas Henkelmann | **Greenwich**	29
Trotters | **White Pl**	24
Ümami Café | **Croton/Hud**	21
Underhills Crossing | **Bronxville**	21
Velvet Monkey | **Monroe**	20
🔲 Vertigo | **Nyack**	18
Vox | **N Salem**	21
Watercolor Cafe | **Larch**	19
🔲 Watermoon | **Rye**	24
West St. Grill | **Litchfield**	21
Zen Tango | **New Roch**	21
🔲 Zephs' | **Peekskill**	26
NEW Zitoune | **Mamaro**	—
NEW Zody | **Stamford**	—
Zuppa | **Yonkers**	23

VALET PARKING

Alpine Inn | **Patterson**	—
Aquario | **W Harrison**	23
Arch | **Brewster**	25
NEW Artist's Palate | **Poughkp**	24
🔲 Baang Cafe | **Riverside**	24
NEW Backals | **Scarsdale**	16
Bastones Italian | **New Roch**	18

Bennett's Steak | **Stamford** _20_

Z Bernard's | **Ridgefield** _26_

Blue | **White Pl** _19_

Z Blue Hill/Stone | **Poc Hills** _27_

Boathouse | **Lakeville** _16_

Ciao! | **Eastchester** _18_

NEW Coco Rumba | **Mt. Kisco** _17_

Z Crabtree's | **Chappaqua** _24_

Deer Park Tavern | **Katonah** _19_

Z Equus | **Tarrytown** _26_

Flying Pig | **Mt. Kisco** _21_

Z Freelance Café | **Piermont** _28_

Gina Marie's | **Eastchester** _19_

Giovanni's | **Darien** _19_

Grande Centrale | **Congers** _19_

Harry's | **Hartsdale** _19_

Z Harvest/Hud. | _22_
Hastings/Hud

NEW Il Teatro | **Mamaro** _21_

Jack & Dyls | **Tarrytown** _18_

Z La Crémaillère | **Bedford** _27_

Z La Panetière | **Rye** _27_

Z Le Château | **S Salem** _25_

Z Legal Sea Foods | **White Pl** _19_

NEW Lejends | **Yonkers** _-_

L'Escale | **Greenwich** _21_

Lighthouse/Hudson | **Piermont** _16_

Louie & Johnnies' | **Yonkers** _22_

Luce Rest. | **Somers** _22_

MacMenamin's | **New Roch** _22_

Maestro's | **Jeff Valley** _16_

Marcello's | **Suffern** _24_

Mayflower Inn | **Washington** _24_

NEW Med 15/35 | **Rye Brook** _-_

Mohonk Mtn. Hse. | **New Paltz** _17_

Z Morton's Steak | **Stamford** _24_

Mount Fuji | **Hillburn** _21_

Z Mulino's | **White Pl** _24_

Olde Stone Mill | **Tuck** _15_

Z Pacifico | **Port Chester** _22_

Pellicci's | **Stamford** _20_

NEW Phoenix | **Mt. Tremper** _-_

Polpo | **Greenwich** _24_

Primavera | **Crot Falls** _23_

Reka's | **White Pl** _16_

Z Rest. X/Bully | **Congers** _27_

Z Ruth's Chris | **Tarrytown** _23_

Samba | **Mt. Vernon** _18_

Z Sonora | **Port Chester** _25_

Spiritoso | **Yonkers** _22_

Stonehenge | **Ridgefield** _23_

Sunset Cove | **Tarrytown** _15_

Z Tango Grill | **White Pl** _23_

Thai Garden | **Sleepy Hollow** _24_

Z Thomas Henkelmann | _29_
Greenwich

Tollgate Steak | **Mamaro** _24_

Tombolino's | **Yonkers** _21_

Tony La Stazione | **Elmsford** _16_

Torches on Hudson | **Newburgh** _15_

Trotters | **White Pl** _24_

Z Valbella | **multi. loc.** _25_

Z Vertigo | **Nyack** _18_

Vuli | **Stamford** _17_

Z Xaviar's | **Piermont** _29_

Zanaro's | **White Pl** _14_

Zuppa | **Yonkers** _23_

VIEWS

Abruzzi Trattoria | **Patterson** _20_

Arch | **Brewster** _25_

Z Bear Cafe | **Bearsville** _23_

Belvedere | **Staatsburg** _17_

Blu | **Hastings/Hud** _18_

Boulders Inn | **New Preston** _21_

Bull's Bridge Inn | **Kent** _16_

Bull's Head Inn | **Campbell Hall** _19_

Cafe on the Green | **Danbury** _23_

Canterbury | **Cornwall/Hud** _23_

Capriccio | **Brewster** _21_

Cascade Mtn. Winery | **Amenia** _24_

Cena 2000 | **Newburgh** _24_

NEW Charlotte's | **Millbrook** _-_

Chart House | **Dobbs Ferry** _16_

China Rose | **Rhinecliff** _21_

Ciao! | **Eastchester** _18_

Cornetta's Seafood | **Piermont** _13_

Creek | **Purchase** _15_

Doc's | **New Preston** _22_

NEW Dragonfly Grille | _-_
Woodstock

Ebb Tide | **Port Chester**	20	Striped Bass | **Tarrytown**	16
☒ Equus | **Tarrytown**	26	Sunset Cove | **Tarrytown**	15
☒ Escoffier | **Hyde Pk**	26	Tavern at Highlands | **Garrison**	23
☒ F.I.S.H. | **Port Chester**	23	☒ Thomas Henkelmann |	29
NEW Flirt Sushi | **Irvington**	20	**Greenwich**	
Granite Springs | **Granite Spr**	20	Torches on Hudson | **Newburgh**	15
G.W. Tavern | **Wash Depot**	18	Traditions 118 | **Somers**	19
Harvest Café | **New Paltz**	24	Troutbeck | **Amenia**	18
☒ Harvest/Hud. |	22	☒ Valley/Garrison | **Garrison**	26
Hastings/Hud		Velvet Monkey | **Monroe**	20
Hopkins Inn | **New Preston**	18	☒ Vertigo | **Nyack**	18
Hudson Hse. Inn | **Cold Spring**	21	White Hart | **Salisbury**	18

WINNING WINE LISTS

Il Sorriso | **Irvington**	20	Alba's | **Port Chester**	23
Imperial Wok | **Somers**	18	Aloi | **New Canaan**	24
Le Chambord | **Hopewell Jct**	22	Aroma Thyme | **Ellenville**	20
☒ Le Château | **S Salem**	25	☒ Bear Cafe | **Bearsville**	23
Lena's | **Nyack**	21	Bennett's Steak | **Stamford**	20
L'Escale | **Greenwich**	21	☒ Bernard's | **Ridgefield**	26
Lia's Mtn. View | **Pine Plains**	16	Bistro 22 | **Bedford**	23
Lighthouse/Hudson | **Piermont**	16	☒ Blue Hill/Stone | **Poc Hills**	27
Locust Tree | **New Paltz**	21	Boulders Inn | **New Preston**	21
Maggie's Krooked | **Tanners**	–	☒ Buffet/Gare | **Hastings/Hud**	26
Main Course/Alum. | **Poughkp**	20	Cafe Tamayo | **Saugerties**	24
Mamma Francesca | **New Roch**	19	☒ Caterina de Medici | **Hyde Pk**	26
Marion's Country | **Woodstock**	22	Cathryn's | **Cold Spring**	22
Mohonk Mtn. Hse. | **New Paltz**	17	Cava Wine | **New Canaan**	22
☒ Monteverde | **Cortlandt**	21	Chez Jean-Pierre | **Stamford**	22
Mount Fuji | **Hillburn**	21	Ciao! Cafe | **Danbury**	21
Old Drovers Inn | **Dover Plains**	23	Cosimo's Brick | **Newburgh**	20
Olde Stone Mill | **Tuck**	15	☒ Crabtree's | **Chappaqua**	24
Pamela's Traveling | **Newburgh**	18	NEW Duo | **Stamford**	–
Paradise B&G | **Stamford**	13	☒ Elm St. Oyster | **Greenwich**	24
Peekamoose | **Big Indian**	25	Emerson | **Woodstock**	18
Raccoon Saloon | **Marlboro**	19	☒ Emilio Rist. | **Harrison**	25
NEW Rani Mahal | **Mamaro**	–	Enzo's | **Mamaro**	18
River Bank | **Cornwall/Hud**	25	☒ Equus | **Tarrytown**	26
River Cafe | **New Milford**	17	☒ Escoffier | **Hyde Pk**	26
River Club | **Nyack**	16	Flames Steak | **Briarcliff Manor**	20
River Grill | **Newburgh**	21	Frankie & Johnnie's | **Rye**	22
Riverview | **Cold Spring**	24	☒ Freelance Café | **Piermont**	28
Ruby's Hotel | **Freehold**	–	Gaia | **Greenwich**	24
Sabatiello's | **Stamford**	18	Harry's | **Hartsdale**	19
NEW Shadows | **Poughkp**	–	☒ Harvest/Hud. |	22
St. Andrew's Cafe | **Hyde Pk**	24	**Hastings/Hud**	
Stonehenge | **Ridgefield**	23		

Hostaria Mazzei | **Port Chester** 21
Hudson Hse. Inn | **Cold Spring** 21
Hudson's Ribs | **Fishkill** 18
Z Il Barilotto | **Fishkill** 26
Z Il Cenàcolo | **Newburgh** 27
Il Falco | **Stamford** 22
Il Sorriso | **Irvington** 20
NEW Il Teatro | **Mamaro** 21
Z Jean-Louis | **Greenwich** 27
La Bretagne | **Stamford** 23
La Camelia | **Mt. Kisco** 21
Z La Crémaillère | **Bedford** 27
Z La Panetière | **Rye** 27
Le Chambord | **Hopewell Jct** 22
Le Fontane | **Katonah** 21
L'Europe | **S Salem** 24
Z Luca Rist. | **Wilton** 27
Z Lusardi's | **Larch** 23
Marco | **Lake Mahopac** 22
Melting Pot | **Darien** 20
Meritage | **Scarsdale** 22
Z Morton's Steak | **Stamford** 24
NEW Napa & Co. | **Stamford** -
Northern Spy Cafe | **High Falls** 16
Ocean 211 | **Stamford** 24

Old Drovers Inn | **Dover Plains** 23
Z Ondine | **Danbury** 26
Peter Pratt's Inn | **Yorktown** 23
Z Rebeccas | **Greenwich** 26
Rustico | **Scarsdale** 20
Z Ruth's Chris | **Tarrytown** 23
Z Sapore | **Fishkill** 26
Sterling Inn | **New Roch** 20
Swoon Kitchenbar | **Hudson** 24
Z Tango Grill | **White Pl** 23
Telluride | **Stamford** 24
Terra Rustica | **Briarcliff Manor** 20
Z Thomas Moran's | **New Preston** 25
Trotters | **White Pl** 24
Tuscan Oven | **Mt. Kisco** 19
Underhills Crossing | **Bronxville** 21
Z Valbella | **multi. loc.** 25
Z Valley/Garrison | **Garrison** 26
Via Nove | **Fishkill** 19
Vuli | **Stamford** 17
Willett House | **Port Chester** 23
Would | **Highland** 23
Z Xaviar's | **Piermont** 29

THE BERKSHIRES
DIRECTORY

	FOOD	DECOR	SERVICE	COST

TOP FOOD

	Restaurant	Cuisine
26	Blantyre	New American/French
	Old Inn on Green	New American
	Wheatleigh	New American/French
24	John Andrews	New American
	Bizen	Japanese

Aegean Breeze, The *Mediterranean* | 18 | 15 | 18 | $37 |

Great Barrington | 327 Stockbridge Rd. (Rte. 183) | 413-528-4001 | www.aegean-breeze.com

Proponents of this "lively" Great Barrington Mediterranean praise the "good grilled fish even though it's far from the ocean" and "tasty Greek dishes" served by a "convivial chef-owner" and "pleasant" staff in a taverna-style setting with white stucco and blue doors; but the less enthused assert "the food has slipped as the prices have risen."

Aroma Bar & Grill *Indian*   ▽ 22 | 12 | 22 | $31 |

Great Barrington | 485 Main St. (bet. Maple Ave. & Pope St.) | 413-528-3116 | www.aromabarandgrill.com

Fans of "authentic" Indian fare "drop everything" and head to this newish spot "slightly removed from the frenzy of Great Barrington", where "well-fixed" "classic" "savory" dishes (with "wonderful vegetarian options") come courtesy of a "gracious" chef-owner and "earnest staff"; if you can't "ignore" the "drab decor", just go for "takeout."

Asters *Steak* | 16 | 20 | 18 | $38 |

Pittsfield | 1015 South St. (Dan Fox Dr.) | 413-499-2075 | www.berkshiredining.net

A renovated 1790s farmhouse with warm, spacious rooms done up in cream and chocolate conjures "casual elegance" at this Pittsfield surf 'n' turfer; while surveyors are split on the quality of the food ("good" vs "uninspired"), wallet-watchers single out the 4–6 PM "early-bird special" at $13.95 as "the best deal."

Baba Louie's Sourdough Pizza *Pizza* | 23 | 11 | 18 | $21 |

Great Barrington | 286 Main St./Rte. 7 (bet. Church & Railroad Sts.) | 413-528-8100 | www.babalouiessourdoughpizzacompany.com

"Mighty tasty" sourdough "pizza with pizzazz", plus "fabulous salads", "great pastas", "good soups" and other organic offerings keep this Great Barrington "hole-in-the-wall" "swamped"; "simple", tiny, "kid-friendly" digs mean there's often a "line out the door", but it's a winner that's "worth the wait"; N.B. there's a newer offshoot in Hudson, NY.

Barrington Brewery & Restaurant *American* | 13 | 13 | 16 | $23 |

Great Barrington | 420 Stockbridge Rd./Rte. 7 N. (off Rte. 23) | 413-528-8282

"Local beers" "have center stage" at this "popular, noisy" Great Barrington microbrewery set in a "barnlike building"; though critics quip the "typical" "all-American chow" is "mediocrity at its finest", some families like the "something-for-everyone menu" and "reasonable" prices and make it a pit stop after skiing.

Bistro Zinc *French*

21 | 21 | 18 | $46

Lenox | 56 Church St. (bet. Franklin & Housatonic Sts.) | 413-637-8800 | www.bistrozinc.com

Lenox's "sophisticated" slice of "SoHo in the Berkshires" offers "enjoyable" French bistro cuisine in a "comfortable" yet "chic" mirrored setting that puts the "beautiful people at ease"; though some say it's "no longer at the top of its game" and find the staff "a bit snippy", it remains "the hot reservation in season", not least for its "happening bar."

Z Bizen Restaurant *Japanese*

24 | 19 | 18 | $37

Great Barrington | 17 Railroad St. (Rte. 7) | 413-528-4343

"Talkative" chef-owner Michael Marcus' "shockingly good" "wacky combo rolls" and "tasty" "grilled items" are the draws at this "always-packed" Great Barrington Japanese; to escape "literally rubbing elbows" at "jammed-in tables", diners can reserve in the adjoining kaiseki section for a prix fixe menu ($40–$150) that's offered in "lovely, serene" tatami rooms.

Z Blantyre M *American/French*

26 | 28 | 27 | VE

Lenox | Blantyre | 16 Blantyre Rd. (Rte. 20) | 413-637-3556 | www.blantyre.com

It's "superb in every way" sigh sybarites about this "absolutely beautiful" Tudor-style Relais & Châteaux inn on 100 Lenox acres; begin with a "cocktail on the veranda", then savor "exquisite" New American–French cuisine, voted No. 1 for Food in the Berkshires, served with "old-world elegance" in a "romantic setting" with "harp or piano music wafting"; natch, such "a wow of a place" requires a "splurge", but "save up and treat yourself" to "life like one should be born to"; N.B. jacket and tie required at dinner and no children under 12 permitted.

Bombay M *Indian*

21 | 15 | 18 | $31

Lee | Black Swan Inn | 435 Laurel St. (Lake Rd.) | 413-243-6731 | www.fineindiandining.com

Curryphiles seeking culinary "nirvana" head to this "top-notch Indian" for "nicely spiced" "tasty morsels" that include a "wonderful lunch buffet" that's an "excellent value" and a "Sunday spread" that the robust declare is "roll-out-the-door good"; the Lee location has a "lake view", but its recently redecorated older sibling in Westport, CT does not.

Brix *French*

▽ 23 | 21 | 25 | $30

Pittsfield | 40 West St. (bet. McKay & North Sts.) | 413-236-9463 | www.brixwinebar.com

"Helping make Pittsfield a new city" is "young, knowledgeable" chef-owner Patrick Spencer's two-year-old French bistro/wine bar offering a "limited" but "tasty", "sophisticated light menu" along with "wonderful wines by the glass or bottle"; industrial-chic decor is warmed up with burgundy banquettes, golden walls and a zinc bar in a narrow space that already "needs to double in size" to fit all its fans.

	FOOD	DECOR	SERVICE	COST

Café Latino *Nuevo Latino* | 22 | 23 | 21 | $25 |

North Adams | Mass MoCA | 1111 Mass MoCA Way (Marshall St.) | 413-662-2004 | www.cafelatinoatmoca.com

"Vibrant" "contemporary" art is an apt backdrop for this "innovative" Nuevo Latino (a sibling of Williamstown's Mezze Bistro) in North Adams' Mass MoCA museum complex; it manages to be both "elegant and kid-friendly at the same time", with "service that raises the bar" for the area, and there are "affordable" prices to boot.

Café Lucia Ⓜ *Italian* | 20 | 17 | 19 | $47 |

Lenox | 80 Church St. (bet. Franklin & Housatonic Sts.) | 413-637-2640

Surveyors are split on this long-standing Lenox Italian; supporters say "excellent" dishes like "the house specialty osso buco", a "respectable" wine cellar and "pleasant" dining porch make it "a favorite for Tanglewood weekends"; but critics claim "overpriced" food, an "overcrowded" interior and "hectic" high-season vibe can make for a "disappointing" experience.

Castle Street Cafe *American/French* | 19 | 18 | 20 | $37 |

Great Barrington | 10 Castle St. (Main St.) | 413-528-5244 | www.castlestreetcafe.com

With "oldsters in the nicely decorated main room and hipsters in the bar", this "popular" Great Barrington American-French gears up to both groups with two menus, one with "satisfying" casual fare, the other with more "upscale" entrees like cassoulet; yes, there's "a din" when it gets "crowded", but it's offset by "friendly service" and outdone by "terrific jazz" on weekends (with nightly shows in summer).

Chez Nous *French* | 23 | 19 | 23 | $43 |

Lee | 150 Main St. (Academy St.) | 413-243-6397 | www.cheznousbistro.com

"Finally, a top-notch restaurant" "in blue-collar Lee" assert admirers of this two-year-old French bistro offering "excellent food" "prepared with great care by the owners" – Franck Tessier oversees the savories, while spouse "Rachel Portnoy bakes wonderful desserts"; the decor in the "converted house" is "a little kitschy but charming" and the service is "really warm", so overall, it's "thoroughly enjoyable."

Church Street Cafe *American* | 20 | 16 | 19 | $38 |

Lenox | 65 Church St. (bet. Franklin & Housatonic Sts.) | 413-637-2745 | www.churchstreetcafe.biz

"Simple", "tasty", "unpretentious" New American cooking draws a "crowd" to this "pleasant", "very Berkshirean" Lenox "classic" where three "casual" rooms exude a "cozy" vibe, as does the "warm greeting"; eating lunch on "the front porch in nice weather is also a treat."

Cranwell Resort, Spa & Golf Club *American* | 21 | 23 | 21 | $50 |

Lenox | 55 Lee Rd./Rte. 20 (Rte. 7) | 413-637-1364 | www.cranwell.com

"Opulent decor" in a "lovely" Gilded Age "manor" plus a staff that "aims to please" create a "refined" atmosphere for "high-end" New American fare, whether it's served in the Wyndhurst or Music Room

	FOOD	DECOR	SERVICE	COST

restaurants at this Lenox resort – "oh, and the food is pretty darn good too"; those who find those settings "a bit stuffy" hit Sloane's Tavern for pub grub, while dieters suggest "try the spa food" in the cafe.

Dakota *Steak*
| 16 | 16 | 16 | $31 |

Pittsfield | 1035 South St. (Dan Fox Dr.) | 413-499-7900 | www.steakseafood.com

Although "not for serious food people", this "no-frills" steakhouse chain is a "family pleaser", delivering "reasonably priced" "formulaic" fare, a "groaning salad bar" and a Sunday brunch that attracts "hordes", especially those with "hungry teens" to fill up; service can be "inept", but the "rustic", "faux -lodge" "rambling room" complete with stuffed animals "entertains fidgety kids."

Dish Café Bistro *American*
| 19 | 10 | 18 | $30 |

Lenox | 37 Church St. (bet. Rte. 183 & Sunset Ave.) | 413-637-1800

At lunch, there are "interesting sandwiches, hearty soups and fresh salads" at this "cute" Lenox New American offspring of Stockbridge's Once Upon a Table; at dinner, tablecloths and candles dress up the tables, but the "teeny" space still remains "cramped."

Egremont Inn **M** *American*
| 21 | 20 | 22 | $43 |

South Egremont | Egremont Inn | 10 Old Sheffield Rd. (Rte. 23) | 413-528-2111 | www.egremontinn.com

It's "quaint and peaceful as long as you don't sit near the band on music nights" is what surveyors say about this "welcoming" South Egremont Traditional American country inn set in a circa-1780 stagecoach stop; the "food is good" in the main dining room, but some regulars prefer to "sit in the lovely Tap Room" and order from "the less-expensive menu."

Elizabeth's **M**⚐ *Eclectic*
| 23 | 11 | 22 | $32 |

Pittsfield | 1264 East St. (Newell St.) | 413-448-8244

This "out-of-the-way" Pittsfield Eclectic offers an "idiosyncratic home-cooked" menu of nine "fresh", "delicious" pastas and two other dishes with international influences, plus a "world-class salad"; owner Tom Ellis is a "likable character", who peps up the "nothing atmosphere", and if the "cash-only policy is off-putting", just write a check or an I.O.U.

Elm Court Inn **M** *Continental/Swiss*
| 22 | 17 | 21 | $47 |

North Egremont | 227 Rte. 71 (Rte. 23) | 413-528-0325 | www.elmcourtinn.com

"If you can't get to Zurich", you'll find "good Swiss-Continental cooking" at this North Egremont "institution"; "once the husband-and-wife owners get to know you", there's such "warm hospitality" in the circa-1790 inn that regulars find they can overlook the "tired", "time-warp" decor and just "linger."

Fin *Japanese*
| ▽ 27 | 17 | 20 | $35 |

Lenox | 27 Housatonic St. (bet. Church & Main Sts.) | 413-637-9171

"Super-fresh, super-good sushi" along with cooked dishes are the draws at this "super-small" Lenox Japanese co-owned by Jason

	FOOD	DECOR	SERVICE	COST

Macioge of Bistro Zinc and his brother; the few who've found the sleek black-wood space with a red-lacquer bar say it "fills up quickly", but if that happens, it's "great for takeout."

Firefly *American*

| 19 | 17 | 18 | $42 |

Lenox | 71 Church St. (Housatonic St.) | 413-637-2700 | www.fireflylenox.com

Is this "the Berkshires or West 72nd Street"? ask those with more than a flicker of interest in Laura Shack's Lenox New American; most maintain the food is "good and getting better", whether for "full meals" taken in the warm-looking dual dining rooms, "small plates" "at the bar" or outside on the patio.

Gideon's Ⓜ *Eclectic*

| 23 | 20 | 21 | $39 |

North Adams | 34 Holden St. (Rte. 2) | 413-664-9449 | www.gideonsrestaurant.com

Chef Bill Gideon "struts his stuff" in the open kitchen of his North Adams Eclectic, turning out "well-executed", "surprisingly good" eats like he once did during his Four Seasons hotel gig; the "comfortable" red-and-black storefront space is "a mecca for those in search of an après-art museum meal" (Mass MoCA is nearby) and "usually crowded", so "you may want earplugs."

Gramercy Bistro *American/Eclectic*

| ▽ 24 | 19 | 21 | $40 |

North Adams | 24-26 Marshall St. (Center St.) | 413-663-5300 | www.gramercybistro.com

The "limited" but "excellent" menu of "first-rate", "creative" New American–Eclectic fare relies on organic and locally grown ingredients, making this "quiet", chef-owned North Adams spot opposite Mass MoCA a "gem"; dark woods, yellow walls and white damask cloths create a chic bistro atmosphere that evokes "New York City style but at Berkshire prices."

Helsinki Cafe *Eclectic/Scandinavian*

| 18 | 16 | 16 | $29 |

Great Barrington | 284 Main St. (Railroad St.) | 413-528-3394 | www.clubhelsinkiweb.com

"Where else can you get borscht and quesadillas on the same menu?" ask aficionados of this "funky" Great Barrington "original" dishing up "homestyle" Scandinavian eats with Eclectic "ethnic" touches; service is "up and down", but the vibe is "cool" "'50s Greenwich Village", tabs are "inexpensive" and the "live music venue" next door is simply "the best."

Jae's Inn of Williamstown *Pan-Asian*
(fka Jae's Inn)

| 22 | - | 20 | $31 |

Williamstown | 777 Cold Spring Rd. (Taconic Trail) | 413-458-8032 | www.jaesinn.com

While there's a name change reflecting its recent move from North Adams to larger Williamstown digs, the menu at this branch of a popular Boston Pan-Asian chainlet remains the same; fans who find it "fun to experiment" with the "consistently good" range of dishes can still choose from Korean, sushi or Thai offerings.

☑ John Andrews *American* | 24 | 21 | 22 | $52 |

South Egremont | Rte. 23 (Blunt Rd.) | 413-528-3469 |
www.jarestaurant.com

This "chic" spot "in the sticks" of South Egremont features "expertly prepared" New American cuisine, "luscious desserts", a "terrific wine list" and service that "generally shines"; the "pretty", "serene" room is warmed by orange walls and a fireplace, although those in the mood "for a lighter, less formal meal" head to the bar or the terrace "when weather permits"; it's "pricey" so perhaps "it's the place to let your weekend guests take you."

Mezze Bistro + Bar *American* | 24 | 22 | 23 | $41 |

Williamstown | 16 Water St. (Rte. 2) | 413-458-0123 | www.mezzeinc.com

"It's amazing that this is the only really good place to eat" "in a fancy college town with frequent visits from lots of wealthy, knowledgeable parents" observe admirers of this "classy" yet "not chichi" Williamstown New American; a "sophisticated menu" of "fantastic" food is served by an "educated" staff in a "warm, low-key" setting done up with chocolate hues and classical columns, so it's no surprise "urban transplants" pile in to "impress their city guests."

Mill on the Floss, The Ⓜ *French* | 23 | 22 | 23 | $51 |

New Ashford | 342 Rte. 7 (Rte. 43) | 413-458-9123 |
www.millonthefloss.com

"Old-fashioned in the best sense", this "country quaint" New Ashford spot "keeps on ticking", turning out "classic" French "feasts" in a "delightful" 18th-century farmhouse; while a few cynics say the menu is "a little faded", romantics revel in the "wonderful service" and "pretty" copper-colored candlelit setting.

Morgan House *New England* | 17 | 17 | 19 | $37 |

Lee | Morgan Hse. | 33 Main St. (Mass. Tpke., exit 2) | 413-243-3661 | www.morganhouseinn.com

Surveyors are split over this New England Regional in an 1817 Lee inn near the Berkshire Mall; loyalists like the "good", "homestyle" fare (like meatloaf and turkey dinners), "cozy" setting and "bargain-for-the-Berkshires" prices, but opponents opine it's "uninspired" and "needs an overhaul"; N.B. a recent change in ownership may outdate the above scores.

Napa *Californian* | 20 | 15 | 16 | $34 |

Lenox | 30 Church St. (bet. Housatonic & Walker Sts.) | 413-637-3204

Like the name says, the wine list emphasizes Napa labels, but there are also "bountiful portions" of "good" "Californian cuisine" (think "fresh salads" and soups) at this "relaxing", "reasonably priced" Lenox spot; the interior is "homey" and there's a "porch for people-watching."

☑ Old Inn on the Green *American* | 26 | 26 | 25 | $60 |

New Marlborough | Old Inn on the Green | 134 Hartsville-New Marlborough Rd./Rte. 57 (Rte. 272) | 413-229-7924 | www.oldinn.com

At this "sublime" New American "in the middle of nowhere" (aka New Marlborough), there's "no electricity" in the 1760 inn's dining rooms, so it's all "candlelight and fireplaces" as a "romantic" backdrop for chef-owner Peter Platt's "outrageously good food" and "exemplary service"; it makes for an "expensively priced" "luxurious night out", but bargain-hunters believe the midweek $30 prix fixe is the "best deal in the Berkshires."

Old Mill *American*
23 | 21 | 23 | $45

South Egremont | 53 Main St. (Rte. 41) | 413-528-1421
A "gorgeous open fireplace" adds to the "warm welcome" at this "classic", "clubby" South Egremont American that's been a "haven" for going on three decades; "well-prepared" "filling" fare is served by an "attentive" staff in a circa-1797 mill where old wood beams and a "comfortable bar" spell "cozy" yet "not too fussy"; the only "drawback": no rezzies for parties under five can make for "a long wait on weekends."

Once Upon a Table *American/Continental*
19 | 15 | 22 | $35

Stockbridge | The Mews off Main St. | 36 Main St. (bet. Elm St. & Rte. 7) | 413-298-3870
"Hidden" in "an alleyway" off Stockbridge's Main Street, this "cute" New American–Continental turns out "nicely flavored" fare via an "attentive" staff; still, claustrophobes complain "talk about cramped" – the space is roughly "the size of a minute."

Pearl's Ⓜ *American*
22 | 22 | 18 | $48

Great Barrington | 47 Railroad St. (Main St.) | 413-528-7767 | www.pearlsrestaurant.com
Great Barrington's "hip" New American "does casual elegance better than most", from an "always-good" "menu that shines" to "stunning", "sleek", "spacious" rooms and a "swank bar" for "snacks"; but detractors who deem it "overrated and overpriced" dis "disorganized" service ("you mean you both wanted your steaks at the same time?") and hiss "hey, guys, lose the NYC attitude."

Prime Italian Steakhouse & Bar *Italian/Steak*
▽ 22 | 21 | 21 | $45

Lenox | 15 Franklin St. (Rte. 7A) | 413-637-2998 | www.primelenox.com
"Come hungry and with a large budget" counsel carnivores crowding into this "cool", two-year-old Southern Italian steakhouse in Lenox for "perfect meat" and "fresh" fare like homemade gnocchi from chef-owner Gennaro Gallo; the "slick" digs include glass-enclosed booths that frost over at the touch of a button and a "crazy-looking bar" with a lit-up top.

Red Lion Inn *New England*
17 | 22 | 20 | $42

Stockbridge | Red Lion Inn | 30 Main St./Rte. 102 (Rte. 7) | 413-298-5545 | www.redlioninn.com
"Still an old charmer", this 1773 Stockbridge "dowager" delivers New England "upscale comfort food" in both its "sedate" main dining room and more casual Widow Bingham's Tavern; even if it's all "a bit touristy" and "tired", the staff is "welcoming" and the pace "leisurely", so go "at least once", if only for "a tall one" "in the courtyard."

Rouge M *French*   22 | 17 | 15 | $47

West Stockbridge | 3 Center St. (Hotel St.) | 413-232-4111 |
www.rougerestaurant.com

There's "a bit of France" in West Stockbridge at this "buzzing" bistro
where "husband William Merelle does good work in the kitchen",
turning out "excellent" "classics", while "wife Maggie charms the
front of the house"; service is "unpredictable" and it can be "noisy",
yet "crowds" still come to the "arty" space, particularly for "inexpensive" tapas in the bar or to "dine alfresco on starry nights";
N.B. dinner only, Wednesday–Sunday.

NEW Rte. 7 Grill *American/BBQ*   – | – | – | I

Great Barrington | 999 S. Main St. (bet. Brookside & Lime Kiln Rds.) |
413-528-3235 | www.route7grill.com

Great Barrington BBQ buffs head to this madeover '50s roadhouse
yearling for local slow-smoked meats (plus occasional pig roasts),
while non-'cueheads queue for burgers, chops and other hearty
American eats; a huge, double-sided granite fireplace forms a
centerpiece in the spacious, woodsy room where there's also a
horseshoe-shaped birch bar to belly up to.

Seven Hills Country Inn &   – | – | – | E
Restaurant M *American*

Lenox | 40 Plunkett St. (Rte. 7) | 413-637-0060 | www.sevenhillsinn.com
"One of the most beautiful places" in the Berkshires, this "elegant"
Tudor-style mansion, near Edith Wharton's estate in Lenox, has dining
rooms with five fireplaces, ornamental carved wood and rich furnishings; some surveyors say the New American fare is "so good",
they'd like to return to "have their wedding here."

Shiro Sushi & Hibachi *Japanese*   ▽ 19 | 16 | 20 | $30

Great Barrington | 105 Stockbridge Rd. (bet. Rtes. 23 & 183) |
413-528-1898

"Though not as fancy as some", this "busy" Great Barrington
Japanese "compares favorably" foodwise, offering a "very large
menu" with "enjoyable" sushi and grilled dishes that "you watch being made"; "sincere service" from a "nice staff" helps warm up a
space that's "sprawling and a little austere."

Siam Square Thai Cuisine *Thai*   18 | 14 | 18 | $27

Great Barrington | 290 Main St. (Railroad St.) | 413-644-9119 |
www.siamsquares.com

"Good" "straight-up Thai" awaits diners at this Great Barrington spot
where "flavorful" noodle dishes, dumplings and other "authentic", affordable eats are served by a "warm" staff; the "roomy" setting is
"quiet" and "simple" but for a few "stylized" Siamese touches.

NEW Spice S *American*   23 | 26 | 21 | $44

Pittsfield | 297 North St. (bet. Summer & Union Sts.) | 413-443-1234 |
www.spice-restaurant.com

An "up-and-comer", this "sophisticated" American newcomer with
"imaginative" fare is "just what Pittsfield needed" to help "spice up"

its revival say supporters; a "well-trained" staff presides over a "spacious" setting in a transformed department store with big windows overlooking Main Street; a "buzzing" vibe, "busy bar" and separate lounge with entertainment make for a "hot"-spot feel.

Spigalina *Italian/Mediterranean*
23 | 18 | 20 | $44

Lenox | 80 Main St. (Franklin St.) | 413-637-4455 |
www.spigalina.com

"High-quality" Southern Italian cooking that "reaches for haute" and "friendly, unobtrusive service" make this "hopping" Lenox bistro "a definite winner"; whether you choose to dine in the "warm" dining room with its tiled floors and ochre walls or out on the "airy, pleasant porch", it's "good before Tanglewood" and "worth the price."

Stagecoach Tavern 🅢 🅜 *American*
▽ 22 | 24 | 19 | $37

Sheffield | Race Brook Lodge | Rte. 41 (Salisbury Rd.) | 413-229-8585 |
www.stagecoachtavern.net

It's "not too fancy, not too rustic", there's just a "nice publike feeling" at this "atmospheric" 1829 Sheffield tavern with its fireplaces, beams and wooden floors; a "friendly" staff delivers "cosmopolitan" American "comfort food" with a focus on natural, organic produce (the "grass-fed burger can't be beat") that's highlighted during Thursday night's three-course community farm table dinners for $36.

Sullivan Station Restaurant *New England*
16 | 16 | 18 | $28

Lee | 109 Railroad St. (Mass. Tpke., exit 2) | 413-243-2082

"As long as you don't expect fine dining", this "kid-friendly" Lee locale turning out "fair-to-good", inexpensive New England classics in an old "restored railroad station" may be the ticket; locomotive-lovers like the "bit of nostalgia" thrown in, especially when the Berkshire Scenic Railway makes a stop.

Thai Garden *Thai*
18 | 14 | 15 | $23

Williamstown | 27 Spring St. (Rte. 2) | 413-458-0004

Surveyors are split over this Asian in Williamstown: wallet-watchers call its "nicely presented", "inexpensive" eats the "best choice for a Thai fix in the sticks" of the "student-oriented" area, but sophisticates sniff it's merely "middle of the road."

Trattoria Il Vesuvio 🅢 *Italian*
17 | 16 | 19 | $34

Lenox | 242 Pittsfield Rd. (bet. Lime Kiln & New Lenox Rds.) |
413-637-4904 | www.trattoria-vesuvio.com

"They love children" at this "cozy", "typical red-checked-cloth Italian" in Lenox that produces "solid" "red-sauce" eats in a rustic, converted stable setting; those less fired-up about the quality of the "no-surprises" cooking suggest the best bet when it comes to ordering is to "stay simple."

Trattoria Rustica *Italian*
22 | 22 | 20 | $45

Pittsfield | 26 McKay St. (West St.) | 413-499-1192 |
www.trattoria-rustica.com

Supporters of this Pittsfield Southern Italian praise the chef-owner's "professional execution" of "excellent", "imaginative" Neapolitan dishes; stone and brick walls, tile floors and lanterns set a "sooth-ing" "Euro cavelike" mood that can make for a "romantic dinner."

Truc Orient Express *Vietnamese*   22 16 19 $31
West Stockbridge | 3 Harris St. (Main St.) | 413-232-4204
"For as long as anyone can remember", the "very nice" family who owns this West Stockbridge "favorite" has been dispensing "excel-lent" Vietnamese cooking" ("try the singing pancakes"); the setting is a "serene", "unpretentious" space dressed up with art and artifacts from their homeland.

20 Railroad Street *Pub Food*   14 13 14 $25
Great Barrington | 20 Railroad St. (Main St.) | 413-528-9345
"Basic" "bar food" is the hallmark at this "pleasantly untrendy" Great Barrington American "standby", an "everyday joint" where "locals" "take the kids" for a "price-is-right" bite; the digs are definitely in need of a "serious redo", but "no fries is the only real complaint."

Union Bar & Grill *American/Italian*   15 15 16 $34
Great Barrington | 293 Main St. (Railroad St.) | 413-528-6228
"Food is secondary" at this "lively" Great Barrington "hangout" of-fering "a few tasty dishes" (like "brontosaurus"-sized ribs) on its Italian-American menu; but "noise", a "trying-too-hard-to-be-hip" attitude and a sense the place is "slipping" cause some to secede.

☑ Wheatleigh *American/French*   26 27 25 VE
Lenox | Wheatleigh | Hawthorne Rd. (Rte. 183) | 413-637-0610 | www.wheatleigh.com
"European grace meets American warmth" at this "stunning" "Gilded Age palace" in Lenox where both the "beautiful" dining room and "glassed-in veranda" overlook mountains and a lake, and "creativity in the kitchen" results in a "divine menu" of "amazing" New American–French fare; while a few sniff about "minuscule por-tions", a "pretentious staff" and "stratospheric" prices, most main-tain "it's worth it for that once-in-a-blue-moon special occasion"; N.B. jacket suggested.

Xicohtencatl *Mexican*   18 18 18 $30
Great Barrington | 50 Stockbridge Rd. (Rte. 23) | 413-528-2002
"Not at all the typical taco and enchilada house", this Great Barrington Mexican offers "the real thing", with some "creative tweaking" for good measure; "large portions", a "huge tequila selection" and a "pleasant" south-of-the-border-style setting add to its appeal.

THE BERKSHIRES
INDEXES

Cuisines

Includes restaurant names, neighborhoods and Food ratings. 🔣 indicates places with the highest ratings, popularity and importance.

AMERICAN (NEW)

🔣 Blantyre | **Lenox**	26
Castle St. | **Great Barr**	19
Church St. Cafe | **Lenox**	20
Cranwell Resort | **Lenox**	21
Dish Café | **Lenox**	19
Firefly | **Lenox**	19
Gramercy Bistro | **N Adams**	24
🔣 John Andrews | **S Egremont**	24
Mezze Bistro | **Williamstown**	24
🔣 Old Inn/Green | **New Marl**	26
Once Upon | **Stockbridge**	19
Pearl's | **Great Barr**	22
Seven Hills Inn | **Lenox**	–
🔣 Wheatleigh | **Lenox**	26

AMERICAN (TRADITIONAL)

Barrington Brew | **Great Barr**	13
Egremont Inn | **S Egremont**	21
Old Mill | **S Egremont**	23
NEW Rte. 7 Grill | **Great Barr**	–
NEW Spice | **Pittsfield**	23
Stagecoach Tavern | **Sheffield**	22
20 Railroad St. | **Great Barr**	14
Union B&G | **Great Barr**	15

BARBECUE

NEW Rte. 7 Grill | **Great Barr**	–

CALIFORNIAN

Napa | **Lenox**	20

CONTINENTAL

Elm Court | **N Egremont**	22
Once Upon | **Stockbridge**	19

ECLECTIC

Elizabeth's | **Pittsfield**	23
Gideon's | **N Adams**	23
Gramercy Bistro | **N Adams**	24
Helsinki | **Great Barr**	18

FRENCH

🔣 Blantyre | **Lenox**	26
Mill on the Floss | **New Ashford**	23
🔣 Wheatleigh | **Lenox**	26

FRENCH (BISTRO)

Bistro Zinc | **Lenox**	21
Brix | **Pittsfield**	23
Chez Nous | **Lee**	23
Rouge | **W Stockbridge**	22

FRENCH (NEW)

Castle St. | **Great Barr**	19

INDIAN

Aroma B&G | **Great Barr**	22
Bombay | **Lee**	21

ITALIAN

(N=Northern; S=Southern)

Café Lucia | **Lenox**	20
Prime Italian | S | **Lenox**	22
Spigalina | S | **Lenox**	23
Tratt. Rustica | S | **Pittsfield**	22
Tratt. Il Vesuvio | **Lenox**	17
Union B&G | **Great Barr**	15

JAPANESE

(* sushi specialist)

🔣 Bizen* | **Great Barr**	24
Fin* | **Lenox**	27
Shiro Sushi* | **Great Barr**	19

MEDITERRANEAN

Aegean Breeze | **Great Barr**	18
Spigalina | **Lenox**	23

MEXICAN

Xicohtencatl | **Great Barr**	18

NEW ENGLAND

Morgan House | **Lee**	17
Red Lion Inn | **Stockbridge**	17
Sullivan Station | **Lee**	16

NUEVO LATINO

Café Latino | **N Adams**	22

PAN-ASIAN

Jae's Inn | **Williamstown**	22

PIZZA

Baba Louie's | **Great Barr**	23

PUB FOOD

20 Railroad St. | **Great Barr**	14

SCANDINAVIAN

Helsinki | **Great Barr**	18

STEAKHOUSES

Asters | **Pittsfield**	16
Dakota | **Pittsfield**	16
Prime Italian | **Lenox**	22

SWISS

Elm Court | **N Egremont**	22

THAI

Siam Sq. Thai | **Great Barr**	18
Thai Garden | **Williamstown**	18

VIETNAMESE

Truc Orient | **W Stockbridge**	22

Locations

Includes restaurant names, cuisines and Food ratings. ⚡ indicates places with the highest ratings, popularity and importance.

Berkshires

GREAT BARRINGTON

Aegean Breeze	*Med.*	18
Aroma B&G	*Indian*	22
Baba Louie's	*Pizza*	23
Barrington Brew	*Amer.*	13
⚡ Bizen	*Jap.*	24
Castle St.	*Amer./French*	19
Helsinki	*Eclectic/Scan.*	18
Pearl's	*Amer.*	22
NEW Rte. 7 Grill	*Amer./BBQ*	–
Shiro Sushi	*Jap.*	19
Siam Sq. Thai	*Thai*	18
20 Railroad St.	*Pub Food*	14
Union B&G	*Amer./Italian*	15
Xicohtencatl	*Mex.*	18

LEE

Bombay	*Indian*	21
Chez Nous	*French*	23
Morgan House	*New Eng.*	17
Sullivan Station	*New Eng.*	16

LENOX

Bistro Zinc	*French*	21
⚡ Blantyre	*Amer./French*	26
Café Lucia	*Italian*	20
Church St. Cafe	*Amer.*	20
Cranwell Resort	*Amer.*	21
Dish Café	*Amer.*	19
Fin	*Jap.*	27
Firefly	*Amer.*	19
Napa	*Calif.*	20
Prime Italian	*Italian/Steak*	22
Seven Hills Inn	*Amer.*	–
Spigalina	*Italian/Med.*	23
Tratt. Il Vesuvio	*Italian*	17
⚡ Wheatleigh	*Amer./French*	26

NEW ASHFORD

Mill on the Floss	*French*	23

NEW MARLBOROUGH/ SANDISFIELD

⚡ Old Inn/Green	*Amer.*	26

NORTH ADAMS

Café Latino	*Nuevo Latino*	22
Gideon's	*Eclectic*	23
Gramercy Bistro	*Amer./Eclectic*	24

NORTH EGREMONT/ SOUTH EGREMONT

Egremont Inn	*Amer.*	21
Elm Court	*Continental/Swiss*	22
⚡ John Andrews	*Amer.*	24
Old Mill	*Amer.*	23

PITTSFIELD

Asters	*Steak*	16
Brix	*French*	23
Dakota	*Steak*	16
Elizabeth's	*Eclectic*	23
NEW Spice	*Amer.*	23
Tratt. Rustica	*Italian*	22

SHEFFIELD

Stagecoach Tavern	*Amer.*	22

STOCKBRIDGE

Once Upon	*Amer./Continental*	19
Red Lion Inn	*New Eng.*	17

WEST STOCKBRIDGE

Rouge	*French*	22
Truc Orient	*Viet.*	22

WILLIAMSTOWN

Jae's Inn	*Pan-Asian*	22
Mezze Bistro	*Amer.*	24
Thai Garden	*Thai*	18

Special Features

Listings cover the best in each category and include restaurant names, locations and Food ratings. Multi-location restaurants' features may vary by branch. ☑ indicates places with the highest ratings, popularity and importance.

BRUNCH

Dakota | **Pittsfield**	16
Pearl's | **Great Barr**	22
☑ Wheatleigh | **Lenox**	26
Xicohtencatl | **Great Barr**	18

BUSINESS DINING

Cranwell Resort | **Lenox**	21
Gideon's | **N Adams**	23
Pearl's | **Great Barr**	22
NEW Spice | **Pittsfield**	23

CATERING

☑ Bizen | **Great Barr**	24
Bombay | **Lee**	21
Castle St. | **Great Barr**	19
☑ John Andrews | **S Egremont**	24
Mezze Bistro | **Williamstown**	24
Red Lion Inn | **Stockbridge**	17
Stagecoach Tavern | **Sheffield**	22
Truc Orient | **W Stockbridge**	22

CHILD-FRIENDLY

(Alternatives to the usual fast-food places; * children's menu available)

Aegean Breeze | **Great Barr**	18
Baba Louie's | **Great Barr**	23
Barrington Brew* | **Great Barr**	13
Bistro Zinc* | **Lenox**	21
Café Lucia | **Lenox**	20
Castle St. | **Great Barr**	19
Church St. Cafe* | **Lenox**	20
Dakota* | **Pittsfield**	16
Egremont Inn* | **S Egremont**	21
Elizabeth's | **Pittsfield**	23
Elm Court | **N Egremont**	22
Morgan House* | **Lee**	17
Old Mill | **S Egremont**	23
Once Upon | **Stockbridge**	19
Red Lion Inn* | **Stockbridge**	17
Rouge | **W Stockbridge**	22
NEW Rte. 7 Grill* | **Great Barr**	-
Shiro Sushi | **Great Barr**	19
Siam Sq. Thai | **Great Barr**	18
Sullivan Station* | **Lee**	16
Thai Garden | **Williamstown**	18
Tratt. Il Vesuvio* | **Lenox**	17
20 Railroad St. | **Great Barr**	14
Xicohtencatl* | **Great Barr**	18

ENTERTAINMENT

(Call for days and times of performances)

☑ Blantyre | varies | **Lenox**	26
Castle St. | jazz/piano | **Great Barr**	19
Egremont Inn | varies | **S Egremont**	21
Helsinki | varies | **Great Barr**	18
Red Lion Inn | varies | **Stockbridge**	17
Seven Hills Inn | varies | **Lenox**	-
Xicohtencatl | varies | **Great Barr**	18

FIREPLACES

☑ Blantyre | **Lenox**	26
Cranwell Resort | **Lenox**	21
Dakota | **Pittsfield**	16
Egremont Inn | **S Egremont**	21
Elm Court | **N Egremont**	22
Helsinki | **Great Barr**	18
Jae's Inn | **Williamstown**	22
☑ John Andrews | **S Egremont**	24
Mill on the Floss | **New Ashford**	23
Morgan House | **Lee**	17
☑ Old Inn/Green | **New Marl**	26
Old Mill | **S Egremont**	23
Red Lion Inn | **Stockbridge**	17
NEW Rte. 7 Grill | **Great Barr**	-
Seven Hills Inn | **Lenox**	-
Stagecoach Tavern | **Sheffield**	22
Truc Orient | **W Stockbridge**	22
☑ Wheatleigh | **Lenox**	26

GAME IN SEASON

Bistro Zinc | **Lenox**	21
☑ Blantyre | **Lenox**	26
Brix | **Pittsfield**	23
Café Lucia | **Lenox**	20
Castle St. | **Great Barr**	19
Church St. Cafe | **Lenox**	20
Cranwell Resort | **Lenox**	21
Egremont Inn | **S Egremont**	21
Elizabeth's | **Pittsfield**	23
Elm Court | **N Egremont**	22
Firefly | **Lenox**	19
Gideon's | **N Adams**	23
Gramercy Bistro | **N Adams**	24

☑ John Andrews | **S Egremont** 24
Mezze Bistro | **Williamstown** 24
☑ Old Inn/Green | **New Marl** 26
Pearl's | **Great Barr** 22
Red Lion Inn | **Stockbridge** 17
Rouge | **W Stockbridge** 22
Seven Hills Inn | **Lenox** –
Stagecoach Tavern | **Sheffield** 22
20 Railroad St. | **Great Barr** 14
☑ Wheatleigh | **Lenox** 26

HISTORIC PLACES

(Year opened; * building)

1750 | Seven Hills Inn* | **Lenox** –
1760 | Old Inn/Green* | 26
  New Marl
1773 | Red Lion Inn* | **Stockbridge** 17
1780 | Egremont Inn* | 21
  S Egremont
1790 | Asters* | **Pittsfield** 16
1797 | Old Mill* | **S Egremont** 23
1817 | Morgan House* | **Lee** 17
1829 | Stagecoach Tavern* | 22
  Sheffield
1839 | Café Lucia* | **Lenox** 20
1840 | Spice* | **Pittsfield** 23
1841 | Chez Nous* | **Lee** 23
1852 | Church St. Cafe* | **Lenox** 20
1893 | Sullivan Station* | **Lee** 16
1893 | Wheatleigh* | **Lenox** 26
1894 | Cranwell Resort* | **Lenox** 21
1900 | Tratt. Il Vesuvio* | **Lenox** 17
1900 | 20 Railroad St.* | 14
  Great Barr
1903 | Gramercy Bistro* | 24
  N Adams
1924 | Brix* | **Pittsfield** 23

JACKET REQUIRED

(* Tie also required)
☑ Blantyre* | **Lenox** 26

MEET FOR A DRINK

Asters | **Pittsfield** 16
Bistro Zinc | **Lenox** 21
Brix | **Pittsfield** 23
Castle St. | **Great Barr** 19
Chez Nous | **Lee** 23
Gramercy Bistro | **N Adams** 24
Helsinki | **Great Barr** 18
Napa | **Lenox** 20
Old Mill | **S Egremont** 23
Pearl's | **Great Barr** 22
Prime Italian | **Lenox** 22
Red Lion Inn | **Stockbridge** 17
NEW Spice | **Pittsfield** 23

Stagecoach Tavern | **Sheffield** 22
20 Railroad St. | **Great Barr** 14

MICROBREWERIES

Barrington Brew | **Great Barr** 13
Red Lion Inn | **Stockbridge** 17

NOTEWORTHY NEWCOMERS

Rte. 7 Grill | **Great Barr** –
Spice | **Pittsfield** 23

OUTDOOR DINING

(G=garden; P=patio; T=terrace)
Aegean Breeze | P | **Great Barr** 18
Barrington Brew | G | **Great Barr** 13
Café Lucia | G, T | **Lenox** 20
Church St. Cafe | P | **Lenox** 20
Egremont Inn | T | **S Egremont** 21
Jae's Inn | T | **Williamstown** 22
☑ John Andrews | T | 24
  S Egremont
☑ Old Inn/Green | T | **New Marl** 26
Red Lion Inn | P | **Stockbridge** 17
Rouge | T | **W Stockbridge** 22
Shiro Sushi | P | **Great Barr** 19
Spigalina | T | **Lenox** 23
Sullivan Station | T | **Lee** 16
Tratt. Rustica | P | **Pittsfield** 22
Tratt. Il Vesuvio | P | **Lenox** 17
Xicohtencatl | P | **Great Barr** 18

PEOPLE-WATCHING

Bistro Zinc | **Lenox** 21
Mezze Bistro | **Williamstown** 24
Pearl's | **Great Barr** 22
NEW Spice | **Pittsfield** 23

POWER SCENES

Bistro Zinc | **Lenox** 21
Mezze Bistro | **Williamstown** 24
Pearl's | **Great Barr** 22

PRIVATE ROOMS

(Restaurants charge less at off times; call for capacity)
Aegean Breeze | **Great Barr** 18
☑ Bizen | **Great Barr** 24
☑ Blantyre | **Lenox** 26
Castle St. | **Great Barr** 19
Church St. Cafe | **Lenox** 20
Cranwell Resort | **Lenox** 21
Dakota | **Pittsfield** 16
Egremont Inn | **S Egremont** 21
Elm Court | **N Egremont** 22
☑ John Andrews | **S Egremont** 24
Mill on the Floss | **New Ashford** 23

Pearl's | **Great Barr** 22
Red Lion Inn | **Stockbridge** 17
Rouge | **W Stockbridge** 22
Seven Hills Inn | **Lenox** –
Stagecoach Tavern | **Sheffield** 22
Z Wheatleigh | **Lenox** 26

PRIX FIXE MENUS

(Call for prices and times)
Z Bizen | **Great Barr** 24
Z Blantyre | **Lenox** 26
Bombay | **Lee** 21
Z Old Inn/Green | **New Marl** 26
Z Wheatleigh | **Lenox** 26

QUIET CONVERSATION

Z Blantyre | **Lenox** 26
Gramercy Bistro | **N Adams** 24
Z John Andrews | **S Egremont** 24
Mill on the Floss | **New Ashford** 23
NEW Spice | **Pittsfield** 23
Stagecoach Tavern | **Sheffield** 22
Z Wheatleigh | **Lenox** 26

ROMANTIC PLACES

Z Blantyre | **Lenox** 26
Z John Andrews | **S Egremont** 24
Z Old Inn/Green | **New Marl** 26
Z Wheatleigh | **Lenox** 26

SENIOR APPEAL

Aegean Breeze | **Great Barr** 18
Asters | **Pittsfield** 16
Cranwell Resort | **Lenox** 21
Elm Court | **N Egremont** 22
Morgan House | **Lee** 17
Red Lion Inn | **Stockbridge** 17
Sullivan Station | **Lee** 16

SINGLES SCENES

Brix | **Pittsfield** 23
Castle St. | **Great Barr** 19
Helsinki | **Great Barr** 18
Prime Italian | **Lenox** 22
Thai Garden | **Williamstown** 18
20 Railroad St. | **Great Barr** 14
Union B&G | **Great Barr** 15

SLEEPERS

(Good to excellent food,
but little known)
Aroma B&G | **Great Barr** 22
Fin | **Lenox** 27
Gramercy Bistro | **N Adams** 24
Prime Italian | **Lenox** 22
Stagecoach Tavern | **Sheffield** 22

TAKEOUT

Aegean Breeze | **Great Barr** 18
Aroma B&G | **Great Barr** 22
Asters | **Pittsfield** 16
Baba Louie's | **Great Barr** 23
Barrington Brew | **Great Barr** 13
Bistro Zinc | **Lenox** 21
Z Bizen | **Great Barr** 24
Bombay | **Lee** 21
Brix | **Pittsfield** 23
Café Latino | **N Adams** 22
Café Lucia | **Lenox** 20
Castle St. | **Great Barr** 19
Chez Nous | **Lee** 23
Church St. Cafe | **Lenox** 20
Dakota | **Pittsfield** 16
Dish Café | **Lenox** 19
Fin | **Lenox** 27
Firefly | **Lenox** 19
Gideon's | **N Adams** 23
Gramercy Bistro | **N Adams** 24
Helsinki | **Great Barr** 18
Jae's Inn | **Williamstown** 22
Z John Andrews | **S Egremont** 24
Mezze Bistro | **Williamstown** 24
Mill on the Floss | **New Ashford** 23
Morgan House | **Lee** 17
Once Upon | **Stockbridge** 19
Pearl's | **Great Barr** 22
Rouge | **W Stockbridge** 22
NEW Rte. 7 Grill | **Great Barr** –
Shiro Súshi | **Great Barr** 19
Siam Sq. Thai | **Great Barr** 18
Spigalina | **Lenox** 23
Stagecoach Tavern | **Sheffield** 22
Thai Garden | **Williamstown** 18
Truc Orient | **W Stockbridge** 22
20 Railroad St. | **Great Barr** 14
Union B&G | **Great Barr** 15
Xicohtencatl | **Great Barr** 18

TEEN APPEAL

Baba Louie's | **Great Barr** 23
20 Railroad St. | **Great Barr** 14

TRENDY

Bistro Zinc | **Lenox** 21
Z Bizen | **Great Barr** 24
Brix | **Pittsfield** 23
Café Latino | **N Adams** 22
Café Lucia | **Lenox** 20
Castle St. | **Great Barr** 19
Fin | **Lenox** 27
Helsinki | **Great Barr** 18
Z John Andrews | **S Egremont** 24

Old Inn/Green | **New Marl** 26

Pearl's | **Great Barr** 22

Prime Italian | **Lenox** 22

Rouge | **W Stockbridge** 22

NEW Spice | **Pittsfield** 23

Xicohtencatl | **Great Barr** 18

VISITORS ON EXPENSE ACCOUNT

Blantyre | **Lenox** 26

Pearl's | **Great Barr** 22

Wheatleigh | **Lenox** 26

VIEWS

Bombay | **Lee** 21

Cranwell Resort | **Lenox** 21

Jae's Inn | **Williamstown** 22

NEW Rte. 7 Grill | **Great Barr** —

Wheatleigh | **Lenox** 26

WINNING WINE LISTS

Brix | **Pittsfield** 23

Castle St. | **Great Barr** 19

Egremont Inn | **S Egremont** 21

Elm Court | **N Egremont** 22

Gramercy Bistro | **N Adams** 24

John Andrews | **S Egremont** 24

NEW Spice | **Pittsfield** 23

THE BERKSHIRES

SPECIAL FEATURES

Wine Vintage Chart

This chart, based on our 0 to 30 scale, is designed to help you select wine. The ratings (by **Howard Stravitz,** a law professor at the University of South Carolina) reflect the vintage quality and the wine's readiness to drink. We exclude the 1987, 1991–1993 vintages because they are not that good. A dash indicates the wine is either past its peak or too young to rate.

Whites

	86	88	89	90	94	95	96	97	98	99	00	01	02	03	04	05
French:																
Alsace	–	–	26	26	25	24	24	23	26	24	26	27	25	22	24	25
Burgundy	25	–	23	22	–	28	27	24	23	26	25	24	27	23	25	26
Loire Valley	–	–	–	–	–	–	–	–	–	–	24	25	26	23	24	25
Champagne	25	24	26	29	–	26	27	24	23	24	24	22	26	–	–	–
Sauternes	28	29	25	28	–	21	23	25	23	24	24	28	25	26	21	26
California:																
Chardonnay	–	–	–	–	–	–	–	–	–	24	23	26	26	27	28	29
Sauvignon Blanc	–	–	–	–	–	–	–	–	–	–	–	27	28	26	27	26
Austrian:																
Grüner Velt./Riesling	–	–	–	–	–	25	21	28	28	27	22	23	24	26	26	26
German:	–	25	26	27	24	23	26	25	26	23	21	29	27	25	26	26

Reds

	86	88	89	90	94	95	96	97	98	99	00	01	02	03	04	05
French:																
Bordeaux	25	23	25	29	22	26	25	23	25	24	29	26	24	25	23	27
Burgundy	–	–	24	26	–	26	27	26	22	27	22	24	27	24	24	25
Rhône	–	26	28	28	24	26	22	24	27	26	27	26	–	25	24	–
Beaujolais	–	–	–	–	–	–	–	–	–	–	24	–	23	27	23	28
California:																
Cab./Merlot	–	–	–	28	29	27	25	28	23	26	22	27	26	25	24	24
Pinot Noir	–	–	–	–	–	–	–	24	23	24	23	27	28	26	23	–
Zinfandel	–	–	–	–	–	–	–	–	–	–	–	25	23	27	22	–
Oregon:																
Pinot Noir	–	–	–	–	–	–	–	–	–	–	–	26	27	24	25	–
Italian:																
Tuscany	–	–	–	25	22	24	20	29	24	27	24	26	20	–	–	–
Piedmont	–	–	27	27	–	23	26	27	26	25	28	27	20	–	–	–
Spanish:																
Rioja	–	–	–	–	26	26	24	25	22	25	24	27	20	24	25	–
Ribera del Duero/Priorat	–	–	–	–	26	26	27	25	24	25	24	27	20	24	26	–
Australian:																
Shiraz/Cab.	–	–	–	–	24	26	23	26	28	24	24	27	27	25	26	–

subscribe to zagat.com